Success Studybooks

Success in
ECONOMIC
GEOGRAPHY

Norman Pounds, M.A., Ph.D.

University Professor of Geography and History,
Indiana University.

CONSULTANT EDITOR

Jonathan Edwards, B.Sc. (Econ.), Dip. U.R.S.

Lecturer in Geography,
Kingston College of Further Education,
Kingston, Surrey.

John Murray

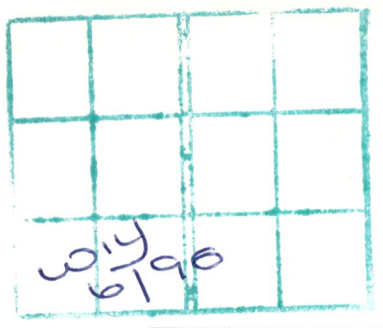
© Norman Pounds 1981

First published 1981
by John Murray (Publishers) Ltd
50 Albemarle Street, London W1X 4BD

Printed in Hong Kong by
Wing King Tong Ltd

British Library Cataloguing in Publication Data
Pounds, Norman John Greville
  Success in economic geography. – (Success studybooks).
  1. Geography, Economic
  I. Title   II. Series
  330.9   HF1025

ISBN 0–7195–3791–6

Foreword

The scope and content of Geography has changed radically during recent years. It has become less descriptive and more analytic; it is now concerned less with productive processes and more with their spatial distribution; less with the individual features and more with the systems of which each forms a part.

In the study of Geography we now try to make analyses in terms of the inter-relationships with the physical and social environment, emphasizing the central role of man as the decision-maker in determining the patterns that emerge. Whether or not we express these patterns as formal models, our method is to collect and examine data, to derive generalizations, and to test them, either by experiment or by further observation. The theories and models used in this book are those which have already been widely discussed, tested and accepted (for the most part) by geographers. Students working for examinations will be expected to use these methods and techniques in their own presentation of material, and as many will be meeting them for the first time, we give full and detailed explanations of the basic facts and principles involved.

Although the focus of much of the material is on Great Britain, the book also deals with the major characteristics of, and contrasts between, the developed and developing worlds. Constraints on space and length of text have meant that some topics have had to be dealt with briefly – such as the European Economic Community – or omitted altogether. But the student is given full guidance on where to go for more specialized study of these topics by the Further Reading list at the back of the book.

This book offers a newer and more up-to-date approach to Economic Geography than the earlier book, *An Introduction to Economic Geography*, which it replaces. It forms a self-contained study course, fully illustrated with photographs, diagrams and maps. It also has sections of self-testing questions at the end of each Unit, and assignments, which make it particularly suitable for students working for BEC National examinations (Economic Geography Option Module) and BEC Higher National awards. The book also covers certain A-level requirements, especially the Principles of Human Geography element of Geography syllabuses, and forms an introductory text for university degree courses.

N.J.G.P.

Acknowledgments

I am deeply grateful to the many people who have helped me, especially the teachers and lecturers who have discussed sixth-form and college teaching. In particular I wish to express thanks to Jonathan Edwards, Consultant Editor, who supplied much valuable advice as well as material, to Dr. John Coyne, who read and criticized the text at its early stages; to Dr. Jean Macqueen who edited it with expert care, and to Rosemarie Burston who researched and collected the photographs.

N.J.G.P.

Thanks are also due to the following for their kind assistance in providing illustrations: Aerofilms (1.6, 4.5(*a*), 5.1(*a*), 5.1(*c*), 5.8, 7.5(*a*), 7.8, 9.4(*a*), 9.4(*b*), 10.2, 13.14); Australian News and Information Bureau (7.3); Automobile Association (13.11); British Petroleum Company Limited (12.17, 13.4); British Steel Corporation (7.6); Camera Press (2.14(*b*), 3.7, 5.9, 9.1(*a*), 12.12, 12.15, 15.3, 15.5); Canadian Government Photo Centre (12.21); Containerisation International (12.20); *Cranes Today* (9.1(*b*), 10.3); D.O.E. Traffic Division (Crown copyright reproduced by permission of HMSO) (12.7); The Electrical Research Association (8.8(*b*)); *The Financial Times* (11.1, 15.1); *Flight International* (12.18); French Tourist Board (14.3); The Greek Embassy (8.8(*a*)); James Holmes (2.14(*a*)); Keystone Press Agency (14.7, 15.4); Leeds City Council (13.5); Leyland Motor Corporation (12.13); Luddington Experimental Horticultural Station (Ministry of Agriculture, Fisheries and Food) (1.3(*b*)); Milton Keynes Development Corporation (13.12); National Film Board of Canada (7.5(*b*)); North of Scotland Hydro Electric Board (8.9); Oxfam (4.5(*b*)); Royal Netherlands Embassy (14.5); Swiss National Tourist Office (6.2, 12.16); The Tesco Group (1.3(*a*)); USDA Soil Conservation Service (5.1(*b*)); United States Steel Corporation (14.6).

Contents

Unit One

Production and Consumption

You—like everyone else in the world—are a *consumer,* that is, you use up a part of the world's resources in the form of goods and services. You consume food, of course, and in addition you consume clothing and other manufactured commodities. Some people consume a great deal more than others, and we speak of them as having a relatively high *standard of living.* Most people consume a good deal less than they would wish, and some less even than that normally considered necessary to maintain life.

Most people are also *producers.* They may grow food or catch fish, or make goods that others will buy, or build houses. Or their production may take the form of performing services: they work in the administration of the community, they provide medical care, they carry on trade, manage insurance, serve in shops, teach, or even write and publish books.

Some people produce more than one kind of commodity or furnish more than one service. In some parts of the world it is normal for a man to work at agriculture as his primary occupation and also to practise a craft, perhaps during the winter months. Or a vegetable grower may sell his surplus at a shop or a market stall and thus, at the same time, be a trader. Many producers themselves consume the greater part of what they grow, like the self-sufficing farmer in south-east Asia; others sell off their produce into the market, as the American wheat-farmer does. There is every gradation from the near self-sufficiency of many African peasant farmers to the narrowly specialized production of a worker on a factory assembly line.

But no individual or family can live wholly to itself. Each is part of a wider community on which it relies for some good or service, and members of the developed, industrialized societies of today are dependent on others for most of the goods they consume and the services they enjoy. Nevertheless, since physical conditions of climate, soil and other resources differ greatly over the face of the earth, productive activities are concentrated at places where they can most easily be carried on. Consumers and producers are often, in consequence, widely separated, and there must be a flow of information and of goods between them. This is made possible by a network of lines of *communication and transport.* Goods and services supplied to people at one point are paid for, or requited, by goods and services supplied to another point. Their movement forms a complex and ever-changing pattern, and it is the analysis of the spatial pattern of production and consumption, and of the linkages between them, which forms the substance of economic geography.

We can represent this system of production–transport–consumption on a small and local scale or on a world scale, and geographers are interested in both.

Take, for example, an isolated community living in the depth of the forests of South America or central Africa—though nowadays few communities are totally insulated from outside influences. There would be some degree of specialization among its members over and above that between the sexes. Some would grow crops, some would make artefacts and some would carry on the traditional practices of the community. There would necessarily be some degree of exchange between the different groups. Those who only performed services would receive goods in exchange, while those who cultivated the land or reared animals would exchange their surplus for the services and surplus production of others. We can represent such a community by a diagram (Fig. 1.1).

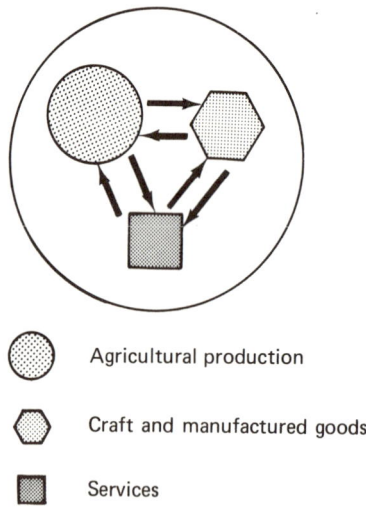

⬤ Agricultural production

⬡ Craft and manufactured goods

▪ Services

Fig. 1.1 The exchange of goods and services within a self-sufficing community

The world community is essentially similar, being made up of producers and consumers linked together by a web of exchange, but it is incomparably more complex. Every individual, at least in the more developed countries, requires some of the services or the surplus production of thousands of other individuals, ranging from the tea-grower in Sri Lanka and the Dutch dairy farmer to the Fleet Street printer and the teacher in the class-room. This worldwide inter-dependence of individuals is so complex as to defy detailed description. We can only represent it by means of a *model* or simplified picture of reality (see Unit 1.8(*a*)). A very small community—a village or a little town, perhaps—might satisfy most of its needs from within, supplementing its own products with small-scale imports, which must of course be paid for by the goods and services which it exports (Fig. 1.2(*a*)). At the other extreme is the industrialized or urban community which generates some of the services it needs, but which is almost wholly dependent on outside suppliers for its food as well as for most consumer goods (Fig. 1.2(*b*)).

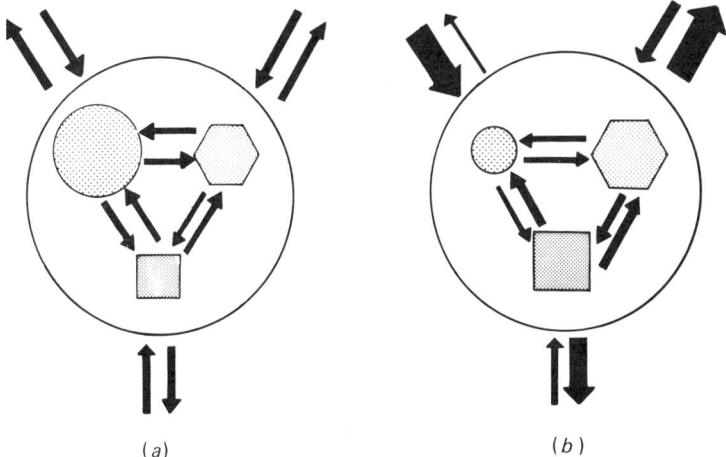

Fig. 1.2 Communities which are (a) dependent to a small degree on external goods and services, and (b) heavily dependent (key as in Fig. 1.1)

1.1   Producers and Consumers

Each of the 4 000 million or so people in the world makes decisions every week, day, even every hour, regarding what he or she shall produce or consume. The range of choice varies greatly from one community to another. For a village community in Indo-China, for example, there is little alternative to a predominantly rice diet, cooked in a traditional way and eaten at the accustomed times of day. But even here there is an element of choice. The rice is commonly accompanied by vegetables or meat, and a decision has to be made — what to grow or purchase in order to supplement the rice. When a housewife in a complex western society decides to have this or that for dinner, however, she is choosing from hundreds of different foodstuffs, representing the marketable surplus of every corner of the earth.

Her decision must in the long run influence producers. Her choice may be very simple: whether to drink tea or coffee at breakfast-time, let us say. She will be influenced both by personal preference and by the prices of tea and coffee in the shops. Those who manage the market have come to assume that, among the millions who make such a decision every day, a certain number will choose tea and another number coffee. It is unlikely that these numbers will change significantly in the short term, and shopkeepers, merchants and tea- and coffee-growers are geared to satisfy a demand of this size. Now let us suppose that the demand for coffee increases — perhaps as a response to hard advertising, perhaps because of a rise in consumers' purchasing power. The coffee-grower in Brazil or Costa Rica or Kenya will in turn have to decide whether or not to increase the area of his coffee plantations in order to satisfy this demand. This is a far more difficult decision than that faced by the housewife, who stands to lose nothing more than the difference in cost between tea and coffee. The coffee-grower

Fig. 1.3 Decision-making: (a) customers choose from a wide range of goods in a supermarket; the results of their choices may well affect

knows that bushes planted now will not come into production for several years. They will represent a capital investment, necessitating perhaps heavy borrowing from the bank, so that his decision may be influenced by the rate of interest which he has to pay. He will also ask whether this increased demand for coffee is merely a temporary trick of fashion which will disappear as suddenly as it came, or a long-term change in people's behavioural pattern. A preference for coffee may well remain for the foreseeable future, but even so, economic factors—a recession, smaller wage packets, unemployment—may reduce purchasing power, thus leading people to save money by substituting tea for coffee.

The nature of popular demand is constantly changing, and it is the role of advertising to wean us away from one product and lead us to adopt another. A choice has to be made, as we have seen, between varieties of foodstuffs or other goods which can in some degree be substituted for one another, and the decision is likely to be influenced by several factors, including the relative prices of the two commodities. We speak of this variability as *elasticity of demand*. It is a highly important concept in economic geography as it greatly influences the geographical pattern of production. Coffee is in *elastic demand*; so also are tea, cocoa, beer, wine and spirits, because none of them is an essential food and in selecting our diet we consciously make a choice between them. Indeed, most foodstuffs are in elastic demand, though basic commodities like bread, potatoes and sugar are probably least so. To the rice-eating peasants of southern Asia rice is in *inelastic demand*: he eats rice or nothing, and he never, as far as his main foodstuff is concerned, enjoys the luxury of choice.

So far we have drawn our illustration from very familiar decisions regarding

(b) the farmer's decisions as to what crops to plant, and the proportion of his land to be devoted to each

food and diet. Similar, though less frequent, decisions must be made in buying clothing and household articles, in deciding whether or not to go to a place of entertainment, and, usually only after long and careful consideration, what cooker, refrigerator or car to buy.

Of no less interest to the geographer than the decision to buy an article is the question of where to go for it. Will it be to the 'friendly neighbourhood store', whose warm welcome is not matched by an abundance of choice, or to the suburban shopping centre where shops are larger and parking usually adequate and possibly even free, or to the shopping centre of a big city, which will necessitate a day's expedition? We may think that we know from our own experience how people behave in all these respects. In fact, the kind of analysis that a geographer can make will show that the decision where to shop is no less complex than the choice of what to buy.

1.2 Decision-making

The task of decision-making is not limited to consumers. We have already seen how an increase in coffee consumption might lead a coffee-grower to consider enlarging his plantation. Just as the consumer decides between goods primarily in the light of personal preference and relative cost, so the producer is influenced mainly by his judgment of what the market can take and the physical conditions of production and marketing (raw materials, transport and so forth). But the scale of a producer's decision-making can be far greater, involving more serious risks and calling for more expert knowledge than that of the consumer.

(a) Decision-making in Agriculture

At the one extreme is a peasant in, let us say, West Africa. He grows most of the food he consumes and may even make many of the articles required in the daily life of his family. His holding covers only a few hectares. On about a fifth of it he grows tobacco which he sells. From the returns on this 'cash crop' he pays his taxes and purchases the few items which he cannot produce himself. On the rest of his land he cultivates subsistence crops—rice, corn, cassava and peanuts, which his family consumes. It might seem that he has few decisions to make. He has, however, to choose a combination of crops which suits both the needs of his family and the conditions of climate and soil. A combination which best satisfies *his* needs might involve taking chances with an unpredictable climate. In northern Ghana the rains are uncertain, and a dry summer might mean severe shortages for his family. On the other hand, to plant those crops which are best suited to a dry summer would mean a smaller production of food. At the same time the market for tobacco is an unstable one. Demand is tending to decline, and the price is falling. This is something which he can neither comprehend nor anticipate, and he and his neighbours react by planting more tobacco in an effort to obtain the same cash income. The effect is to depress the market yet more. Here the peasant is competing with physical conditions which he cannot anticipate and a market which he cannot understand.

At the opposite end of the agricultural scale is a Kansas wheat-grower, cultivating perhaps one or two thousand hectares of rolling prairie with every mechanical and scientific aid available to help him. Unlike the peasant, he has a very large capital investment in his farm, both in the land itself and also in equipment. He watches the grain market closely and follows prices on the Chicago Exchange. He is encouraged when his government contracts to sell immense quantities of grain to China or the Soviet Union, and depressed when he learns that wheat stocks are high or when drought affects the yield of his crops. He may have borrowed from his bank in order to finance developments on his farm, so that he is equally interested in fluctuations in the rate of bank interest. He too is continually faced with the need to make decisions: whether to hold his corn or sell it, whether or not to plough and sow an additional hundred hectares, whether to increase or diminish his use of fertilizer. These are difficult decisions. Kansas farmers plough and sow in October, and the crop is unlikely to be ready for harvest before July. The wheat will not be in the market until August, and if the railroads are slow in handling it he may not be able to sell it before the autumn. His decisions are therefore complicated by the need to assess the conditions of the market a year ahead. He draws on the expert advice of agronomists and economists, but errors of judgment are possible and may cost him dearly. At worst, the bank may deny him further credit, or even foreclose.

There is one fundamental difference between the peasant and the large-scale, highly capitalized, specialist farmer. In an emergency the peasant can always live off his land, provided his farm is large enough. Also he is used to hardship and to improvising from the little he has. But the wheat-farmer cannot live only on wheat. Although in times of prosperity he can make enormous profits, he is ill equipped to survive when times are bad.

(b) Decision-making in Manufacturing

Decisions regarding food consumption and food production are made more frequently than decisions in any other field. This is because people spend more on food than on other commodities and services, and also because about half the human race is engaged in food production. The most far-reaching of all decisions are probably those made by the industrialists who manage the great factories of the world—automobile concerns, steel works, chemical works and so on. Small-scale craft industries are still carried on, even in the most highly industrialized countries, but most manufactured goods come from factories which in much of the world are managed by a 'board' and owned by thousands of faceless shareholders. (There are important exceptions to this, discussed in Unit 1.7(b).) Industrial management has to decide when to expand or to contract production, when to introduce new 'models' and how to price them. It therefore needs to know how much money people are likely to have to spend both in the immediate and the more distant future, their probable tastes and preferences, and what kind of competition may be expected from other manufacturers, both at home and abroad.

The manufacturer relies on the advice of skilled market analysts. He tries to stimulate and guide the pattern of demand and, through advertising, to persuade people that his product is better, safer, cleaner than all others, that it confers greater advantages and gives more pleasure. Our social standing, we are even told by some manufacturers, depends on the clothes we wear, the food we eat or the car we drive. Some advertising is misleading, in spite of efforts to maintain high standards; all advertising represents an attempt to influence the decisions made by the consumer.

The manufacture of cars is one example of large-scale factory industry, with perhaps thirty major manufacturing companies in at least a dozen countries engaged in it. They are in direct competition with one another throughout the world, and their success depends in large measure on their ability to anticipate public demand in a highly elastic market. It is not surprising that many companies have gone out of production during the past half-century, nor that the geographical pattern of car production (Unit 10.4(d)) is very different today from what it was in 1950, and we may be sure that it will again have changed radically by the year 2000.

1.3 Man against Nature

We can thus represent the farmer, in whatever part of the world he may be, as attempting to get the maximum output from his land, but always working under certain constraints. These can be summarized as (i) *market conditions*, or the demand for the kinds of farm goods that he is capable of producing, and (ii) the changing *physical conditions* under which he operates. In neither instance can he foresee these conditions for more than a few months at most, and natural hazards—flood, hailstorm or drought—may overtake him and destroy his crops without warning.

Farmers almost everywhere have a choice of crops, some of which can be expected to do well in a wet year, others in a dry. For instance, Table 1.1 represents the quantities (in arbitrary units) of various crops that would be produced from a given area in Ghana under different conditions.

Table 1.1   Cropping under wet and dry conditions

Crop	Yield Wet year	Dry year
Yams	82	11
Maize	70	49
Cassava	12	38
Millet	43	32
Hill rice	30	71

Source: Gould, P. R.: 'Man against his environment: A game theoretic framework'. *Annals of the Association of American Geographers*, vol. 53 (1963), pp. 290–297

Table 1.1 shows that yams, maize and millet do best in a wet year, and cassava and hill rice in a dry. How is a farmer to react to this situation? He is playing a game against nature, in which the stakes are his own livelihood and that of his family He might gamble on the coming season being wet and plant only yams, maize and millet, or he might expect a dry year and grow only the alternative crops. Or he might divide his land between the two groups of crops, thus assuring himself of a moderate return which might be enough for his needs whatever the weather. He has to choose a combination of up to five crops in such a way that, under weather conditions that he cannot foresee, he secures a sufficient return for his needs. He will have two conflicting goals: minimizing his risks and yet maximizing his output. In the face of climatic uncertainty the resolution of this conflict requires that he select the crop combination which yields the highest output under the worst possible conditions.

It is possible to determine the 'mix' of crops he should grow by using a procedure called *game theory*, which is now an important technique for determining the ideal cropping pattern under given physical conditions. A simple graphical solution to the farmer's dilemma has been suggested by Gould (Fig. 1.4), in which yields for each crop are plotted on two axes representing wet and dry years respectively and the corresponding points on the axes are connected. The crop combination that is best for the farmer to plant is indicated by the lowest point on the upper limit of the graph—point X in Fig. 1.4, indicating maize and hill rice in proportions which may be mathematically calculated from the data in Table 1.1.

It may be that such a crop combination is normally cultivated, but if this is so then it certainly derives from the community's collective experience rather than from any game-theoretical analysis. Game theory may suggest ways in which a cropping system might be improved in order to ensure a more regular supply of food. Choice of crops is, however, likely to be influenced also by palatability, ease of preparation and traditional attitudes to food. One fact is clear: it is

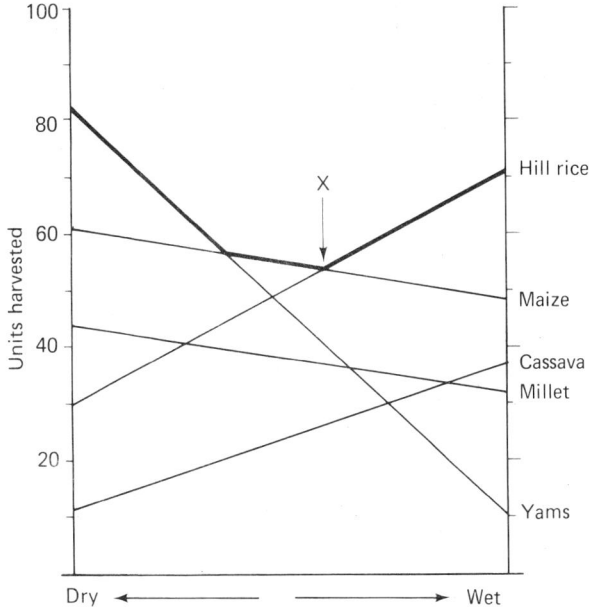

Fig. 1.4 A game-theory solution to the problem of what to grow in a tropical environment in order to minimize loss through abnormal weather; the farmer's safest gamble will be to grow the combination indicated by the heavy line (after P. R. Gould)

unwise for the farmer to concentrate on a single crop. Monoculture has more often than not proved disastrous for the cultivator.

The manufacturer plays a similar game to the farmer's, though his opponent is not the physical environment but the market and the uncertainty of supply and demand. The decision to manufacture a new 'line' or a fresh 'model' differs from that to grow a particular crop only in the greater scale of the operation and the larger amount of capital involved. It is based on someone's *perception* (see Unit 1.5) of market trends, popular taste and the availability of capital. Throughout this book we shall return at intervals to this twofold concept: every producer plays a game against an opponent whose moves cannot be fully anticipated, and each individual acts according to his perception of physical and economic conditions.

1.4   Comparative Advantage

There is probably no *ideal* site for any economic activity, in the sense of satisfying its every possible requirement at all times. There are good sites and less good sites, and it is often necessary to choose the latter. The hills of southern Brazil have often been cited as ideally suited to the cultivation of coffee, but even here in 1975 unusually severe frosts gravely reduced the crops and inflated world prices. It is therefore best to think of a zone or region of *optimum* conditions for a given activity, within which are found most of the requirements for the successful cultivation of a crop or the management of a factory. This area may be surrounded by a zone in which conditions are less than optimum, but nevertheless broadly satisfactory. Beyond this might lie a third zone where the activity could be pursued, but with less success: crop-yields would be lower or manufacturing costs high as the case might be. The undertaking would be less profitable and therefore less likely to be carried on.

To take an example from agriculture: suppose that two neighbouring regions have respectively optimal conditions for two different crops, *A* and *B*—say

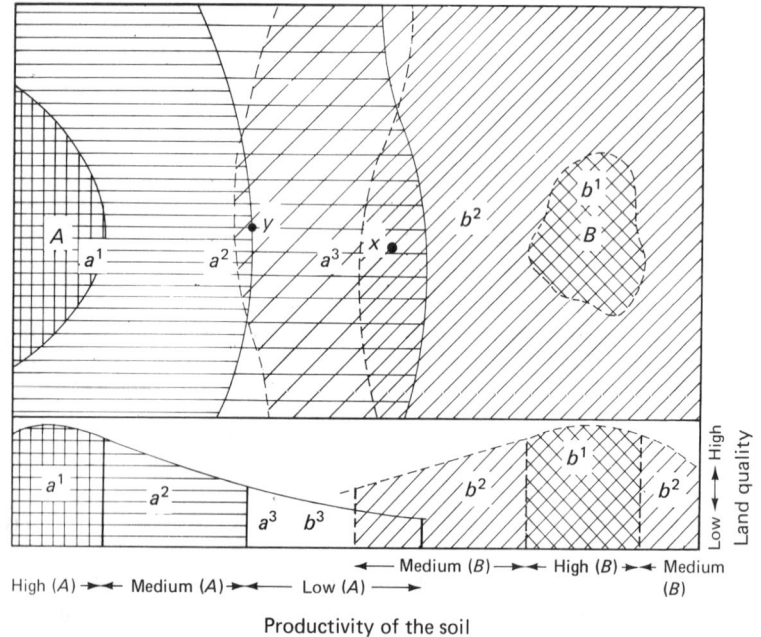

Fig. 1.5 Comparative advantage in agriculture. Point x lies in an area moderately well suited to crop B but poorly suited to crop A; even so, A may be grown at point x if its market value is sufficiently above that of B

wheat and maize in the Great Plains of the United States. The situation is represented diagrammatically in Fig. 1.5. Crop *A* predominates in a^1 and is widely cultivated in a^2, but is only rarely seen in a^3; crop *B* is similarly cultivated in b^1, b^2, and b^3. Now let us assume that the demand and the price of crop *A* rises. For technical reasons—the need to rotate crops and to maintain soil fertility, or the capacity of their storage facilities—farmers in a^1 cannot greatly increase production, though they do receive a higher price for their crop. Those in a^2, however, can—and do—sow a much larger area, and at the same time the crop becomes very much more conspicuous in a^3. The higher prices received make it profitable to cultivate less suitable land, and as the price rises cultivation is pushed steadily into less desirable areas. In the end, frost or drought or some other natural constraint will probably limit the diffusion of the crop.

Meanwhile, the prices of crop B have been falling; cultivation has ceased in zone b^3 and is contracting in b^2. Only in b^1 has it suffered no loss, though here the farmers are complaining, as farmers do, that falling prices will drive them out of business. The geographical limit of *profitable* cultivation of B has receded, just as that for crop A has advanced.

The marketability of crop A is taking it into areas which are more suited on physical grounds to producing crop B. At point x, which lies in both b^2 and a^3, crop A is preferred because, under existing market conditions, it enjoys a *comparative advantage* over crop B. Of course, market conditions might within a few years be reversed, so that farmers at y might then find themselves choosing to grow crop B instead of crop A which, so the textbooks tell them, is more suited to their physical conditions.

Fig. 1.6 The geographical limit of profitable cultivation, clearly visible here in the hills of County Kerry, Ireland

Similar conditions apply to the decisions taken in manufacturing industry. The optimum site of a factory—measured by transport facilities, nearness to market and to source of materials, and labour supply—will often be preferred, but a less suitable site may be chosen if long-term prospects for the industry seem particularly good. Whether in agriculture or manufacturing, however, a location is not forced upon the producer by its physical characteristics. Rather, he is the decision-maker, who chooses the place where a particular activity can most profitably be pursued in the light of his perception of both physical and economic conditions.

1.5   Perception

Let us take two neighbouring towns, *A* and *B*. *A* is twice the size of *B* and has proportionately more shops, services and facilities. It might seem that, logically speaking, a person living equidistant from both is likely to prefer to shop in *A*; but not everyone acts entirely logically. Each individual has preferences, prejudices and sometimes quite irrational likes and dislikes. While common sense might lead him to *A*, the one-way traffic system, the location and cost of car parks and the atmosphere of the town might all serve to repel him. Moreover, the individual does not perceive distance in quite the same way as the car's trip-recorder. A more distant town may *seem* nearer because the road is better or more attractive.

This is a simple and familiar example of how in all our activities as producers and consumers we do not react to actual events and phenomena in the real world, only to reality *as we perceive it*. We all look at the world through glasses tinted by ideas drawn from our history and traditions, our social class, our education and our concepts of what pleases us, and we make decisions in the light of these perceptions. If we all perceived the world with accuracy and precision, our behaviour would no doubt conform more closely with what our models predict. It is that 'irrational' element in all of us which not only gives variety to life but also compels us to deal in terms of probabilities (see Unit 1.8(*c*)) when discussing human behaviour.

1.6   Types of Economic Activity

It is convenient to divide the many forms of economic activity into three groups known respectively as *primary*, *secondary* and *tertiary*.

(*a*) Primary Activities
Primary activities are those which relate to the cultivation of the land and the extraction of minerals and fuels from the rocks. They include forestry and fishing as well as quarrying and drilling, and all processes yielding raw materials for subsequent processing.

(*b*) Secondary Activities
These embrace all forms of manufacturing and processing of raw materials. It is usual to include under this head the generation of power, because it uses raw materials—coal, oil, uranium—to produce energy.

(c) **Tertiary Activities**

Tertiary activities include all the services which make primary and secondary activities possible. Transport, for instance, is essential to most extractive and all manufacturing activities, and such services as brokerage and insurance are necessary to many. Shipping and dock-working are tertiary activities, as also are secretarial and administrative services.

It is not always easy to distinguish between these three broad groups of economic activity. Is, for example, hydro-electric power-generation a primary or a secondary process? and to which group do ore-processing, oil-refining and the petrochemical industries belong? are they part of the extractive process, or do they belong to manufacturing industry? At the other end of the spectrum do the personal services provided by teachers and doctors, lawyers and policemen belong to the tertiary sector? Most people would agree that they do because they contribute to the well-being of those engaged in primary and secondary activity.

The importance of such demarcation lines lies in the practice of grouping the working population according to the kinds of activity in which they are engaged, and hence categorizing and comparing cities, towns and even countries. For example, in some towns the primary activity of mining is the dominant occupation; in others, secondary activities like car manufacturing are dominant. Yet others are dominated by service activities: dock towns like Harwich, for example, and business centres like the City of London. We can draw similar distinctions between countries. Primary activities—chiefly agriculture—

Table 1.2   Relative contributions of primary, secondary and tertiary activities in rich and poor countries (per cent)

	Primary	Secondary	Tertiary
Group A:			
Bangladesh	59	8	33
Ghana	51	14	35
Malawi	47	13	40
Ethiopia	48	9	43
Chad	50	8	42
Rwanda	59	6	35
Nepal	69	10	21
Yemen	61	3	36
Haiti	44	15	41
Group B:			
United States	3	28	69
United Kingdom	3	30	67
West Germany	3	43	54
Belgium	3	31	64
Sweden	4	32	64

Source: *Statistical Yearbook 1976*, UN (1977)

predominate in the countries of the developing world. The industrialized countries have, by definition, a higher proportion of their population in secondary activities, and the richest countries—the USA, Switzerland and Sweden, for example—have large tertiary sectors.

Table 1.2 compares the contributions made by primary, secondary and tertiary occupations to the wealth of two contrasted groups of countries.

Group A is made up of countries which are very poor, and Group B of countries which are among the richest in the world. In the poor countries, roughly a half to two-thirds of the working population is engaged in primary activities, chiefly agriculture, but a much smaller proportion in manufacturing. In the developed or rich countries, only a very small fraction of the population is in primary activities; from a quarter to a half is in manufacturing, whereas more than a half is employed in tertiary activities, many of which are related to manufacturing.

As a general rule, primary activities are rewarded by lower incomes and command a lower standard of living than secondary, and secondary occupations are generally less well rewarded than tertiary. There are of course exceptions: the miner and oil worker are rising in the scale of remuneration, and some are very highly paid. Nevertheless, industrialization and the expansion of the secondary sector are seen in the Third World countries as the most important—indeed as the only—steps toward higher income levels.

1.7   Types of Economy

The *economy* is the system of production and consumption, including the means of decision-making and the allocation of resources, which prevails in any particular country. This unit has emphasized that economic activity results from the decisions taken to produce, to consume or to perform or receive services. It has been implied that such decisions are taken by the individual either in his private capacity as a member of the public or in a more official role as member of a board or management. In every country, however, some part in these decisions is played by the government acting ostensibly in the interests of all its citizens. The extent of government involvement in the economy varies from almost complete control in the communist countries to the relative freedom of private enterprise in the western world.

(a) Market Economies
The concept of the *market economy* evolved in the early nineteenth century. Its theoretical basis had been propounded by Adam Smith in *The Wealth of Nations* (1776). Its prescription for government was to remove all obstacles to the freedom of trade and the exercise of private initiative. The profit motive was seen as the guiding factor in the economy, and what was good for the entrepreneur was deemed to be good for the country. No country ever accepted the extremes of *laissez-faire*, but for a period the governments of western Europe and the USA did little to restrain the freedom of private initiative.

As the nineteenth century advanced, however, the governments of Great

Britain, France, Germany and other European countries gradually withdrew from their *laissez-faire* policies. Social legislation restricted the freedom of employers, planning legislation imposed controls on land use and selective import duties were introduced to protect agriculture and certain manufactures.

There is now no country in which the market system operates entirely unfettered by government controls or supervision. Even in the United States, which claims to be the 'freest'' country in the world in this respect, large areas of economic life are under governmental control. The Federal Government in effect operates the railways, and a series of supervisory bodies serves as watchdogs over other sectors of the economy. There is a battery of legislation designed to prevent price-fixing and other offences of which the capitalist system is said to have been particularly guilty, and the government itself negotiates and fixes prices for some of the largest commercial transactions, such as the bulk sale of wheat. There are also more subtle ways in which the government can influence the decision-making process and thus the development and location of production and consumption. For instance, it can—and does—support the prices of certain agricultural products, and it influences very strongly the rates of interest charged by banks on money lent for the expansion or improvement of services and production; moreover, through the orders which it is able to place it can profoundly influence the decisions reached in the board room.

Within the very large group of market economy countries two important sub-groups can be distinguished.

(*i*) **Mixed economies.** In this group, which includes the United Kingdom and others having related political systems, the state has taken over certain branches of production and exercises a limited role in planning the economy as a whole. The railways, the coal-mines, power production and steel manufacture are in public hands, and the patterns of land use are broadly controlled by the government. Direct support of agriculture and direct financial grants to certain sectors of industry ensure particular help for some in the competitive struggle which all must face. Much of the decision-making process in mixed economies is thus carried out by branches of the government, and decisions of private enterprise are tightly constrained by government regulation and supervision.

(*ii*) **Developing countries.** No less than two-thirds of the countries of the modern world are described as 'developing' or 'Third World' countries (see also Unit 15), though no precise line of division can be drawn between them and the developed nations—whether managed or market economies. They are the countries with a relatively low gross national product (GNP; see Unit 4.2) per head. In most of them agriculture is the dominant productive activity, and in all of them capital investment is relatively small; as a general rule their population is rising more quickly than is their agricultural and industrial production. In varying degrees their spokesmen claim that they have been either exploited or neglected by the more advanced countries and that this is the cause of their relative backwardness. It can be argued that without the expertise and capital supplied by the advanced countries, the Third World would be even less developed. Most developing nations, however, perceive their backwardness in terms of past exploitation, and expect the developed world to help to remedy their situation.

The developing countries have formed a number of overlapping political organizations and, despite their many internal differences, press their claims for economic aid with considerable vigour and some success (see Unit 15.3).

(b) Managed Economies

In fourteen countries, embracing as much as a third of the human race, no market economy exists. These countries are communist in their political and economic structure, and are organized on lines which are sometimes described as Marxist–Leninist. The communist revolt against the market economy was founded on the assumption that the free enterprise system was wasteful and unfair, that companies and firms were primarily interested in maximizing profits rather than in making goods more widely available to the public, and that the mass of the people—the workers—were exploited by those who controlled the means of production and made the critical decisions.

Few would deny that there is a large element of waste in the free enterprise system. For instance, advertising is sometimes carried far beyond the simple process of informing the public of what is available, and its cost must ultimately be borne by the consumer. The existence of several competing brands of a certain commodity may make for cheapness and efficiency, but the effect may be to bring the size of the producing unit below that which is desirable for efficient management (see Unit 9.2(a)). There is always the risk that competing companies may agree among themselves to keep prices artificially high. Many countries have 'anti-trust' legislation to prevent this, and acts 'in restraint of trade' can be severely punished, but it is not always easy for the long arm of the law to reach into company board rooms.

In the *managed* or *planned economies* most of the natural resources have been taken over by the government. The only significant exception is the land, which in Poland and Yugoslavia remains largely in the hands of the peasants (Unit 5.4(b)). All means of industrial production, with the exception of the smallest handicraft workshops, belong to the 'people', which in fact means the state, and the state also runs the banking, commercial, medical, educational and other services. The effect is to transfer the decision-making role from the individual entrepreneur or the board of management to government planners. Communist apologists would add that the worker under the free enterprise or capitalist system was merely contributing to the profits of management and shareholders, while the worker in the communist system was striving for the betterment of his state and nation. This rather theoretical distinction does not appear to have any very conspicuous practical effects.

In simple terms, the method in the planned economies is for government agencies to decide how much of a given commodity should be produced, and make available the labour and material resources necessary. The amount of a particular consumer good put on sale thus depends on the government's allocation of resources rather than on an uncertain consumer demand. In most planned economies during the past quarter of a century, the production of garments and footwear has been inadequate to meet domestic demand, while the shelves in bookshops are plentifully stocked with books on political philosophy. In most market economies, the relative supplies of clothing and philosophical textbooks are reversed.

A vitally important decision in both free enterprise and managed economies is: how much money should be invested in renewing and extending plant and equipment? Suppose that a company in western Europe makes a small profit in a certain year. Is this profit to be distributed to shareholders, or is only a small dividend to be paid and the rest 'ploughed back' into the enterprise, perhaps to be used to replace an old workshop or foundry? The latter is, in the long run, the wiser choice, though in the United Kingdom far too many enterprises have not taken this course, and are therefore burdened today with obsolete plant and the resulting high production costs. In the managed economies this decision is made at the governmental level. It may be decided that 5 per cent of the gross national product (see Unit 4.2) shall be reinvested, that it shall go towards extending certain factories, establishing new plant and in laying down railways and building docks. The plan may go even farther: it might even specify the amount of steel and the number of cars, pairs of shoes and metres of cloth to be made during a given period.

There is no obvious reason why government officials should not be able to estimate the size of future demand at least as well as the market analysts employed by private companies. But this is not the really important issue. In most managed economies there has been an under-supply of consumer goods, in other words a grave shortage of such things as footwear, clothing, housing and household appliances and even of some foodstuffs. This has been because the planners have allocated too few resources for such products, diverting them instead to capital investment. The building of new factories has been at the expense of the living standards of the mass of the people, and this has been made possible by the tight control exercised by the Party over all aspects of political and economic life. It is unlikely that the diversion of resources on such a scale would be tolerated in a democratic country, except in wartime.

1.8   Geographical Concepts and Techniques

In the course of this book, you will find that certain specialized concepts and some simple statistical techniques are used in the discussion of geographical topics. Some of these are described or explained in the text, but others that are of general application are considered in the following pages of this Unit.

(a) Models
This Unit has emphasized the extreme complexity of the real world. We cannot possibly comprehend the entire range of its complexity so we resort to generalizations: 'this is what we expect to find', or 'this is what is likely to happen'. The geographer is always seeking to simplify, to establish valid generalizations regarding the distribution of different forms of human activity and to

demonstrate relationships between them. Is there a relationship, for example, between the distribution of farms of varying size and the variety of crops grown in a particular country? between the whereabouts of a man's home and his place of work? or between the sizes of cities and towns in a region or a country? Each of these distribution patterns is highly complex and detailed. It could perhaps be presented on a map, but to *describe* the relationships it incorporates would be immensely difficult, if not impossible. But it is possible to abstract from the real world's complexity the essential distributions and relationships and to present them as *models* of reality.

Models have been described (by Chorley and Haggett in their book on the use of models in economic geography) as 'simplified structurings of reality which present supposedly significant features or relationships in a generalized form'. They are not precise pictures of reality. They make no allowances for local and incidental factors; they are only approximations, embodying general principles rather than the specific detail of the real world. They have to be tested against reality, and if reality is found in a particular instance to diverge widely from an accepted model, then the geographer would do well to examine his data with care with a view to discovering the reason for the exception.

Models assume many forms. They may be models in the strict sense of the term—miniature replicas of reality, like 'model' railways or aircraft. A map is a kind of model insofar as it is a pictorial representation of part of the real world from which much incidental detail has been suppressed. The amount that has been omitted, and hence the level of generalization, is likely to vary with the scale of the map. Most often, however, the term *model* is reserved for attempts to represent in a generalized way the relationships that exist between phenomena. Let us look at a simple example.

The gravity model. This is one of the most frequently used models in geography. It defines the ways in which people and human activities are attracted to each other, in a manner superficially analogous to the gravitational forces that exist between all bodies. People journey from their homes both to places of work and to shopping centres and places of recreation, and the attraction of such places draws people into them from considerable distances. Empirical evidence—that is, evidence collected on the spot by means of questionnaires or observation— shows that the number of people making the journey to a particular factory or shopping centre declines as the length of the trip increases, but that this decline is not usually a uniform one. Instead, the fall-off, or decay, is at first steep and then increasingly gentle. The attractive force of a shopping centre to a person living one kilometre away from it is a great deal more than twice that to another living two kilometres away. Moreover, the larger the centre the greater the attractive force it exerts. In fact, we can write

$$G = \frac{P}{d^2}$$

where G is the attractive force exerted by the centre, P is its size and d the distance of a particular point away from the centre.

This simple model of human behaviour can be manipulated to predict the sphere of influence of a shopping centre (see Unit 2.5(*b*)), the movement of commuters to a city, the attraction of a park or other recreational area or the interaction between two towns, whether in terms of rail services, road traffic, telephone calls or any other form of movement or communication between them (see Unit 2.5(*c*)). The gravity model suggests that we can expect to find a clustering among related activities, and in later Units we shall find that the tendency to cluster is a strongly marked feature of many forms of economic activity.

(*b*) Sampling

In this Unit we have referred several times to the decisions people make and to the ways in which they respond to external influences. But when we speak of farmers in a particular region as growing a certain range of crops, or of housewives as going to their nearest shopping centre, we cannot say that *all* farmers or *all* housewives act in this way. We are not automatons. We react in differing ways to certain stimuli, and our perceptions of what is cheapest, easiest, most profitable or most pleasurable vary greatly.

Let us take an example. Suppose that a chain of grocery stores is considering the possibility of opening a new branch in a developing suburb. Before it acquires land, obtains planning consent and begins to build, it must first find out where local people do their shopping, whether there is a need for a new store and whether shoppers' habits can be changed to allow them to use it. (It is easy to say that the shopper will choose the nearest store, and that if a new store would have the effect of shortening her journey, then she will use it. But this is to make the elementary mistake of assuming an automatic response to a particular situation: we should know that with human beings anything is *possible* and that some reactions are *probable*.) So the chain store conducts a survey, aimed at finding out the present pattern of shopping behaviour.

To obtain an accurate, complete picture of the situation, it would be necessary to ask everyone within the neighbourhood of the proposed store a number of questions: where do you buy your everyday necessities, and if you use more than one shop, what is their relative importance? where do you make exceptional purchases such as household appliances, furniture or a suit of clothes? This is of course impossible. The chain store would ask a small number of people a few particularly searching questions. This is the essence of *sampling*, the selection of a small but representative portion of a population. A *sample* is a small number taken from a population for the purpose of surveying. A large sample is more likely to give accurate results than a small one, but accuracy depends more closely on the method of selection of the sample than on its size. If a sample is carefully selected, it should provide information from which reasonably precise conclusions on the characteristics of the total population can be drawn.

A sample must be chosen in such a way that every member of the population has an equal chance of being selected—that is, it must be *random*. A properly constructed sample must contain realistic proportions of men and women, rich and poor, young and old: it should, in other words, be a replica or *cross-section* of the real population. We can ensure that such a cross-section is obtained by *stratifying* the sample by dividing the population into meaningful groups or classes—perhaps in terms of age or occupation—and taking a random sample from each group in proportion to the size of the group within the total population, *Stratified random sampling*, while it requires more time and effort on the researcher's part, normally yields the most reliable results.

Systematic sampling is a convenient way in which to take a sample by selecting members of a population at regular intervals—for instance, by questioning every tenth or twentieth shopper in the shopping survey mentioned above. Unfortunately the gain in convenience is offset by a loss in reliability, since there may be regularly occurring variations or similarities in the population which systematic sampling might emphasize or obscure.

A simple way of achieving randomness in a sample is to use a printed table of random numbers—that is, a list of numbers selected electronically in such a way that each digit from 0 to 9 has an equal chance of being selected every time a selection is made. Once a way has been found of identifying individual members of a population numerically, the list can be used to select a random sample of its members. For instance, in an analysis of spatial distributions using data illustrated on maps, random numbers can be used to select co-ordinates of points or areas to be sampled, such as grid references on Ordnance Survey maps.

Nevertheless, however carefully a sample is taken it is unlikely to mirror precisely the composition of the whole population being surveyed. Thus a statement about a population based on a sample taken from it is generally qualified by an estimate of the degree of probability (see Unit 1.8(*c*) below) of that statement being true.

(*c*) **Probability**

Geographers are always looking for regularities in the distribution of human activities; as we saw in the last section, however, no population ever behaves uniformly. We must therefore be very careful when we make generalizations about people's spatial behaviour. We must ask *how* likely a given statement is to be true, for only when we know this does it begin to have real meaning. In most aspects of economic geography we are dealing with human reactions to opportunities to produce, sell and buy, and these can never be predicted with absolute certainty. We can only say that people will *probably* act in this way, or, much more precisely, that there is a certain *degree of probability* that they will do so. For example, it is highly probable that a housewife shopping for her family will visit a large store or shopping centre at least once a week, and furthermore that she will go to the nearest. There are likely to be exceptions, but in perhaps nine weeks out of ten she will act in this way. In other words, there is a 90 per cent probability that she will do her shopping like this, or, expressed somewhat differently, that 90 per cent of all housewives in her position will act in this way in any given week; it is upon calculations like these that markets and stores are located and their size determined. Similarly, it is possible to estimate the percentage probability that the Ghanaian farmer will grow this crop or that, and hence to predict both inputs (seed and fertilizer) and output or crop.

(d) Correlation

Geographers examining two or more sets of data will look for any kind of correspondence that may exist between them. We can say, for example, that the birth rate is higher in poor countries than in rich, that the consumption of energy is greater in rich countries than in poor, and that developed countries carry on more foreign trade than the less developed. We can be more precise than this. We can say that there is a simple, direct relationship between the GNP per head of a country and its energy consumption: an increase in one is likely to lead to an increase in the other. This implies that one variable is independent and the other dependent, meaning that movements of the latter depend upon, or are the result of, movements of the former. When we say that crop yields vary with the amount of fertilizer used by the farmer, there is no doubt about which of the two variables is independent and which dependent. On the other hand, when we look at the connection between birth rate and poverty the causal relationship is less clear. Poverty might be the consequence of overpopulation; equally, overpopulation might result from ignorance and lack of social responsibility which are in turn the result of poverty. But the empirical evidence, nonetheless, shows that they are related.

Sometimes a change in one variable brings about a precise and predictable change in another; increasing the temperature, for instance, always brings about the expansion of a copper bar. Here we can speak of a *perfect correlation*, or a correlation of 1·0, between the two. When we are considering human affairs, however, correlation is usually a good deal less than perfect. Fortunately we can measure the *degree of association* or *correlation* between sets of data. We can say that a correlation of 0·9 is good, and that there is very likely to be a causal connection between the two sets of data; but one of 0·3 or 0·4 is so weak that a causal connection has not been demonstrated.

We can demonstrate correlations by plotting one variable against another, as in Fig. 8.12 showing the relationship between energy consumption and GNP per head of population of many of the world's countries (there are several other instances in this book as well). If all the points lie on a line, whether the line is straight or curved, there must be a perfect correlation. In fact, none of them do, and the correlation must necessarily be less than unity. Most points, however, cluster close to the line (known as a *regression line*), so that we can see by inspection that the degree of correlation is a high one. On the other hand, a very few points, called *residuals*, lie at a great distance from the regression line. Clearly, the data which these points embody do not fit the generalization represented here. There must be some further factor to explain why the dependent variable does not correlate more or less precisely with the independent variable. Away to the left of the regression line is a point representing Panama where the GNP is relatively very high compared to the energy consumption, while to the right of the line is a point representing Korea, where the reverse is true. There are good reasons why this should be so. In other words, there are factors which have not been taken into consideration in the simple analysis represented by the regression line.

The graph is the simplest way of demonstrating a correlation, but there are ways of calculating and expressing it numerically. One of these, the *Spearman rank correlation*, consists in taking two sets of data, placing each in rank-order and then comparing the two ranked groups. Suppose we take a list of ten countries, chosen at random. We can look up the GNP and the energy consumption per head for each, and then set them in order as in the first three columns of Table 1.3. We then take the difference *d* between the two rankings for each country (column 4), calculate d^2 and sum the results (column 5).

Table 1.3   Calculating the Spearman rank correlation coefficient

	Energy consumption per head	Rank-order GNP per head	d	d^2
Canada	1	2	1	1
Kuwait	2	1	1	1
Australia	3	5	2	4
Belgium	4	4	0	0
West Germany	5	3	2	4
Italy	6	6	0	0
South Africa	7	7	0	0
Brazil	8	8	0	0
Zaïre	9	9	0	0
India	10	10	0	0
				$\Sigma d^2 = 10$

We now apply the formula

$$R = 1 - \frac{6\Sigma d^2}{n^3 - n}$$

where R is called the *rank correlation coefficient*—a measure of the degree of correlation—and n the number of countries:

$$R = 1 - \frac{6 \times 10}{10^3 - 10}$$
$$= 1 - \frac{60}{990}$$
$$= 0 \cdot 939$$

which is a very high degree of correlation indeed.

(*e*) **Lorenz Curves**
There are occasions when it is useful for us to be able to study the ways in which a particular characteristic is distributed among the population we are examining.

We might, for example, want to know whether all the farms in a particular country are roughly the same size, or whether there are some very large and some very small ones. Let us imagine that the sizes of all the farms in the country are the same (a highly improbable circumstance). If we draw a graph to show the relationship between their numbers and their cumulative area, it would be a straight line: a quarter of the farms would embrace a quarter of the agricultural land of the country, three-quarters of the farms would have three-quarters of the land, and so on. We know that, in fact, there is no country where all the farms are of the same size: they vary from smallholdings to large estates. Suppose that we rank all farms in order of size, beginning with the smallest. We might find the poorest 25 per cent (*quartile*) of farmers had only 6 per cent of the land between them, the next 25 per cent had 8 per cent and the next, 10 per cent. The richest quartile would thus hold no less than 76 per cent of the land.

This was the actual state of affairs in Egypt before 1952, with a few very rich landowners and a very large number of impoverished peasants. A programme of land reform was then introduced. Land was taken from large estates and used to make more medium-sized holdings, while at the same time the number of very small holdings was reduced. Complete equality of farm holdings was certainly not achieved, but they became less unequal than they had been: Fig. 1.7 represents the size of farm holdings before 1952, and also in 1965 when the land reform was complete. The straight line represents a perfect equality of all farm holdings. The diagram shows that as a result of the land reform, farm sizes were brought closer to perfect equality, but nevertheless remain a good distance from it.

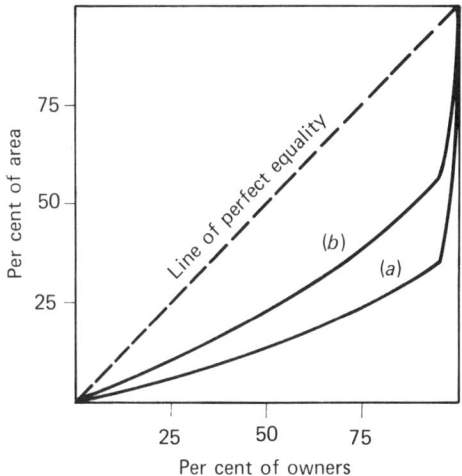

Fig. 1.7 Lorenz curves showing the distribution of sizes of Egyptian farm holdings (a) before the land reforms of 1952, and (b) in 1965 (after Agrarian Reform and Rural Power, *ILO, 1977)*

The curves in Fig. 1.7 are known as *Lorenz curves*; they are used to show graphically how a particular distribution of land, or jobs, or wealth differs from a perfectly equal distribution. A further example is discussed in Unit 10.5.

Detailed discussion of what can be done with information once collected and of its manipulation to yield useful conclusions is beyond the scope of this book. There are many useful texts on elementary statistics that cover techniques for collecting, describing and comparing data, some of which are listed at the end of the book.

Questions

1. What factors would (*a*) a Kansas wheat-farmer, (*b*) a Malayan rubber-planter be likely to consider if he contemplated expanding his activities?
2. Explain, giving examples, what you understand by the law of comparative advantage.
3. 'Economic geography is the study of the location, distribution and use of scarce resources.' Discuss.

Unit Two

Towns and Urban Functions

In the United Kingdom and, indeed, in most of the developed world, a large proportion of the population lives in cities and towns and is employed in factories and offices and in service activities. No less than 78 per cent of the British population is classed as urban. Over north-western Europe as a whole the proportion is about 68 per cent; in the United States it is 74 per cent, and in Australia as high as 86 per cent. Even in some of the developing countries as much as half the population lives in cities and towns, and the urban fraction is steadily increasing. Only in the least developed countries is less than a quarter of the population urban. This is because agriculture and rural pursuits are employing a steadily diminishing proportion of the population of the world. In most developed countries less than 5 per cent of the working population is employed in agriculture. Most of the remainder work in manufacturing and service industries and live in cities and towns.

Towns began to develop in the ancient civilizations of the Middle East and Orient during the third millennium B.C. From the start they served many functions: some were centres of government, and all were market centres in which the rural population could sell their products and purchase the goods fabricated by urban craftsmen. Towns grew in numbers and have spread over much of the world. Today there are few major regions which are not in some degree urbanized, and very nearly half the world's population lives in towns.

The Romans introduced the concept of the city to Britain, and some thirty cities of modern Britain derive from Roman origins. Foremost among them are London, York, Canterbury, Bath and Exeter. The number of towns increased during the Middle Ages to several hundred, but most remained small until the nineteenth century. Then, with the development of modern industry and commerce during the later nineteenth and early twentieth centuries, they began to expand rapidly. Few new towns were established, but the urban population in England and Wales grew from about 49 per cent of the total in the mid-nineteenth century to about 80 per cent on the eve of the First World War, and the proportion has since remained roughly the same. Cities and towns must therefore be central to the study of economic geography. They constitute important centres for both the consumption and production of goods, and for this reason they must necessarily be the focal points in the network of transport and communication. Furthermore, their rapid growth and the concentration of large numbers of people within quite small areas have created serious problems: those of congestion and crowding, of transport and the supply of food and water, of the provision of recreational amenities and of pollution and the disposal of waste. The problems of the city must occupy an important place in our studies.

We can all recognize cities and towns, but they are nevertheless difficult to define. They are concentrations of people among whom agricultural employment is of minor importance and most of whom are engaged in secondary and tertiary activities. The problem of description largely arises because towns are defined and delimited in different ways in different countries, so that their sizes are not strictly comparable. Some towns are, for statistical and administrative purposes, taken to include not only their suburbs, but also part of the surrounding rural areas: these are *overbounded*. There are many such instances in the United Kingdom, especially since the local government reorganization of 1974. Others—Chicago, for example—consist of a closely built and densely settled urban area, which extends far beyond the defined limits of the city itself: these are *underbounded*. In some countries it is the practice to measure the population not only of each city and town, but also of these 'metropolitan areas'. Greater London, reaching almost as far as Slough in the west and Brentwood in the east, might be considered such a metropolitan area. In the United States, the city of New York has a population of about 7 800 000, but lies embedded in a sprawling metropolitan area twice this size.

At the lower end of the urban spectrum the smallest towns, both in the United Kingdom and in the rest of the world, resemble villages in their function and appearance. Many are predominantly agricultural and are so closely bound up with their rural surroundings that they can be difficult to recognize as towns. There were many such rural towns in the United Kingdom. Most were merely medieval towns that had failed to grow and develop a broader range of functions in the nineteenth century. Some, however, retained their self-governing status, which alone distinguished them from villages, until the local government reforms of 1974.

2.1   Central Places

Whatever other functions it may have assumed, the town originated as a market centre, a place where people from the surrounding countryside could meet to exchange goods and services. Centrally placed in most towns is the market place, where villagers once laid out their goods for sale, though today it may well have been converted to a car park. As specialized crafts developed, many of the craftsmen established their business in the towns, from which they could most conveniently serve their surrounding areas.

If towns are to function as market centres for their local areas, they must be accessible to the farms and villages they serve. In medieval England it was assumed that the peasant's journey to market would not exceed $6\frac{2}{3}$ miles (about 10·7 km). The reasoning ran thus: a day's journey was reckoned to be 20 miles (about 32 km), and a peasant could spend up to a third of the day travelling to market and a similar time returning home, while the remaining third would be spent in the varied business and distractions of the market place. The maximum journey which the peasant might be expected to make to market was therefore a third of 20 miles, or $6\frac{2}{3}$ miles. The area served by a market might thus be thought of as a circle with a radius of $6\frac{2}{3}$ miles. Since it is not possible to cover the ground with a pattern of circles without overlaps or unserved zones, a hexagon of comparable size can be substituted for the circle (Fig. 2.1). We might thus expect a pattern of central places to develop such that no point would be more that $6\frac{2}{3}$ miles from the nearest central place, with each central place serving a hexagonal market area.

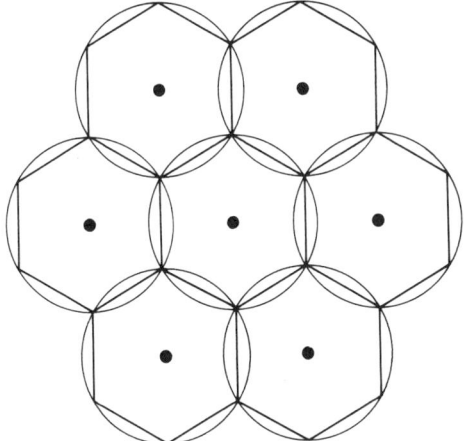

Fig. 2.1 A simple network of central places

This hexagonal pattern is the basis of the *central place theory* first proposed by the German scholar Walter Christaller in 1933. His theory assumed that the land was flat and of uniform quality, that movement was equally easy in all directions, that the purchasing power of the population was equally distributed, and that consumers followed the principle of least effort and minimized the distance travelled to obtain a service. Given these conditions, Christaller claimed, the result would be an absolutely regular pattern of urban centres, or *central places*, providing services for the population of the surrounding areas.

Central places display a hierarchical structure. Different services require different populations to sustain them. The minimum population necessary for the economic provision of a good or service is termed the *threshold population*. In the retail sector, the circumstances of say, a bread shop, whose products are required almost daily by most of the population, are quite different from those of a camera shop, whose wares are required much less frequently (see also Unit 2.2(*b*)). Furthermore, different services have different *ranges*. The range of a service is the distance over which consumers are prepared to travel to obtain it, and it depends on the impact of transport costs on the final price of the good or service to the consumer. Bread shops have low ranges, as bread is a low-cost item in frequent demand. Consumers are not prepared to travel far to obtain it because transport costs would add greatly to the total cost. Camera shops, on the other hand, have high ranges as cameras are relatively expensive and are bought infrequently, so their price to the consumer is less affected by transport costs. You will easily arrive at a concept of range by asking yourself how much more likely you are to travel 10 kilometres to save 10 per cent on the cost of a new camera than to travel 10 kilometres for the same saving on bread purchase.

   Low-order goods and services are those with low ranges and thresholds, and are provided from *low-order central places*. Similarly, *high-order goods and services* have high ranges and thresholds and are provided from *high-order central places*. There are fewer high-order central places; they are further apart and serve larger market areas than low-order places. High-order centres are larger than low-order centres because they offer all the goods and services provided by lower-order centres and more besides, and size is related to employment in the provision of services. A number of different orders of centre may be identified, depending upon the characteristic services they offer the surrounding population. Christaller identified eight orders in his study of southern Germany, ranging from the smallest village to a regional capital such as Munich.

   In the real world there is no perfectly uniform or *isotropic* surface. Nevertheless in areas such as East Anglia which is fairly flat and primarily agricultural there is a certain regularity in the number, size and spacing of settlements. The smallest villages, although widely distributed, do not provide more than the basic services. More specialized services may be obtained from market towns such as Thetford and Cromer. Above these, in turn, are a few larger centres, such as Bury St Edmunds and King's Lynn, above which are the two regional capitals Ipswich and Norwich. At the apex of this East Anglian *urban hierarchy* is London, outside the region and providing the highest-order services not only for East Anglia but for the whole United Kingdom. (Detailed research, of course, might well reveal more than these five orders of centres.)

   It is important to consider the relationship between the settlements and market areas of different orders, and the settlement pattern that emerges. According to Christaller's theory, there will be a fixed relationship between central places, depending upon the primary function to be achieved by the settlement arrangement. This relationship he expressed as a k value—k being a constant fixing the ratio of settlements and market areas of one order to those of the next. Christaller identified three principles that could be served by a settlement network of central places, each having a different k-value: the functions of marketing, transport and administration.

(a) The Marketing Principle

The function of marketing would best be served by a network in which low-order centres lie on the boundaries of market areas of the next higher-order centres (Fig. 2.2). Each place is thus surrounded by six places of the next lowest order, but each of these is, as it were, shared with two other places of similar order. The ratio of the lower-order to the higher is thus 2:1, and each higher-order market area is made up of *three* lower-order market areas: the market area of the place itself plus one-third of the market areas of each of the six surrounding lower-order centres $[1 + (6 \times 1/3) = 3]$ and thus $k = 3$. In this network—assuming that

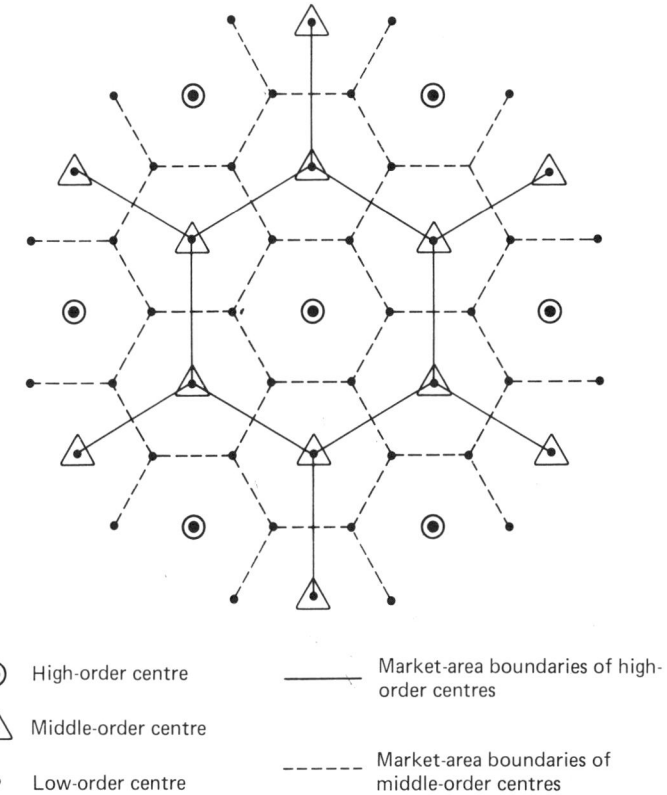

◉	High-order centre	———	Market-area boundaries of high-order centres
⬛	Middle-order centre		
•	Low-order centre	------	Market-area boundaries of middle-order centres

Fig. 2.2 Network of central places organized on the marketing principle (k = 3)

consumers are evenly distributed on the isotropic surface—the total distance travelled by all consumers to obtain services from central places is minimized, and thus this settlement network is most efficient for the purposes of marketing.

(b) The Transport Principle

An arrangement which was most efficient for transport purposes would involve locating each place in the middle of a straight line connecting the two adjacent higher-order places. Direct transport routes between two centres of similar order pass through centres of the next lower order at the boundary of their market areas (Fig. 2.3). (This is clearly not the case in Fig. 2.2, where $k = 3$.) If the transport principle applies, then $k = 4$, because each central place is surrounded by six places of the next lowest order but each of these is shared by only one other central place of similar order. Each market area is made up of four lower-order areas: that of the place itself and half the market areas of the six surrounding centres $[1 + (6 \times \frac{1}{2}) = 4]$. This arrangement minimizes the number and length of transport routes connecting central places.

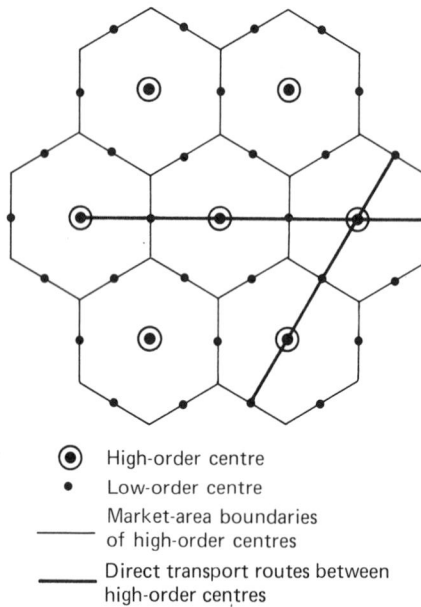

Fig. 2.3 Network of central places organized on the transport principle (k = 4)

(c) The Administrative Principle

The purposes of administration would best be served by a $k = 7$ settlement network, in which the market areas are arranged so that lower-order central places lie entirely within the market area of the next higher-order centre (Fig. 2.4); in this way there are no 'divided allegiances', and administration can be

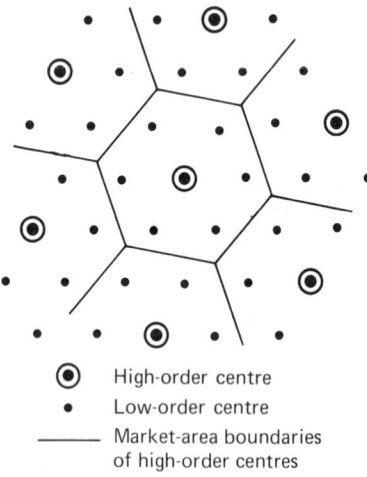

Fig. 2.4 Network of central places organized in the administrative principle (k = 7)

carried out efficiently. For this network $k = 7$, because the higher-order market area contains the equivalent of seven market areas of the next lowest order — one of its own plus six of the surrounding lower-order centres.

Table 2.1 shows the relationship between the market areas of successive orders according to each of the three principles described above: for a $k = 3$ network, for example, the first-order area contains the equivalent of three second-order areas, nine third-order and so on. Each market area has a central place and so the relationship between the number of central places of successive orders is similar; because the theory assumes that the distribution of population is uniform, there is also a similar relationship between the numbers of people served by central places of successive orders.

Table 2.1   Numbers of market areas in successive orders

Order	Marketing principle $(k = 3)$	Transport principle $(k = 4)$	Administrative principle $(k = 7)$
1 (highest)	1	1	1
2	3	4	7
3	9	16	49
4	27	64	343

How close is this central place theory of Christaller to reality? People are not evenly distributed over an isotropic plain and do not always behave rationally, and so a perfectly ordered network of central places can be found nowhere in the world. When Christaller tested his theory in southern Germany, he of course found no regular settlement pattern, nor any uniform ratio of smaller places to larger. But he did find a hierarchy of settlements and each larger place had a number of smaller places dependent upon it. The density of settlements clearly varied with such factors as the quality of the land and the adequacy of the means of transport. It was very much denser in the Rhine and Neckar valleys than it was over large areas of Bavaria, but overall it seemed that the marketing principle was the most important of the factors influencing the pattern.

Christaller's theory should not, however, be judged inadequate because of its failure to explain reality exactly. It is a formalized and rigorous theoretical statement of the relationship between settlements and their surrounding areas and as such has been further developed by other workers and widely used in urban and regional planning.

2.2   Urban Functions

Christaller, and those such as Lösch and Berry who have elaborated and developed his theory, have stressed two significant aspects of urban development. Settlements form a hierarchy of size and function, and each has a market-area or *sphere of influence* which varies in extent according to its function. Reality is, of course, vastly more complex than theory. In the first place, as we have seen, the distribution of central places is never regular or uniform; moreover, settlements have other functions apart from providing services for the surrounding populations. Furthermore, the sizes of settlements form a smooth gradation from large to small: we rarely find any step or break dividing one order from the next and there is no question that places of the same order are necessarily of similar size.

(a) Rank-order

In almost every country, there is one city which in size greatly overshadows all others. It is sometimes called the *primate* city: London in Great Britain is an instance, and so are Paris in France and Chicago in the American Midwest. If, however, we rank the other towns in the country according to size, we usually find them to be closer and closer together as we go down the scale. We can represent this graphically: Fig. 2.5, for example, shows the rank-size of towns in

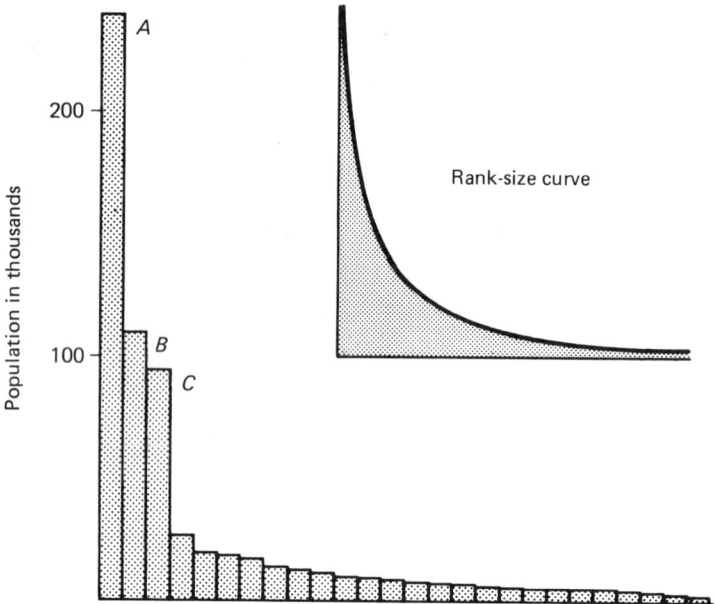

Fig. 2.5 Rank-order of towns in south-west England, and a theoretical rank-order graph

south-western England. The largest town, Plymouth, (A), is roughly twice the size of the second largest, Torbay (B), roughly three times the size of the third, Exeter (C), and so on. This can be expressed in the formula

$$p^n = \frac{p^1}{n}$$

where p^n is the size of the nth largest town and p^1 that of the largest. A graph drawn strictly according to this formula has been superimposed on Fig. 2.5, and it can be seen that the towns of south-west England accord very closely with the model.

This, however, is not always so. There are sometimes quite wide divergences from the model. In Australia, for example, there are two primate cities of approximately equal size—Sydney and Melbourne—while in England the primate city, London, is no less than eight times the size of the second largest, Birmingham. Much depends, however, on how we define a city or town. If we compare Greater London with the West Midlands conurbation, we find a relationship that accords very much more closely with the rank-size model. As a general rule, the rank-size model is very approximately satisfied; it even fits quite closely the sizes of the cities of Roman Britain. Though we cannot ever expect it to fit a particular case precisely, any wide departure from it calls for special investigation and explanation.

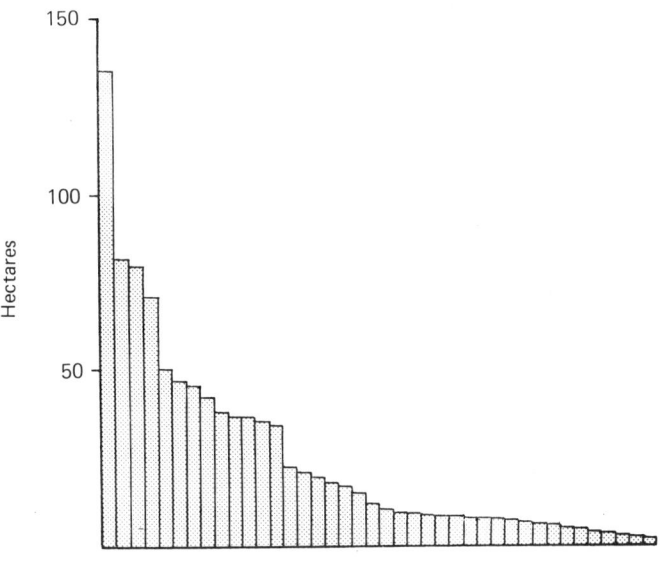

Fig. 2.6 Rank-order of cities (civitates) of Roman Britain

(b) Thresholds

With so even a gradation from large towns to small, it becomes very difficult indeed to differentiate between first-, second- and third-order places on the basis of their size alone. It occasionally happens that a small jump in the graph may serve to distinguish them, but a categorization on the basis of population must in general remain very arbitrary. Towns should therefore preferably be classified on the basis of function; Christaller, after all, defined his higher-order places not in terms of their greater population, but in relation to. the more diversified services they provided.

This idea is expressed in a different way when we say that a branch of Boots the Chemists requires a catchment area of 10 000 people—perhaps more in a low-income area—in order to remain in business. A smaller population will not generate enough trade; a larger population might lead the branch to take on more staff. There is a similar, though lower, threshold—perhaps 500–1 000 people—for a large grocery store, whereas Marks and Spencer appears to require an appreciably higher threshold. While banks vary greatly in size, a branch bank probably requires a population of 5–10 000. Certain highly specialized shops such as antique dealers or jewellers serve a very large population; they are readily found in large towns, but seldom in small. Each of these functions serves the needs not only of the town in which it is carried on, but also those of a surrounding market area. Higher-order functions require a larger population to support them than those of a lower order.

If towns are classified according to the functions they perform, and the result plotted on a graph, a gradation will still be found but thresholds are more likely to become apparent, separating the urban spectrum into a small number of orders of magnitude. There remains, however, a number of problems. In the first place, how do we measure the functions performed by a central place· of whatever order? What weight should we give to banks, department stores, specialist shops, public libraries, newspapers, local government offices and schools? Their catchment or service areas are likely to differ from each other, and it is impossible to set a value on some of the services rendered. Employment may be used as a measure of their size, but statistics are unlikely to be available through the whole range of urban functions. We are likely to be left with a number of approximate measures of the significance of central places, and must not be disappointed to find that our study area lacks the elegant simplicity of Christaller's model, with its attendant assumptions.

2.3   Markets and Service Functions

In this section we shall examine the categories of services provided by urban centres: *professional services, personal services* and *retail services and marketing*. There are, of course, others: the provision of transport and communication facilities, the operation of commodity, financial and wholesale markets, and government service and administration. Lack of space prevents a fuller discussion of these service functions beyond that given in Unit 11.

(a) Professional Services

These include the services of doctors and dentists, of lawyers, bankers and brokers, teachers and architects. Their services are largely of an individual or face-to-face nature; they are based upon a prolonged period of training and are generally relatively highly remunerated. In a developed society such as that of the United Kingdom there is a predictable ratio of professional people to the total population: there is on average a doctor for every 800 of the population, a dentist for each 4 000, and a lawyer for every 3 000–4 000. This is a rough measure of the frequency with which the public calls upon them. It might therefore be assumed that in a relatively homogeneous society their distribution would show a high correlation with that of the population itself. This is not, however, supported by the evidence. The ratios of, for example, doctors, dentists and lawyers to the total population varies very considerably from one area to another. You can work out some of these for your own town quite easily, using the relevant professional directories or the yellow pages of the telephone directory. You will probably find that the ratios are much higher in good residential areas than in poorer, and in middle-class and service-oriented towns rather than in those that are working-class or industrially based.

(b) Personal Services
These include the services supplied by, for instance, hairdressers, laundries and tailors. Their ratio to the total population varies greatly, as does the social level at which they are pitched. They are most often associated with shopping centres, as though the once- or twice-weekly shopping excursion might take in also a visit to the hairdresser or the collection of laundry.

(c) Retail Shopping and Market Centres
Everyone is a consumer, and almost everyone has at some time to purchase goods from shops. In Great Britain in 1977, about 20 per cent of each family's expenditure (on average) went on food, with roughly 10 per cent on housing; most of the remainder was spent on clothing and other 'durables'. This at once introduces an important distinction between two categories of retail shops. *Convenience stores* are those which we visit frequently, usually to buy perishable foods and articles of daily use like soaps and detergents. We do not want to travel far to purchase such goods, and trips to the central business district (CBD; see Unit 2.4(a)) are rarely made solely to buy groceries. Instead, we use the 'corner store' or the shopping centres which lie scattered through the residential areas of the larger towns.

Durable goods, often known as *shoppers' goods*—articles like a new suit, a television set or a suite of furniture—are bought much less frequently. Each represents a relatively large financial outlay, and the buyer usually pauses to compare competing brands, patterns and qualities. The purchase of durable goods is commonly the objective of an expedition. The purchaser is usually prepared to travel a considerable distance, and he likes to be able to move from one competing shop to another in his search for a particular commodity. This is an important reason why durable goods shops tend to cluster in the Central Business District (CBD), which has usually the further advantage of good transport facilities from suburban and residential areas.

A small town, or low-order central place, is likely to have a few shops which sell durable goods, together with a number of chain stores like Liptons, Sainsbury's or International, and a few other convenience stores, with a scatter of convenience shops outside the area of the CBD. A large town will have a more extensive and varied CBD, in which shops selling luxury goods will be mingled with 'shoppers' shops' but the convenience store will be comparatively rare. For day-to-day purchases people will not go to the CBD, with its travel problems and parking difficulties, but rather to the 'corner shop' or to a shopping centre which is likely to be made up of convenience stores—grocers, newsagents and shops selling fruit and vegetables, sweets and tobacco, hardware and ironmongery. The largest shopping centres may break into the lower ranges of the durable goods trade, perhaps with a store selling mass-produced furniture, domestic appliances and television sets.

Shopping centres are adjusted, if only approximately, to the needs of the public who use them. Shops which fail to serve these needs are likely to have only a short life. The centres themselves assume many forms. One may consist of a row of small shops, whose customers come mainly on foot; another may be made up of large stores arranged, not necessarily elegantly, around an open space which serves as a car park. In its most modest form it takes the shape of a shabby one-man store, trying desperately to fight the competition of a group of modern shops half a mile away.

Fig. 2.7 illustrates diagrammatically the structure of retail shops in a variety of settlements, ranging from the large town to the village. The first diagram (*a*), represents a large town or high-order central place in which the CBD, apart from its financial and professional services, is given over largely to the sale of durable goods, with only a small fraction of the retail area devoted to food stores (apart from restaurants and delicatessens). Convenience shopping is largely done at centres in the residential areas of the town. In the medium-size town, (*b*), the CBD is likely to have more food stores and convenience shops, but peripheral

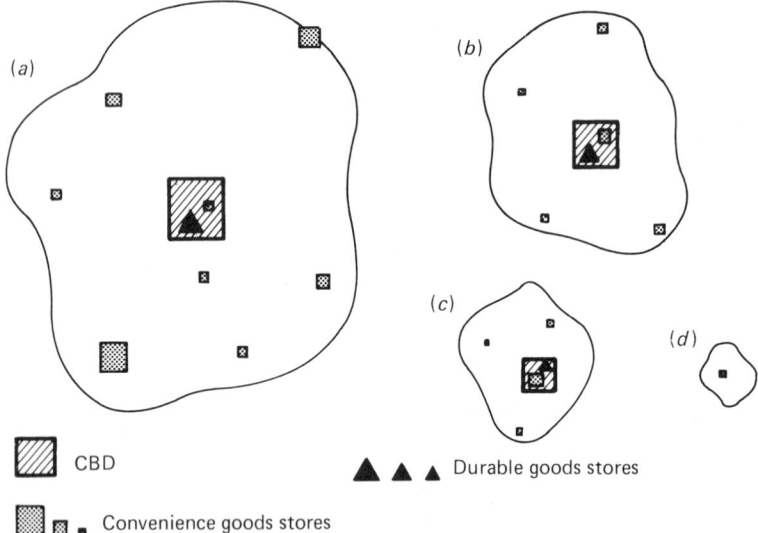

Fig. 2.7 *Models representing the location of retail shops in (a) a large town, (b) a medium-sized town, (c) a small town and (d) a village*

centres and stores will still be relatively important. In the small town, (c), which is unlikely to be larger than the area (or population) served by a large-town suburban shopping centre, the town centre is likely to contain both the convenience and the durables shops, but the latter are not conspicuous as the shopper is more likely to go for durable goods to the nearest large town. Lastly the village, or lowest-order central place, (d), is likely to have only one or two shops selling convenience goods, leaving shoppers' goods entirely to the larger urban centres.

There is, in fact, a steady gradation from type (a) to type (d), with shops selling durables of diminishing importance both absolutely and relatively towards the smaller end of the 'spectrum'. This is illustrated in Fig. 2.8. At a certain point—x in Fig. 2.8—the sale of durable goods disappears for practical purposes. This is

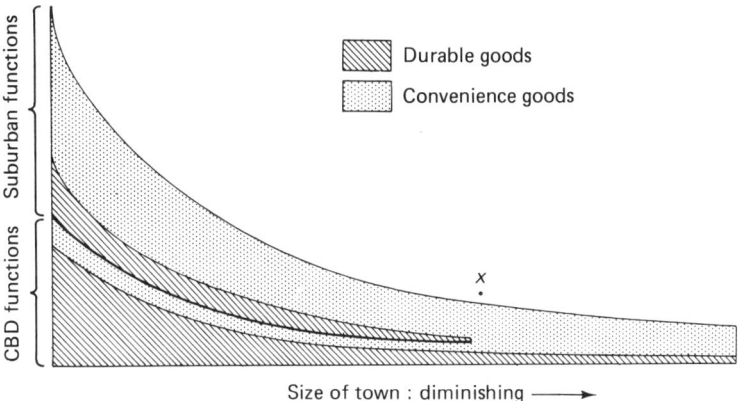

Fig. 2.8 The relationship between the CBD and suburban functions in towns graduated from the very large to the very small

a hypothesis, to be tested against the evidence of towns and centres. Where is the boundary to be drawn between large and medium towns, or between medium and small? Can a suburban shopping centre in a large town so increase in size and become so diversified in function that it becomes in effect a CBD in its own right, with its own hierarchy of shopping centres? American evidence suggests that it can.

Urban Population

One aspect of the city is, however, comparatively well known. We know with a high level of accuracy how big it was when the last census was taken, and we also know, perhaps slightly less precisely, what its inhabitants do for a living. These data are published in the census reports and are commonly kept more or less up to date by local authorities between one census and the next. But they record categories of employment for local government units, not for the streets or districts of a city, and so only allow comparisons to be made between cities and regions, not between one suburb and another. This does not, however, prevent the student from making his own survey. Employment in a suburb, ward or street, obtained by random sampling, can be compared with published figures for the census unit as a whole. It can thus be shown to be more or less working-class, say, or professional-class than the average.

There are ways of checking or testing such conclusions. Inspection of the housing itself, inquiry into rateable values and checks on commuters (made at the appropriate times of day at bus stops or railway stations) can all throw a great deal of light on the occupational structure of a town. It is particularly illuminating to relate housing, occupational structure and other such parameters to the quality of shopping available. Simple questions to be answered or hypotheses to be tested might concern the relationship between specialist shops or department stores, or even newsagents, betting shops or post offices, with the income–employment structure of the areas of a town where they are found.

Population statistics serve, in particular, to highlight the functions of a town. The census uses an accepted classification of types of employment. We can see at a glance what fraction of the employed population is engaged in clerical work or in a particular type of manufacturing industry. We can tell whether a town contains a high or low proportion of professional people, or whether it serves as a dormitory for those who commute to offices in the nearest big city. In a highly industrialized region it might be desirable to map, in addition, the numbers of those employed in specific sectors of industry. This was done on an ambitious scale in the *Atlas of Britain* (Oxford Clarendon Press, 1963) though the data on which these maps were based are now obsolete. Such statistics and maps are, however, only descriptive. It is by the correlation of distribution patterns with one another that our understanding of the functioning of the city is deepened, and we discover added meaning in the distribution of the services it provides.

2.4   Urban Structure

It is a useful exercise to prepare an urban land-use map. This may be done on a small scale, using only the generalized categories of land use—industrial, residential, recreational and so forth—employed in the published land-use surveys. Alternatively, every property in a given district may be listed and classified, using a large-scale map (6″ or 25″ to the mile, for example). Shops can be shaded according to the goods they sell—groceries and convenience goods, clothing and footwear, furniture and other durable consumer goods. Financial houses (banking, insurance) and professional services (legal, medical, dental) can each be given an appropriate colour or symbol. Domestic housing can be classified in several ways—by quality (low-, middle- and high-income), by style (terraced, semi-detached, detached) or by density, which may range from 1 to 40 dwellings to the hectare. The result is a 'picture' of the urban scene.

The next stage is the analysis of this pattern, the explanation of why it takes on a particular form, and the formulation of generalizations regarding it. This can be done in two ways. The first consists in comparing the present urban pattern with early patterns constructed from such sources as old maps, directories and photgraphs. This may suggest the trend of development; it may, for example, provide a measure of the decay of the inner city and the spread of urban blight, or, alternatively, of the spread of the suburbs into surrounding countryside. The second method is the comparison of the urban pattern with whatever measurable parameters are available. The student will ask questions: what, for example, is the relationship between the quality of housing and the physical terrain? what effect has public transport on the quality of housing, as revealed in rateable values? how are shops and shopping centres related to residential areas? and what factors govern the pattern of people's behaviour when they go to market?

(a) Urban Models

From such studies emerge models of urban structure, simplified pictures of urban land use.

At the centre of every town is a cluster of shops, banks and business houses. This is the *central business district*, or CBD. It is usually quite easy to delimit it. It may cover only a few blocks in a small town, but in a larger centre it may spread over one or two square kilometres. Its buildings are often taller and more pretentious than those in the surrounding area. Few people live here, and space is taken up mainly by shops or offices. The shops themselves are commonly larger than those outside the CBD, and are likely to include clothing, furniture and luxury goods stores. Outside the CBD are found factories, warehouses, shopping centres and mile after mile of residential streets. These may at first glance seem to be arranged in a haphazard or random fashion. Nevertheless, geographers and urban sociologists have sought to find a pattern in this confusion, to establish a generalized picture or model of the spatial structure of the city.

One of the first of such attempts was made by Burgess, an urban sociologist working in Chicago, on the shore of Lake Michigan. He claimed to find a series of concentric rings around the CBD, here known as *the Loop*. Adjoining the CBD was a second zone of older and generally decaying residential buildings, sliding downwards into slums and tending to attract poor immigrant settlers. Beyond this, in zone three, was a belt of working-class housing, inhabited largely by people who had moved outwards from zone two. Lastly came a zone of better-class residential property and, on the outer fringe of the metropolitan area, the spacious homes of those who could afford to 'commute' the relatively long distances to the centre (Fig. 2.9).

While we can recognize in this model some common features of British and other cities, it failed to consider some important factors in urban growth. The Burgess model was refined by Hoyt, again on the evidence of American cities. Hoyt did not deny a certain zonal character in the spatial character of the city, but he emphasized the tendency for sectors—industrial, low-cost residential, high-quality residential and so on—to develop *across* the zones (Fig. 2.10). He claimed that, once established, a certain type of land use was likely to spread outwards from the centre along established lines of communication. Industrial

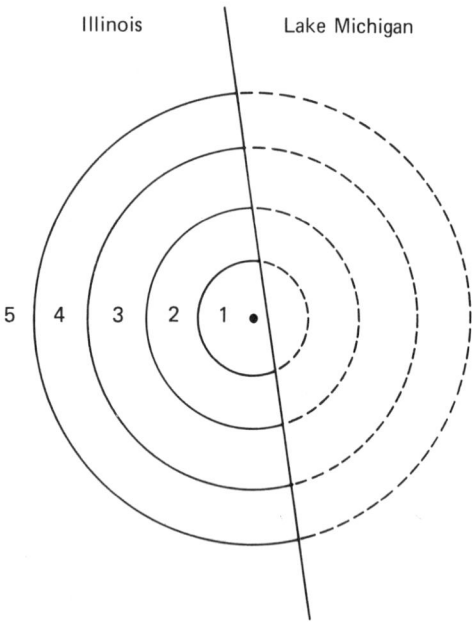

Zone 1:   'The Loop' (Central Business District)
Zone 2:   The zone in transition
Zone 3:   The zone of working men's homes
Zone 4:   The residential zone
Zone 5:   The commuter zone

Fig. 2.9 Burgess's concentric model of urban functions

sites, for example, might be developed along a railway or canal, and middle-range housing along a commuters' line or close to a trunk highway. It is easy to find examples of this pattern of development. It is often said that better-class housing developed on the windward side of industrial cities, while factories and working-class housing were relegated to opposite and less salubrious quarters, and this thesis can certainly be illustrated by London, Birmingham, Bristol and Coventry. There were doubtless other factors than wind direction, but qualities of housing and location of factories nevertheless tended to form belts lying at right angles to Burgess's concentric zones.

A further refinement of this model has been suggested by Harris and Ullman (Fig. 2.11). They point to the separate or autonomous development of 'nuclei', each of which concentrates a certain type of human activity. Heavy industry and high-class housing, for instance, are mutually incompatible, and are often found at opposite extremities of a town. Low-cost housing is likely to be found where land is cheapest—on the flood-plain of a river, for example—and amenities are least. This view of the town has much in common with that proposed by Hoyt.

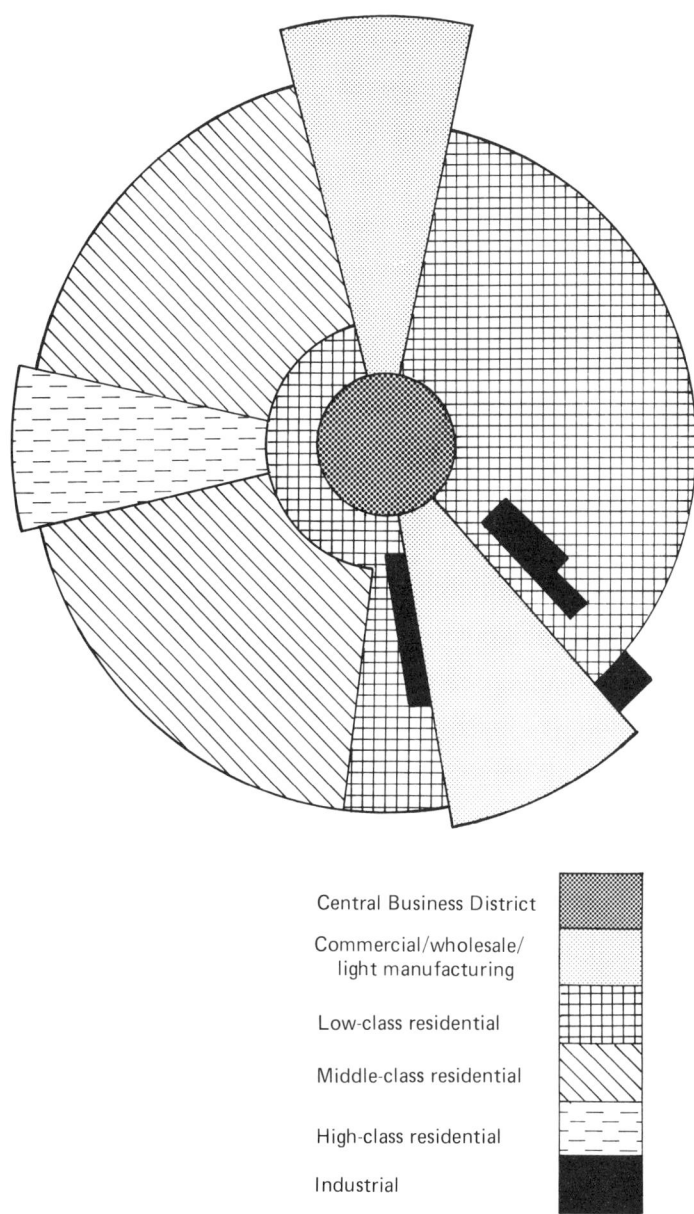

Central Business District

Commercial/wholesale/
    light manufacturing

Low-class residential

Middle-class residential

High-class residential

Industrial

Fig. 2.10 Hoyt's sector model of urban functions

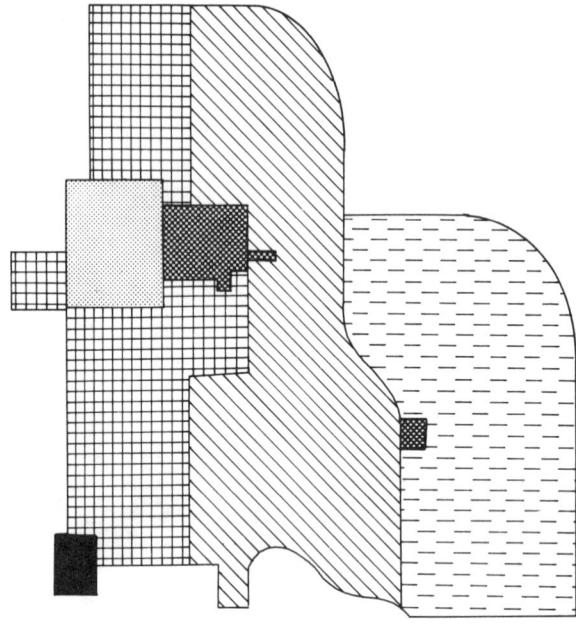

Fig. 2.11 The model by Harris and Ullman of urban functions (key to shading as in Fig. 2.10)

Another attempt to reconcile the concentric pattern of Burgess with Hoyt's radial pattern was made by Mann in 1965. He postulated the division of the city into a series of segments within each of which there was a concentric organization (Fig. 2.12). Mann's model is particularly useful in the British context because it was based on the study of three British cities and took into consideration, among other things, the very active role of the local authorities in determining urban land-use patterns through the provision of municipal housing and public amenities. It is worth noting that Mann's model of urban structure follows Hoyt's in predicting the sectoral development of better-class housing in the west—because of the prevailing westerly winds—and the confinement of industry and lower-class housing to the east.

(*b*) Accessibility and Urban Land Use

The chief factor in determining the arrangement of land uses in urban areas is *accessibility*, although in any individual city land use zones will reflect the particular topographic, social and historical background. Different activities have different accessibility requirements and some are better able to pay for the use of more accessible land. The most accessible area in a city is at the point

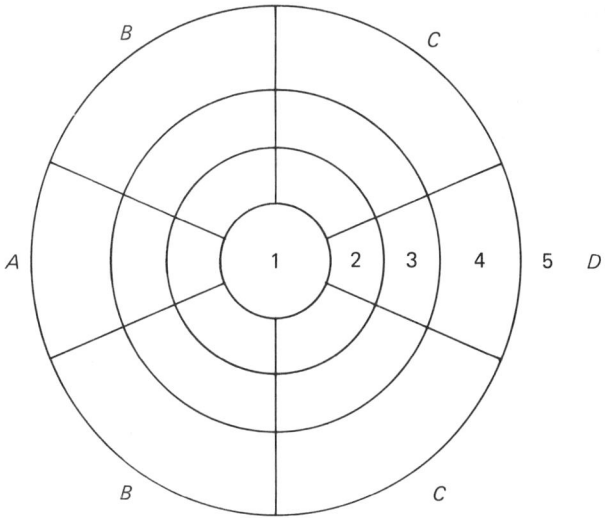

Zones

Zone 1: City centre/CBD
Zone 2: Transitional zone
Zone 3: Zone of small terraced
houses in sectors C and D,
larger bye law houses in B,
large old houses in A
Zone 4: Interwar residential
development, peripheral
post-1945 development
Zone 5: Commuters' dormitory villages

Sectors

Sector A: Middle-class sector
Sector B: Lower-middle-class sector
Sector C: Working-class/municipal
housing sector
Sector D: Industry and
lowest-working-class sector

Fig. 2.12 Mann's model of urban structure

where transport routes converge and this is usually near the topographic centre. This area becomes dominated by commercial activities such as retailing and financial services which require good access to their many consumers throughout the urban area and beyond. In this way the central business district referred to in Unit 2.4(*a*) develops. Here space is limited and there is great competition for the use of land, so land values or rents are high. Only those activities able to pay high rents obtain the use of this space, and industrial and residential activities are forced outwards to more peripheral locations. One response to high land values is to use the land more intensively—it is common knowledge that the central areas of towns are frequently characterized by high-rise buildings. Conversely, land is used more extensively—building heights decrease and plots increase in area—with greater distance from the centre because, in general, accessibility and thus land values decline towards the periphery.

Accessibility does not decline at a uniform rate, however (one of the faults of

Burgess's model is that he assumed that it did and therefore proposed perfectly concentric zones), but depends on the disposition of the transport network (see Unit 12.2). There will be ridges and peaks of accessibility and land values along transport links and at transport nodes (intersections and junctions). Thus the land value surface of an urban area resembles an irregular tent with a peak at the centre, ridges along the main roads and localized peaks at road junctions, railway stations and at areas with some particular amenity or advantage (Fig. 2.13). Such peaks are characterized by smaller concentrations of business

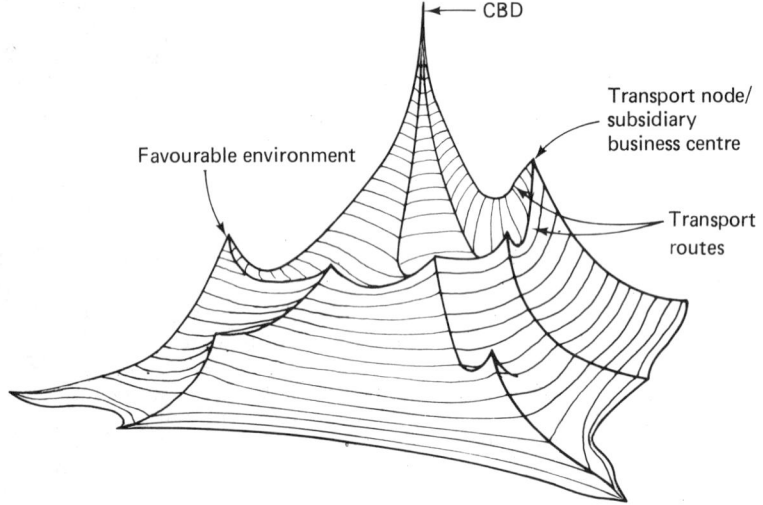

Fig. 2.13 The surface of land values in a hypothetical city; note the highest values at the centre and 'peaks' at other points

activity or high-class housing; other users are relegated to cheaper, less desirable sites. In this way, the varied mosaic of urban land use emerges.

(c) Local Urban Studies
You might find it interesting to make a study of the distribution of functions within your own (or the nearest) city or town, and to discover which of these models applies most closely to your own.

Up to a point you can discover the functions and quality of the many parts of a town by inspection—that is, by going about the streets with map and notebook in hand. You can, however, supplement this visual evidence by more quantitative and precise data. It would be very useful to know the value of land or of property and to plot its variations on a map, but in general too little comes on to the market at disclosed prices for this to be possible. On the other hand, the rateable value of property can be looked up by any citizen in the offices of the local authority. Residential suburbs can be compared; variations in the average rateable value for each street or block can be plotted on maps, and in this way a measure of social structure devised. The rateable values of business properties in the CBD can be obtained in the same way. It is possible—though not easy—to work out the average rateable value per square metre of floor space. Far more practicable, however, and no less useful is the calculation of the rateable value per metre of street frontage. Rateable values would be a great deal higher in the CBD than in the surrounding 'inner city', which is so often an area of blight. Even within the CBD, variations in rateable value—and thus in property values—are certain to be found. Rateable values, as the most readily available and usable measures of personal wealth and way of life, play a vital role in the analysis of urban patterns. Indeed, the Hoyt model of urban development was based to a large degree on variations in the tax value of property.

(*d*) The Problem of the Inner City and CBD

The motor car has brought about a revolution in the spatial structures of city and town. It is a major reason for the decay of the inner city (Burgess's zone two), whose inhabitants have moved to the suburbs to live, while they commute to the city centre for their work. Though this movement is in part by public transport, the private car also plays an important role. It at once raises the question of urban traffic congestion and the provision of car parks, for which large areas adjacent to the CBD and even within it are needed. City workers' cars thus rest by day where an earlier generation of city workers slept by night.

The retreat to the suburbs of the urban middle class has been followed by a shift in shopping facilities. We often find in the inner city only the decaying corner store, while new shopping centres are built in the expanding suburbs. The newer centres are usually served by good roads and have ample car-parking space. They have competed successfully with the small corner shop for the business of all except the lowest-income groups, and American evidence suggests that they are also tending to replace the CBD. In countless cities the CBD is of declining importance in retail trade. Large stores, especially those dealing in clothing and furniture, establish branches in the shopping centres, which are often found to be larger and to be carrying a wider range of goods than the parent store 'downtown'. There are many reasons for this trend, including the greater space for parking and for the display of goods at the centres as compared with traffic congestion, one-way streets and parking difficulties in the CBD. The latter all too often bears a faded image, belonging in terms of style and décor rather to the turn of the century than to the 1970s, while shopping centres by contrast are adapted in style and plan to the present day. Shops are being followed in their flight to the suburbs by banks and insurance houses, legal firms, doctors and dentists.

The predicament of the CBD and the inner city in many parts of the United States is a very unhappy one. Some newly built shopping centres lie outside the jurisdiction of the city administration and pay no local taxes to the urban authorities. The disappearance of business from the centre thus represents a net loss of revenue. Many great American cities—New York in particular—are thus in desperate financial straits, some having become unable to pay for their own essential services; indeed, Cleveland, Ohio, was in early 1979 on the edge of

Fig. 2.14 (a) A modern suburban shopping centre, with dozens of different shops beneath a single roof;

bankruptcy. In the United Kingdom the city centres have not reached this plight, because methods of raising revenue are different, and because the central government makes large direct grants to local authorities. The trend is none the less apparent towards larger suburban shopping centres with a steadily increasing share of total business. The subject deserves very careful investigation by geographers.

It is urgently necessary to find a solution to the problem of the inner city and CBD. In the bigger cities of the United Kingdom large sums of public money have been spent on modernizing property in inner urban areas and the central government runs 'partnership' schemes with inner city local authorities designed to boost economic activity and improve the living environment. Another solution, much favoured in the United States, has been to build tower-blocks of flats, often of luxury quality, in and near the CBD.

None of these measures, however, has been particularly effective in bringing business back to the centre of the city.

2.5   Inter-urban Relations

Christaller, as we have seen, postulated a series of closely similar autonomous territorial units, each bounded by a line which represented the maximum travel distance to its market centre. This concept had a certain validity when goods

(b) the main shopping street of a country town

travelled at the speed of an ox-drawn waggon. It has little relevance to conditions today, when 100 km may represent merely an hour's drive. The compulsion to use the nearest market town has declined throughout most developed countries, though no doubt it remains significant in those which are developing. The catchment areas of towns and shopping centres are thus more fluid than ever before, and it becomes increasingly important to establish a model representing the normal or expected pattern of relations between urban centres.

(a) Catchment Areas

We can assume that lower-order goods of the kind which are normally obtained from a 'convenience' shop (see Unit 2.3(c)) will always be purchased locally, and that no one will drive 30 km for groceries that can be bought in the next street. It is the need for higher-order goods and services which leads people to travel to a distant town, for instance to purchase durable goods, to use professional services, or to visit the theatre, some sporting occasion or other forms of entertainment. Underlying and supporting the attraction of distant urban centres will be the provision of good roads, the availability of public transport and the circulation of newspapers with their advertising services.

Fig. 2.15 shows the trading and service areas of a town of intermediate size. They vary a great deal from one town to another, as might be expected, but most are larger than might have been inferred from the size of the town and that of its

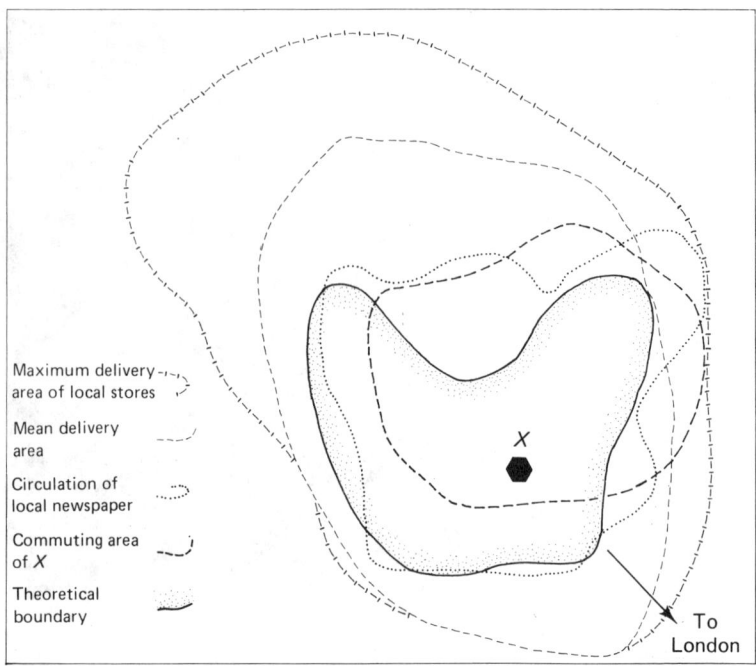

Maximum delivery
area of local stores

Mean delivery
area

Circulation of
local newspaper

Commuting area
of *X*

Theoretical
boundary

X

To
London

Fig. 2.15 Catchment area of a town in south-eastern England; note that the area is elongated to the north-west, that is, away from London (based on field work by Barbara G. Young)

neighbours. Two features deserve comment. The first is the tendency for the town's sphere of influence to be elongated towards the north-west, while extending only a short distance to the south and south-east, and this tendency is particularly evident in the delivery area of local retail stores. This is because the West End of London lies within 50 km to the south-east, and exercises a powerful attraction on people living on this side of the town; the effect of the capital is thus to push the town's sphere of influence away in the opposite direction. A second feature is the considerable difference between the *mean* delivery area of local stores and the *maximum* area served by one of them. This discrepancy is greatest towards the north-west, showing how broad is the belt of territory within which the desire to shop in *X* slowly diminishes with increasing distance.

(b) Theoretical Sphere of Influence

Towards the margin of *X*'s sphere of influence is a zone of indifference, within which shoppers are as likely to go to *Y* or *Z*, or to some other town, each of which offers facilities and services not radically different from those provided by *X*. This suggests that there might be some way, other than by laborious and often unreliable field observation and inquiry, to determine the respective spheres or catchment areas of X, Y, Z and other towns. Two theories have been devised to measure the respective 'pulls' of neighbouring towns.

(*i*) **Reilly's break-point theory.** The first derives from the gravity model discussed in Unit 1.8(*a*), which defines the attractive force G of a town as

$$G = \frac{P}{d^2}$$

where P is its population and d the distance from it. Let us consider two neighbouring towns X and Y, with populations respectively of P_X and P_Y—say, 70 000 and 40 000 (Fig. 2.16). It is inherently probable that the former will have

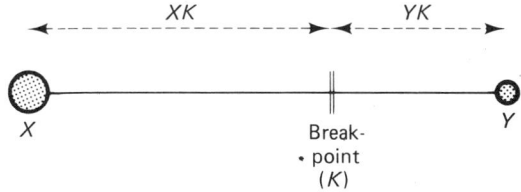

Fig. 2.16 Diagram illustrating Reilly's break-point theory

larger and more numerous shops and services than the latter, and that its sphere of influence will be greater. People will be prepared to travel farther to shop or do business in X than to use the corresponding services of Y, and the *break-point* between the two centres, K, where their respective attractiveness is equal, will be closer to Y than to X. But how much closer?

The gravity formula given above can be manipulated to give

$$d_{XK} = \frac{d_{XY}}{1 + \dfrac{P_X}{P_Y}}$$

where d_{XK} and d_{XY} are the distances between X and K and between X and Y respectively. The theoretical break-point between X and each of its nearest neighbours can thus be calculated quite simply and the several break-points joined together to give a *theoretical* sphere of influence, which may not, however, agree closely with the results of field observation. One reason may be the use of straight-line distances in the theoretical calculation, whereas the shopper necessarily has to follow a road which may be far from direct. The model fails also to make allowance for either the relative attractiveness of the physical difficulties of the road to a nearby town. These may modify very greatly the *perceived* distances, for in all human behaviour there is a strong psychological factor, impossible to measure and sometimes difficult to identify. Lastly, a small town may offer some particular attraction: easy (or free) parking, a good restaurant, a pleasant shopping precinct or merely an atmosphere which the shopper enjoys but cannot define. Nevertheless, wherever you find that the *real* zone of influence departs significantly from the theoretical, you should try to elucidate the reason.

(*ii*) **Huff's probability model.** Alternatively the sphere of influence of a town may be estimated by calculating the probability (see Unit 1.8(*c*)) that a shopper in any intermediate location will go to each of the rival centres. Fig. 2.17 illustrates

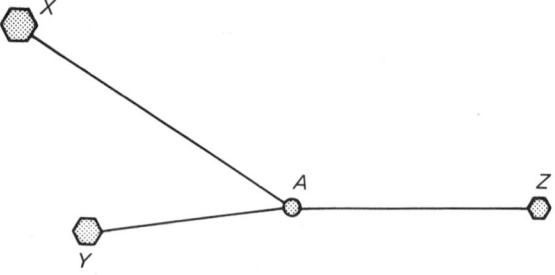

Fig. 2.17 Diagram illustrating Huff's probability model

the situation: the shopper is at A, and for practical purposes has the choice of X, Y and Z in which to purchase a suite of furniture. Assuming that delivery of the goods to A presents no problem, his decision is likely to be influenced by (1) the relative distance of the centres, and (2) the range of choice, that is, the number of shops at each. The probability that he will make a purchase at one centre amounts to a certainty, which we can express as 1·0. The customer is attracted to X despite its somewhat greater distance by the larger range of choice offered there. Let us say then that there is a 50 per cent chance—a probability of 0·5—that the purchase will be made at X. But Y and Z have a certain attraction, especially Y, which is on balance preferred to Z. Let us say that the probabilities of buying at Y and Z respectively are 0·3 and 0·2. The probabilities are thus:

$$0·5+0·3+0·2 = 1$$

which excludes any other possibility.

These are only subjective estimates of probability, reflecting what is happening in the mind of the shopper who, we can safely assume, has never heard of Huff or Reilly. Can we quantify these probabilities entirely on the basis of factors which we can measure? These can only be distance (or travel time) and the number, size and attractiveness of shops at X, Y and Z, and on these we can surely put a value. It can be shown that the probability that the purchase will be made in X (p_X) is:

$$p_X = \frac{S_X/T_X}{(S_{X,Y,Z})/(T_{X,Y,Z})}$$

or, in words:

$$p_X = \frac{\text{Number of shops in } X/\text{Travel distance (or time) to } X}{\text{Total shops in } XYZ/\text{Total travel distance (or time) to } XYZ}$$

The relevant data can be tabulated, as in Table 2.2, and the probability worked out for each of the three places.

Table 2.2   The probability of choice of a market centre

	Distance from A (km)	Number of shops, etc.	p_{XYZ}	Percentage probability
X	8	40	1·22	42
Y	5	20	0·97	33
Z	6	18	0·73	25
Totals	19	78	2·92	100

Table 2.2 shows that it is probable that the shopper will go to X, and A can thus be said to lie in the catchment area, in this respect, of the market centre X. But this is only a statement of probability; the shopper might easily change his mind and go to Z. We can only say that, of all shoppers for this particular item who live at A, 42 per cent are likely to go to X to make a purchase.

(c) Urban Linkages

We have so far been considering the measurement of competition between urban centres. Co-operation and interchange between them are no less important. Is there, for example, a more frequent movement of people between large towns than between small? Is the volume of movement related directly either to the relative sizes of the towns, or to their distance apart, or to both? The motorway system of Great Britain is designed to interconnect all the larger cities, and when the system is complete will link all urban centres of more than a quarter of a million people. Linkages with small or medium-size towns are incidental, and the system makes no effort to include them. Similarly, British Rail publicizes its 'Inter-City' services almost to the exclusion of those between small places. Are these developments justified? Is most of the traffic flow in fact between the larger centres of population? The evidence suggests that it is.

Statistics of inter-urban travel are most readily available for rail and bus, the frequency of which can be obtained from the time-tables. Table 2.3 gives the frequency of rail service between London and a number of cities lying beyond the normal range of the commuter services.

Table 2.3   Rail connections with London

City	Population	Distance from London (km)	Trains per day
Birmingham	1 004 000	180	40
Bournemouth	147 460	174	34
Bristol	421 800	190	28
Coventry	334 440	151	31
Edinburgh	449 632	633	14
Leicester	287 350	159	39
Liverpool	574 560	312	16
Manchester	530 580	295	21
Plymouth	249 800	364	11
Portsmouth	200 380	118	39

It might be suggested that the attraction of towns for one another could be expressed in terms of the gravity model discussed in Unit 1.8(*a*). The gravity formula can be manipulated to give the expression

$$\text{Interaction between town } A \text{ and town } B = \frac{\text{Population of } A \times \text{Population of } B}{(\text{Distance from } A \text{ to } B)^2}$$

or

$$I_{AB} = \frac{P_A \times P_B}{(d_{AB})^2}$$

For instance, the population of London is about 7 600 000, that of Glasgow is roughly 1 000 000 and that of Nottingham 300 000. London interacts both with Nottingham and with Glasgow: does the comparative nearness of Nottingham compensate for its smaller size? You can obtain some idea of the answer for yourself by using the formula above, together with an atlas. The answer is, however, a theoretical one, based on our ideas of what is normal behaviour. But how close is it to reality? This can only be determined by comparison with the empirical data, obtained by counting the numbers of trains, cars, passengers or telephone calls passing between them. In fact, if the real frequency of train services, which we assume is adjusted to demand, is plotted against the interaction predicted by using this formula, a relatively high correlation is obtained. But rail traffic is only a part of the interaction between cities. For cities that are fairly near to each other, especially if there is a motorway between them, the use of private cars must cut significantly into the demand for rail services. This applies especially to London and Birmingham, for which the interaction index is very low.

The use of means of communication offers considerable scope for study as an index of interaction between cities. The volume of mail passing between them is not published, but it is possible to find out the number of telephone calls; a map of the frequency of trunk calls was published in the *Atlas of Britain and Northern Ireland*, Clarendon Press (Oxford, 1963). The data relate to 1958 but are nonetheless significant as confirming the general validity of the model presented above.

Questions

1. How important is central place theory to the economic geographer?
2. What services and functions commonly characterize (*a*) large towns? (*b*) medium-sized towns? (*c*) small towns?
3. How would you measure variations in the occupations of the inhabitants of the various districts or wards of a city?
4. Examine the adequacy of the commonly used models of urban structure.
5. What is the 'problem of the inner city'?
6. How would you measure the sphere of influence or the catchment area of a town?

Unit Three

Four Billion Consumers

There are about 4 000 million people in the world today, and their number is increasing at the rate of about 75 million, or nearly 2 per cent, each year. By the year 2000, if the present rate of increase is maintained, the world's population may reach 7 000 million. Three hundred years ago it probably numbered less than a quarter of its present total. The most rapid growth has taken place in the past century, during which the world's population doubled. In all continents the population has increased in modern times, least rapidly in Africa, fastest in Europe. While we often think of Asia as a generally overpopulated continent with a high birth rate and a rapidly rising population, it has in fact a smaller proportion of the world's peoples than it had when Europeans first reached the Far East in about 1500. The rapid increase in the population of Europe—from perhaps 100 000 000 in 1650 to 473 128 000 (1977 estimate, excluding the Soviet Union)—was made possible only by an expansion of food supply, since any increase in consumption must be balanced by an increase in production. This expansion was made possible by the agricultural revolution of western Europe, associated first with the enclosure movement and then with the improvement of seed and of farm stock, the introduction of crop rotation and the gradual elimination of fallow, and, later in the nineteenth century, by the import of grain and meat from the 'new' countries such as Australia and the Americas, and of sugar, fruit, fats and oils from the intertropical dependencies of European countries. The population of Europe is still rising, though far more slowly, while the populations of India, Pakistan, Bangladesh, Indonesia and south-east Asia are increasing very much more rapidly.

An increasing population always represents an increasing demand, and today there is grave anxiety for the future food supply. As population grows larger, the nature of its consumption must inevitably change. There may not be enough of some commodities to satisfy human needs; more and more people will go short, and most people throughout the world are likely to notice a decline in their living standards.

3:1   The Malthusian Dilemma

In the closing years of the eighteenth century, the population of Great Britain was rising sharply. Despite growing industries there was every sign of unemployment, distress and surplus population. It was at this time that Thomas Malthus turned his attention to population problems. In 1797 he published *An Essay on Population*, one of the most important contributions ever made to the subject. In it he argued that there is a tendency inherent in the human species to increase and multiply, and that the rate of increase would, unless checked, be in a geometrical progression, with a *doubling* of the population with each successive generation. The restrictions on such growth, he claimed, were threefold. The first was moral restraint, which, he admitted, was not likely to be a powerful deterrent. Then there was what he termed 'vice': abortion, infanticide and the use of contraceptive devices. If these failed to hold back the rising tide of population, there were the positive checks which would inevitably arise: starvation, disease and war.

As far as most of the world was concerned, the gloomy prophecies of Thomas Malthus remained unfulfilled during the nineteenth century. Agriculture spread to new lands, new and better strains of seed were developed, fertilizer was manufactured in ever-increasing quantities, and agriculture began to be studied scientifically with a view to producing greater quantities of food. The emergence of a Malthusian situation, with an increasing population pressing against a stable level of food production, seemed to have been postponed indefinitely. In the United Kingdom, where population growth was especially rapid, domestic agriculture was revolutionized. It was put on a commercial basis, and began to supply food to the growing cities. At the same time, the 'new' lands of Canada, the American Midwest, Argentina, Australia and New Zealand were brought into production, and began supplying bread grains, meat and other foodstuffs to the developing industrial population of Europe.

The situation was less satisfactory in Third World countries, even then. Their population was very much smaller than it is today, but the primitive agricultural practices combined with the violent climatic fluctuations, especially of rainfall, did lead to serious famines in India, China and many parts of Africa. As the demographic transition (see Unit 3.4) began to influence these countries and western medicine reduced the incidence of disease, the population began to increase. Pressure on agricultural resources increased, and famines became more frequent and more severe.

Food production has been increased in these countries, but, as Malthus emphasized, the *rate* of increase in food supplies can never be as great as the growth rate of the human population. If the human population is capable of growing in geometrical progression, the food supply can increase at no more than an arithmetical progression; in other words, the annual increments would be uniform (see Fig. 3.1). It cannot be doubted that there was, and still remains, abundant scope for expanding the production of foodstuffs in countries like India and Indonesia. The 'Green Revolution' in plant breeding (see Unit 5.2(*b*)) of recent years has saved millions of people from starvation, but if the demand for food continues to increase, as indeed it must do until far into the twenty-first century, the farmer will eventually run out of cultivable land; there will be no more water available for irrigation, and innovations and improvements in agriculture will have run their course. This is the Malthusian dilemma: how to expand the production of food to keep pace with a rapidly growing population; or, conversely, how to hold back population growth and keep it in harmony with the expansion of agriculture. The question of the world's food supply is discussed further in Unit 6.8.

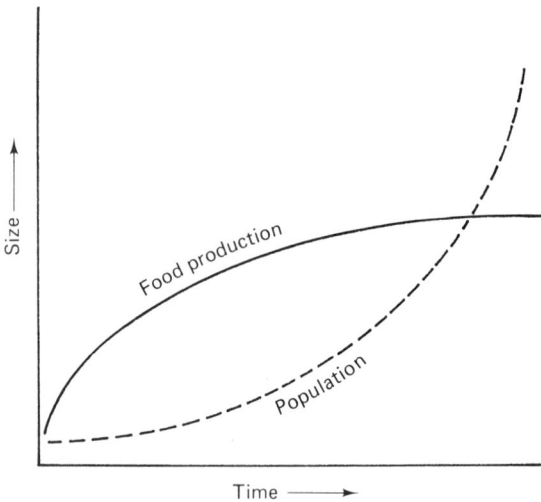

Fig. 3.1 The differential increase in (a) population and (b) food production, as postulated by Thomas Malthus

3.2   Characteristics of the Population

The size of the population is an essential basis for a discussion of the economic geography of a country. The measurement of population is, however, a modern science, and over many parts of the world it is still applied very imperfectly. The first English census was held in 1801, and was taken in part because of Malthus's gloomy forebodings. The United States had held a census in 1800, and Sweden had anticipated this by about half a century. In the course of the nineteenth century most European countries came to hold censuses at regular intervals. The British dominions and colonies followed their example, but elsewhere estimates of population were conjectural or based on inadequate data. The totals commonly given for China, the Indian subcontinent and south-east Asia, as well as for some African republics, may today be very wide of the mark.

We need to know, however, not only the actual size of the population but also its age-structure, since this does much to influence production and consumption at present and the number of people forecast for the future. The size of the future population is directly related to the number of people of child-bearing age today and tomorrow. The high birth rate of the years immediately following the Second World War was reflected in another period of increased birth rate twenty to thirty years later. We need to know the total income of a society or community, and how it is distributed between the various sectors within it, since the rich have a very different pattern of demand from the poor. The census, at least in most of the developed countries, therefore asks supplementary questions intended to throw light on standards of living and patterns of behaviour.

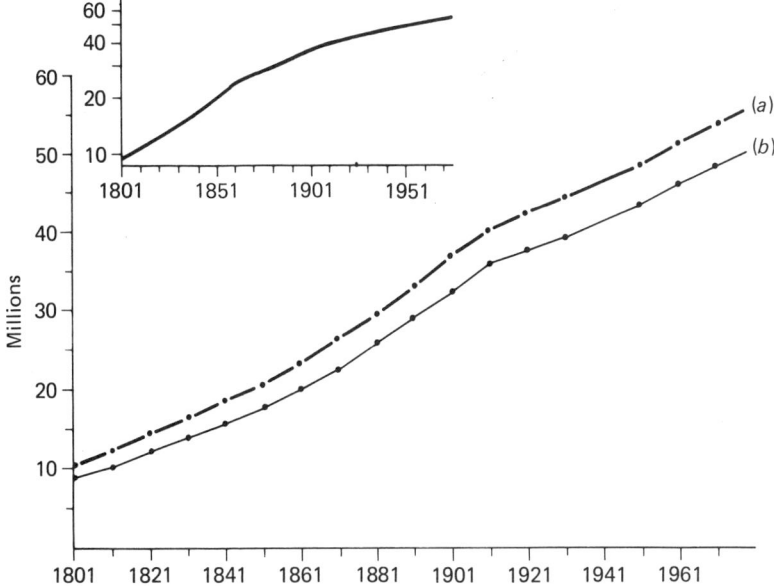

Fig. 3.2 The increasing population of Great Britain since the first census was held in 1801; the inset shows the same data plotted on a logarithmic scale: (a) Great Britain; (b) England and Wales

3.3 Birth and Death Rates

The most important thing which we need to know about a population is the frequency with which people are born and die, because this tells us most about its tendency to grow or to decline. There is now, in fact, no country in which the population is continuously declining, though that of East Germany was falling for a period after the Second World War, and that of Ireland is approximately stable. This vital information can be, and commonly is, expressed in several different ways.

The simplest way is the statement that the population of a given country is increasing at the rate of *x* per cent a year. This is not really very informative, because it tells us nothing about the reason for the change, which may in part be due to immigration or to a lowered death rate and consequent increase in the number of the aged.

Far more helpful is the *birth rate*, expressed usually in terms of the number of live births per thousand of the population during the year in question. Current birth rates range from about 12 to over 50. It can generally be assumed that the higher the birth rate the steeper is the rate of population increase. This, however, is not always true, because against the birth rate must be set the *death rate*. The deaths of old men and of women beyond the child-bearing age are of no importance for the *future* of the population: what matters most in this respect is the death rate among the young. In other words, we need to know the *age-specific* death rates, or the death rates for each age group. Countries with a very high birth rate tend to have a high infant mortality rate.

A more precise measure of population trends is the *net reproduction rate* (NRR). This concept recognizes that many people do not live long enough to become parents; that many women die before the end of their child-bearing period, and that some of those who live to a considerable age have, in fact, no children. The NRR is defined as the number of female children born on average to every woman, and is thus a measure of whether that society is in fact reproducing itself. A stable population should thus have a NRR of unity. An index of more than one must represent a growing population; if it is less than one, the population is declining. Table 3.1 shows population data for two groups of countries, the developed (including the People's Democracies) and the developing.

Table 3.1   Population and birth rates in selected countries

	Population (thousands, 1974 estimate)	Rate of increase per year (%)	Crude birth rate (live births per thousand population per year)
Developed countries:			
United Kingdom	55 968	0·2	13·3
Belgium	9 772	0·3	12·7
Sweden	8 161	0·4	12·6
People's Democracies:			
USSR	252 064	0·9	18·2
Poland	33 691	0·9	19·0
Yugoslavia	21 153	0·9	18·1
Romania	21 029	0·9	20·3
Developing countries:			
India	586 266	2·1	34·6
Indonesia	127 586	2·3	42·9
Egypt	36 417	2·2	35·5
Colombia	23 952	3·2	40·6
Libya	2 346	4·2	45·0
Paraguay	2 572	1·9	39·8

Source: *Demographic Yearbook*, UN (1975)

The contrast between the countries in these two groups is both striking and alarming. Rates of population increase in developing countries range from 2 to 4 per cent a year, and birth rates from 30 to 50 per thousand. Such high birth rates might have been necessary to maintain a stable population when famine was an ever-present danger and disease was endemic. It is so no longer, and at a time when most children may be expected to survive and grow up, these high birth rates present perhaps the most dangerous threat to the future well-being of the human race.

The countries listed in Table 3.1 form a rather small sample, and the categories are somewhat arbitrary. Let us therefore plot a graph of birth rate against the gross national product per head for as many countries as provide reliable data (Fig. 3.3). (The concept of gross national product or GNP per head

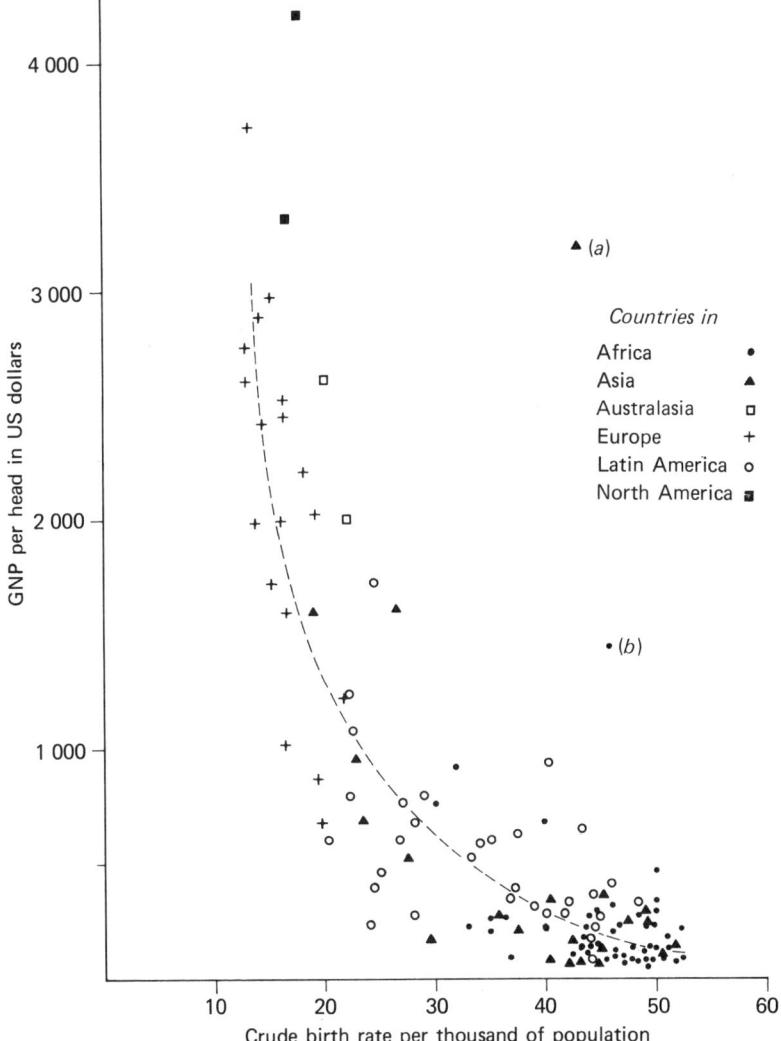

Fig. 3.3 Birth rate plotted against gross national product per head; the highest birth rates characterize the poorest nations

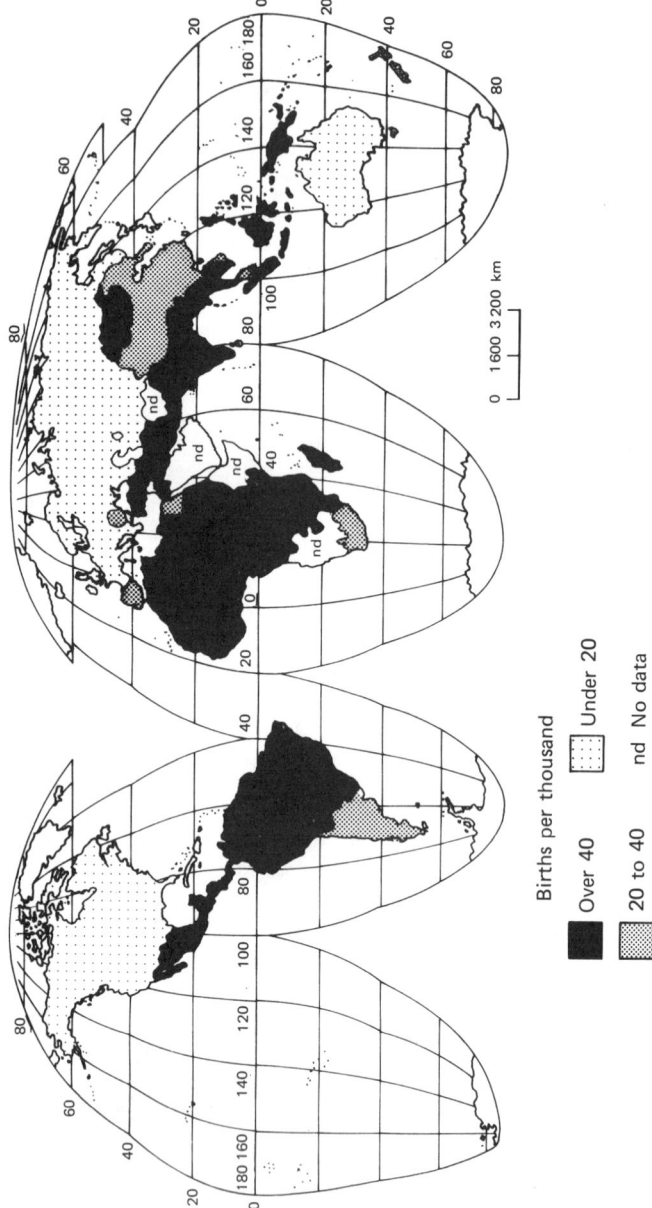

Fig. 3.4 World map of annual birth rates per thousand of population; the symbol 'nd' indicates that a government has not collected (or published) reliable data

is examined in Unit 4.2; it is the most reliable measure we have of the average wealth of individuals in a particular country.) The points on such a graph do not lie exactly along the line—they could hardly be expected to do so; but a 'best fit' line or *regression line* (see Unit 1.8(*d*)) can be drawn through them, and most of them cluster near it. There are two evident exceptions, the points *a* and *b*, which represent Kuwait and South Africa respectively. Clearly these two countries do not fit into the general pattern; such cases are called *residuals*.

The line in Fig. 3.3 shows the relationship between wealth and poverty on the one hand and low and high birth rates on the other, and it emphasizes the scale of the problem of population growth. Another way of relating these two sets of data is to compare the world map of birth rates (Fig. 3.4) with the world map of GNP per head (Fig. 4.1).

3.4 The Demographic Transition

Two centuries and more ago, western societies were characterized by a very high birth rate and a high death rate. Families of ten or more children were not uncommon, but it was also usual for half or more of them to die before reaching adulthood, mainly because of poor diet, inadequate housing and the prevalence of disease. Epidemics—notably of smallpox, typhus, cholera and, in an earlier age, bubonic plague—would sometimes sweep away a quarter of the younger generation. A very high birth rate could thus be regarded as a biological compensation for a very high death rate among the young. The biblical injunction to 'be fruitful and multiply' was a necessary one in a society in which famine, disease and war inflicted so great a toll.

In the late eighteenth century and throughout the nineteenth, public health gradually improved in western Europe and North America. Epidemic disease was gradually conquered, diet and housing conditions were improved and hospitals and medical attention were provided for an increasing proportion of the population. In consequence the death rate began to decline, especially among the young, and expectation of life increased.

In these changing circumstances, the human behavioural pattern itself began to change. Parents had fewer children since a higher proportion of those born might be expected to survive into adulthood. This adaptation was not immediate because social and religious pressures in favour of a continued high birth rate were powerful, so that there was a period when the death rate was declining but the birth rate remained high. It was then that population began to increase sharply. Fig. 3.5 illustrates these changes in England and Wales, where the death rate continued to drop until early in the present century. After 1870 the birth rate began to fall, and continued to do so until 1931. Thereafter it rose slightly, but again declined and today is about 12 per thousand, one of the lowest in the world.

This change from a low total population experiencing high birth and death rates to a high total population experiencing low birth and death rates is known as the *demographic transition*. In most western societies the nineteenth and twentieth centuries were characterized by sharply rising populations as the fall

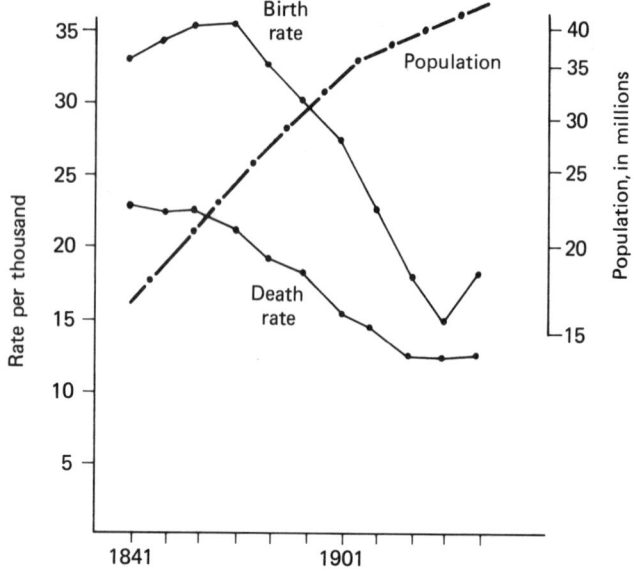

Fig. 3.5 The demographic transition in England and Wales

in birth rates lagged behind that in death rates while they moved through the demographic transition. In the end most of them successfully adapted to the conditions of a lowered death rate and by the mid-twentieth century achieved stable—or only slowly rising—populations.

The demographic transition was not only a behavioural response to a diminished death rate. It marked also a change to a consumer-oriented society. People began to look for more material advantages in life, and found themselves making a conscious choice between an addition to the family and the purchase of goods—for example, a larger home or foreign travel. Not everyone chose one of the latter alternatives, but enough did so to bring about a further reduction in the birth rate.

The demographic transition occurred in most of western Europe: a little earlier in France and Sweden, rather later in central and southern Europe. In Ireland it was masked by the disastrous potato famine of 1846–8 as a result of which the population was cut by famine and emigration from about 8 300 000 to less than 6 million in the space of ten years.

Outside Europe, the demographic transition has been made in North America, Australia, New Zealand and, in recent years, in Japan. The Soviet Union is in the process of adjusting its birth rate to the diminished death rate. The problem today is that most developing countries have now reached the stage which the United Kingdom passed through more than a century ago. Their death rates have been greatly reduced through the application of modern medicine. Diseases like smallpox have, for practical purposes, been eliminated.

Others, like cholera, typhus or typhoid, may occasionally break out in epidemic proportions, but are by and large kept under control. At the same time birth rates remain high, and in many developing countries (India, for example) there is great popular resistance to any artificial means of reducing births.

The task of inducing a lower birth rate in the poorer and more crowded lands is a difficult one. Among such people large families are regarded, not as an excessive drain on the resources of the land, but as a mark of prestige and social standing. People's lives centre in their families. Education may release them from this over-riding dependence on traditional modes of behaviour, but the illiteracy rate is often high, so that printed means of persuasion are ineffective, while all too often religion and such schools as there are only reinforce long-established social prejudices. China, with its highly organized and disciplined population, is one of the few developing countries that have met with success in their efforts to reduce the birth rate in harmony with the declining death rate.

The Age-structure of Population
In a country in which the death rate is high and the expectation of life short, there will be far more people aged up to 10 years than those of 10 to 20; the latter will similarly exceed the age-group 20 to 30. The sizes of older age-groups will then diminish rapidly. A man of 40 will be accounted old, and few indeed will be found able to withstand the buffetings of life for threescore years and ten. This kind of data is best represented in a diagram called a *population pyramid*, and an increasing number of countries now include such a diagram in their statistical yearbooks.

Fig. 3.6(*a*) represents the population of a typical developing country, the Philippines. Each consecutive age-group is smaller than the one lower in the pyramid, until the total population aged over 50 is only a fraction of that below 5. Compare this with the diagram for the relatively stable population of the United Kingdom (Fig. 3.6(*b*)), which can hardly be called a pyramid. Age-

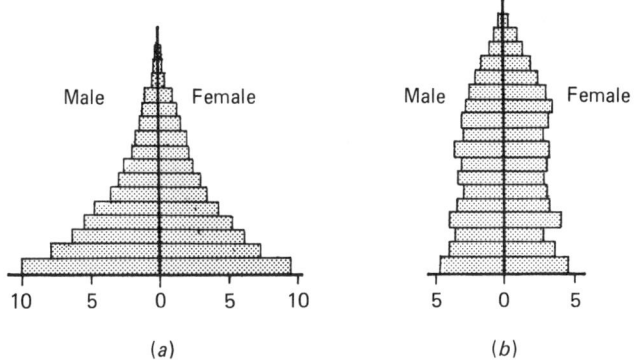

Fig. 3.6 Population pyramids showing the contrasted population structures of (a) the Philippines and (b) the United Kingdom; the figures represent percentages of the total population

Fig. 3.7 The rush hour in Manila; note the high proportion of young people in the crowd

groups below the age of 55 or 60 differ very little in size; there is no evidence of acute mortality among the young, and variations in the sizes of age-groups are due mainly to such factors as the reduced birth rate in wartime. Even age-groups above 60 are much larger than the corresponding age-groups in the Philippines. It is very easy to fit these contrasting pyramids into the evidence presented in Table 3.1 and Fig. 3.3. It is clear, too, that the average age of the people of the Philippines is low, whereas the United Kingdom has an old population, with a smaller proportion of children and a larger proportion of the elderly and the retired. This in turn is likely to influence both the pattern of consumption and of governmental obligations and expenditures. In the Philippines expenditure on

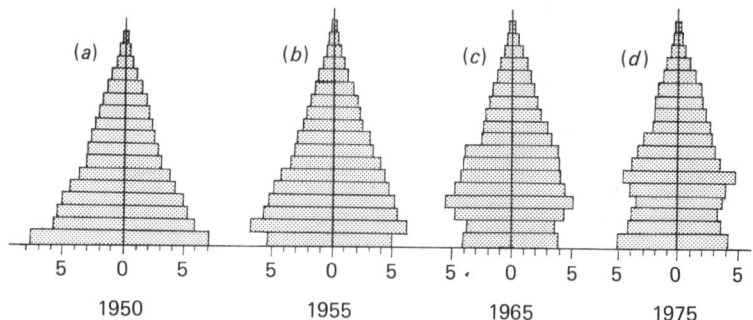

Fig. 3.8 Population pyramids showing the age–sex structure of the population of Japan (a) before and (b), (c) and (d), after the initiation of a policy to restrict family size (Males to the left of the pyramid, females to the right)

schools *ought* to be high and that on pensions low, whereas in the United Kingdom the reverse is in fact the case.

Let us look, lastly, at a series of population pyramids for Japan. The graph for 1950 resembles somewhat the graph for the Philippines: it has a large base and suggests a very high birth rate. Thereafter, however, the government did its utmost to encourage its people to have smaller families, and for more than twenty years the birth rate has been much lower. As a result, the pyramid for 1975 resembles that for the United Kingdom.

3.5   Population Density

Another measure of population is *population density*, the average number of people living in each unit area. The most densely populated states are Hong Kong and Singapore, with respectively 4 000 and 3 500 people per sq km. Among the most sparsely settled are Australia with 2 and Libya with 1; the United Kingdom has about 229 per sq km. Among the Common Market countries, France, Italy, Denmark and Ireland are less densely populated than the United Kingdom, and Belgium–Luxembourg and the Netherlands more densely, while the density in West Germany is almost the same (see Fig. 3.9). No one seriously considers any of these countries to be overpopulated, despite varying levels of unemployment. The United Kingdom has been the recipient of a steady flow of immigrants, and several other members of the Community employ immigrant labour from southern Europe and North Africa.

By contrast, India has a density of 175, Pakistan 83, Indonesia 84, and Egypt 36 per sq km; yet many would consider these countries to be far too populous. Clearly the concept of population density needs to be refined before it is of any significance to the economic geographer.

In the first place, dense population can be of two kinds, which are commonly—though not always—distinct from one another. In Bangladesh (density 502), for instance, some 76 per cent of the population is rural and occupied mainly on the land. Population density is largely controlled by the quality and extent of agricultural land and by the size of farm holdings. Many of the Bangladeshi population are peasant farmers, whose holdings are on average no more than 2 hectares in size. A family could scarcely be supported by a farm as small as this, so that the population density of Bangladesh must be considered very high indeed. India has a much smaller overall density than Bangladesh, not because farm population is less crowded or farms larger, but rather because a large part of the country—about 45 per cent of its area—is forest, mountain or desert without any agricultural value, and much of the rest has only limited agricultural usefulness. The same is true of some other densely peopled countries, such as Egypt and Pakistan, in both of which much of the territory is desert, and Indonesia where it is mountain and dense forest.

At the opposite extreme are highly urbanized and industrialized countries and regions, such as the Netherlands (density 340 per sq km). Obviously, more people can live in any area if most of them are employed in factories or offices. The example cited of exceptionally high population density, Hong Kong and

Singapore, are abnormal in being very small and very highly urbanized, with no significant agriculture. Most densely peopled countries, such as the Netherlands, Belgium and the United Kingdom, have an important agriculture which, largely on account of efficient management and a high level of mechanization, employs only a small fraction of the working population—less than 4 per cent in the United Kingdom. The rest are engaged in secondary and tertiary activities.

Industrialization and Population
The United Kingdom and the Low Countries can thus show far greater population densities than comparable areas in India or China without being seriously overpopulated. There are clearly certain conditions under which a country's population can outstrip its food supply without detriment to its standard of living: for example, the United Kingdom has not only increased its population eightfold but also its standard of living by almost as much during the past three centuries. By selecting carefully her lines of specialization and by pursuing them methodically and efficiently, Great Britain was able to produce certain goods on a large and increasing scale by means of a relatively small expenditure of labour, and these were exported to pay for large quantities of imported foodstuffs and raw materials. (The complete inadequacy of the domestic output of food and raw materials mattered little as long as the import of these goods was uninterrupted.) The reward for efficient and effective labour and labour management was thus a higher standard of living.

It has been assumed a little too readily that the western model—the solution of the population problem by means of industrial development—can be imitated in all backward and overpopulated countries, and that a rising population constitutes no problem provided it can be absorbed into industry. This assumption ignores the need for such an industrialized country to find a market both for its imported foodstuffs and raw materials and for its exports. This it is unlikely to do in a world of growing scarcities. Industrialization can, admittedly, lead directly to increased agricultural production. This is achieved in part by the greater use of good tools and equipment—cloches, for example, for the more rapid growth of vegetables, pipes and pumps for irrigation—and, more important, by the increased production of chemical fertilizer. Nevertheless, industrialization is a palliative rather than a cure for the problem of overpopulation. It has enabled certain countries—those first in the field—to achieve a high standard of living; it is not a magic process which will bring security and prosperity to all the poor, ignorant and crowded masses of the world. At best it may postpone for a while the day of Malthusian doom.

3.6   Overpopulation

Despite its dense population of over 300 to the square kilometre, the United Kingdom is not overpopulated. Its population of about 55 million could not be employed on the land, nor could it be fed from domestic agricultural production. But its efficient and intensive farming is able to supply approximately half of its food needs, and it can import the remainder from overseas and pay for it with current exports and services to other countries. Nevertheless, a problem could arise if growing scarcities in the world at large were to force up the price of imported foodstuffs to the point at which the United Kingdom would find it difficult to pay for them. At that point, however, that same increase in food prices would have made it profitable to cultivate marginal land within the United Kingdom (see Unit 5.3(*b*)), so that domestic food production would have been increased.

Happily, this situation is remote as far as the United Kingdom is concerned. In the Netherlands, however, an acute shortage of agricultural land has developed. This is the most densely populated country in Europe, with about 340 people to the square kilometre, and 6 per cent of the population—high for a developed country—is employed in agriculture. This was an important consideration when, after the First World War, the Dutch planned to reclaim that shallow arm of the sea, the Zuider Zee, which divides their country. This project is nearing completion, and will, when finished, have added almost 2 000 square kilometres to the area of cropland.

Other countries have faced up to the problem of population growth running ahead of the supply of food in different ways. A decade or two ago it would have been said that Japan was seriously overpopulated, and Japanese expansion both before and during the Second World War was motivated in part by increasing population pressure. During the past quarter of a century, however, there have been two important changes. In the first place, a campaign to educate the public to the dangers of a continuing population rise has achieved a very considerable measure of success. The birth rate is today very little above that found in western societies, and the total population is increasing only very slowly. At the same time agriculture has become more intensive and manufacturing industries have been greatly expanded. Japan is the only non-western country to have made the demographic transition from high birth and death rates to low. This it was able to do through the control which its government was able to exercise over an intelligent and well-disciplined population.

Other very populous countries, notably China and India, have attempted to follow the Japanese example. Both had been subject to disastrous famines, and, unless population growth was controlled, these could be expected only to get worse. In China, a high minimum age for marriage has been set and is strictly enforced by the government. The effect has been to reduce drastically a birth rate which had previously been one of the highest in the world. The government of India met with less success. Its policy of encouraging family planning encountered strong popular resistance and was an important factor in the defeat of Indira Gandhi's government in 1977. The population is at present about 635 million, and is increasing at the rate of about 13 million a year. The country's resources are inadequate to support or employ so many. The situation is no less serious in Pakistan, where agricultural resources are more restricted, and in Bangladesh where population density—about 60 per square kilometre—is very much greater. In all of south Asia population restriction offends the social values and practices of too many of the people for it to have much efficacy at present.

Overpopulation and Migration

Finally, we should consider the extent to which overpopulation can be relieved by *migration*. During the nineteenth century an incipient overpopulation problem in Europe was in part averted by large-scale migration to the Americas, Australia, South Africa and elsewhere. It has been estimated that within a hundred years about 60 000 000 people left Europe, and that no more than 20 000 000 returned. Indians, Chinese and Japanese have also left their countries, though in smaller numbers, to settle in East and South Africa, south-east Asia and the East Indies. More recently the Chinese have spread into Inner Mongolia and Manchuria, on the northern borders of their country, in perhaps the greatest population movement in history.

But there are serious obstacles in the way of further migration. Barriers to immigration have been established. The USA has limited drastically the total annual number of immigrants. Britain has received West Indians, Indians and Pakistanis in considerable numbers, but restrictions have now been placed on their entry. Other countries impose tests on would-be immigrants, designed to exclude people of a low level of education and low standard of life. Against the willingness of, say, Australia to receive skilled British craftsmen as immigrants, there must be set the unwillingness to permit the settlement of coloured labourers. Wherever a relatively high standard of living has been achieved there is reluctance to admit people whose standards are appreciably lower. This is because the immigrant may be content to accept a wage which, though higher than would be paid in his native country, is below the general level in the country of his adoption. This in turn threatens local wage levels, especially those of the indigenous unskilled labourers; the problem has become acute in parts of the USA and in South Africa, and has only been avoided in Australia by the strict application of the 'White Australia' policy, designed to exclude cheap immigrant labour.

A further obstacle to migration is the relatively high cost of travel, especially for a family with its accompanying impedimenta. Few of the poorer peoples can take part in overseas migration unless some financial assistance is provided by a government or by an international relief organization.

Lastly, there are few remaining areas of the world which can receive migrants, and these are likely in their turn to fill up: the myth of the 'great open spaces', like that of industrialization, is not a cure for all the ills of overpopulation, though it may well provide a palliative for some of them.

3.7   The Future Population

The world's population is today increasing at the rate of about 1·9 per cent annually. This yearly rate of increase is highest—about 2·5 per cent—in southern and south-eastern Asia and in Latin America, with the highest rates in the West Indies and the republic of central America (compare Table 3.2). The lowest rates of increase—about 0·2 per cent—occur in the countries of Scandinavia and eastern Europe.

Table 3.2   Annual rates of population increase in the major land areas (per cent)

Africa	2·7
Asia	1·9
North America	0·6
Latin America	2·7
Europe	0·4
USSR	0·9
Australasia	1·2
World	1·7

A Malthusian situation is likely to arise if the rate of population growth is higher than that of the increase of food production. In recent years these two have grown at closely similar rates. But food production *per head* has not increased, and the improvement in living standards apparent in areas like North America and western Europe has clearly to be balanced by a decline in countries such as India, in which the expansion of food production has failed to keep pace with population growth.

Crop yields vary from year to year, and even in India food production is sufficient in a very good year to provide on average a diet that is almost adequate. But bad years come as frequently as good, and when they do there is widespread famine. The droughts which struck parts of India in 1966 and 1967 revealed, through the famines in Bihar and other provinces, the severity of the overpopulation problem.

Land reclamation, irrigation, the use of fertilizers and better seeds and improved farming techniques are only palliatives; population problems as serious as those of India or central America are beyond amelioration by such measures as these. The only remedy, as the Indian government has realized, lies in the restriction of births. Birth-control—by whatever means it is achieved—is easy to practise in those countries which need it least; it is far more difficult to convince the Indian peasant, conservative in outlook, untravelled and often illiterate, that a large family is not in all respects a blessing, and that in giving himself the pleasure of several sons he is probably condemning them to slow starvation.

3.8   The Population Map

The map of the world's population (Fig. 3.9) shows a small number of areas of dense population, separated by great regions in which population is sparse or even non-existent. Relatively dense areas occur in (*a*) western Europe, (*b*) India, Pakistan and Bangladesh, (*c*) China, Korea and south-east Asia, (*d*) Japan and (*e*) north-eastern USA and neighbouring areas of Canada. Two of these areas, the North American and the European, are areas of manufacturing industry and relatively high standards of living; a third, Japan, has developed factory industries on a large scale but has not yet achieved as high a standard. The

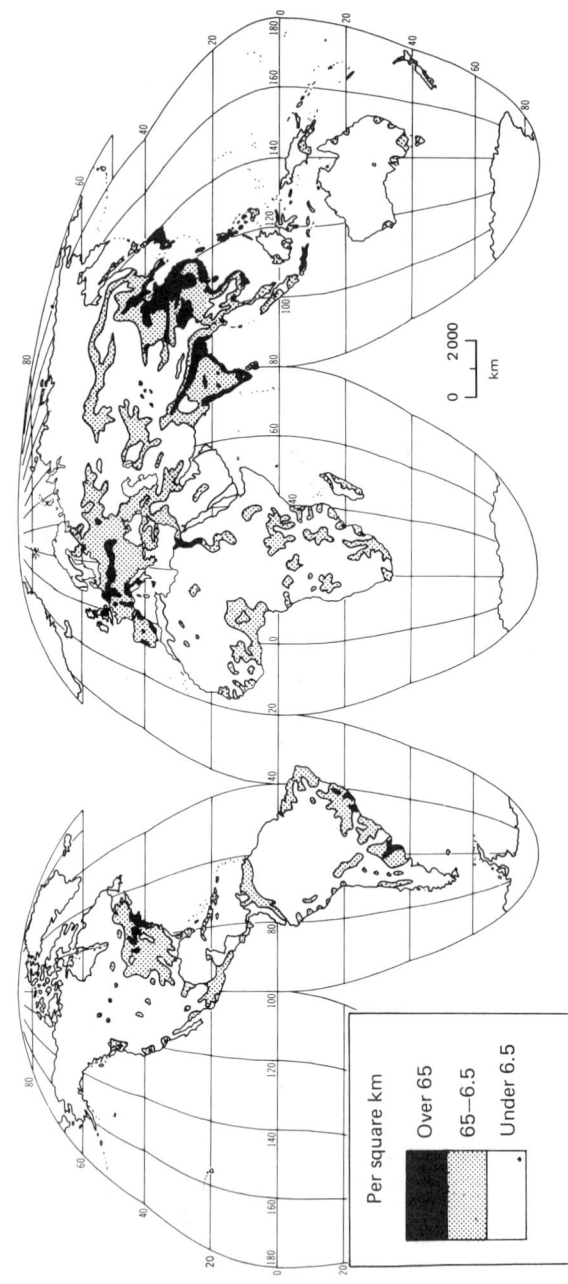

Fig. 3.9 World population density; note the very sparse population density of the greater part of the land surface of the earth

remaining areas are in the main regions of peasant farming, with a low subsistence level. None of these large areas is uniformly populated. Each contains areas of exceptionally high density, and each contains also regions of mountain and waste land, where agriculture is difficult and industry is not practised. By contrast, the much vaster area of sparse population has its local areas of concentrated settlement. Across the great waste of the Sahara desert flows the Nile, in whose valley are found agricultural populations as dense as any in the world. Fig. 3.9 is, however, on too small a scale to show the distribution of population in anything but a generalized and simplified way. Only a large-scale map can give an accurate impression of the distribution of population in any given area.

It is impossible to explain the distribution of population in any simple fashion. The monsoon lands are favoured in soil and climate, but Thailand, Burma, Laos and Cambodia have achieved no great density. There is a strong contrast between densely populated Java and most other parts of Indonesia. In Europe and North America, the areas of dense population accord neither with areas of high fertility nor with those of mineral production. Densely populated areas, if they are primarily agricultural, normally have a climate that encourages plant growth, a soil that supports it and possibilities for irrigation or drainage, insofar as these are necessary. But what determines whether such a land shall support a small population of efficient farmers, cultivating with all the aids of modern science, or a dense struggling mass of impoverished peasantry? what gives rise to the 'rice-bowl' of Louisiana or the Ganges delta? The answers can scarcely be found in environmental influence. They lie rather in the history, traditions and behavioural characteristics of the people.

A dense industrial population, on the other hand, is built up in a certain region because local conditions favour the growth of industry. It may be encouraged by the presence of some specific resource like coal or salt, but the *absence* of inhibiting or restricting features is probably more important than any positive consideration. But no simple explanation has been found of the patterns of high density in western Europe, north-eastern USA and Japan, and perhaps none is possible.

The presence of the open spaces of the world, the vast unshaded areas on the population map, is more easily explained than that of the very densely populated areas. Very considerable parts of these regions are uncultivable; their populations can be engaged only in mining, manufacturing and transport, and if agriculture is impossible, other pursuits will not attract very many people. It has been estimated that about 44 per cent of tropical land is uncultivable under present economic and technological conditions and that a further 34 per cent is too dry for crops. The area under cultivation is less than 9 per cent of the total, though half as much again is described as cultivable. But much of this additional land is of low fertility and remote from transport facilities. The picture of agricultural potentialities in temperate and cool lands is not dissimilar: almost 80 per cent of the area is uncultivable for either climatic or soil reasons. The possibilities for the extension of agriculture are small, and in marginal areas of the world the point of diminishing returns has probably been reached.

Questions

1. Summarize the theories of Thomas Malthus on the relationship of population to resources. Is the world today in a 'Malthusian' situation?
2. What question would you, as a geographer, like to see included in the next census?
3. Compare the demographic pattern in western Europe with that in southern Asia.
4. Explain how a population pyramid is constructed. Why is the age-structure of a population of significance to a geographer?
5. A population density of 40 per km² in Egypt is too great; one of 321 in Belgium is not. Why?
6. What is overpopulation?

Unit Four

Consumers—Rich and Poor

The four billion people in the world live at widely differing standards of living. The gulf between rich and poor is wide enough within the limits of a single country; it is far greater between the rich of the developed countries and the poor of the Third World. A few countries—no more than 20 or 25—are classed as developed. Most others are described as 'developing', though the developmental process has made very little progress in some of them. There is no simple explanation of why some countries are advanced and relatively rich and others are backward and poor. No doubt the answer lies partly in the natural endowment of the land—its soils, minerals and climate—and partly in human initiative. We can, however, devise certain measures of advancement and backwardness and thus can study the spatial distribution of wealth and poverty.

4.1 Standards of Living

Standard of living is a convenient term for denoting the volume of goods and services received by an individual or a community, compared with that obtained by other individuals and groups. It cannot easily be expressed in numerical terms, though there are certain measures of living standards, such as the kind of television set or car which a family owns. We can normally say only that one group has a higher or lower standard than another.

The characteristics of a high standard of living differ from one society to another. In a western society they might include a second car, colour television and holidays on the Costa Brava, while to other people a larger family, a better house and an attractive garden might be ideals to strive for. Within most communities in Africa, Asia and much of Latin America, the possession of a radio or an old car might represent a fairly high level of well-being, and the possession of a bath or indoor sanitation an almost unheard-of luxury. To certain less-advanced people, the possession of more cattle or a second or even third wife would be a mark of wealth and status. The census-takers sometimes collect data of this kind to be used in making estimates of levels of welfare, but they can at most count the symbols which we accept as representative of a satisfactory or a good living standard.

4.2 National Income

Data are collected for political units, or states, because only governments possess the power to collect statistics and to compel people to answer their questions. As geographers, we should also like to have such data for the different parts of a city—to be able to compare, for example, the London districts of Bermondsey with Bethnal Green. We know subjectively that living standards are higher in Hampstead than in Stepney; but how much so? and what difference does it make to people's choice as consumers? and how, in their turn, do wholesalers and retailers react to such differences? The variations in income and in living standards are clearly very great between different districts of a single city. They are, however, difficult to measure and plot on maps. We are usually obliged to use alternative measures like the rateable value of homes and the distribution of two-car garages. In the United States, statistics are published giving the average income in each county, but even a single county may contain wide extremes in wealth and welfare.

We can, however, obtain an estimate of the income of each of the 170-odd political units of the modern world. Most calculate and publish the figures of their *gross national product* (GNP). This can be defined as the net value of all goods produced and of all services rendered in a particular country in the course of a year, the country's exports being subtracted and its imports added to give the final figure. There is an immense range between the richest countries and the poorest, almost as great as the difference between the very rich and the very poor within each of them. Each contains rich people, able to indulge every whim, and poor who can barely satisfy their most elementary needs. In some countries, such as the United Kingdom and Sweden, it has been the policy to redistribute wealth by means of taxation, and differentials within them are therefore less extreme. They are probably least in the communist countries.

National income is difficult to compute. In many instances the necessary data are unavailable or unreliable. In any case, they are interpreted differently in differing countries, and in all they necessarily exclude all personal services that are not paid for in money. The communist countries, furthermore, make no calculation of their GNP as this is understood in the west. National income statistics must therefore be regarded as only approximate measures of the wealth of nations. It is, moreover, of little use to compare the national income of, let us say, the United Kingdom with that of Belgium, the one having several times the population of the other. To overcome this difficulty the national income of each country is divided by its total population, and in this way the GNP *per head* is obtained.

This gives us a measure of the *average* income of each person in every country for which the necessary statistics are available. The 'average individual' (if he exists at all) does not, however, receive this amount. It is his average *gross* income. It includes expenditure on defence, interest payments on government debts and many other obligations whose value to the individual is not at first apparent. Governments differ greatly in the ways in which they subtract from the gross income in order to finance such undertakings. In most countries they levy direct and indirect taxes, thus reducing substantially the income of individuals and corporations. In the socialist countries the government itself determines the price of its products and services and can charge for these far more than their real cost. The consumer's range of satisfactions is thereby reduced and the government has a sum of money to use as it chooses. This is

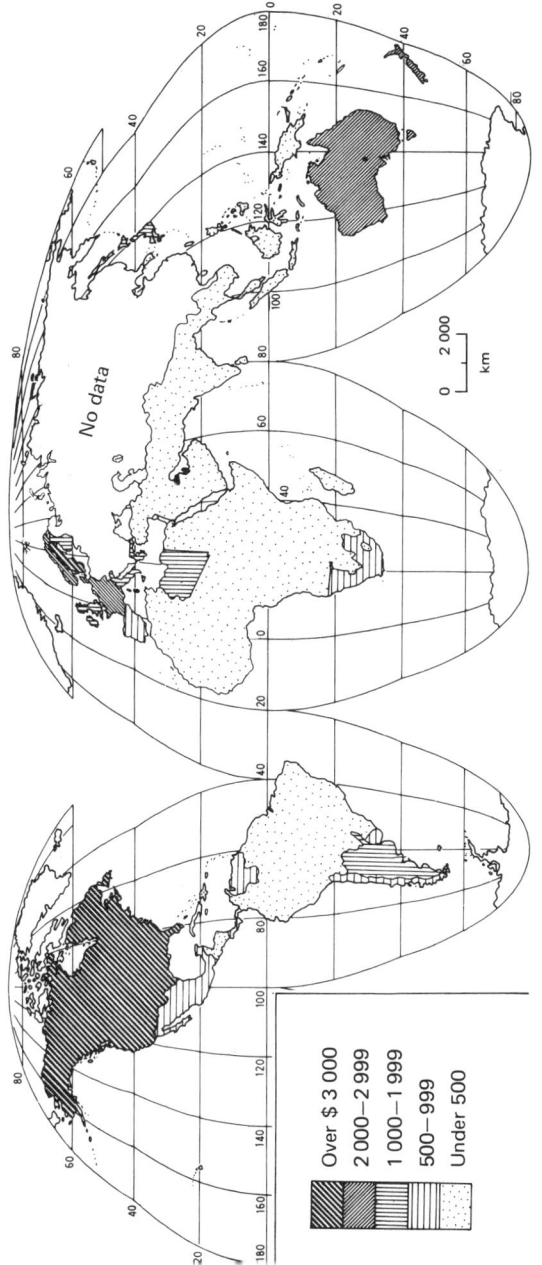

Fig. 4.1 World map showing gross national product per head, by political units

how, in general, the government of a communist country carries through its development plans (see Unit 1.7(*b*)): the gross national product is not altered, but its proportionate allocation to capital investment and the satisfaction of consumers' needs and desires is changed in favour of the former.

This can be represented in the two simple models shown in Fig. 4.2. The first, which very approximately represents the United Kingdom, shows only a very small fraction of the GNP directed towards capital investment, a sizeable defence expenditure, a large export, and the remainder distributed in goods and services. By contrast, the second diagram can be taken to represent one of the People's Democracies. It shows a very large expenditure on capital stocks and a much smaller allocation to the consumers' sector. Individual purchasing power is smaller than in the United Kingdom, and by every subjective measure we might use the standard of living is lower. Expressed in different terms, this means that if a country wishes to expand its capital stock or to industrialize rapidly, it must cut back on the private ability to spend on consumer goods and at the same time increase expenditure on capital account.

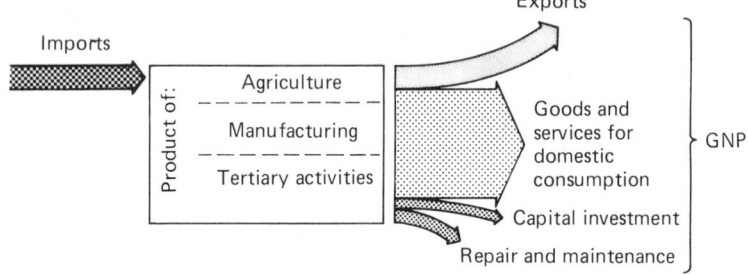

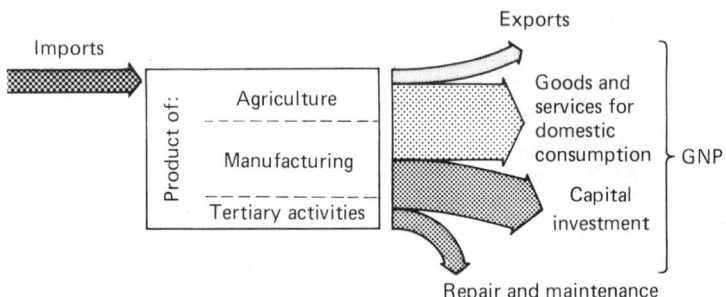

Fig. 4.2 The composition of gross national product: (above) for a country like the United Kingdom and (below) for a 'People's Democracy'

Table 4.1 shows GNP per head of three groups of countries representing respectively the high-, middle- and low-income countries. Though selected arbitrarily, these countries show an immense range, the richest having a *per capita* income over 80 times that of the poorest in the list. More significant, however, are the data shown in the last column, representing the proportion of the active population engaged in agriculture. In all the high-income countries this is well under 10 per cent and in the low-income countries over 50. Indeed, the relationship between GNP per head and the proportion of the population in agriculture is so close that we might generalize and say that GNP per head varies inversely as the percentage employment in agriculture.

The same information is presented graphically in Fig. 4.3. Here GNP per head is plotted against the proportion of the employed population that is engaged in agriculture. If the relationship between the two factors were constant, the points would all lie along a line. They do not, but most are clustered close to it.

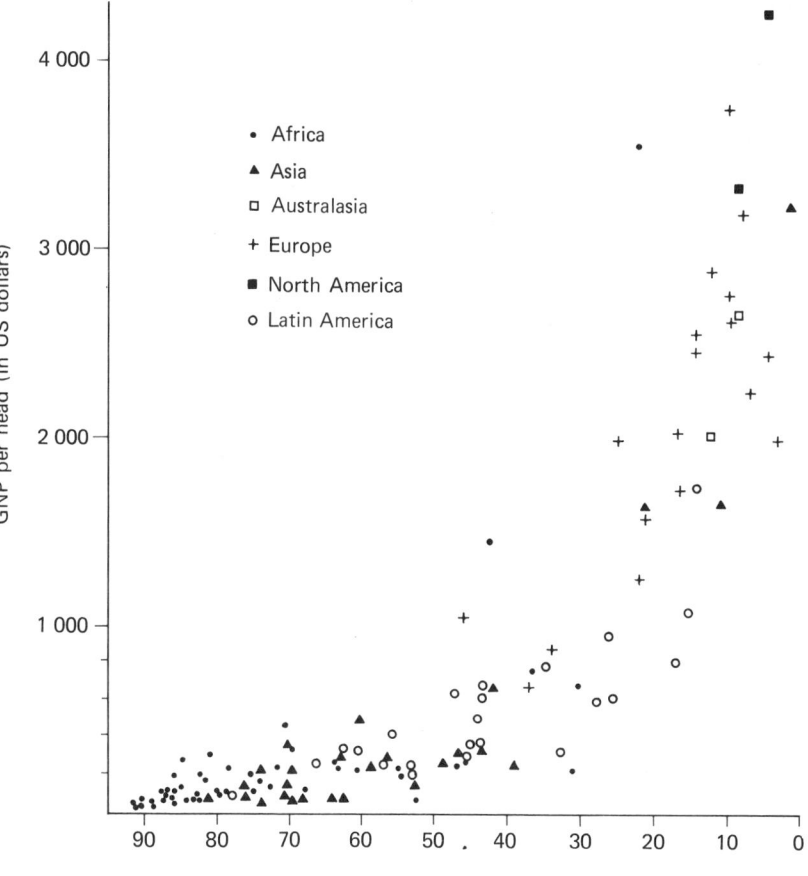

Fig. 4.3 The percentage of employed population in agriculture, plotted against GNP per head for most of the countries of the world; the proportion of agricultural employment diminishes with increasing wealth

This *regression line* (see Unit 1.8(*d*)) can be taken to represent the normal or expected relationship between GNP and employment in agriculture.

Table 4.1   GNP per head and employment in agriculture in selected countries (1974)

	GNP per head (in US dollars)	Percentage of population employed in agriculture
High-income (developed) countries:		
USA	5 941	3·7 ⎤
Canada	5 672	8·2 ⎟
Denmark	5 402	11·2 ⎟ under 20%
Australia	4 994	8·1 ⎬ in
Belgium	5 029	4·8 ⎟ agriculture
France	4 486	13·7 ⎟
United Kingdom	3 072	2·8 ⎟
Japan	3 562	19·6 ⎦
Medium-income (developing) countries:		
Ireland	2 015	26·5 ⎤ 20–40% in
Spain	1 605	26·0 ⎦ agriculture
Low-income (underdeveloped) countries:		
Ghana	220	58·4 ⎤
Paraguay	457	52·7 ⎟ over 50%
Bolivia	206	55·5 ⎬ in
Pakistan	121	58·9 ⎟ agriculture
India	103	69.3 ⎟
Bangladesh	74	85·9 ⎦

Sources: *Statistical Yearbook*, UN (1975) and *Production Yearbook*, FAO (1975). Owing to variable exchange rates and lack of published data this kind of calculation is not possible for many countries, including those of the communist bloc.

(*a*) Variations in National Income

Table 4.1 and Fig. 4.4 show how extreme are the variations in GNP per head over the world. The United States is commonly described as the richest country on earth, and the average American is, indeed, about seventy times better off than the average Nepalese or Ethiopian. The income per head in the United States is, however, exceeded by that in Kuwait, a very small territory (16 000 sq km) with a population of only about 738 000 and immense reserves of oil. Its income from oil has raised Kuwait to the status of one of the richest countries and allows it to invest heavily in hospitals and education, as well as to spend lavishly on consumer goods. The life of the oilfields may prove to be short, however, and unless the Kuwaiti government diverts a large part of its current income to capital investment—unless, in other words, it builds factories, desalination plants and other works, and develops irrigation agriculture—it may within a decade or two find its income declining and its extravagant way of life no longer supportable.

We pointed out earlier that the best and most reliable national income statistics are only approximations. The figures published for the poorer countries are the least reliable, not because of errors in their compilation— though these are unquestionably present—but also because it is impossible to set

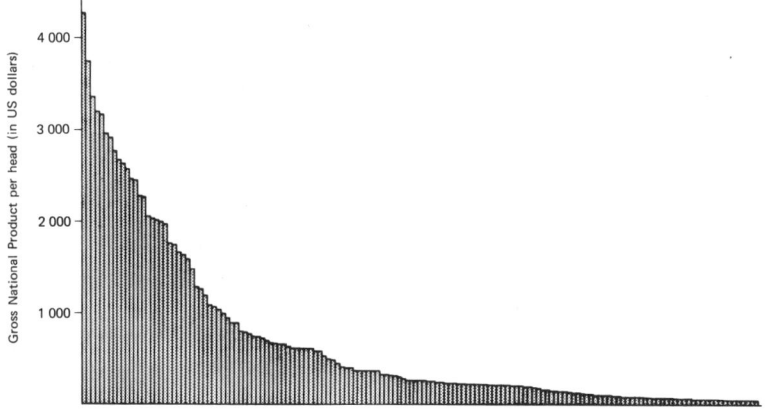

Fig. 4.4 Rank-size graph showing the GNP per head of those countries which publish comparable statistics (the communist countries are omitted)

any value on the services which members of simple communities perform for one another. In our society, you pay a builder to erect your house, and if you are ill you pay the doctor, either directly or through the National Health Service. In some non-western societies, these services would not be paid for and would not appear in national income statistics. One would build one's own house with the help of neighbours, and even some of the materials would require no payment. Thus a complex system of mutual self-help can provide goods and services without any statistical record ever appearing in national income tables. The poorest countries are thus somewhat less poor than the statistics might suggest.

(b) Wealth and Population in Agriculture

The poorer countries, as we have seen, are more agricultural than the rich, in the sense that a higher proportion of the population is engaged in farming; Fig. 4.3 shows this relationship. Conversely, the poorer countries have only a small industrial sector, which may largely be made up of craftsmen working at home. The developed countries, by contrast, have developed manufacturing industries in which, together with ancillary services such as transport and power generation, the greater part of the population is employed. Not surprisingly, developing countries see industrialization as the golden road to wealth, prosperity and the good life (see Unit 15).

(c) Wealth and the Birth Rate

Lastly, a comparison of the data represented in Fig. 4.1 with that in Fig. 3.3 shows that there is a high correlation between the GNP per head and the birth rate. This is a *negative correlation*, that is, the lower the GNP per head the higher the birth rate (*BR*):

$$\frac{\text{GNP}}{P} \quad \propto \quad \frac{1}{BR}$$

This means that the largest rates of population increase are occurring in countries whose incomes are too small to support them and that the pressure of population on the land in heavily agricultural countries will continue to increase.

(d) Causes of Backwardness

We have just considered three variables or *parameters*: (i) GNP per head, (ii) percentage of the population engaged in agriculture, and (iii) birth rates; and we have seen that statistically speaking there is a close relationship between them. We may now ask whether any one parameter is the cause of the variations observed in the other two. For example, do the differences between GNP per head for particular countries stem from their respective birth rates? in other words, do high birth rates lead to poverty, or *vice versa*? Alternatively we may ask whether the poverty of some countries results from the high proportion of their population which is engaged in agriculture, or, on the other hand, whether a high employment in agriculture leads inevitably to poverty.

It cannot be demonstrated that any one of these variables is directly dependent in every case on one of the others. The three are so interwoven that each influences the others:

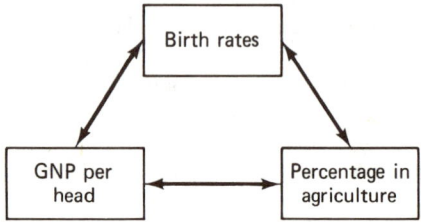

For example, the GNP per head may be low because the population is increasing too fast, or the birth rate may be high because the GNP is too low to permit adequate educational and family planning facilities to be made available. You can think of other ways in which each variable may influence the other two. It would be unwise to generalize by saying that any of these variables is *independent*, determining the size or value of one of the other two. More progress can be made toward answering the question by studying the *factors of production*.

4.3 Factors of Production

In the richer and more developed countries workpeople produce factory goods by using power-driven tools and machines to fashion the materials which they handle. Minerals are obtained by men who use mechanical devices to cut away and crush the rocks of the earth's crust and to separate the valuable minerals from the waste, and farmers use machines to cultivate the soil and reap the crops. All these activities, manufacturing no less than agriculture, require space or land, and the availability or price of land influences the ways in which the activity is carried on. Here we see the three *factors of production*: labour, capital and land. We will discuss these one by one.

(a) Labour

Labour is always of the first importance. Without it the productive processes, however highly automated, cannot be fully accomplished. Some activities, such as the oil industry, call for relatively little labour in relation to the scale of the operation. Others employ a great deal of labour in proportion to the value of the product, especially those which call for a large amount of hand labour, like lacemaking and the assembly of electronic goods. The price of oil, however, incorporates only a small amount for labour, whereas the selling price of lace largely represents labour costs. The one branch of industry is said to be *labour-extensive*, the other *labour-intensive*.

Similar generalizations can be made for agricultural activities. The large Canadian wheat farm of several thousand hectares may employ only a handful of men who work the land with the help of the most sophisticated agricultural machinery, and is labour-extensive. On the other hand the peasant family in monsoon Asia might work a holding of 5 or 10 hectares with the simplest tools but employing the whole family every day of the year: the holding is labour-intensive (Fig. 4.5).

Clearly, in activities like the oil industry or the Canadian wheat farm, each unit of labour is responsible for a large output. Conversely, the domestic lacemaker or the peasant farmer, however hard he or she works, produces only a very small volume of goods or foodstuffs. The reward to labour for the work performed must bear some relationship to output, and varies from a very high return to the worker in the oil industry or on a large farm to a very low return to the domestic craftsman or peasant farmer.

Labour furthermore varies in its capacity to perform work. Some tasks call for higher skills than others. The highest skills in industry and the professions are acquired only with difficulty and are possessed by few; they thus have a scarcity value and can command a proportionately high price or wage. Most of the world's population has been able to acquire only the most rudimentary skills. The peasant farmer has neither the technical nor the scientific knowledge to manage a North American wheat farm, nor could a simple craftsman, however delicate his or her workmanship may be, work at a steel mill or drill the earth's crust for oil.

We see here two separate though related factors which determine whether

Fig. 4.5 Labour-extensive and labour-intensive farms: (a) harvesting wheat on a prairie farm in Manitoba;

labour is well rewarded or not: firstly, the level of the skill which it possesses, and secondly, the volume of production for which it is responsible.

(b) Capital

No productive activity can be carried on without tools and equipment and some stock of materials. The peasant farmer has a draught animal and a simple plough as well as the materials which he uses: seed and fertilizer. At the opposite end of the agricultural scale, the wheat-farmer uses expensive mechanical equipment and owns a much larger stock of materials. A similar but greater contrast exists between those who practise craft industries with the simplest of tools and the oilman or steelworker, who operate some of the most expensive pieces of industrial equipment to be met with anywhere in the world. Such materials and equipment constitute *capital*. Factories and machines are fixed equipment. Once built or installed, they are generally used until their useful life is over, when they may be scrapped and replaced.

We can make two important generalizations regarding capital. Firstly, most productive activities can be carried on with the help of an amount of capital which may vary from very small to very large. Secondly, the volume of output will increase with the size of the capital investment. Thus mechanized production yields a higher return to each unit of labour employed than a comparable process carried out by hand. The use of power-driven tools and

(b) plucking millet plants in Mysore

machines is the secret of greater industrial output, as agricultural machinery and fertilizers is of farm production.

(c) Land
The third factor of production is the land itself. Every productive process takes place in geographical space; it occupies land. This is conspicuously true of agriculture, but land is no less important in manufacturing, transport and commerce. How often do we hear that a factory site is too constricted, or that a shop or office block lacks space for storage or parking? In general, the more abundant the land, the more adequately will the other factors of production be employed.

(d) Interchangeability of Factors
This discussion points up two highly important considerations

(i) The factors of production can be combined in any one industry in almost any proportions. Table 4.2 shows in very general terms how the factors of production are combined in four types of agricultural production.

Similarly, in the field of manufacturing we can distinguish between branches of the same industry. Table 4.3 is a rough comparison of the factor inputs in four branches of the cotton textile industry.

Table 4.2   Factors in agricultural production

	Land	Labour	Capital
Peasant farming (India	small	very large	small
Wheat-farming (Canada)	large	small	very large
Ranching (Argentina)	very large	very small	small
Market gardening (England)	very small	large	small

Table 4.3   Factor inputs in the cotton textile industry

	Land	Labour	Capital
South Carolina (USA)	fairly large	small	very large
India	small	fairly large	fairly small
South-east Asia: domestic	very small	very large	very small
Lancashire	small	small	large

(*ii*) The factors of production can in some measure be substituted for one another. The mechanization of an industrial process may throw people out of work because it substitutes the factor capital for the factor labour. On the other hand, an abundant and cheap labour force is likely to hinder the introduction of labour-saving machines. Capital and labour can also replace land. If land is scarce, it is likely to be highly intensively used. For instance, on the Great Plain of China immense human effort is put into agriculture, using hand planting, weeding and reaping and the restoration to the soil of all available vegetable waste and human excreta. Similarly, on Manhattan Island higher and ever higher buildings are constructed at a great cost in labour and capital. In Egypt there is, for climatic reasons, a grave shortage of agricultural land. A solution, perhaps only temporary, of the problem of food scarcity has been to build a high dam on the river Nile at Aswan, using the impounded water to irrigate land during the dry season: agricultural production has thus been increased by investigating a very large volume of capital.

The relationship of the three factors of production is illustrated in Fig. 4.6. In both craft industries and peasant agriculture the factor of capital is small, since both make use of the simplest tools and equipment. The craftsman's workshop covers only a minute tract of land, and the peasant's farm is far from large. In both, labour represents the largest input, and since the total productivity of the operations is small, the labour must be poorly rewarded. But in a developed country, manufacture is carried on in factories and agriculture mainly on comparatively large and highly capitalized farms. Productivity in both cases is high in relation to the labour input, and labour is, in consequence, relatively highly rewarded. Generalizing from these examples, we can say that the workers in the developed countries are highly productive and well-paid, because they always have at their command a large stock of capital and in some instances an abundance of land. In the poorer countries labour is relatively abundant and

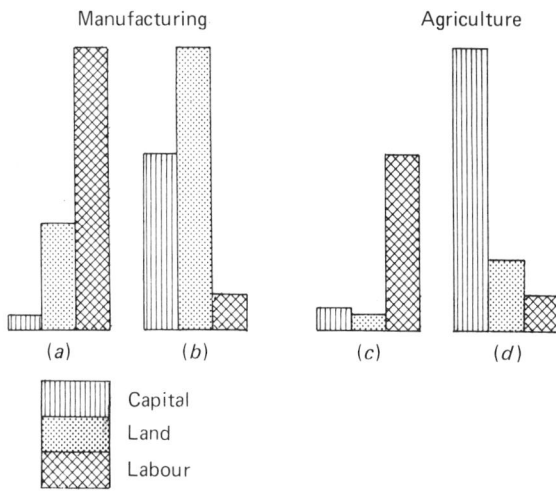

Fig. 4.6 Factors of production (left) in manufacturing: (a) craft industry and (b) factory production; (right) in agriculture: (c) peasant agriculture and (d) highly mechanized farming

capital scarce. Labour, in consequence, achieves relatively little, and the total income of the country is small.

The process of development consists in turning a low-level producer, such as those illustrated by Fig. 4.6(*a*) and (*c*) in which there is a high ratio of labour to capital, into a high-level producer with a very much higher productivity, as in Fig. 4.6(*b*) and (*d*). Essentially this consists of increasing the factor of capital relative to that of labour, and the ways in which it can be done are discussed in Unit 15. In this sense change and development are taking place in all countries. They change not only the geographical pattern of production, but also that of consumption. Workers in a developed country consume a greater volume and a wider variety of goods than those in one that is underdeveloped, because their labour is more effective and their real income higher.

In the foregoing discussion of the factors of production we have used the term *intensive*: we speak of the intensive use of the land and refer to a branch of manufacturing as labour-intensive. The word must, however, be used with care. Chinese agriculture is described as intensive and that of the Prairies as extensive. Chinese agriculture is, however, intensive of land, in that it makes the greatest possible use of it, and also of labour, which it uses in vast quantities, but non-intensive, or extensive, in its use of capital in the form of tools and equipment. Prairie agriculture is extensive of land and of labour, but intensive of capital.

4.4   The Map of Demand

The world map of gross national products (Fig. 4.1) is, in some measure, also a map of the ability to consume goods and services. But we need, in economic geography, a much more detailed map than this. We want to know what are the differences in effective demand between, let us say, Gwent and Kent, or between the East End and the West End of London. We should be safe in assuming that total demand and also demand per head would be larger in the second of each of these two pairs than in the first, but would the patterns of demand be essentially different? Would people in Kent, for instance, require goods and services for which there was no real demand in South Wales? Clearly, when total demand is low a high proportion of the income must be spent on necessities, among which there is little effective choice. On the other hand, high incomes have a very much wider margin to be spent on luxuries—both goods and services—and here the range of choice is almost unlimited. We might thus expect to find a far greater variety of shops, and of goods in the shops, in Kent and the West End of London than in Gwent and the East End.

We can take this argument a stage farther. Within the limits of a single city there are low-income districts, where most of the stores sell only basic foodstuffs and consumer goods, and high-income districts which also have delicatessen, antique shops, art shops and many others catering only for the sophisticated taste of the well-to-do. The study of consumption and production within small and *local* areas and their correlation with levels of wealth, as measured by the quality of housing and other indicators, is an important aspect of economic geography.

It is more important at this stage to look at the *regional* variations in purchasing power. Fig. 4.7 shows the GNP per head, and thus, broadly, the income and consuming power within the major administrative divisions of western Europe. The difference between the wealthiest and the poorest regions is a great deal less than that between the richest and poorest countries of the world, but is nonetheless considerable. A belt of high incomes and high purchasing power extends from south-eastern England across north-eastern France and the Low Countries into north-western Germany, with the areas around Paris and the German port cities of Bremen and Hamburg as outliers of this region of wealth. It is a highly urbanized and industrialized region, in which agriculture, though of secondary importance, is itself highly capitalized and productive. From this west-to-east belt, incomes decline both northwards and southwards, and the lowest levels are found in southern Italy, Sicily, Sardinia and Corsica, with low levels also in the outermost fringe of the British Isles. This fact is recognized within the individual countries of western Europe, which have made provision in varying degrees for capital investment in and the economic development of these more backward areas. The United Kingdom, for example, has its 'development areas' and its 'special regions' (see Unit 13.5), and Italy its *Casa per il Mezzogiorno*, its Department for the South, entrusted with the task of raising the economic level in southern Italy and Sicily. These countries have hitherto had considerable success in investing capital in agriculture and industry, and thus securing fuller employment and higher production and purchasing power in their less-developed regions.

The European Economic Community has established a special commission to handle the development of the Community's relatively backward areas,

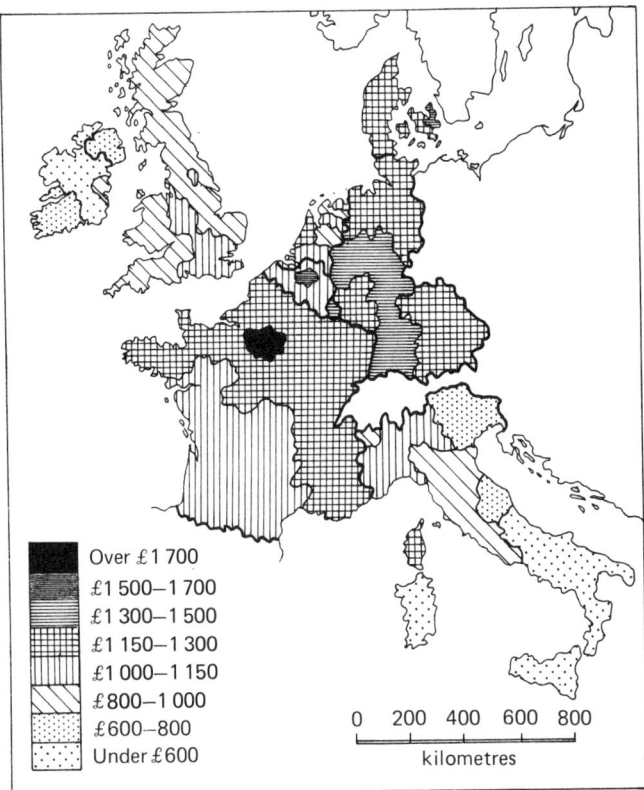

Over £1 700
£1 500—1 700
£1 300—1 500
£1 150—1 300
£1 000—1 150
£800—1 000
£600—800
Under £600

0   200   400   600   800
kilometres

Fig. 4.7 Regional variations in average income in western Europe (the countries of the European Economic Community)

including the Scottish Highlands, the Central Massif of France and southern Italy. The objective of the Community is to raise the level of welfare, and hence that of consumption, throughout the territory of its member states. It cannot do this if there remain depressed 'islands' within it, with a low consuming power. The wealth of West Germany, for example, is today being used to develop such areas wherever they may be within the Community, and West Germany will eventually reap its reward in larger markets for the products of its factories.

Fig. 4.8 shows the variations in income between the various states of the USA. The richest states have incomes per head considerably more than twice that of the poorest state, Mississippi. The greatest wealth occurs in a belt across the country from New England in the east, through Ohio and Illinois, to the rich farm states such as Kansas and Nebraska, and also in the Pacific States of California and Washington. The poorest states lie in the south-east of the country, the so-called 'Old South'.

The effect of this variation in levels of wealth on the consuming pattern is

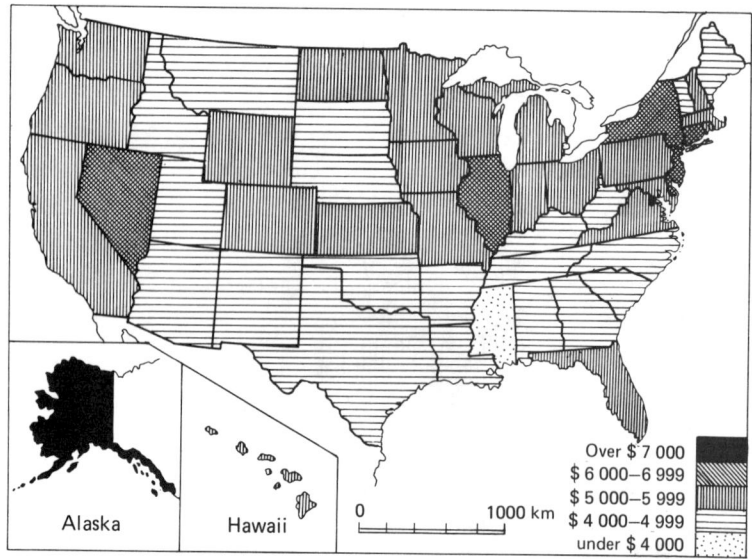

Fig. 4.8 Variations in average income between the states of the USA (based on US Statistical Abstract, *1975)*

immense. Huge, richly provisioned shopping centres, sleek new cars and elegant clothing are common features of the 'rich belt', but are rarely seen in the poorer parts of the country, where shops carry little more than bare necessities and houses are meanly built and ill-equipped. Here, as in Europe, however, a relatively backward area—the basin of the Tennessee river—has been helped by using part of the wealth of the rest of the country, channelled through the Tennessee Valley Authority (TVA) for resource development and the improvement of living standards.

Almost two centuries ago Arthur Young in the course of his travels through France found abundant evidence of poverty and distress alongside luxury and wealth. After noting the poverty of many rural areas he wrote:

> The wealth of a nation lies in its circulation and consumption; and the case of poor people abstaining from the use of manufactures ... ought to be considered as an evil of the first magnitude ... a large consumption among the poor being of more consequence than among the rich.

His words are no less true today. What manufacturer does not look with eager anticipation to the potential market provided by the less-developed regions of his own country and even more to the vast, unsatisfied market of the developing countries? Moreover, if the governments of France, Italy and the United Kingdom are interested in developing their own relatively backward enclaves, the western world as a whole should be concerned for the welfare and prosperity of the developing or Third World.

4.5   The Map of Regional Development

Economic development is never uniform over the territory of any given country. It occurs at certain points, and if distant places are influenced by it at all it is often in a negative sense: the development of *A* draws to itself as it were the life blood of *B* and *C*. The reasons for the initial economic growth may be obscure in detail. They can, however, be summarized as, on the one hand, the presence of resources and, on the other, human perception of their value coupled with the technical capacity to use them.

Development is accompanied by the movement of both labour and capital. Workers migrate toward the point of development, attracted by the prospect of employment or perhaps of higher wages than they can earn at home. Investment capital has also to be mobilized. In the earlier phases of western industrialization profits from agriculture were channelled through banks to the newly established factories and industrial undertakings, and these in their turn supplied the means for further growth.

The point at which growth is initiated may not, in the long term, be the most suitable. Its choice may have arisen from an incomplete realization of the nature and extent of resources or from dependence on a technology which was later superseded. Some of the earliest textile mills in the north of England were established in the Derbyshire Dales, where water power was relatively abundant, rather than on the Lancashire coalfield, which eventually became the major source of industrial power in the region.

But having been established, the point of economic growth is extraordinarily difficult to shift. It represents a fixed capital, which might be broken up or destroyed but is incapable of being transported. Such a development, furthermore, attracts to itself an infrastructure made up of transport and ancillary services, which tends yet more strongly to fix it and encourage its further growth at the same site. This is what we mean by the term *industrial inertia*. Change in the general location pattern of an industrial activity is most likely to come about only when plant is obsolete and about to be written off, or when technological change has made its operation uneconomic. Both these factors influenced, for example, the shift of the United States cotton textile industry from New England to the south, or that of the British steel industry from the Welsh mining valleys and the English Midlands to coastal sites (see also Unit 9.4).

Economic development is likely to lead to growth in quite unrelated fields. By a kind of *multiplier effect* the expansion of the industrial workforce leads to a growth in the number of shops, teachers, public employees and so forth. The industrial nucleus may continue to be dominated by a particular manufacture, but the activities carried on there must in time become increasingly diverse.

As one branch of industry attracts another, the centre of growth expands into a cluster (see Unit 10.5). Competition for land at the centre forces some enterprises into the surrounding countryside. But the influence of the developing region spreads yet more widely. The demand for food stimulates agriculture, the rural area provides homes for many who work in the industrializing region, and in other ways also a *transitional area* emerges in which there is some growth, though less rapid and less concentrated than in the developing core (Fig. 4.9(*c*)).

Beyond the transitional area there is likely to be one of economic decline. This area lacks the resources to attract new undertakings, it is too remote to share the

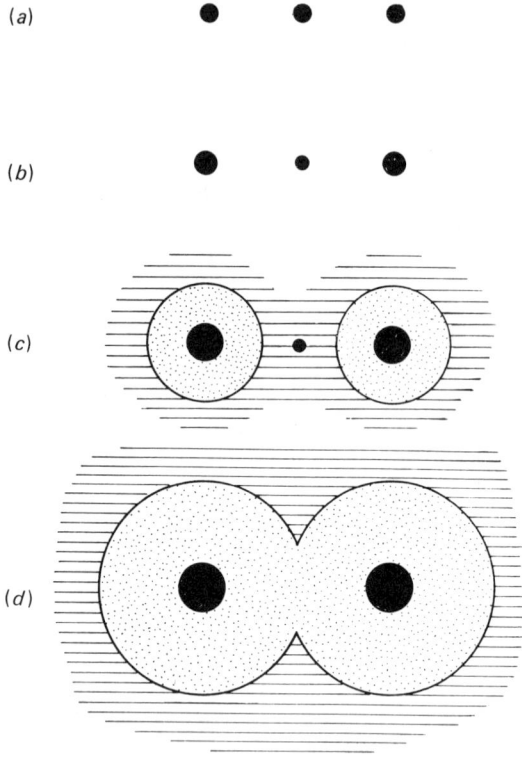

Fig. 4.9 A theoretical model of the development of an industrial region: (a) a series of small centres of development; (b) the further growth of some of these; (c) formation of transitional areas of less intensive development around growing centres; (d) merging of transitional areas to form industrial or developed regions

limited prosperity of the transitional area, and there is a selective migration of the younger and more active and enterprising elements in the population. In this general way a 'depressed' area forms. Indeed, most instances of economic growth have been balanced by economic decline in peripheral regions. This is reflected in, for example, the migration of the Scottish Highlander from his croft to the factories of Glasgow, of the mountaineer from the Alps to the developing urban centres of Germany, Switzerland, France and Italy, and of the 'hill-billy' from the Cumberland Mountains or the Ozark Plateau to the industrial belt of the north-eastern USA.

(a) Regional Patterns

These examples differ greatly in scale. The first took place over a distance of only a few dozen kilometres, the last over many hundreds. In the first example the developed area covered little more than a few counties, but in the second, almost half a continent: we can recognize a north-west European belt of vigorous development and high standards of living, extending all the way from the Paris region to the border with East Germany, and from Switzerland to the North Sea. Similarly the North American industrialized belt extends for over 1 600 km from Chicago to New York or Boston.

Each of these regions has a higher level of industrial development and a more productive and richer population than those outside them. Yet there are wide variations within each. Inside the north-west European region are relatively poor and depopulated areas such as the Ardennes and Eifel plateaux, the Sauerland and the Central Massif. Similarly within the north-eastern USA lie the depressed region of much of New England and the forested wilderness of the northern Appalachian Mountains.

Our model needs to be modified. Instead of a single developed core, surrounded by its transitional region and embedded in a depressed peripheral region, we are more likely to find a series of cores. Their transitional areas merge, leaving regions of underdevelopment between them (Fig. 4.9(d)). This is the situation which we find in the north-eastern United States and north-western Europe.

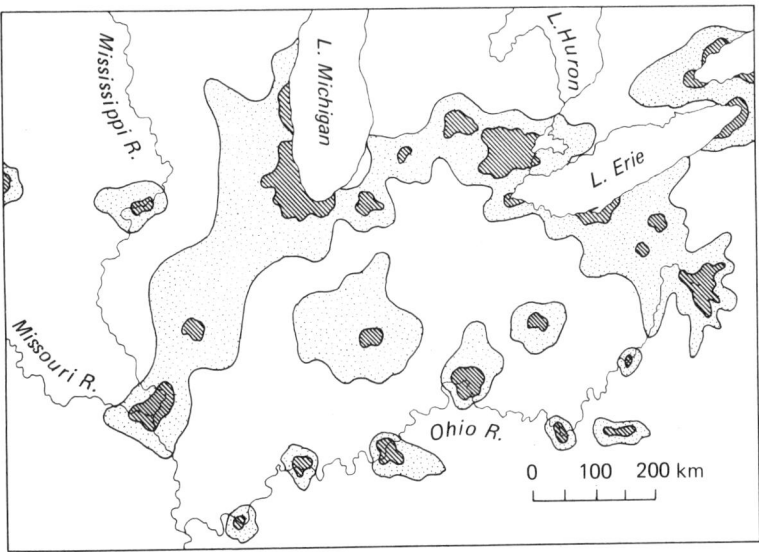

Fig. 4.10 The development of an industrial region: a simplified example from the American Midwest. The darkest shading indicates developed areas and light stippling the transitional zones, while the unshaded areas are regions of non-growth or even of decline

(b) The Changing Pattern of Development

Classical economic theory tells us that the gulf between the developed core and the depressed periphery will continue to widen, the rich becoming richer and the poor poorer. The process will only be reversed when the very cheapness of the labour and land factors in the depressed region attracts entrepreneurs away from the core, where these factors are dear, to areas where their cheapness more than compensates for difficulties in transport and in procuring materials. In this way West German industry has established branches in Portugal, western entrepreneurs are turning to the cheap labour of Hong Kong, Taiwan and other parts of the underdeveloped world, and manufacturing industry is now moving into the American South.

We must not, however, expect this trend to revolutionize either the location of manufacturing or the relationship of rich and poor countries: the infrastructure of the older developed nuclei, at least, will continue to exercise some attraction. Growth may be less rapid, but in only a few instances—industralized New England is one of them—is expansion likely to give way to economic decline.

Government intervention. In very few parts of the world is economic growth left wholly to private enterprise; in most the government plays a significant role either in setting guidelines within which the entrepreneur must operate, or in establishing factories, creating the infrastructure and directing development plans. The objective of private enterprise is the maximization of profits. Governments, on the other hand, aim (or should do so) at improving social conditions, relieving unemployment and raising living standards. They would claim that it is their duty to balance the private net profit of the entrepreneur against the public good. A government may decide that depressed areas can no longer be tolerated and may thus restrict the freedom of manufacturers to locate their activities anywhere they wish and may direct them to less profitable sites instead of waiting for the operation of economic forces.

In this way decline may be arrested and growth initiated, as in the 'development areas' of the United Kingdom, the Italian *Mezzogiorno* (south) and parts of the southern USA. The effect is to blur the simple model presented here, and to create new centres of growth, incipient cores each surrounded by its restricted transitional area.

In some instances the underdeveloped periphery has been a source of raw materials—vegetable, mineral and fuel. One of the grievances of the underdeveloped world has been that in the past inadequate compensation was paid for the supply of these to the developed core regions—that it has, in other words, been exploited. The current trend would reverse this. The establishment of aluminium-smelting in Ghana, steel-making in Brazil, Venezuela and Egypt, and the production of cotton textiles in India represent not only the movement of manufacturing to the source of at least part of its raw materials, but also the development of previously poor and underdeveloped areas.

The government, lastly, may restrict the further expansion of developed and industrialized cores. Further growth might be thought to place too great a strain on the infrastructure, increasing pollution and posing dangers to health—

factors which private enterprise might not be willing to take fully into consideration. Government might thus limit the growth of the core by interposing 'green belts' between it and the transitional region, as happens in Great Britain. It might accompany this with the creation of 'new towns' in relatively less-developed areas, as has been done in Great Britain and in several other countries of the developed and communist worlds (see Unit 13.4(*b*)). Social policy is thus beginning to play a role comparable with that of market forces in the slowly changing pattern of economic regions.

Questions

1. What outward measures and symbols are there of standards of living?
2. 'GNP per head varies directly with the size of the urban sector and inversely with employment in agriculture.' Discuss.
3. 'Economic backwardness merely means that the capital factor in production is present in only small amounts.' Discuss, quoting examples.
4. Compare, from the point of view of capital inputs, agriculture (*a*) in India with that in England, (*b*) in Canada with that in the Soviet Union.
5. Compare the nature of demand in the West End of London with that in the East End. What would you expect to be the resulting differences in shops?
6. 'Every developed country has its backward or depressed areas.' Discuss why this is so, and show what attempts are being made to remedy the situation.

Unit Five

Agricultural Production

The cultivation of the soil is the most widespread and the most important of all human activities. It employs at least half the human race: though in the developed countries only 10 per cent or less of the population works on the land, the proportion rises to 75 per cent and even higher in some parts of the developing world. Agriculture is basic to every other activity since, apart from the sea foods, it provides the whole of mankind's diet. Furthermore, agriculture is for very many people not just an occupation which yields a livelihood, but a way of life. It is still in many countries hedged about by customs and traditions which demonstrate that its roots reach far back in human history. There are few countries which do not in some way protect agriculture and the farmer. To some extent they are assuring the continuance of their food supply, but they are also supporting a class of people who have traditionally formed the backbone of their stock.

5.1   Conditions of Agriculture

Agriculture differs in certain very important respects from other productive activities like manufacturing or mining, or even forestry.

(a) Size of Farms

Agriculture is carried on by an immense number of separate farming enterprises: there can hardly be less than 500 million of them. They range in size from large wheat farms and ranches in the American Midwest, which may cover thousands of hectares, to small subsistence holdings of a hectare or less, each cultivated by a peasant family. This fragmentation of agriculture has important consequences. The decisions that have to be made are as diverse as the farms; but the advice available to factory managers is out of the reach of most farmers. The majority have no access to commercial or market reports and so cannot easily gauge the future demand for their products, and they respond only very slowly, if at all, to changes in demand. In general, large-scale farmers who are highly capitalized and well trained are best able to modify their farming practice to take advantage of shifts in demand and fluctuations in the world economy. Most small farmers are at the mercy of every change in the market for their products.

(b) Agricultural Self-sufficiency

The majority of the world's farmers are in some degree *self-sufficient*. Whereas the car or textile manufacturer produces for the market, and all his output is sold by dealers and shop-keepers, most farmers keep a part of what they produce and use it in their own households. On an English farm this may be only a very small proportion of total production, though the farming family is often self-sufficing in eggs, milk and perhaps vegetables. The specialized wheat-producer of the North American Prairies may be the extreme case of the farmer who derives no part of his subsistence directly from his own land. Indeed, he commonly lives on his farm for only a few weeks in each year, to supervise ploughing, sowing and harvesting.

As a general rule, however, the smaller the undertaking, the larger is its contribution to the feeding of the farming family. Among the subsistence farmers of much of Africa and of southern and south-eastern Asia, almost all the agricultural production is consumed on the holding, and only a small and variable surplus is sold. Conversely, the holding supplies all, or almost all, of the food consumed in the household. The subsistence farmer is thus to a large degree insulated from the world market; its fluctuations involve him only marginally, and his decisions are chiefly concerned with satisfying his own and his family's needs.

(c) Flexibility of Agriculture

Agricultural production is not usually tied to one particular commodity. The factory is geared to one type of product, and even small design modifications call for extensive and costly retooling. A few farmers are similarly restricted: for example, the proprietor of a rubber, coffee or tea plantation, or a North American wheat-farmer. Most, however, can change from one crop to another, from maize to soy beans, perhaps, or from dairy or mixed farming to corn-growing. Some such changes amount to little more than substituting one seed for another. Other changes, such as that from arable farming to livestock-rearing or vice versa, may call for a larger capital investment and will take place more slowly.

This does not mean that the farmer makes such changes readily. He tends to be conservative, keeping to traditional practices because time has shown them to be the most reliable amid shifting markets and uncertain weather conditions. Nonetheless, the farmer is continually being faced with the need to make decisions, perhaps by changes in the market or in the physical conditions in his district. He may have to decide, for instance, between growing a crop which best suits his soil and one which appears to offer a greater market advantage. He makes his decision according to his perception of physical, social and economic conditions, and his choice is as likely to be unwise as it is to be farsighted and intelligent.

(d) Joint Production

Few forms of agriculture produce only one commodity: most of necessity produce more than one crop or practise crop-farming along with animal-raising in such a way that each is dependent on the other. There are many reasons for this. The maintenance of soil fertility may require a sequence or rotation of crops. Or, as in parts of southern and south-eastern Asia, it may be practicable to take two or even more crops within a year from the same land, their choice depending upon the season of the year when they are planted. Or animals may be kept to provide manure for the crops, and certain crops may be grown as fodder for the animals.

An immense number of such crop or crop–animal associations are known and are regularly practised. Two or more such interdependent commodities are said to be in *joint production*: examples include summer rice and winter wheat in parts of India, wheat, barley and sugar-beet in East Anglia, and maize and bread grain in the American Corn Belt. The production of a given quantity of one such crop must necessarily be accompanied by a corresponding amount of the associated crop. One is the *primary crop*, the chief object of the farmers' system of cultivation, while the other can be considered a by-product. It is by definition less profitable and is grown chiefly in order to make the cultivation of the primary crop practicable. It may even be sold at a price below prime costs—that is, its directly related costs of production—since a farmer is not concerned that *each* of his crops should show a profit, but that his farm's products should *together* bring him a sufficient return. Thus he cannot easily control the volume of production of the secondary crops: it may even be larger than the market can bear and its price may fall correspondingly.

5.2 The Physical Constraints on Agriculture

Agriculture is restricted more narrowly than most other human activities by physical conditions. The farmer has learned through many generations of trial and observation which crops and practices best suit his soil and climate. But these conditions are themselves not stable. Drought, flood and frost, fungi and insect pests may lead to fundamental changes in farming practice.

Physical conditions do not in themselves determine a farmer's crops and practices. But they set limits within which he operates, and he must reconcile his needs with the physical conditions of his land and the opportunities offered by the market. The physical conditions influencing his choice include the nature of his soil, the climate and its expected fluctuations, the terrain and the aspect of the land, and to these must be added his location with regard to markets and means of transport.

(a) Soil

In farming the soil is used as a medium for germinating seeds and growing crops, and the fundamental problem in agriculture is the maintenance of soil fertility. Each crop removes nutrient materials from the soil, and though crops may be taken for many years from the same tract of land without apparent diminution in the yield, as in the rich lake basin of Winnipeg, returns will nevertheless eventually decrease unless as much is put back into the soil as is taken out. This applies as much to pastoral farming as to arable; meadows have to be manured no less than cropland. Our ancestors attempted to maintain soil fertility by *fallowing*—that is, allowing the land a year's 'rest-cure' during which, left without growing crops, it recovered naturally something of what it had lost. The various crop rotations and long 'leys' are adaptations, under differing conditions of soil and climate, to the urgent necessity not to take too much of any plant nutrient from the soil too quickly.

The study of fertility was wholly empirical until the various soil constituents were identified in the early nineteenth century. In 1840 von Liebig gave scientific recognition to the principal elements essential for plant growth: nitrogen, phosphorus, sulphur, potassium, magnesium, calcium and iron, also a number of 'trace elements'. More recently the trace elements have been found to be necessary only in very small amounts. The proportions of the vital elements in soils vary from place to place, partly because of the different compositions of the rocks from which the soils were derived, partly because of different climatic conditions which hasten or retard the breakdown of the rock constituents, and partly because soluble minerals can be washed out of the soil by percolating water and carried away in streams and rivers to the sea.

We thus know, or have the means of discovering, what needs to be put back into the soil in order to offset the losses due to cropping. We can change the texture and composition of a soil in order to render it fitter for certain crops. Good agricultural practice replaces what it takes from the soil. The most obvious and natural means is by restoring to the land, in the shape of excreta, just what the soil has given to animals and men. This practice has been carried to its extreme in Chinese agriculture, but is quite impracticable over most of the world. The deficiency has to be made good, in the long run, by the use of artificial fertilizers. In most developed countries a farmer will submit samples of his soil to a soil scientist who will test it, discover its deficiencies and prescribe the right quantities of a suitable fertilizer to remedy them.

No cultivated soil remains in its natural condition; it may be improved by manuring, deep digging, draining and liming, or it may deteriorate through careless cultivation. It becomes, in the words of the American geographer Carl Sauer, a 'response to management'. A good piece of allotment garden may have an almost completely man-made soil. The minerals have been recombined and redistributed by the vegetation, which draws salts from the soil, manufactures complex organic substances, and returns these to the soil when it withers.

Soils are most often classified according to the features which do most to determine the crops to be grown in them: (*i*) their texture, (*ii*) the ways in which the soil constituents are arranged within them, and (*iii*) their degree of acidity or alkalinity.

(*i*) **Soil texture.** This is a consequence primarily of the nature of the parent rock, and the range includes the fine particles of clay and silt at one extreme and coarse sand at the other. Texture determines the porosity and water-holding properties of a soil. Clay soils, like those of the clay belts that lie across England from Somerset to Yorkshire, are slow to drain, so that they may remain waterlogged far into the spring and thus be difficult to plough in time for sowing. Though certain crops—notably wheat—do well on clay soils, such soils are generally left under grass and commonly support dairy farming. Lighter soils, developed on limestone and chalk, as in the Cotswolds and Chilterns, are usually well drained and are sometimes too dry for certain crops. With very few exceptions, any crop *can* be grown on any soil, but the results may be poor. Every type of crop has a range of soil types which suit it best and on which it will produce most heavily. Market factors may make it a wise decision to grow certain crops on soils that are less than ideal: high wheat prices, for example, might be expected to push wheat-growing on to poorly drained valley soils, the lower yields being offset by higher prices (see Unit 1.4).

(*ii*) **Soil structure.** This is the vertical arrangement of the soil constituents within the soil itself. *Leaching*, the process whereby soluble constituents are dissolved and carried downwards beyond the reach of many plants, results in the *podsols* of the cool damp climatic regions and the *laterites* of the intertropical lands. (Both podsols and laterites are highly-leached soils of very low fertility.) On the other hand, soluble materials are drawn by capillary movement towards the surface, producing at best the fertile *chernozem* soil of the Russian Steppes and the American Prairies, and at worst the salt-encrusted desert. Intermediate between these extremes are the well-structured soils of midlatitudes, in which leaf mould and other organic matter have produced a rich *humus* in the upper layers of the soil.

The soils of the wetter parts of the British Isles are generally podsolized, though in some areas deep ploughing is used to break up the structure and bring darker, lower horizons to the surface. The climate is too wet in the British Isles, or indeed anywhere in Europe except its eastern borderland, for chernozem to develop, and over most of the area brown forest soils prevail, much modified by very long periods of cultivation.

(*iii*) **Acidity–alkalinity.** The acid or alkaline properties of the soil are dependent both on the nature of the parent rock and on the moisture content and chemistry of the soil itself. They are usually expressed in terms of the *pH value*, a numerical measure of acidity or alkalinity: neutral soils have a pH of about 7, that of an acid soil is lower than this and that of an alkaline soil is higher. It often varies widely within short distances: surveys sometimes show variations from acid to strongly alkaline soils within the limits of a single farm. Though a few crops do well in acid soils, most prefer neutral or alkaline conditions, and it is a common practice in the more developed countries to spread lime—an alkali—in order to raise the pH.

Within limits the farmer adapts his crops to the qualities of his soil. Alternatively, he attempts to modify these qualities by drainage or by using chemical additives, especially in the richer countries, where money and scientific knowledge are more readily available. Some soils, however, almost defy the efforts of the soil scientist to alter them: for instance, the podsols and the lateritic soils cannot easily be improved, and the agricultural return from their cultivation is likely to remain small.

Soils within the United Kingdom are strongly alkaline in limestone regions, and acid over much of the hilly west and north. Even in the clay lands, soils are generally neutral or mildly alkaline.

Soil erosion. Soil is formed by the slow breakdown of the underlying rock. In time a balance is reached whereby the wind and rain remove no more soil from the surface than can be replaced by the weathering of the rock below. It is the vegetation that maintains this balance, and any interference with the natural plant cover may accelerate the removal of soil. Lord Boyd Orr once said: 'It takes nature from 300 to 1 000 years to build up one inch of fertile soil. Man by his wanton misuse can destroy eight inches in one or two generations.'

Soil erosion occurs everywhere. It is serious when the rate of removal exceeds that of replacement, and this probably happens to some extent wherever the land is cultivated. In its extreme manifestations soil erosion shows itself in deep gullies cut by torrents through the soil to the bedrock, and in huge areas of useless, stony wilderness stripped by the wind of topsoil and left infertile. But it can be very serious long before it reaches so advanced a stage. Even in England, where climatic conditions are not especially conducive to soil erosion, topsoil blowing is known, and in the Fenland has become quite serious.

Soil erosion has been most spectacular in the North American continent. Here large areas in the Appalachian Mountains and elsewhere have been laid waste by gullying, very largely as a result of the destruction of the natural forest cover. Extensive areas in Kansas, Nebraska and other states have lost their topsoil through wind erosion, as a result of tilling land that is climatically too dry for regular cultivation. Erosion extends northwards into Canada, and has also reached serious dimensions in Venezuela, Brazil, Uruguay and Argentina. In Africa marginal land has been destroyed by overcultivation but more often by the overgrazing of the poor grasslands. The *loess* lands (where the soil consists of a fine-textured, wind-blown deposit) of northern China are being stripped of their soil, and the menace is felt elsewhere also. In Australia, the government has come to take a serious view of the problem and is doing its utmost to restrict its ravages.

Good farming aims not merely at preserving or increasing the natural fertility of the soil but at retaining the soil itself *in situ*. Any system of farming must be considered a misuse of the land if it does not pass on its soil and fertility unimpaired to the next generation.

(b) Climate

Climate is a much more important constraint on agriculture than is soil. An unsuitable soil does not make it impossible to grow a particular crop; it only makes its cultivation less profitable. Climate, on the other hand, may present an absolute barrier. Plants do not grow if the temperature is below about 7° Celsius, and some are killed or their flowers blighted even by a slight frost. All have a particular growing period, and if this is cut short by drought or frost they cannot produce their seed and propagate themselves. Nevertheless, many cultivated plants are remarkably tolerant of climatic conditions. Wheat, for example, grows well in climates as diverse as that of the Mediterranean, with its dry summers, of mild, wet countries like Britain, and of the North American and Soviet heartlands which represent continental extremes.

For all cultivated plants, however, there is an *optimum* climate. It does not of course follow that any particular crop will be important in areas where the

Fig. 5.1 Soil erosion: (a) deep gullies have been cut by torrents pouring down steep hillsides—the gentler slopes have been terraced to minimize soil losses (Madeira); (b) topsoil is carried away in a high wind (USA); (c) the results of erosion: wind and rain have removed much of the topsoil between the rows of maize in this field

climate suits its cultivation; this depends on market and social conditions. But there is nonetheless a rough adjustment of crops and farming systems (discussed in Unit 5.4) to climatic conditions.

We shall consider three aspects of the relationship between agriculture and climate: the divergences of climate from the expected conditions, the adaptation of plants to a wider climatic range, and the modification of the environment to accommodate a wider variety of crops.

(*i*) **Climatic fluctuations.** The climate represents the conditions which might, on statistical grounds, be expected to occur. Most crops can tolerate small climatic variations; but wide divergences are infrequent and may be beyond the capacity of the plants to resist. They may be frozen or parched, rotted by abnormal rainfall or prevented from ripening by a cool summer.

Such abnormal conditions can always be found on a local or regional scale somewhere on the earth's surface: frost in the Florida orange groves or the Brazilian coffee plantations, drought in parts of India or the Sahel of tropical Africa, or flood in the Great Plain of China. Catastrophes like these always give rise to scarcities, high prices and, especially in regions of subsistence agriculture, famine. Throughout history the lean years have always followed the fat, and the only significant change of recent years has been the provision of relief for stricken areas.

(*ii*) **Plant breeding.** Although natural conditions such as soil and climate can be varied only minimally, the plants themselves may be susceptible of a more profound alteration. The practice of plant-breeding has not only succeeded in increasing the volume of return from each tree, plant or seed but has developed varieties able to withstand more severe or more exceptional physical conditions. A well-known example is the production of a wheat that could germinate, grow, produce its fruit and ripen during a short summer, between the last killing frost of spring and the first of autumn. This success has permitted the extension of wheat-growing in Canada northwards into the Peace river valley, where the growing period is usually less than 100 days.

Scarcely less spectacular have been the improvements in cotton, potatoes, sugar-beet, maize and other cereals, and their acclimatization in regions differing in some degree from their native habitat. At the same time grain and other crops are being bred with useful characteristics such as a stronger stalk or greater resistance to fungus and pests, as well as with a heavier yield.

(*iii*) **Environmental modification.** Control or even modification of the climate has not yet come within the range of human capability, though a great deal of work has been done to develop techniques for inducing rainfall, such as cloud-seeding. On a small and local scale, however, the effects of abnormal weather can be ameliorated. Smut pots, for example, are sometimes used to spread a blanket of smoke and thus to ward off frost from orchards and citrus groves. Crops—coffee in the hills of southern Brazil, for example—are planted on the hill slopes to minimize the effects of frost settling in the valleys. Clay lands can be improved by laying porous drainage pipes beneath the surface, and the growing period of plants can be shortened by raising the soil temperature in glasshouses and under *cloches*: large areas in England are covered by glasshouses or polythene sheeting, under which crops like tomatoes are grown. In the Isles of Scilly and in southern France, hedges or rows of trees are planted as windbreaks to protect tender crops. In regions of small and unreliable rainfall dry-farming methods are sometimes practised by allowing soil moisture to accumulate for two years before taking a crop.

These methods and devices all have this in common: they overcome the vagaries of the weather only at a high cost in labour and capital. They can be used only for crops such as fruit and early vegetables for which there is a strong demand and for which high prices can therefore be expected.

The most important and the most widely practised environmental modification is *irrigation*. The most irrigated parts of the world are the areas of seasonal rainfall. India is the outstanding example, and here the great irrigation works of the Punjab alone render cultivable very large areas of semi-arid and arid country. The irrigated oases, large and small, in otherwise uncultivated lands are too numerous to count. It is hard to estimate what proportion of the world's agricultural output comes from irrigated lands: if with these is included the rice-lands of monsoon Asia, it may well be over a quarter and perhaps a third.

There are two modes of irrigation: first, the accumulation of water during the wet season for use during the ensuing dry, and second, the abstraction of water from rivers or reservoirs for crops throughout the year in areas where the rainfall is insufficient at any time. The small reservoirs which feed the *vegas* and *huertas* (irrigated gardens) of south-eastern Spain and the tanks of India belong to the first category; the great irrigation projects of the Punjab, the Imperial valley scheme of southern California and the irrigation works of the Orange and Vaal rivers of South Africa, of the Murray in New South Wales and, above all of the Nile and the Sudan belong to the second.

Serious technical and economic problems, however, set geographical limits to the use of irrigation. The primitive irrigation works of the Indian, Chinese and Japanese peasants call for a certain skill and, above all, for a vast supply of labour, which in these countries is not lacking. But it is doubtful whether the area now under irrigation can be extended further without the use of elaborate civil engineering works. While an immense number of irrigation projects are technically feasible, no more than a few could ever be financially practicable. Whether irrigation is a private venture or a government undertaking, the expected gain from the improvement of the land must be sufficient to yield a reasonable interest on the capital invested in a dam and its related works. Even the developments financed by the World Bank (see Unit 15.3(*b*)) are expected to show a profit and pay interest to the bank as well as to repay the capital loan.

Judged by this criterion, many visionary projects collapse. The soil may be too poor or too alkaline to yield much return even if irrigated, or the technical difficulties and high cost of the construction may outweigh the advantages offered by a good soil, or the scheme may be expected to have a relatively short life because the reservoir is likely to silt up or because the irrigated land may deteriorate with the accumulation of alkalis in the soil as a result of repeated inundation and evaporation. On the other hand, a project deemed uneconomic might come within the bounds of possibility if money could be borrowed at a lower rate of interest.

Whether to irrigate or not is thus a complex problem with many variable factors, none of them easy to evaluate. The answer depends on the climatic conditions, the river regime, the physical conditions of the river basin, the volume of silt and dissolved material which it carries, and the availability of labour and capital, in addition to the market demand for the crop.

5.3 The Land Factor in Agriculture

Agriculture, as we have seen, demands all the three factors of production discussed in Unit 4.3, but land is of especial importance: this is why physical factors impose severe constraints on agricultural practices. As a factor, land has certain characteristics: it is finite in quantity, its quality varies greatly from one place to another, and its food-producing capacity can be diminished or exhausted by careless or improper use.

(*a*) Diminishing Returns
The factors of labour and capital vary greatly in relation to land. A heavy use is made of labour in monsoon agriculture (see Unit 5.4(*a*)); there is a large capital investment in, say, a rubber plantation or an orange grove. If there is a

comparable increase of *all* the factors of production, including land, the level of production per unit area is likely to remain unchanged. If however only *one* factor is increased there is likely to be some expansion in yield, but not in direct proportion to the increase in the factor in question. The first application of fertilizer, for example, may yield a handsome dividend; the second, however, may give a somewhat smaller increase, and the third, one that is smaller still, until the addition of yet more fertilizer gives no appreciable increase in crop-yield (Fig. 5.2).

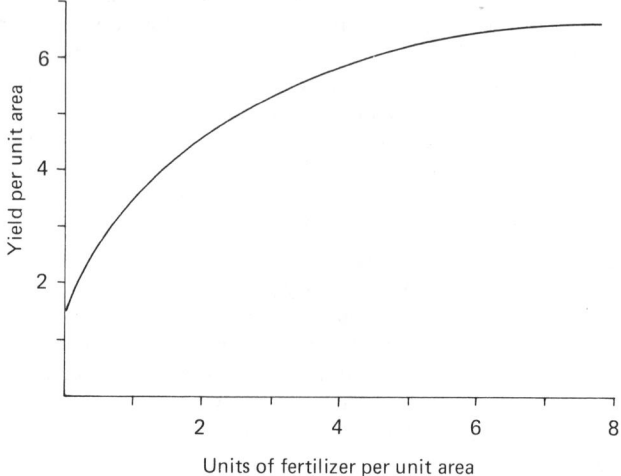

Fig. 5.2 Diminishing returns: each additional increment of fertilizer gives a smaller increase in yield until the point of no increase is reached

This is what we understand by *diminishing returns*. The developer or investor has at some point to decide whether it is worth his while to add more capital in the face of continued diminution of yield. It pays to add a great deal of fertilizer and to invest large sums in field-drainage or other development projects in the Netherlands or the United Kingdom; it would not be profitable to do so in, for example, much of Pakistan or Ecuador, because the physical conditions of soil and climate are such that the point of diminishing returns would be reached early in the process.

The same situation would arise if the labour factor were increased. An additional unit of labour on a farm gives rise to no increment in production beyond a certain point—a point already reached in many overpopulated regions.

(b) Margin of Cultivation

Let us consider any area of commercial agriculture, such as that of wheat-growing in the Fenland of eastern England, of maize-growing in the United States Corn Belt, of wool production in Australia or of mutton and lamb production in New Zealand. Let us assume that somewhere within this area the physical requirements of the particular crop are as fully satisfied as seems possible and that transport facilities could not readily be improved upon. Here the profit from producing this commodity would be at a maximum. Since conditions are so ideally suited to this form of agriculture, the land might be expected to have a relatively high value. The farmer would have a great deal of capital invested in it, or, alternatively, he would be paying a high rent for it, which would cut into his profits.

These ideal conditions would, however, only be met with over a very restricted area—too small to satisfy demand for the product. Production therefore spreads beyond it into other areas which may be satisfactory, but do not offer optimum conditions. They may lack adequate transport facilities, the soil may lack certain nutrients and need fertilizer, or the risk of frost or uncertainty of rainfall may be great. Nevertheless, farming is carried on. Yields are lower and farm income smaller, but the value of the land is less and rents are lower. So production of this crop moves outwards from the optimum area into areas which yield less and less well, until total production satisfies total demand. If demand is great enough, production will spread into land which is increasingly unsuitable, until at last a point is reached where the land is no longer cultivated. Does agriculture cease high up on a mountain side or on the dry plains of the American West because of the natural barriers to its further advance, or because demand has ceased to expand? The answer is that the *margin of cultivation* lies where the last farmer can be expected to break even. Beyond it, farming would be carried on at a loss under prevailing market conditions. If prices were to rise the margin would advance; if they were to fall, it would retreat. Fig. 5.3 illustrates this concept of the 'margin', which is of the highest importance in the study of economic geography.

(c) Economic Rent
Fig. 5.3 shows how, in a time of rising prices for a particular crop, its cultivation expands into areas which are not optimally suited to it: for example, where the

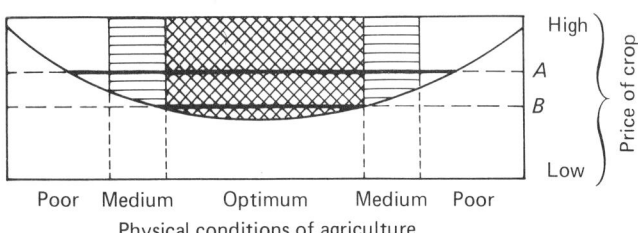

Poor   Medium   Optimum   Medium   Poor
Physical conditions of agriculture

Fig. 5.3 The concept of the 'margin'. Provided a crop is in demand, it will always be grown in areas with optimum conditions. Increasing demand, reflected in a high price, will lead to the extension of cultivation into areas with less than optimum conditions until, with heavy demand and very high prices (A), cultivation spreads into areas fundamentally unsuitable for it. With falling prices (B), the margin recedes towards the area of optimum conditions

extra land brought into cultivation yields less well or requires an increased expenditure in fertilizer. It is, in other words, less valuable land, and the rent which a farmer could be expected to pay would be lower than that for the optimum land. The highest rents would be charged for the land offering the best conditions, and rents per hectare might be expected to decline as one moves outwards from this land.

Fig. 5.4 illustrates the concept of *economic rent*. It assumes that the farmer's costs are the same for each hectare of land irrespective of its quality (an assumption unlikely to be valid in practice). The total height of each column

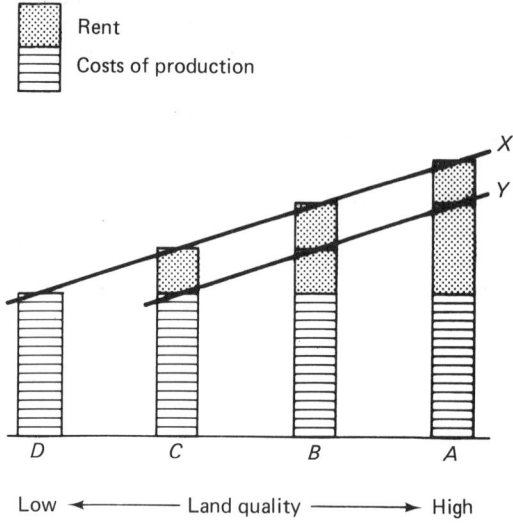

Fig. 5.4 The concept of 'economic rent'. In the marginal unit of cultivation the yield just covers the costs, leaving no surplus for rent. If C is the marginal unit, the line Y indicates the theoretical rent for land of different qualities; if D is marginal, line X indicates the rent

represents the income per hectare obtainable from land of differing qualities (line X). The yield from the land at D exactly covers the costs of production, leaving nothing over for the payment of rent; this land thus represents the marginal unit of cultivation. For the other farms, the stippled sections at the top of the columns represent the theoretical economic rents which might be expected from the farmers of the best land, A, and of the less good lands B and C. Suppose however, the prices fall; the income per hectare from all the land falls too (line Y). Farming at D now becomes unprofitable, and the margin moves to C.

The rents which a farmer or industrialist (or anyone else who occupies land) might be expected to pay may not accord completely with this model. They may be stabilized by law or by leasehold contract. They cannot in any case be adapted to short-term fluctuations in the market and in the margin of cultivation. Nevertheless, behind all considerations of rent lies the concept of the *margin*, the line beyond which it does not pay to use the land and the land in consequence can have no rental value.

Von Thünen's theory. The classical theory of rent was developed by the economist David Ricardo in 1817. He conceived of land as varying in quality, with the better-quality land bearing the higher rent. At about the same time a German landowner, von Thünen, developed a theory which was in many ways complementary of that of Ricardo. He postulated a discrete area of land—the *isolated state*—with a centrally placed town and soil of equal quality throughout, and he assumed that there were no improved means of transport, and that all goods had to be carried by peasant waggon except where a small river was available.

Von Thünen suggested that the value of land, and hence its rent, depended on its distance from the town which served as market. Land close to the town was more valuable than that lying further away because its products had to bear the cost of only a short journey. Since it was more valuable it was cropped more intensively, and the least intensive use was made of the most distant land. Von Thünen thus conceived of a series of six concentric zones around his ideal town (Fig. 5.5). The innermost was given over to market gardening, the stall-feeding of animals and other such intensive forms of agricultural land use. Beyond this lay a belt of woodland, preserved thus close to the town because in von Thünen's world it supplied building materials and fuel, which were difficult to transport over long distances. Beyond this came in turn zones of intensive arable farming, combined arable and pastoral, rotational arable and animal-rearing. He traced furthermore a belt of more intensive land use along the valley of the small river, which, he imagined, would provide transport. Later he extended his model from the isolated city-state to the individual farm. Here too he found that, both in logic and in practice, the most intensive use was made of land lying closest to the farm buildings, while rough grazing was relegated to the periphery.

We may quarrel with von Thünen's categories, which do not seem to accord with the spectrum of intensive–extensive land use we recognize today. They were, however, based upon his own observation and experience in the German province of Mecklenburg. We must accept too that von Thünen presented an idealized set of conditions which could never have been fully achieved in reality, if only because distance is not the only variable affecting the value and hence the rent of land. Nevertheless, his emphasis on transport charges as part of the total costs of production was of great importance (see Unit 9.4(*a*)).

Countless studies have been made of land use in the light of von Thünen's model. If today it fits the farming practice in lowland England only imperfectly, this is largely because cars and tractors have reduced the significance of distance, and also because increasingly intensive use of the land has made it hard to distinguish rigidly separate categories of land use. In less crowded areas, however, it is not difficult to detect a zonal pattern in the use of the land, though one which is clearly less regular than von Thünen's theoretical postulate.

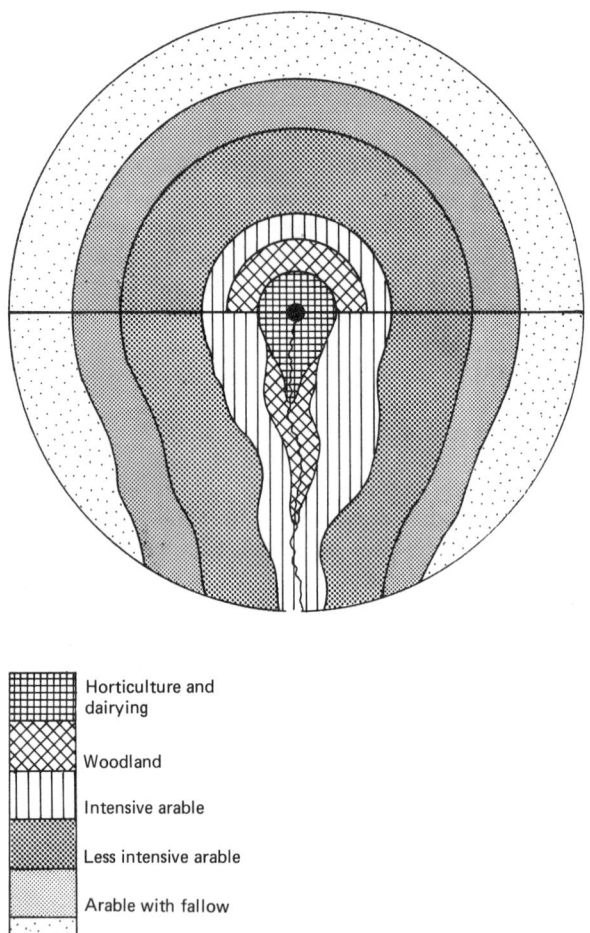

Horticulture and dairying

Woodland

Intensive arable

Less intensive arable

Arable with fallow

Grazing

Fig. 5.5 The von Thünen model of land use

5.4   Agricultural Systems

Unit 4.3 showed how the factors of production are brought together in agriculture in varying proportions and in different ways, how cropping is adjusted to physical conditions and how physical conditions may be modified to suit crops. The result has been the creation of *agricultural systems*, or ways in which these elements are combined in order to produce crops and rear livestock (Fig. 5.6). Each system is immensely complex. Inputs of labour and capital vary greatly. Crops are associated in joint production. One agricultural product may

0 1600 3200 km
Plantation
Commercial gardening, fruit
Commercial dairying
Commercial crop and livestock
Commercial grain
Mediterranean agriculture
Intensive subsistence
Primitive cultivation
Ranching
Nomadic herding
Little or no agriculture

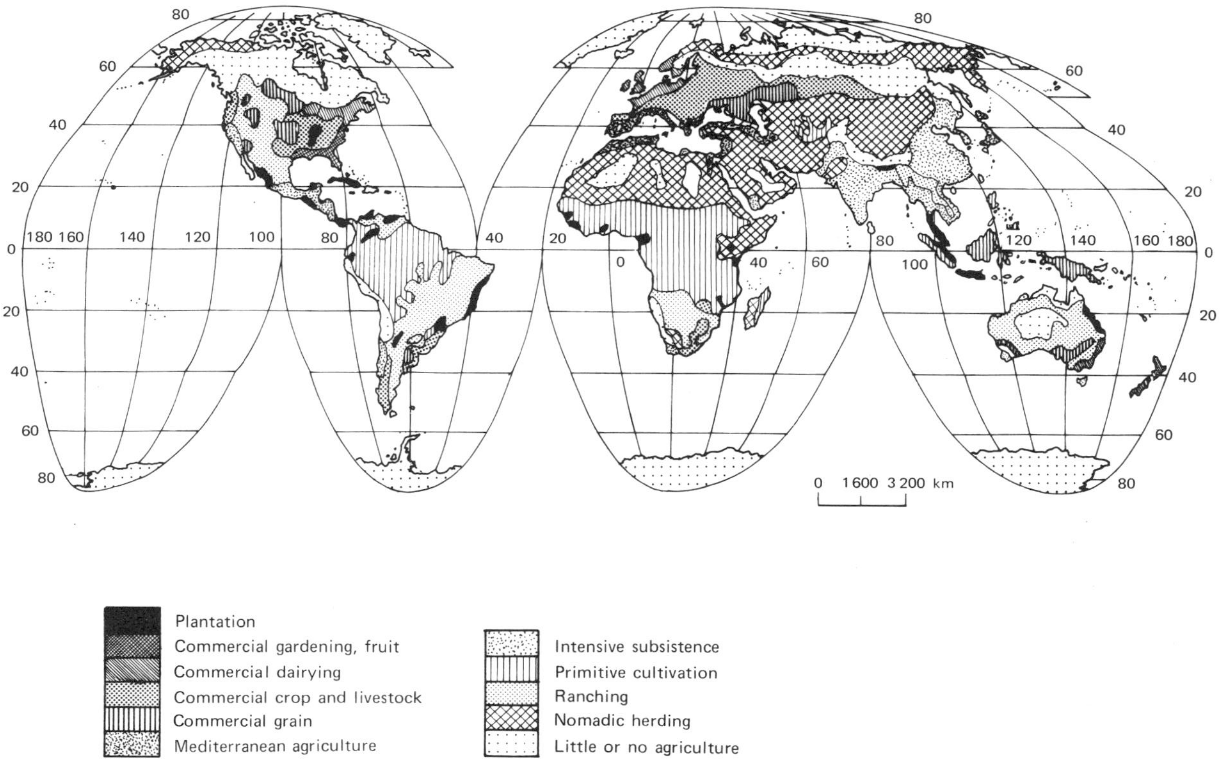

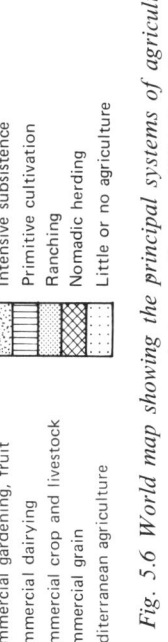

Fig. 5.6 World map showing the principal systems of agriculture (based with permission on Derwent Whittlesey)

serve as an input in another branch of the same system; for instance, fodder crops, grown in rotation with corn, help to feed dairy cattle.

An agricultural system can be represented by a diagram showing the inputs entering the system and outputs leaving it. Fig. 5.7 is a very simple model of midlatitude mixed arable and dairy farming. You should try to prepare similar

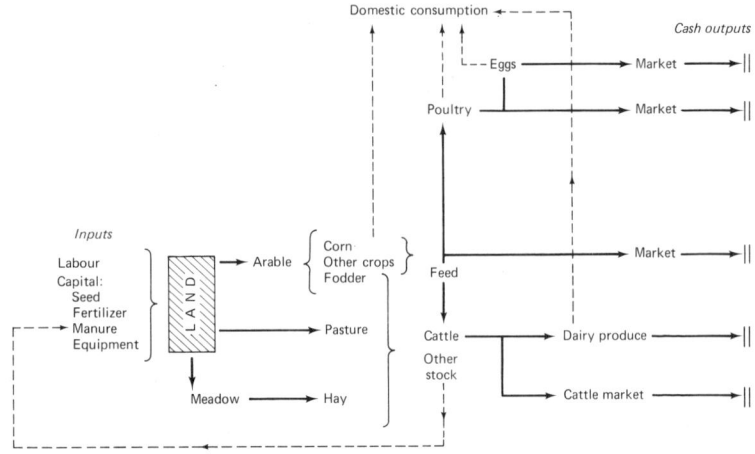

Fig. 5.7 A flow diagram for a farming system in north-western Europe

flow diagrams for other agricultural systems described later in this unit. Sometimes a value can be set upon each input, allocating it to each stage in the system, as well as upon the marketable outputs. In this way a simple *input–output analysis* can be carried out, and the farmer can thus find out the relative profitability of each division of his total operation.

It is usually a simple matter to make substitutions within a system: for example, to grow sorghum instead of maize, or to use soy beans instead of a fallow. Indeed, any farmer regularly makes a choice between available crops, deciding which to put into a particular slot in his agricultural system. Such a choice may necessitate minor changes in the system—in the date of sowing or harvesting, perhaps, or in the use of fertilizer. But the system is not dislocated thereby, and the change can be and often is, reversed. But drastic changes in a system can introduce substantial difficulties, because modification in one part usually brings about changes in others. Peasant societies rarely make such a change unless compelled to do so. Even a change such as that from dairy to beef farming imposes a strain on the system, and few farmers choose to face the resulting disorientation unless driven by economic necessity.

Every agricultural system represents an adjustment to climatic conditions, and it is convenient to group the more important systems practised in the world today according to the physical conditions in which they are carried on.

(a) Tropical and Equatorial Agricultural Systems

The intertropical areas of the earth's surface are characterized by great heat, a seasonal range of temperature which is negligible on the equator and nowhere considerable, and a rainfall whose incidence and distribution varies widely. The agricultural economies are adjusted in varying degrees to their physical conditions; they differ also in the ways in which skills and techniques, capital and labour are represented in their management and organization.

(*i*) **Primitive shifting agriculture.** This agricultural system has received an attention from geographers and anthropologists out of all proportion to its slight economic importance today. It continues to be practised, mainly in equatorial regions, by primitive subsistence farmers. They cultivate a small patch of land with crops such as yams, cassava and sorghum until its natural fertility is exhausted. They then abandon it and make another clearing, which they cultivate until it too loses its fertility. Such cultivators use only the simplest methods, and very rarely produce for the market. They have few or no animals, and their frequent movements restrict the volume of goods that they can possess.

(*ii*) **Tropical peasant farming.** This system makes a more effective and continuous use of the land. It is found throughout the intertropical world. The peasants cultivate holdings which may range in size from one to a dozen or so hectares with crops such as millet, sorghum, rice, ground-nuts, cassava and yams. Although they may leave a small area fallow for a time, their settlements are permanent and their holdings change little if at all. They may produce small amounts of ground-nuts, cacao or palm oil for the market, though this depends on transport and marketing facilities. In many areas where this system is practised, there is scope for improving methods of cultivation and for increasing its marketable surplus.

(*iii*) **Plantation agriculture.** The plantation represents the intrusion of a western style of capitalist organization into tropical agriculture. The agricultural unit is large; it usually concentrates on a single crop, such as rubber, cacao, hemp, coffee or tea, and is worked with hired labour. It represents a large capital investment. Its crops—frequently tree crops—take many years to mature, and often require careful processing before they can be marketed. The plantation is usually an efficient method of production, but its concentration on one crop may harm the soil, while the fact that it is usually subject to foreign control, and is in effect a kind of imperialism, is likely to raise political problems.

(*iv*) **Monsoon agriculture.** This is, in reality, a special case of tropical peasant agriculture. Its particular circumstances are the concentration of rainfall, sometimes very heavy, into a short rainy season. It is characterized by intensive, irrigated cultivation of rice during the hot, wet season, except where this is precluded by the terrain. It is common for a dry-season crop to be taken after the rice harvest, and sometimes even a third crop in spring. Monsoon agriculture is

Fig. 5.8 Plantation agriculture: a large oil-palm station in Malaysia

capable of supporting a very dense population and south, south-east and east Asia have the densest rural populations to be found anywhere in the world. Limits are set to monsoon agriculture by increasing cold and diminishing rainfall, and monsoon peasant agriculture disappears against the arid mountains and plateaux of the interior of Asia.

(b) Midlatitude Agricultural Systems

In the agricultural regions discussed so far, most of the population is rural and is directly dependent on cultivating the soil for its livelihood. Though Japan and parts of China have in modern times become urbanized and industrialized, and an urban market has thus developed for farm products, elsewhere in these countries subsistence agriculture predominates. In the temperate areas of the earth, on the other hand, very large urban and industrialized societies have developed during the last 150 years, and the demand they create is a great and sometimes dominant factor in agricultural organization and production.

In this section, the agriculture of temperate lands is divided arbitrarily into three types, but these are extremely difficult to separate from one another either spatially or on the basis of their organization. Furthermore, each of the four categories could be subdivided into distinct cultivation patterns for local regions of perhaps only a few square kilometres each.

(*i*) **Mediterranean agriculture.** The Mediterranean region is the most distinctive of the major climatic regions of the world, and has evolved a distinct agricultural system that has changed little in 2 000 years. Rainfall comes mainly in winter, and the hot summer is generally a period of drought, when plant growth ceases unless irrigation is practised. Corn crops are winter-sown and ripen during the dry summer; spring-sown crops are excluded by the summer drought. There is a heavy dependence on tree crops such as olives and grapes, which are able to survive and even flourish in the dry season. In some Mediterranean areas irrigation from rivers permits the cultivation through the summer of such crops as maize and cotton.

(*ii*) **Mixed farming of north-west Europe and the north-eastern United States.** The farming pattern in these areas is dominated by the presence of large urban markets. Subsistence farming is not important and most of the farm produce is sold off the farms to the nearby towns. The large and still-growing demand for foodstuffs has set a premium on intensive production. The high yields thus obtained have encouraged a rise in land values and this increase brings about even more intensive use of the land. In general the intensity of land use diminishes with the increase in the effective distance from the towns; as the time and cost of transport to the town market increase, the more intensive dairy farming, vegetable- and fruit-growing and glasshouse cultivation tend to give place to mixed and arable forms of husbandry.

In north-western Europe, this highly complex pattern of agriculture has evolved during the past two centuries from one which was at once simpler and more self-sufficient and less dependent on urban markets. In general it is intensive and highly capitalized, though there remain many areas of relatively backward farming. The organization of agriculture varies from a predominance of dairy farming in moister areas and close to large cities, to arable farming which concentrates on 'cash grains', grains sold off the land directly to the buyer. Between these extremes is the true mixed agriculture, in which arable farming provides the fodder for sheep and cattle.

(*iii*) **European peasant farming.** This is distinguishable from mixed farming, which in some ways it resembles, in being largely subsistence, with only a small dependence on the market. It was once widespread in Europe and was not unknown in eastern North America. The peasant holding was commonly small, fragmented and under-equipped. It yielded only a small livelihood, and is today giving place to commercially organized mixed farming. The peasant remains of great importance, however, in parts of central and eastern Europe, notably in Poland and Yugoslavia.

(*c*) **Dry Land Agricultural Systems**
Dry lands occupy the interiors of most continents. Intensive use of the land is in general precluded by the lack of moisture, and the predominant forms of land use are ranching and commercial grain cultivation.

Fig. 5.9 A Sardinian shepherd with his flock ; the standard of living of these peasant farmers is among the lowest in western Europe

(*i*) **Ranching.** This is today confined to the more arid margins of the temperate grasslands. It has already lost much of the exotic colouring and romantic appeal of the last century, and is now under pressure from the encroachment of arable farming. The ranching areas of Canada and the USA now breed cattle, which are sent in large numbers to be fattened in the arable farming areas.

(*ii*) **Commercial grain farming.** Large areas of midlatitude grasslands are given over to the cultivation of a single crop, most often wheat. Wheat is the predominant crop over great tracts of the North American and Soviet grasslands, as well as on those of Australia, South Africa and South America. Farming is, generally speaking, highly mechanized but does not make intensive use of the land. There is a tendency for rotational farming, which makes a much more intensive use of the land, to encroach on the region of commercial grain agriculture wherever the amount of rainfall is adequate.

(*d*) **Arctic and Sub-arctic Regions**
These regions can scarcely be said to have agricultural systems. The climate nearly everywhere is too severe for agriculture, and cultivation is practicable only in a few well-favoured spots. Mixed farming does, however, tend to encroach on these regions, aided by the development by the plant-breeders of quick-growing species.

(For questions on the material in this Unit, see the end of Unit 6.)

Unit Six

Problems and Policies in Agriculture

In Unit 5 we considered the broad pattern of the world's agriculture against its physical background of soil and climate. In this Unit we shall examine the social and economic factors in agriculture: land tenure, capital, credit, co-operation, collectivization and other systems and practices, whose influence on the prosperity of the agricultural community is immensely significant. No distribution pattern of production is controlled wholly by the physical factors of soil, climate and labour. In theory these set no limit that cannot be overstepped if the price structure is sufficiently favourable, but in practice physical circumstances set an outer limit to the production of every crop, beyond which production is possible only at prohibitive cost (see Unit 5.3(b)). While physical influences certainly help to determine the precise areas of cultivation of a given crop, social and economic factors also have a large if not predominant influence.

These factors are, for the greater part, the product of centuries of evolution, and only in recent years has there been any deliberate interference by governmental agencies in their development. The break-up of large estates, the resettlement of peasants in intertropical countries, the formation of co-operatives, the encouragement of certain crops by bounty or subsidy, and above all the collectivization of agriculture, are examples of such intervention. Such actions are evidence of the tendency, increasingly marked during the present century, for economic development to be 'planned' with, as its ultimate objective, an increase in either the general level of welfare or the military security of the state.

6.1   Land Tenure

This is perhaps the most fundamental and important of these influences on agriculture.

The concept of the individual's ownership of land is comparatively modern. Primitive peoples regard land as owned by the community; the individual has the right to occupy and cultivate his share and he has a part interest in areas of uncultivated but potentially useful land. His land is not usually saleable, nor may he bequeath it to his heirs. This is the traditional tenurial background of the intertropical tribal economies. In recent years the concept of the communal holding has broken down, partly because the chiefs have been tempted to sell that to which they had no absolute right, and partly because of the appropriation by European powers of all uncultivated land. The effect of both has been to check the old practice of shifting cultivation, producing at worst a landless class, readily 'detribalized' and a focus of discontent if not also a serious economic liability. A further consequence may be the establishment of plantations on lands often acquired in defiance of local tradition. The development of a tropical peasantry, settled on holdings which are either owned outright or rented for a payment in cash or kind, shows clearly the influence of European example.

In Europe, land tenures evolved from a medieval system by which land was held by a variety of services and dues in kind, which came eventually to be commuted for a money payment. Modern European tenancies are principally *freehold, cash tenancy* or *share-cropping*; we will consider these one by one.

(*a*) Ownership or Freehold

About half the farmed land of western Europe is held in this way. Some freeholds were purchased from feudal owners; in France many were acquired forcibly at the Revolution. This is the dominant form of land-holding in all the more advanced countries; only Great Britain is an exception. It is accompanied, as a rule, by a more developed agricultural technique backed by a greater capital than is found in most areas of primitive cultivation. The peasant owner, eager to extend his holding, often buys land which he cannot afford to equip adequately; where this happens (most commonly probably in France), the agricultural technique may be of a lower order.

(*b*) Cash Tenancy

Cash tenancy is the commonest mode of land tenure in those countries whose social and economic development lies between that of the primitive shifting agriculturist and that of the owner-farmer. The cash tenant is relatively at a disadvantage in that his outgoings in rent are fixed, whereas his income from cultivation may vary widely. A slump always produces an epidemic of bankruptcies in an area where cash tenancies are common. The cash tenant usually takes his land for a period of years, but generally without any assurance that the lease will be renewed at the end of that time, nor, if it is, that the rent will not be raised. The tenant in occupation can sometimes be induced to pay an increased rent rather than face the dangers and difficulties of moving with his stock. Where the pressure of population on the land is very severe, as in the monsoon lands of Asia, the level of rents is forced so high that the tenant is left with a bare subsistence in return for his labour.

The tenant, furthermore, has little incentive to maintain the full productive powers of his holding during the last years of his tenancy. He is deterred from making capital developments which are likely to remain unexhausted at the expiry of his lease, because he knows that no payment will be made to him for them if he leaves, while if he remains a higher rent will probably be demanded. Many countries have taken steps to protect tenants in such respects by restricting rises in rent or by guaranteeing some payment for improvements of permanent value to the land.

(*c*) Share-cropping or *Métayage*

This form of tenancy has been important at some time or other in most parts of the world. The share-cropping tenant cultivates the land, giving to the owner a proportion, often a half, of its produce. Frequently the landowner contributes a part or all of the farm stock and equipment. The practice is valuable in that it often allows the cultivator with little or no capital to farm on his own. It also protects him to some extent from fluctuations in the yield and price of his crops.

In Europe, where the practice grew up in the Middle Ages, it survives in parts of Italy and France, but is clearly on the decline. On the other hand, the share-cropper is still an important member of the farming community in the southern USA, though his role is diminishing.

6.2 Size and Distribution of Holdings

The average size of agricultural holdings in a particular country is governed in large measure by the pressure of population, and is clearly much smaller in, say, India, China or Greece than in Canada or Argentina. Figures of the average size of holdings, however, can be misleading. In some countries where most holdings are small, the presence of a number of very large estates raises the average level. In Belgium and Denmark smallholdings predominate, though they are highly capitalized and intensively used; but in western Europe in general the average size of holdings is larger and there are few minute holdings.

In Middle and Far Eastern countries the average size of holdings is very much less than in Europe. In Egypt it is about 1·6 hectares. In China (when statistics were last available) a quarter of all farm holdings were under 1·7 hectares and over half were of less than 2·9. The average Indian peasant farms about 2·5 hectares, but the average Japanese, little more than 1.

Holdings as small as these clearly cannot give full employment to the families which occupy them, and *under*employment is in consequence severe. Output is small in relation to the human effort expended, and standards of living are low. Improved farming techniques are likely to intensify the underemployment problem because they cut down on labour needs. Domestic industries can to some extent relieve the poverty, but the only thorough-going solution is to remove the surplus labour from the land, either by migration to another country or by absorption into industry. Migration may be regarded as impracticable on any scale adequate to provide more than the most modest relief to the dense populations of parts of Latin America and Asia. Absorption into industry is often hailed as the panacea for all the ills that beset the small peasant farmer. Nevertheless, many schemes for the industrialization of backward countries are a little naive. The compulsory merging of smallholdings into larger units of cultivation, like the mechanization of farming, is not by itself a solution, because it would diminish the demand for agricultural labour. Nor is collectivization, unaccompanied by industrialization, a remedy for rural overpopulation. On the other hand, in recent years many of the surviving large estates have been broken up and the land distributed among the land-hungry peasantry. After 1918, considerable areas were thus distributed in eastern Europe; similar land reform has been introduced in Mexico and Iran and is long overdue in other countries.

The small size of holdings was often accompanied by acute fragmentation or *morcellement*. Each holding would be made up of a number of scraps of land scattered through almost as many fields. This system, wasteful of time and of land, originated firstly in a profound respect for equality: if the quality of land varied within the manor or commune, then all must share in good and bad alike. It also derives from the practice of dividing an inheritance between the heirs. This was common in parts of eastern France before the Revolution, and was extended to the whole country by the *Code Napoléon*. It figures in Islamic law and is widespread in just those countries where a poor and backward peasant agriculture is found. A factor in leading the French peasant to limit the size of his family has certainly been his fears of the evil of further break-up of already divided and scattered holdings. Fragmentation, lastly, arises as a result of the peasant's piecemeal acquisition by purchase or inheritance of small plots of land.

Fragmentation is an undoubted evil. It survives only where labour is so abundant that there is no point in saving it. In France, however, considerable progress has been made in consolidating scattered holdings; Fig. 6.1 illustrates the concentration of holdings in a commune in Meurthe-et-Moselle. Scandinavia, over the last two centuries, and more recently Germany and the Low Countries have made even greater progress in consolidation.

6.3   Rural Indebtedness

We said in Unit 6.1(b) that the farmer's income fluctuates more than his outgoings. Living close to the margin of subsistence, the peasant of Europe or of monsoon Asia will in some years inevitably earn from his crops considerably less than he must spend, and to cover this deficit he must resort to the money-lender—a necessary evil, none the more loved because he is indispensable. There are several reasons for rural indebtedness.

(a) A mortgage may be contracted by an heir in order to buy out the claims of brothers and sisters, a necessary decision where the holding has already shrunk to an uneconomically small size. Under such conditions of population pressure, land values are likely to have reached such heights that the mortgage may well be more than the holding can conveniently bear.

(b) In bad years, the peasant may contract debts which he hopes to discharge in good. Money-lenders, however, often demand interest rates so high that a sequence of supremely good years would be needed to wipe out the debt accrued in the bad. A peasant who contracts such debts is unlikely ever wholly to free himself from them.

(c) Often local custom obliges the peasant to participate in costly social and religious festivities, such as marriage feasts; public opinion demands that local traditions be honoured whatever the cost. This is probably the most serious by far of the avoidable causes of indebtedness, though individual recklessness and lack of attention to crops and stocks are certainly significant.

(d) The farmer may contract a mortgage for purposes of development. Rural indebtedness of this kind is more common in the United Kingdom and the 'new' countries, and indicates that farmers are concerned to increase and improve their stock and equipment. Unfortunately, however, such debts are most readily

Peasant holdings

Gardens, orchards

0   200   400   600   800

Metres

Fig. 6.1 The consolidation of scattered and fragmented holdings in a French commune

contracted during 'boom' periods when both prices and interest rates are high. Such debts become burdensome during the succeeding depression when farm prices have fallen markedly.

It is impossible to exaggerate the extent of agricultural indebtedness, which is chronic in the monsoon lands of Asia and scarcely less serious in parts of southern Europe. Even in the 'new' countries it exists on a substantial scale: some farmers borrowed in order to purchase the heavy equipment which enables a few men to cultivate great areas, while others bought land at inflated prices during boom years. The effect of indebtedness is to increase farming costs and to diminish the margin on which the farmer and his family have to live. The purchasing power of the peasant is reduced and in the long run industrialization is retarded by the smallness of the domestic market.

6.4   Co-operation

Co-operation offers a means by which the peasant and the smallholder may try to offset some of the disadvantages of their lack of economic security. The community buys and sells collectively, pledges its collective credit and acquires for joint use pieces of equipment which no single member could either afford or fully utilize. Competition between members of the group is avoided, and better terms of trade are obtained. There are three forms of co-operation in agriculture.

(a) Co-operative Provision of Credit
This assists those who would otherwise be forced to turn to the money-lender. Where a banking system has already been developed, money could of course be raised on the security of the land itself, but such banks exist for the profit of their shareholders, not for the peasant in need of credit.

Most co-operative banks follow in essentials the pattern set up by the Rhinelander Raiffeisen, who raised capital on 'the universal unlimited liability of the associating members'—the peasants themselves. The credit society was limited to the village, within which both the necessity for loans and their proper use were guaranteed by 'the immaterial asset of mutual knowledge'. Raiffeisen banks became common in south-western Germany, and the method was copied in the Low Countries, especially in the *Boerenbond* of Belgium. Credit co-operatives have grown rather less quickly in Ireland, France and Switzerland. Elsewhere they are few or non-existent.

The co-operative bank can develop and flourish only where there is a vigorous and progressive peasantry whose credit is good. Liability, however, unlimited, of the Asiatic peasant could never guarantee loans of the kind he wants. Thus, as so often, the farmer in greatest need has the most difficulty and pays the highest price in trying to satisfy that need.

(b) Co-operative Purchase of Goods
The collective purchase by a group of peasants of fertilizers, fodder, tools or equipment is the simplest form of co-operative activity. It is widespread among

the more prosperous peasants of western Europe, and the buyers can thus save up to half the normal cost of the goods.

(c) Co-operative Processing and Marketing

The *fruitière*, or co-operative cheese-making unit, already existed in some form in Switzerland and France in the Middle Ages. It became more common in the nineteenth century, as the demand for cheese increased. In Denmark the system was extended to bacon-curing, and in France to the making of wine and the distillation of spirits.

Fig. 6.2 A Swiss cheese-making co-operative is able to process milk from a large number of individual farms and to market the product on the farmers' behalf

Denmark has become the classic exponent of co-operative processing of farm produce. Here the farmer confines himself strictly to agricultural duties, while the separating of his milk, the making of his butter and cheese, the curing of his bacon and hams and the grading of his eggs and poultry are carried out by co-operative factories, which then market the goods. The advantages of the system are obvious: the farm produce is prepared and marketed cheaply and efficiently and quality is guaranteed and maintained, while the farmer is not obliged to concern himself with market conditions. The system requires a farm unit big enough to give full employment to the farmer and his family, and settlements close enough together and linked by adequate roads for the daily deliveries to the factory to be made cheaply and expeditiously. Denmark, a small country of medium-sized farms, satisfies these requirements.

The co-operative processing and marketing of agricultural goods has spread to several similar countries, notably Finland, the other Scandinavian countries, the Netherlands and Belgium, and to a smaller extent, France, Switzerland and Ireland. Private and voluntary societies of producers grade and market much of the fruit in California, much of the dairy produce in the eastern and central states of the USA, and some of the tobacco and cotton in the south. In Canada, the wheat 'pools' are co-operatives, adjusted to the geographical and economic problems of grain marketing. Much of the meat, wool and wheat of Australia and of New Zealand's dairy produce, fruit and bacon are handled by co-operatives.

But the co-operative method of handling and marketing agricultural produce has made little progress outside north-westen Europe and those overseas countries which have inherited the European tradition. It increases the wealth and prosperity of those areas where the standard of farming and the level of rural welfare are already good. It has hitherto been given little opportunity to show how far it is able to promote the welfare of the densely populated and backward agricultural countries.

6.5   Government Marketing

Certain governments have chosen to involve themselves in the collection and marketing of produce. In many countries and at various times, farmers have been obliged to sell their surplus through state agencies, either in order to restrict output (see Unit 14.3(c)) or to subsidize production by the farmer. The marketing boards in the United Kingdom, such as the Egg and Milk Marketing Boards, combine these two objectives. In the USSR part of the agricultural surplus of the collective farms has been collected and marketed by the State, and during wartime many governments have resorted to the compulsory purchase and distribution of agricultural produce.

The importance of such measures to the geographer lies in the extent to which they alter the price structure and so bring about a change in the pattern of cropping.

6.6   Collective Agriculture

We have referred to the problems, common to peasant cultivators, of the small size and fragmentation of holdings and the not unrelated problem of marketing agricultural surpluses. The collectivization of agriculture is—all ideological considerations apart—an attempt to resolve these difficulties. The background of the Soviet enterprise was the urgent need for more food for the people of the towns, and to obtain it, as far as possible, with a smaller input of labour. The method was to throw all the holdings of a community, however parcelled and fragmented, into a single farm which would be worked collectively by those who had formerly toiled uneconomically on the small scattered strips. In the Soviet Union the objectives of collectivization were largely achieved. The yield of the soil was not greatly improved, but the productivity of labour was increased immeasurably.

The collectivization and mechanization of agriculture is only practicable where land is relatively abundant. The system makes the most of each unit of labour, but not of each unit of land. Collectivization has been extended to the countries of eastern Europe and China, and more recently to Cuba and some countries in south-eastern Asia. In each, the private ownership of land has been terminated, except for small gardens, and the fields have been consolidated into large units. Only in Poland and Yugoslavia was opposition to collectivization sufficient to halt the process. In these two countries a number of state farms have been established, many of them on land that had been confiscated from the Germans and from large landowners, but most farmland continues to be owned and cultivated by the peasants.

Collectivization completely changes the countryside. The picturesque, uneconomical strips vanish; instead, there are large fields, and huge barns and sheds for the mechanical equipment. In eastern Europe mechanization remains incomplete; a great deal of hand labour is still used in the fields, but draught animals are yielding place to tractors. The farms no longer grow large quantities of fodder, so that capacity is released for the production of food for human consumption. There has been little expansion in agricultural production, but the labour demands of farming have been very much reduced, thus making labour available for factory and construction work.

Table 6.1 Employment in collectivized agriculture

	Percentage of agricultural land in the socialized sector	Percentage of labour force in agriculture	
		1930–44	1973
East Germany	89·1	23	12·4
Czechoslovakia	91·1	33	15·5
Hungary	97·0	49	25·4
Romania	95·0	no data	51·9
Bulgaria	c. 95·0	73	42·2

Sources: *Production Yearbook*, FAO (1973), and national statistical yearbooks

6.7 Political Influences in Agriculture

State intervention in the affairs of agriculture, of which the collectivization of Soviet agriculture is probably the supreme example, may be guided by one or more of several considerations. The state may wish to maintain the prosperity of its farmers or to produce foodstuffs as cheaply as possible for the satisfaction of an industrialized population, or, in time of war, its object may be self-sufficiency and security. Such a choice of policy is only open to the more advanced countries; the great majority of the world's cultivators can have only one objective—the satisfaction of their material wants.

The import into Europe in the 1870s and 1880s of large and increasing quantities of foodstuffs from the 'new' countries brought about a crisis in European agriculture. The question was whether to protect the agricultural community against this competition or to allow farmers to adjust themselves as well as they could to conditions in which it no longer paid them to grow wheat on their previous scale.

Great Britain adopted the latter course; the 'golden age of English farming' melted away in the depression of the seventies. Some farmers began to specialize, for instance in the production of milk, green vegetables and fruit; but while in the manufacturing towns corn was cheap, the old stronghold of the four-course rotation decayed.

In France, the agricultural depression was scarcely less acute, but the peasant was rescued from it by the state, determined to preserve the rural classes, the 'backbone of France'. From 1885 onwards, French agriculture was protected by a tariff-wall of steadily increasing height. In the end, state action resulted in the preservation rather less of the sturdy peasant farmers than of the out-of-date agricultural methods which they practised. From this condition, itself the consequence of government action, French agriculture has been rescued since the Second World War by a government plan for its modernization and re-equipment.

In Germany, too, agriculture was protected, though less so than in France, and perhaps for this reason has been more progressive in its methods. The updating of West German agriculture had to wait a little longer than in France, and has now been carried through as a protection against competition from other Common Market countries.

In modern times there has been a tendency in some north-western European countries towards self-sufficiency. Self-sufficiency is itself both undesirable and unattainable in our industrialized society, but, in one way or another, many countries gave their agricultural policy a twist in this direction. Their object—to diminish dependence upon overseas supplies—could be attained only at a price. If, instead of buying in the cheapest market, goods are grown at greater cost at home, the real price to the consumer inevitably rises. Extension of the area under cultivation can only mean that marginal land is brought into production, and this in turn leads to increased costs. During the 1930s, for example, marsh and heath were cultivated in Germany at a high price in fertilizers and labour. In Great Britain, bounties were given to assist the farmer in the otherwise unprofitable ploughing up of grassland. Individual crops have sometimes been singled out for governmental encouragement, as in the subsidizing of British sugar-beet cultivation, largely because it was thought advisable to increase domestic output in the interests of national security.

The determination of wages has similarly been a field of state intervention. Wage levels in agriculture always tend to be lower than those in other occupations, primarily because the development of agricultural techniques continually permits farms to be worked with fewer 'hands'. There is thus a tendency towards the accumulation of redundant labour, and a commodity in abundant supply is cheap. Legislation by a state in favour of higher wages would result in higher prices for its agricultural produce and thus diminish its competitive position in the world market.

6.8   Agriculture and Population

For at least three centuries the population of the world has been increasing rapidly (see Unit 3). At the same time there has been a slow, uneven rise in the general standard of living, more marked in industrial than in agricultural countries. The two movements, taken together, have resulted in a greatly increased demand for food. The industrializing countries of Europe created a demand which local agricultural resources could in no way satisfy. A stream of foodstuffs and industrial raw materials of vegetable origin began to flow to Europe from the Americas and Australasia, supplemented by smaller amounts from India, south-east Asia and Africa.

In Unit 6.7 we saw how this influx changed the pattern of European farming. Nevertheless industrialists, schooled in the doctrines of free trade, welcomed it and encouraged the 'new' countries to produce more and more. World production of all the major foodstuffs rose sharply, as did the proportion entering into world trade. The fraction taken by Europe was increasing all the time, and despite periodic depressions, demand appeared to be insatiable and producers had no fears of not finding a market in the long run.

This period of expansion lasted until the 1920s. But confidence in a future of unlimited growth was shaken. Investment fell, and demand for manufactured goods shrank. The market contracted, and the world was faced with serious *over*production of many commodities. The resulting depression had not been fully overcome before the Second World War again led to increased demand. Since 1945 demand has grown steadily, owing at first to the wartime destruction of resources, but more recently to the mounting pressure of population.

For a century a Malthusian situation (see Unit 3.1) had been disguised by the diffusion of agriculture in lands newly opened up and by the developments in agricultural technology. It was confidently hoped that a succession of achievements in plant-breeding, together with the use of fertilizers and the creation of new cropland, would lead to an endless expansion in crop production. These hopes were false: although under carefully controlled conditions crops can be grown in the most hostile environments, huge inputs of resources and expertise are necessary.

The world's population today is twice that of 1930, and its food requirements have at least doubled. Food production has not, however, increased proportionately, and people are *on average* less well fed now than they were then. Some 75 per cent of Asians, it was claimed in the 1960s, have a diet far below the minimum standard recognized as being necessary for good health.

The future for human welfare is not made more hopeful by the reckless and destructive exploitation of natural resources over a very long period, particularly during the last century. Examples are the progressive deterioration and erosion of the soil, the felling of timber at a rate exceeding the normal rate of replacement, the overfishing of certain seas, and the near-extermination of some species of whales and seals over large areas.

The restoration of these damaged resources is not only costly in labour but also slow, and over many parts of the world deterioration continues. On the other hand, further extension of agricultural production is possible in certain areas, including much of Brazil and parts of adjoining countries, considerable areas of intertropical Africa, New Guinea and the Outer Territories of Indonesia. But in each, the climate hinders the employment of immigrant labour, and in few such areas is the local labour force adequate either in numbers or in efficiency. Diseases of men and animals present problems, and often means of transport are few or non-existent. The soils, moreover, are often poor, lateritic and unproductive. While an immense development of agricultural production in these areas is technically possible, the probable cost is so high that it would be undertaken only if market prices were to rise considerably above present levels. In other words, the labour required for the provision of a given quantity of food from such marginal areas would be far greater than that on present-day farms; the ratio of output to labour would thus be so low that the yield from such lands would be insufficient to support the life of those who cultivate them.

Of course, a remedy might lie in the use of more and better tools and fertilizers, more rational methods of farming and cheaper marketing and transport facilities, and what is lost by cultivating marginal and submarginal land might be saved by the application of human ingenuity to the situation. Man's ingenuity, however, has not so far allowed him even to keep soil erosion under control, and its rapid extension in the United States has been prevented only by immense expenditure of labour and capital, expenditure which must be abstracted from some other field. It would be rash to prophesy that man, armed with the new tools of chemical and biological science, has it in his power greatly to increase the general level of well-being. Malthus's model is as relevant to the twentieth as to the eighteenth century, and in the race between an exploding population and world hunger, the latter will inevitably win.

Malnutrition and Food Supply

There was widespread malnutrition before the Second World War, at a time when governments were attempting to restrict food production. It was assumed, however, that the problems could be solved by better distribution and the stimulation of purchasing power among the underprivileged. The League of Nations and later the United Nations pledged themselves to stimulate agricultural production and make an adequate diet available to all.

The Food and Agriculture Organization (FAO) was the outcome. The report of its Preparatory Commission stressed the means of attaining an increased output of food: improvements in farming methods, and in equipment, seed and stock. But such developments are most easily effected in just those countries where standards are already highest. The report pointed out that increasing yields in such countries as the USA, Canada, Australia and New Zealand solves no problem unless there is a simultaneous increase in the buying power of the less developed nations which are expected to purchase the surplus. The level of real wages, and hence of consumption, in many poorer countries is so low that the margin for purchasing imported foodstuffs is virtually non-existent. Until labour in these countries is made more effective it is difficult to see how it can possibly afford a higher level of consumption. The granaries of North America may burst, but, apart from the doles which charity may prompt, the grain can scarcely make its way to India until India has the means to pay for it.

Among the tasks assumed by the FAO has been the collection and publication of statistics of agricultural production and the preparation of reports on world agriculture. These demonstrate convincingly the steadily increasing gap between world population and the necessary supply of food to support it at an adequate level. Global figures are, however, deceptive because they are aggregate totals, including luxury products as well as essential foodstuffs. Luxury products are in demand chiefly among the rich minority of the world's population. For instance, the production of tea, coffee and cocoa has almost doubled within ten years, largely in response to the market demand of a few developed countries. Production of wine and of many semi-luxury foodstuffs, including certain fruits and out-of-season vegetables, has also increased. But outputs of rice, maize and the bread grains—the basic foodstuffs of most of the human race—have risen very much more slowly, in some years scarcely at all.

Fig. 6.3 shows the expansion in the output of food per head of the world

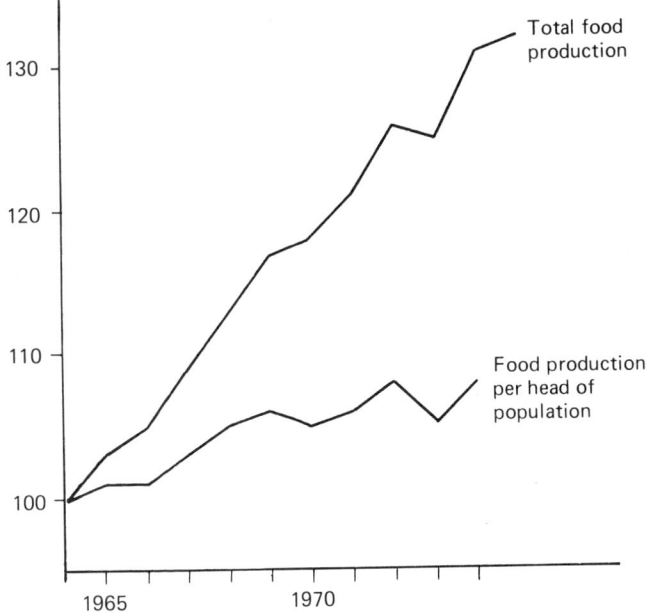

Fig. 6.3 The growth in world food production in arbitrary units (1964 = 100) (based on United Nations statistics)

population and of total food production as a percentage of 1964 levels. Total food production, including of course that of luxury foodstuffs, increased by 32 per cent between 1964 and 1974, but food production *per head* increased by only 7 per cent, with virtually no increase at all for eight years, during which food output barely kept up with the growth in population. The annual rate of population growth is tending to rise; that of the expansion of food production can only decline. The outlook for the human race, if it continues to increase at its present rate—which in the short term it cannot avoid—is bleak indeed.

Questions

1. In England farms are becoming larger; in India, smaller. What are the causes and consequences of this development?
2. Explain, with examples, what you understand by (*a*) joint production in agriculture, (*b*) diminishing returns in agriculture, (*c*) monoculture.
3. 'Soil is a response to management,' wrote Carl Sauer. Discuss.
4. What developments do you consider to be most likely to bring about an expansion of agricultural production in any particular region? Quote examples.
5. Discuss the relationship between rent, land use and crop yields.
6. Examine the relative advantages of (*a*) tropical peasant agriculture and (*b*) plantation agriculture.
7. What effect does the presence of a very large city have on agriculture in its region?
8. To what extent can rural co-operatives compensate for a small average size of farm holdings?
9. Is collectivization a remedy for too dense a rural population and too low a level of capitalization in agriculture in some parts of the world?
10. To what extent does government policy influence the organization and practice of agriculture? Give examples.
11. What do you consider to be the importance of (*a*) irrigation and (*b*) soil erosion in influencing the future level of food production?

Unit Seven

Minerals and Mining

The extraction of minerals from the earth's crust is, like agriculture, forestry and fishing, a primary activity (see Unit 1.6(*a*)). Mining, however, differs from the other primary activities in certain vital respects.

In the first place, the raw materials which are extracted from the ground are not renewed. With careful management the soil may be expected to continue cropping, and the sea will continue to yield fish, provided reasonable conservation measures are adopted. The extraction of minerals leaves only a hole in the earth, and it will take millions of years for the slow geological processes to happen which will form new mineral deposits in the earth's crust.

In the second place, mining is highly restricted geographically. Whereas agriculture in some form can be carried on over most land surfaces, mining and quarrying can be practised only over the minute proportion of the earth where useful minerals are found.

Minerals of economic importance can be divided into four very broad classes:

(*a*) the metalliferous minerals or *ores* from which metals are obtained;

(*b*) such minerals as clay and gravel, building and road stone, which occur very much more widely and in far greater quantities than the metalliferous minerals (discussed in Unit 7.5);

(*c*) water, one of the most plentiful substances on earth, which is nevertheless a resource of supreme importance that is perhaps only properly valued in conditions of its scarcity (see Unit 7.6);

(*d*) the common fuels—coal, oil and natural gas—which all occur within the earth's crust and are obtained by various mining processes (see Unit 8).

7.1 Metalliferous Minerals

Very few metals occur naturally in a pure or *native* condition. Gold is the most familiar example, but native copper and silver are occasionally found. All other metalliferous ores consist of the metal in chemical combination with other elements such as sulphur, oxygen, carbon and silicon. The resulting mineral is very often found mixed with unwanted substances, such as quartz or clay, from which it must be separated. Sometimes two or more economic minerals are found associated with one another, and are extracted together from the same mine: the ores of lead, zinc and silver are examples. They are thus in joint production, and this raises marketing problems analogous to those met in agriculture (compare Unit 5.1(*d*)).

Most mineral deposits have a complex geological history, which greatly influences the economics of mining. They have been formed within the earth's crust in a variety of ways, and they assume a number of different forms to which mining methods must be adapted.

(a) Mineral Lodes

Certain periods of the earth's history, notably the Pre-Cambrian, the Carboniferous and the earlier Tertiary, saw widespread fracturing of the land and the intrusion of lavas of varying chemical composition. Large masses of granite and related rocks were formed deep in the earth, and liquids and gases were forced upwards towards the surface, cooling as they ascended and crystallizing in the cracks and fissures through which they passed, to form *veins* or *lodes*. Each constituent solidified at a characteristic temperature, and thus at a particular level, so that in some deposits there is a marked zonation of minerals (Fig. 7.1). Copper may give place in depth to tin, and lead and zinc, to copper.

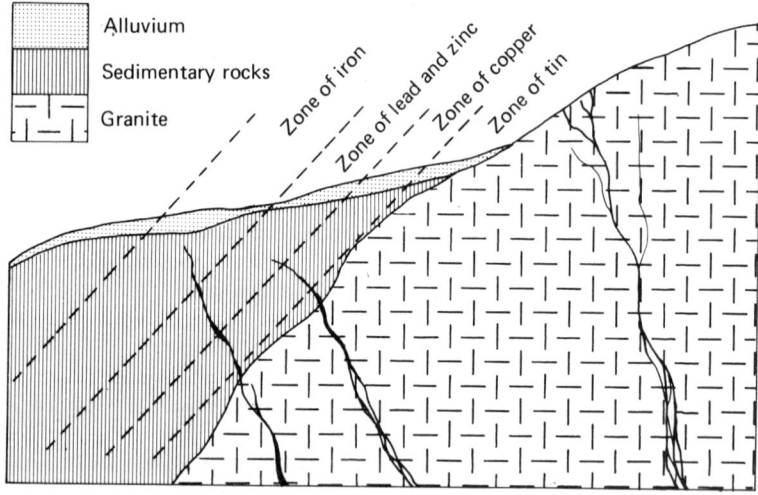

Fig. 7.1 Metal zone in the earth's crust

Certain groups of minerals are commonly found in close association: silver with lead and zinc, copper with nickel, iron with manganese. The productive section of a lode usually has a narrow vertical range. Pursuing a lode to a great depth, even if technically possible, is unlikely to be economically worthwhile. Lodes may diminish and almost disappear, or they may break up into interlacing veinlets far too small to be traced individually; they may be *faulted* or fractured in such a way that one side has slipped and cannot easily be traced, or they may divide and subdivide, or lead on into large masses of ore.

(b) Impregnations and Replacements

These are often related to lodes, from which mineral-bearing fluids have passed into the surrounding or *country* rock, impregnating it with small quantities of finely divided ore. *Impregnations* may be limited to narrow regions around a lode, or they may permeate vast areas. The heated solutions may act on certain minerals in the neighbouring rocks, *replacing* them with others which may be of greater or lesser value.

(c) Bedded Ores

These occur in level sheets rather than in veins or irregularly shaped masses. Some—certain iron ores, for instance—have been formed by direct deposition in lakes and on the sea-floor. Others, notably gypsum, celestine, common salt and the potash salts, were left behind after the evaporation of shallow seas. Still others, including most bedded iron ores, owe their origin to water percolating downward through rocks, dissolving and then redepositing certain minerals in concentrated form. Lastly, surface rocks may decompose, their soluble constituents being carried away by water to leave the residual mass which may contain naturally concentrated ores. Bauxite (the principal ore of aluminium) is such a deposit, and some beds of manganese and nickel originated in this way.

(d) Alluvial Deposits

Metalliferous minerals occur, finally, as *alluvial* or *placer* deposits. These have been eroded by rivers and streams from ore-bodies and laid down in the sands and gravels of valley floors or along the coast. Some become covered by deposits of later date, and become compact, hardened and workable under conditions similar to those of bedded ores.

Alluvial deposits are necessarily restricted to minerals which resist corrosion in water. Gold and tin ores, which are chemically inert, have always been the most important of these; others include wolfram (tungsten), diamonds and many less important minerals such as zircon, selenium and monazite.

7.2   Mineralized Regions

The injection of metalliferous and other minerals into the earth's crust is intimately associated with the movement of the *plates* or slabs of continental rock of which the crust is composed. *Magmas*—the fluid material from beneath the crust in which the metalliferous ores were concentrated—tended to reach the surface of the earth around the margins of the plates, especially where these were being forced against one another. It appears furthermore that the process of concentrating these minerals in the crystalline rocks was more active very early in the earth's history, and this is reflected in their relative abundance in the vast masses or *shields* of ancient rock. Many of the concentrations of metalliferous ores are thus found in close association either with areas of ancient rock, or with areas of recent tectonic movement in the course of which magma rose to the surface (Fig. 7.2).

(a) The United Kingdom

Great Britain was at one time one of the world's most important sources of the metalliferous minerals. Most of the ore reserves have now been exhausted and abandoned, and, except for iron ore, they have ceased to be worked. Merchants

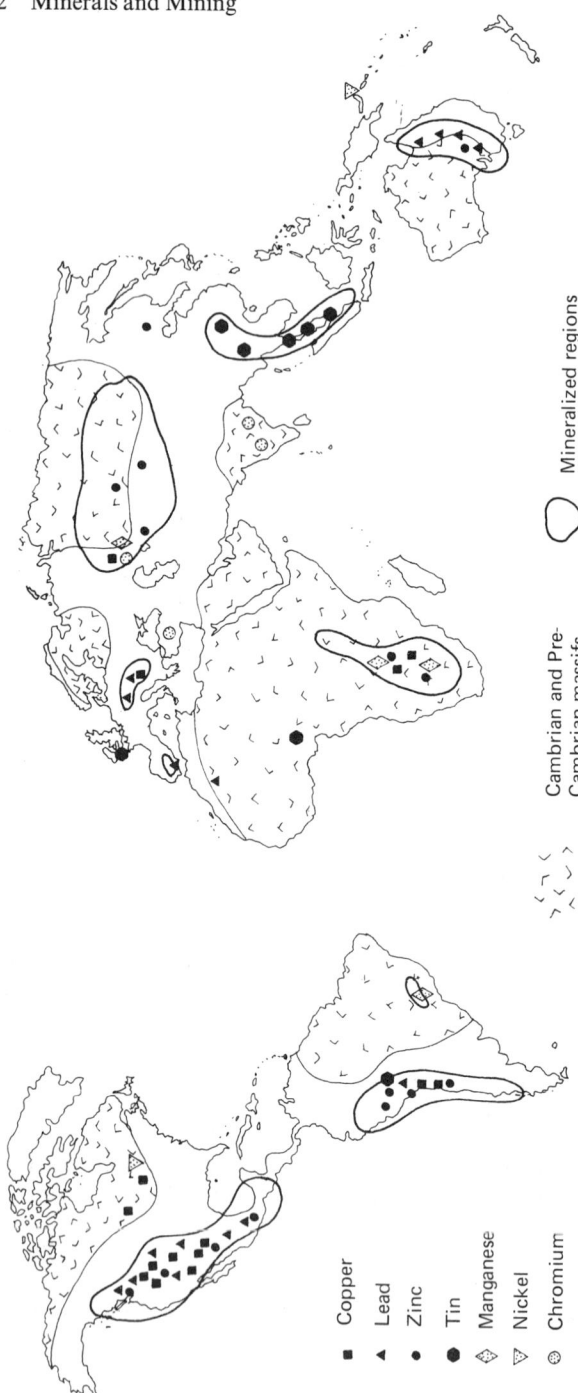

Fig. 7.2 World map showing the more important mineralized regions: the most richly endowed occur within the ancient (Cambrian and Pre-Cambrian) massifs or shields

Copper ■
Lead ◀
Zinc ●
Tin ⬤
Manganese ◈
Nickel ▷
Chromium ◉

◯ Mineralized regions

◯ Cambrian and Pre-Cambrian massifs

came to Cornwall in ancient times for tin; the Romans worked the lead of the Mendip and Pennine hills, and later zinc and copper were mined. Reserves of iron ore were widespread, and until the second half of the nineteenth century they satisfied all the country's domestic needs.

Most of the non-ferrous ores were associated with the Palaeozoic rocks which make up the Highland Zone of western Britain, with the intrusive granite masses of the south-west and with the areas of Carboniferous or Mountain limestone. Gold has been mined in North Wales, but resources are minute and output negligible. Welsh gold cannot compete on economic grounds with South African, and nowadays it is only mined because of its sentimental value.

Cornwall and south-western Devon were for long the chief source of tin in the western world. At first alluvial tin was panned in the sands and gravels of the valleys; then the miners worked their way up the hillsides to where the tin-bearing lodes came to the surface. Here they sank mines along the lodes so that tin ore hewn from the rock gradually replaced alluvial. During the nineteenth century the reserves of tin ore by degrees became exhausted; only a few well-endowed mines have been able to continue in production, and these are now being threatened with closure in the face of Malaysian competition. In 1978 an unprofitable mine ceased production, and at once the burden of pumping water was greatly increased at a neighbouring and still profitable mine. Within a few months, the latter was also forced to close. This instance demonstrates how marginal are some mining enterprises; at the time of writing, only two tin mines in the whole south-west remain active.

The mineralized lodes of south-western England also contained copper, lead, zinc and tungsten. There was a period in the nineteenth century when Cornwall was one of the world's leading sources of copper, until competition from the mines of Africa and South America, coupled with increasing costs, led the mines to close.

Other formerly important sources of non-ferrous metals have been the Mendip hills of Somerset, the Pennines, and the hills of Shropshire and southern Scotland. Here lead, accompanied in some instances by silver and zinc, occurs as replacements in the limestone. Reserves have in many places been exhausted; elsewhere, rising costs and overseas competition have forced the closure of the workings.

Only iron ore among metalliferous minerals remains important in the United Kingdom. Deposits were formerly numerous and widespread but none was especially large and most—notably those of the Weald, the Forest of Dean, Cumbria and the coalfields of Yorkshire and the Midlands—have for practical purposes been exhausted. Most recently the mines in the Cleveland hills, which once supported the important industry of Middlesbrough and Teesside, have closed. The only remaining source of iron ore today is the bedded deposits of the scarplands of the East Midlands. The ore is of low grade, generally less than 30 per cent metal, but occurs close to the surface and can be extracted relatively cheaply by opencast methods. The ore is smelted in the furnaces at Scunthorpe and Frodingham; but it supplies less than a tenth of Britain's iron ore requirements.

(b) Continental Europe

Like the British Isles, continental Europe was formerly endowed with a great many deposits of the metalliferous minerals, but many are now exhausted and abandoned. Most lay in the belt of ancient rock which extends from the Meseta (plateau) of Spain, through France and Germany to Czechoslovakia and Poland. Lead, zinc and copper remain of some importance. A second highly mineralized region is the 'shield' of very old rock which makes up much of Finland and northern Sweden. Many metalliferous ores are obtained here, but the most important is the high-grade Swedish iron ore. Europe also contains extensive deposits of low-grade bedded iron ores, similar to those worked in the English Midlands; the most extensive and important are those of Lorraine in eastern France and of the Harz region in West Germany.

(c) Soviet Union

The Ural Mountains and the rocks of the Siberian 'shield' are highly mineralized, and the Soviet Union has very large reserves of iron ore and of some non-ferrous metals.

(d) Asia

Metalliferous resources in Asia, outside the Soviet Union, do not appear to be very extensive. China has large reserves of tin and tungsten, Malaya of tin and India of iron ore, but Japan, the most highly industrialized Asian country, is also one of the least well endowed.

(e) Africa and Australia

These two land masses are both made up largely of massifs or shields of hard, ancient rocks, intruded by numerous lodes or ore bodies. Africa, especially that part of the continent that lies south of the Sahara Desert, is richly endowed. Among its most important resources are the copper of Zambia and Zaïre, the gold and diamonds of South Africa and the tin of Nigeria. But there are also important reserves of chrome, zinc, manganese, cobalt, the radioactive minerals and of bauxite, the ore of aluminium.

Australia has a number of rich sources of lead–zinc–silver. Its gold-mines are no longer of great importance, but Australia is now one of the world's leading sources of iron ore, much of which is mined in Western Australia and shipped to Japan.

(f) North America

This is probably the most richly endowed of all the continents, and in none have mineral resources been exploited more actively during the past century. There is today very little active mining in the eastern half of the United States, but there are large reserves of copper, lead, zinc and the alloy metals in the mountainous west. In Canada copper, nickel and iron are being worked in the old rocks of the Laurentian Shield, and further discoveries may confidently be expected.

Fig. 7.3 Ore being loaded on to a train at Iron Knob, a vast iron-ore mountain in South Australia

(g) Latin America

Gold and silver, which attracted the early explorers, are today of little importance except in Mexico. Far more important are the copper of Chile, the tin of Bolivia, the bauxite of Guyana, Surinam and some of the West Indian islands, and the iron ores of Venezuela and Brazil.

7.3 The Size of Reserves

For any orefield or ore-body, the initial opening up of mines is likely to be followed by a period of rising production, as more and more capital is invested in the workings. A peak of production is then reached, after which technical problems arising from the gradual exhaustion of the ore lead to a gradual diminution of output. The deposit becomes, for practical purposes worked out though small-scale production may continue for a very long time. But all mineral deposits are exhaustible: if exploited long and intensively enough, the richest ore-body will be worked out.

The theoretical curve of production from a single reserve or a group of closely related deposits is shown in Fig. 7.4. The life of the mines may be prolonged by introducing new technological developments permitting low-grade or marginal ores to be worked economically, and this may even lead to a secondary peak of

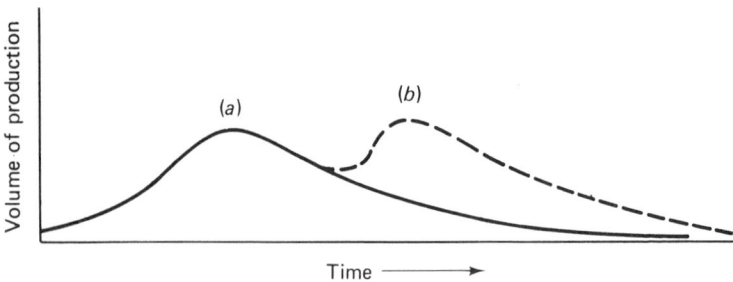

Fig. 7.4 Graph showing the expansion and contraction of mineral production from a typical orefield; (a) represents the climax under normal conditions, and (b) a secondary climax resulting from the introduction of new technology or the discovery of new reserves

production. Exhaustion within the limits of profitable mining will nevertheless ultimately be reached.

(a) The Exhaustion of Ores

The developed countries are strewn with the debris of former mining activity, and throughout Europe mining has been abandoned in many once-famous

Fig. 7.5 Mining moves on: (a) the Cornish tin mines are becoming worked out and abandoned;

mining areas. In none of these, however, has the ore been wholly removed from the mine-working. There always remain masses of low-grade ore and of ore which it costs too much to reach. The stage at which mining ceases on any particular ore-body or orefield is a function of both the rising costs of extraction and the market price obtainable for the ore. There are many places where mining has been revived by an increase in the ore price. Technological innovation—for example, the introduction of improved drainage of workings—can bring an abandoned mine back into production because it lowers the working costs. Exhaustion is thus a relative term, dependent on price and technology.

While the price of metalliferous ores is likely to rise in relation to the prices of other commodities, the question arises: at what point will the cost of mining be greater than the market can afford? Some economic minerals, such as iron ore and bauxite, form so high a proportion of the earth's crust that eventual exhaustion is inconceivable; nevertheless the grade (see Unit 7.4(*b*)) of these ores is very low and costs of extraction and processing proportionately high. There would be little demand for iron if its relative price approached that of the precious metals today.

At the opposite extreme are the relatively rare ores of metals like cobalt, vanadium, nickel, chrome—all of them of great importance in the manufacture of ferrous alloys. Known reserves are small and at the present rate of use are unlikely to last for more than 100 years; those of cobalt, for no more than 50.

(b) new mines are being opened up in previously inaccessible and difficult terrain (Ontario)

The European reserves of all important metals except three—aluminium, magnesium and titanium—are unlikely to last for more than 50 years, and in the United States no less than nine significant metalliferous ores will be exhausted within this time. The prospect for the world as a whole is somewhat brighter, in part because mining has been pursued less intensively and for a shorter period in many well-endowed regions such as South America, Africa and Soviet Asia. Nevertheless, reserves of gold, tin, tungsten, molybdenum, lead, nickel, zinc, chrome and vanadium are likely to be exhausted within 200 years, and those of medium-grade iron may not last much longer.

The developed countries, not excluding even the United States, are heavily dependent on the import of metals and metalliferous ores. In particular, the metals used in the production of high-quality and special steels have a very erratic distribution, with much of their reserves occurring in the Soviet Union and in developing countries. The supply of such materials will probably come to depend as much on politics as on geology and mining economics. In any event it is likely to become difficult in the near future and very precarious in the next generation.

(b) Recycling of Metals

The conservation of the earth's reserves of metalliferous minerals thus becomes a matter of great urgency. It is also a question of economics, of the relative cost of recovering metals which have been used and discarded as against that of mining and smelting new metal. Some metals are, of course, destroyed in the course of use, and recovery and re-use are inconceivable; examples are the lead used in paint and petrol, the steel reinforcement in concrete, the ship lost at sea, and those metals which are consumed in chemical processes. In a strictly controlled society, the only *new* metal required might be that needed to replace such losses. But in practice much of the recoverable metal exists in small amounts: metal containers in a rubbish dump, the rusting harrow in the corner of a field, old car batteries. The cost of collecting such scattered pieces of scrap is, under present market conditions, greater than the price of new metal, and is likely to be undertaken only when, as may happen in wartime, there is a 'drive' to gather and recycle old metal. Today the scrap market is almost entirely restricted to large pieces, such as ships or heavy mechanical equipment, which can be broken up economically. Exceptions are the precious metals—gold, silver, platinum—very little of which is ever lost in the course of circulation, and, to a very much smaller extent, lead, copper and zinc: the scrap market in lead piping, for example, is substantial.

This is unfortunate, because the world's stock of metals is too small to be trifled with in this way. The neglect of the recycling of metals is an example of a familiar phenomenon, the disregard of long-term benefits in favour of short-term savings: even though the net cost of recycling exceeds the *immediate* value of the metals recovered, in the long run the advantage might be incomparably greater.

The recovery and re-use of old metal offers advantages over and above the conservation of the world's mineral supplies. It has already been smelted, and

Fig. 7.6 Scrap steel being lifted by an electromagnet for transfer to the steelworks for recycling

usually requires only to be melted down again and recast. There is thus a considerable saving of fuel—an important consideration—in the re-use of old metal. In the United States steel industry, the amount of scrap making its way back to the open-hearth furnace or the foundry is slightly less than that of new metal brought into circulation; but in Italy and Japan the ratio of steel scrap to new steel is much higher, because both countries are almost entirely without iron-ore reserves and are thus dependent on imports of ore and scrap. It is clearly more economic to import scrap metal if this is available. Many of the ships which are taken out of service are destined for the scrapyards of Japan. Fig. 7.7 demonstrates the increasing use of scrap metal in steel manufacture during the past 100 years.

A note on the logarithmic scale. Most of the graphs in this book use *linear* scales—that is, the axes of the graphs are marked off into divisions of equal length, each division corresponding to one unit of the variable concerned. But sometimes we find this simple method of plotting graphs is inadequate. Suppose, for instance, that we are considering the world's production of steel over the past century, as in Fig. 7.7. A hundred years ago, steel production was very small; nowadays it is of the order of 700 million tonnes annually. No ordinary graph can adequately handle so enormous a range of numbers; we must therefore look for an alternative way of manipulating them.

One way might be to plot the *logarithms* of the numbers concerned, rather than the numbers themselves. (We can regard the logarithm of a number as that power of 10 that is equal to the number; thus the logarithm of $100 = 2$, since $100 = 10^2$, the logarithm of 1 000, or 10^3, $= 3$, and so forth.) Rather than looking up the numbers in logarithm tables, however, it is simpler and quicker to plot the data on special graph paper printed with a *logarithmic scale*, on which consecutive *powers* of numbers (rather than consecutive numbers, as usual) are equally spaced: for instance, in Fig. 7.7, successive equal divisions of the *y*-axis correspond to 10, 100. 1 000 million tonnes of steel, and so on. On this scale all the numbers with which we have to deal lie within the space of 9 divisions; the graph becomes manageable and remains wholly intelligible.

A great advantage of a logarithmic graph is that it enables us to measure the *rate* at which a variable is changing. Suppose that a population is increasing by a certain percentage every year. Plotted on a linear scale, the graph of population growth would be a sharply rising curve (cf. Fig. 3.2). On a logarithmic scale, however, the graph is much closer to a straight line (inset on Fig. 3.2), from which the rate of population growth can be calculated and the probable future population predicted. Growth of this kind is called *exponential*, meaning that the annual increments are a *percentage* of the amount of, say, steel or numbers of people at the beginning of the year, rather than a fixed quantity each year; a very familiar example of exponential growth is that of world population.

On the graph paper used to plot Fig. 7.7, the vertical scale is logarithmic while the horizontal scale is linear; it is called *log-linear* paper. Sometimes, however, it is convenient to use paper with two logarithmic scales, or *log-log* paper. An instance is the graph of the energy consumption against the GNP per head of a sample of countries (Fig. 8.12). Ordinary graph paper could not be used, because both sets of data cover so great a range, but log-log paper serves very well.

7.4   Economic Factors in Mining

Long-term considerations of metal supply are rarely of primary interest to mining companies: the first consideration is the relationship of their costs to the world price of metal. In the 1930s output was voluntarily restricted to some extent, in the interest of maintaining the world price in a contracting market. Today, however, the market is expanding rather than contracting, and any form of agreement to restrict production is improbable. We will consider the factors which influence the production of metal one by one.

(*a*) Capital Investment and Ore-body Size
Most forms of modern mining require a heavy capital investment in sinking shafts and in installing hauling, pumping and ore-dressing plant. It may well

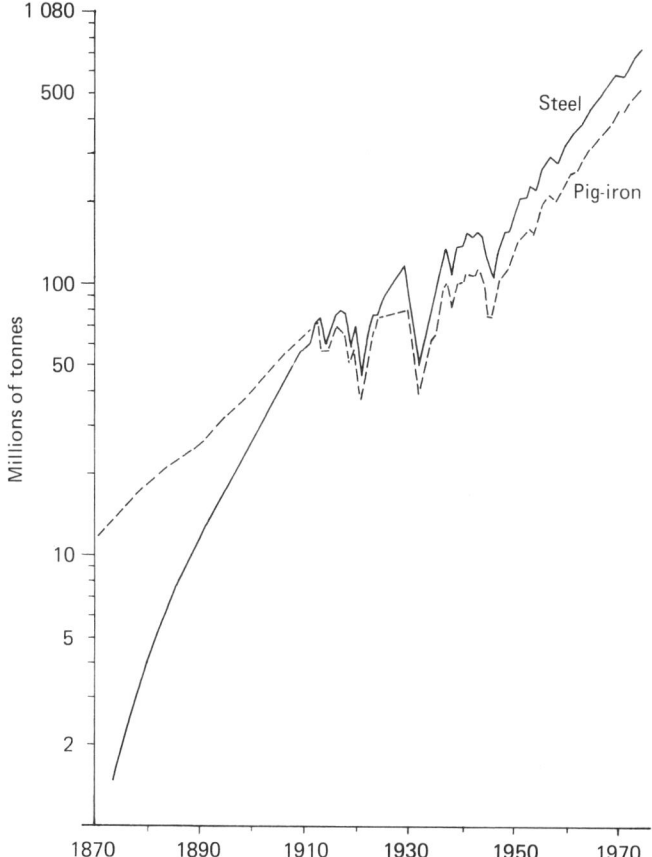

Fig. 7.7 Steel production has grown more sharply than that of pig-iron during the past century, partly because of the development of steel technology and partly because of the use of scrap for the direct manufacture of steel

even be necessary to build a railway into the mine or a dock on a river bank. These installations, however, will have no value except to the mine they serve, and they must be paid for entirely from its earnings. A small ore-body might not justify the capital outlay, because it might become exhausted before the equipment had been paid for or amortized. It is thus probable that large ore-bodies will be worked rather than small, and that the bulk of the world's minerals will be obtained from a relatively small number of extensive deposits.

(b) Grade of Ore

A crucial economic factor is the *grade* of the ore, that is the ratio of metal to the volume of rock which has to be processed in order to extract it. Native copper consists of 100 per cent metal, and thus requires no smelting. The richest iron ores cannot contain much more than 60 per cent metal, but the percentage ranges downwards to 25 per cent or less in the 'scarplands' ore of the East Midlands or of eastern France, and to as little as 10 per cent in the so-called taconite deposits near Lake Superior in North America. Some ores are mined which contain only 1 or 2 per cent of metal; in the case of precious metals the figure is usually even less. At what point does a mineral-bearing rock cease to be an ore and its exploitation become unprofitable? This depends on mining and transport costs, on political considerations and the market price of the ore. Both Nazi Germany and Japan, because of wartime shortages, exploited iron ores far poorer than those worked today.

Other disadvantages of using low-grade ores, besides the higher costs of extraction, include greater transport costs (because of the greater volume of waste to be carried) and higher fuel consumption in smelting (because the waste has also to be melted down). Nevertheless, with ever-climbing metal prices, increasingly low-grade ores are being brought into production. In 1800 the average grade of copper ores mined in the United States was about 3 per cent; by 1970 this had sunk to 0·7. The industry has been obliged to mine ever larger tonnages of progressively poorer ore. Very low-grade ores, such as the Lake Superior taconite, is *beneficiated* before shipment in order to reduce transport costs, that is, the metal content is increased either mechanically or by a process of partial smelting.

(c) Nature of the Ore-body

The nature of the ore-body itself greatly influences the profitability of mining. Some lie at a great depth, or reach downwards far into the crust of the earth; these can only be reached by shafts, with the attendant costs of ventilation, drainage and haulage to the surface. Some bedded deposits, however, lie at or very near the surface, and many of these are worked by opencast methods, which require nothing more costly or complex than excavating machines.

Ore taken directly from the mine is rarely in a fit condition for smelting. It has first to be freed from most of the foreign matter it contains. *Ore-dressing* consists of crushing the ore and separating the metalliferous minerals from the waste. In the past, separation of the desired minerals was achieved by methods exploiting their higher specific gravity. These were usually cheap but not particularly efficient, and many of the waste heaps of one generation have been reworked later to provide ore for another. More recently chemical methods have been used to dissolve and remove the desired minerals, which can then be recovered from solution. The *flotation* process has, however, brought about a revolution in ore-dressing. The finely crushed ore is placed in 'cells' containing oil and water, and air is forced through the mixture so that a froth is formed at the surface; certain minerals having a particular affinity for the oil used are concentrated in the froth and can be removed. The process is particularly effective with low-grade ores of copper, tin, lead and zinc. The equipment is, however, costly to install and has the effect of increasing yet more the relative importance of large ore-bodies.

A few minerals, notably gold and tin, occur as alluvial or placer deposits (see Unit 7.1(*d*)) that can be recovered fairly inexpensively by dredging. During the late nineteenth century cheap alluvial tin from Malaya effectively closed the Cornish tin mines, in which, by contrast, production costs were steadily increasing.

Mines differ greatly in their costs of exploitation. Intensive faulting increases the costs of mining and adds to the difficulties of transport underground. The temperature gradient in the earth — the rate at which temperature increases with depth — may be sharp, thus adding to the burden on the ventilating and cooling system. On the other hand, an unusually gentle temperature gradient has helped to make mining economic on the Rand even at the depth of 2 300 metres. Other local factors are the strength of the roof and the need, or otherwise, to provide supports, and the tendency of the floor to 'heave'. Heavy pumping costs may be incurred if water flows into the mine from the cavities of the rock or from abandoned mines nearby; and costs can also be affected by the hardness of the rock and any need there may be to provide protection from such occupational diseases as silicosis and arsenical poisoning by installing dust-extraction equipment.

(d) Transport Costs

The tendency of mineral deposits to occur in remote and sparsely populated parts of the earth is to be attributed, in part at least, to the fact that the rocks of which they are composed tend to produce a rugged terrain and to yield only poor soils. From the days of the Phoenician tin trade to the contemporary search for uranium in the hard rocks of the Laurentian Shield, transport has been a major factor in the success of mining operations. The development of most great mining areas has been dependent on railway-building. In Africa, the lure of precious metals 'drew' railways across the continent. The exploitation on modern lines of the copper of Katanga, the iron of northern Sweden, the deposits of Kalgoorlie, Cloncurry and Broken Hill, Cerro de Pasco and Oruro, Sudbury and Noranda, and the iron ores of Labrador were all forced to await the building of railways, and other areas are still waiting in northern Quebec, Western Australia, Brazil, Siberia and elsewhere. The grade of the ore and the cost of fuel will, in large measure, determine whether smelting operations are carried on at the mine, at the port, or in western Europe or North America.

(e) Labour Supply

Most mining of metalliferous ores is carried on in sparsely populated areas; only the mines of south-eastern Asia can command an ample supply of labour. The Rand mines, for instance, employ a large force of recruiting agents in the South African tribal lands. There are, however, both political and social problems in training African labour to high levels of skill. Moreover, though African miners' wages are low, European and American technicians and professional engineers expect to be paid high salaries and allowances to induce them to work in remote and often uncongenial surroundings.

(f) The Market

Minerals are worked not because they are technically convenient to mine or are well situated with regard to transport but because the demand for them has raised their price sufficiently to make their exploitation potentially profitable. The demand for specific minerals fluctuates, and is strongly affected by technological developments. The electrical industry during the present century has absorbed vast quantities of copper, and the aircraft industry, large amounts of aluminium and magnesium; the development of alloy steels has stimulated a demand for tungsten, chrome, nickel, cobalt and molybdenum. At the same time the demand for some metals shows signs of contracting relatively if not also in absolute terms, as other and cheaper materials replace them. While certain metals, notably steel and aluminium, are absorbed more and more in building construction, they are losing ground in other respects to plastics. Substitutes may well be found in the future for some of the scarcer metals in demand at the present time.

Complications arise, however, when two or more minerals occur in the same ore-body: the common association of lead with zinc, for example, or the association of silver with both. Most of the world's arsenic is obtained as a by-product, and copper is a prominent by-product of the Sudbury (Ontario) nickel mines; the International Nickel Company cannot avoid producing some copper, however low its price, as long as it continues to work nickel. In such a situation the prices of the minerals produced jointly may vary widely; the requirement is simply that the *joint* price covers costs of production. This phenomenon was of importance to the attempts to control mineral output made between the two world wars.

(g) Political Considerations

Minerals, particularly iron, copper, aluminium and the alloy metals, are of such importance in war that the possession of reserves is of great military significance. Essentially economic considerations ceased to apply when Germany, in the interests of her war economy, developed the low-grade iron-ore reserves of Peine and Salzgitter and subsidized production from the poor copper ores of Mansfeld. At various times, the United Kingdom has assisted tungsten production. There are many examples of the politically enhanced value of mineral deposits, from Rhodesia's chrome to Japan's copper and Canada's uranium.

(h) Environmental Considerations

The mining and extractive industries have been destructive of the environment on a scale perhaps greater than any other category of industry. Most governments watch the activities of mining companies with considerable care, and must continually balance the economic benefits of mining against the social and economic losses to the environment. In this section the environmental consequences of extracting solid fuels (other aspects of which are discussed in Unit 8.3) are considered along with those of other forms of mining since closely similar problems are raised.

Environmental damage arises mainly in the following ways:

(*i*) **Subsidence.** The extraction of ore or fuel leaves a cavity and, unless this lies at a very great depth, it is likely to lead to the subsidence of overlying rocks. This is especially important in the mining of bedded deposits, such as coal. Shallow depressions may form at the surface, accumulating water and interfering with the natural drainage of the land. Most coal-mining areas have been in some degree sterilized in this way. The only solution to the problem is to return waste material to the worked-out cavities underground, as is done in some of the coal-mines of Upper Silesia (Poland); but the method is too expensive to be widely adopted.

(*ii*) **Waste disposal.** Every form of mining results in the extraction of a great deal of material of no economic value. This has to be disposed of as cheaply as possible, and the simplest way is to allow it to accumulate in vast spoil heaps near the mine (Fig. 7.8). These sometimes occupy potential cropland; they are

Fig. 7.8 Environmental damage from coal-mining: spoil tips disfigure the Welsh countryside in Ebbw Vale

unsightly and often so sterile that vegetation is slow in covering them. In recent years many such heaps—the 'Wigan alps' in Lancashire, for example—have been cleared at very great expense, but others, such as the huge piles of china clay waste in Devon and Cornwall, still cover vast and still-growing areas.

(*iii*) **Superficial damage.** Some bedded deposits of iron ore, coal, gravel and mineral salts lie just below the surface. These can only be worked by strip-mining or opencast methods (Fig. 7.3), in which large machines move slowly forwards across the land, stripping first the soil and superficial rocks, then removing the mineral and lastly dumping the waste material behind them on the worked-out ground. This process is highly destructive, leaving behind it a landscape of ridges of unconsolidated rock. Even if the land is then levelled and the topsoil conserved and replaced, the surface has been lowered by several metres and the natural soil profile and drainage destroyed. In any case, the cost of restoring the land to agricultural use may fall only a little short of the value of the minerals extracted. Since much of the most easily accessible coal—especially in North America—as well as of iron ore and bauxite occurs as bedded deposits near the surface of the ground, we may anticipate much further environmental damage from this source.

(*iv*) **Smelting.** The concentration and smelting of non-ferrous ores can also damage the environment. Most are sulphides, and during smelting these give off sulphur dioxide which, in the atmosphere, forms sulphuric acid, which is poisonous to plants and wildlife. More recently attention has been focused on more insidious forms of destruction, such as lead poisoning in districts close to lead works. Although most governments attempt to limit the deleterious effects of smelting, few are wholly successful, and some areas, notably in North America, have been denuded of vegetation and disastrously eroded.

The preceding discussion makes it clear that not all technically workable orebodies can, in practice, be mined, though most ore-bodies may some day acquire a real value even if they do not yet possess it. Minerals are a wasting asset. The real costs of mining increase with each tonne of ore extracted up to the point where they exceed the market value of the product and the mine is abandoned as uneconomical. Price changes may, however, make its working profitable again, as some of the Rand mines were rejuvenated in 1932 by the rise in the price of gold. More recently, a rise in tin prices appears to have given a new lease of life to some Cornish tin mines.

In the long run the richest mineral area inevitably begins to show signs of exhaustion. The present pattern of world production is undergoing a slow change as the focus of the production of one mineral after another shifts from older centres to newer. Even the United States, still the world's largest mineral-producing area, will be faced with shortages, though perhaps not until the distant future. A few years ago the exhaustion of many economic minerals was regarded as imminent, but more recently fresh discoveries in the United States and Canada have postponed the danger, perhaps for a long period. The progress of exploration, together with the interacting geographical and economic factors we have outlined, will determine future trends, but it is reasonable to expect Canada, South America, Africa and Asiatic Russia to become increasingly important producers of the ores of the common metals.

7.5   The Non-metalliferous Minerals

These constitute a large and varied group of substances, including salt and sulphur, potash and nitrates, clay, sand, gravel and stone. The problems posed by the extraction of these materials are broadly similar to those of metalliferous mining. Reserves in the long run become exhausted; only the largest are used, and their exploitation, like metalliferous mining, scars the face of the land and destroys or impairs other resources. Here, however, the similarity ends. Most of these materials are abundant and, though individual deposits may be exhausted, no general scarcity can be anticipated. On the other hand, there is little likelihood of re-using them, with the possible exception of bricks and building stone.

(a) Salts

Common salt, gypsum, potash and *nitrates* are more or less soluble in water, and most deposits have been formed by the drying up of shallow lakes and seas. They thus tend to occur as bedded deposits. They can be mined, but salt is most often extracted today by dissolving it, pumping the solution to the surface, and recovering it. *Sulphur* (though not a salt) is extracted in a rather similar way, using superheated steam to melt it and them pumping the liquid sulphur into vats. Nitrate salts have sometimes been concentrated at the surface of the ground under desert conditions, so that their extraction is a matter of quarrying rather than of mining.

In the United Kingdom there are extensive and important deposits of common salt beneath the Cheshire plain near Nantwich and Middlewich—the suffix '-wich' denotes a salt-spring. These are worked to supply the important chemical industries of Cheshire and southern Lancashire.

(b) Sand, Gravel, Clay and Stone

These minerals are of great importance to the construction industry because they are essential components of concrete. Vast quantities are found in the flood-plains of many river valleys, and can be extracted with relatively simple mechanical equipment. The problem is not so much the exhaustion of beds of sand and gravel, but the consequent destruction of the land surface. Old gravel pits, now filled with water and constituting a dangerous attraction to children, are to be found in the vicinity of many of our larger cities. They are especially numerous and extensive along the Lea valley north-east of London, where attempts are being made to convert them into a public amenity.

Clay is dug for three broad purposes. Some clays, smooth in texture and lacking in impurities such as iron oxide, are used in potting. The Etruria Marls at Stoke-on-Trent yield an excellent clay which was the basis of the Stoke pottery industry. Coarser clay is dug in vast quantities to be burned into bricks and tiles, especially near Bedford and Peterborough. Clay is, lastly, an essential raw material of cement, and is worked for this purpose in northern Kent and along the foot of the Chiltern hills, where it occurs in close proximity to chalk, the other raw material of cement.

China clay is derived from the decomposition of the felspar crystals in granite. It occurs only in the granite areas of Cornwall and south-western Devon. It is obtained from vast open pits, and clay-working yields an enormous volume of mineral waste which accumulates in high conical heaps. In addition to its use in pottery, china clay also serves as a filler in paper and rubber and has many other uses as well. It constitutes today the United Kingdom's most important mineral export.

Stone is a traditional building material, and much of our vernacular architecture shows how local styles have been adjusted to the qualities of the stone available. The most important among building stones are the limestones which are found in a belt lying across England from Yorkshire to Dorset. They have been used in an immense number of magnificent buildings, but today are tending to be replaced by brick, concrete and synthetic materials. Some of the hardest stones, notably granite in Cumbria and the south-west and the rocks of Charnwood in Leicestershire, are crushed and used as roadstone.

7.6   Water as a Resource

Metals, minerals, and fuels are all natural resources: substances which occur naturally in limited amounts, and are exploited and used by man. Water, despite its apparent abundance in certain places, is also a scarce resource, and its scarcity is a factor of immense importance in many parts of the world. Water is more important than fertilizer to agriculturalists, few industrial processes can dispense with it, and life is impossible without it. Water can be used as a source of energy as it flows downhill, and is the medium in which many important forms of life exist. Its scarcity limits agriculture and human settlements in all arid regions of the world and everywhere influences crops. It has been fought for between nations, as in India and Pakistan, and between tribes at desert waterholes.

Water, like all other resources, is distributed unevenly in space. Its availability also varies from season to season. It is transported from relatively wet areas, like the northern parts of California, to relatively arid regions, like the south of the same state. In countries like India, it is accumulated behind dams during the wet season for use in the dry. In many ways, the spatial distribution of water can be modified by the use of dams and barrages, canals and pipelines.

Like metalliferous ores, water also exists in many qualities or grades. There is soft water and hard, each with its respective problems and uses. There is water with large quantities of dissolved minerals which are likely in time to poison the land it irrigates, or to corrode the pipes through which it flows, and there is salt water in the oceans, seas and certain inland lakes which cannot be drunk or used to water crops. Sea water is 'refined' naturally by being evaporated from the sea and condensed as rain over the land. The supply of such water is variable, but limited. It can be supplemented by water from reservoirs locked up in the rocks of the earth's crust, and by the desalination of sea water, a costly process of eliminating the dissolved salts but one which is necessary if civilized life is to be lived in such areas as the Middle Eastern deserts.

Water differs from other resources in that, apart from artesian and some other forms of underground water, it cannot be exhausted as long as rain continues to fall and rivers to flow. But it is unlikely that the volume that is thus made available can be increased. There is much scope for improving the *use* made of available water, but its *amount*, apart from year-to-year fluctuations, is fixed. In most developed societies water is becoming increasingly scarce and expensive. The construction of storage facilities in order to prevent its waste and loss may reduce the availability of other scarce resources—agricultural land and amenities. Water is piped great distances, especially in the United States, where there are ambitious plans to bring it from the Northern Rocky Mountains to the eastern cities and the dry plains. Immense investments, some of them by the World Bank, have been made in projects to conserve and supply water in India and Pakistan, Egypt and Israel.

The converse of the problem of water supply is that of removing excess water from the land. The two problems are, indeed, interconnected since flooding in one season is commonly balanced by drought in another. The chief means of reducing the risk of flooding lies in holding water behind dams and barrages for liberation during the dry season when river levels are low. One can perhaps look to a time when relatively little of the world's rainfall flows unused to the sea. Only then will the maximum use of this scarce resource have been achieved.

Questions

1. 'Metalliferous minerals are a wasting asset.' Examine as a geographer the past and future consequences of this.
2. Explain, with examples, the influence of the grade of an ore and the mode of its occurrence on the profitability of mining.
3. Where do you think that future finds of metalliferous minerals are likely to be made?
4. 'Recycling must become of ever greater importance.' Discuss this with reference to the metals.
5. 'The exploitation of minerals is necessarily injurious to the environment.' Discuss.

Unit Eight
Fuel and Power

The industrial civilization of the nineteenth and twentieth centuries is based upon the availability of cheap mechanical power: the invention and improvement of the steam engine is the central thread running through the whole Industrial Revolution. Without steam power a limit would soon have been set to the invention and use of machines for spinning and weaving. Coal-mining would have declined without steam engines to pump water from the mines and haul coal to the surface, and the carriage of bulky goods would be restricted to the slow-moving barge. The use of coal made today's machine civilization possible: until recently it was argued that the exhaustion of the coal measures would, within the foreseeable future, bring about its end. But the development of other sources of power, notably oil and natural gas, hydro-electricity and nuclear power, has postponed, though not altogether removed, this threat.

8.1   Forms of Power

In the course of 3 000 years of history, new sources of power have successively been exploited. An early dependence on manual power to turn the potter's wheel and to work the loom and spinning-wheel was followed by increasing use of water and wind power. The first steam engines were at work in England early in the eighteenth century, and steam has since remained the dominant source of industrial power. The internal-combustion engine, using liquid fuel, made its appearance about 1880, the steam turbine was invented in 1894 and the diesel engine was first used in 1892. Meanwhile the generation of electricity had been placed on a commercial footing. Electricity generated via the steam engine and steam turbine, and later hydro-electricity, have increasingly replaced the direct use of mineral fuel. Attempts have been made to derive power from solar energy, from wind, tide and waves, and by concentrating the low-grade heat of the atmosphere, of streams and rivers and of the rocks; but these have met hitherto with only limited success, although they offer possibilities for the future. More recently, the generation of electric power via the heat produced by the disintegration of atomic nuclei, and perhaps at some future date by nuclear fusion, offers an immense potential, though at a high cost in research and capital investment.

(a) Direct and Indirect
Energy may be used in two ways. The first may be termed the *direct* use of energy, because the source—a waterwheel or steam engine—is geared directly to

the machine which it operates. The power produced is not transferable, and must be used where it is generated. The second is the *indirect* use of energy. The energy of flowing water, the combustion of fuel or nuclear fission is converted into electrical energy which is transferable over great distances. The power generated by a hydro-electric station or a nuclear reactor is always used indirectly.

The use of sources of non-transferable power—for example, the simple steam engine—tends to encourage the concentration of industry; the availability of transferable power tends to encourage the dispersion of the industrial units that use it. The trend during the past century has been strongly away from the use of direct power and towards the indirect supply of power from an electric motor linked by cable with a distant generator.

(b) Exhaustible and Inexhaustible
An important distinction must be drawn between exhaustible and inexhaustible sources of power. In the absence of climatic change or human interference, a stream may be expected to continue to flow indefinitely. A coalfield or a reserve of radioactive minerals may have a long, but nevertheless limited, life. A superficial deposit of peat or lignite may last for a shorter period, and an oil-well may have a life of only a few years or even months. Not only is each mineral deposit exhaustible, but the cost of working it is likely to increase as the mines become deeper and the galleries longer. The last tonne would cost far more to extract than the first, and is in fact very unlikely to be worked at all. Power derived from burning mineral fuels must increase in cost relative to other commodities, and there is therefore great interest in methods of using non-exhaustible sources of power, in particular the waves of the seas, the tides and the energy of the sun.

Another recent trend has been towards a greater efficiency in the use of energy. Some ways in which this has been achieved are the reduction of friction in the moving parts of machines, in the improved design of boilers and hearths with a view to fuel economies, in the development of larger and more efficient machines for power generation, and in the use of high-tension transmission of electricity.

8.2   Wind and Water Power

The direct use of wind and water power to drive machines is now of only trifling importance in much of the world, and has almost disappeared from the more advanced countries. Before the extensive use of steam power, however, running water provided the greater part of the mechanical power used in Great Britain and elsewhere, and in the eighteenth and early nineteenth centuries factories of considerable size were powered by one or two waterwheels. The availability of water power determined the original location of several manufacturing industries which have since turned to other sources of energy: the earliest textile mills in northern England, for example, were powered by large waterwheels, not by steam engines.

Nevertheless, water power has severe disadvantages. Flood or drought could bring a works to a halt, and without the use of a turbo-generator even the largest rivers could produce relatively little power. Wind power is even less reliable, and can be developed only in very small units (see also Unit 8.6(*a*)). The Dutch drained their meers with wind-driven pumps and windmills were also used in the reclamation of the Fenland of eastern England, but elsewhere the windmill has served for little beyond the grinding of corn and the fulling of cloth.

8.3   The Solid Fuels

These fuels consist of carbon mixed with various carbon compounds, and are derived from fossilized plant remains. They can for convenience be classified as *peat*, *lignite* and *brown coal*, *bituminous* or *soft coal*, and *anthracite*, though there are many intermediate varieties. The value of any solid fuel is related to its heating capacity or *calorific value*, and this is in turn dependent upon the percentage of 'fixed' carbon in the fuel. This percentage may be from 92 to 98 in anthracite, but as low as 50 in the poorest bituminous coal, and even lower in brown coal. The quality of coal is closely related to its geological age, the coal with the highest calorific value occurring lowest in the geological table. Lignite, brown coal and peat, fuels with the lowest heating power, are of Tertiary or even Recent date, but can often be extracted from shallow pits relatively cheaply, thus compensating in some degree for the low price corresponding to their low calorific value.

Like the grade of an ore (Unit 7.4(*b*)), the fixed carbon content of coal tells us how much of the fuel contributes to its economic value. It may not pay to extract a low-grade ore, and certainly not to transport it far. Similarly with coal: fuels of the sub-bituminous and lower categories are never moved more than a few kilometres from the pits from which they are obtained.

(*a*) Peat and Turf
These, the humblest of the solid fuels, illustrate the inability of the lowest grades to bear the costs of transport. In the past, however, they have been of considerable local importance in fenland areas; many of the Dutch meers, as well as the Norfolk Broads, were produced by peat-digging. In the Irish Republic peat is used—on the site—to fuel an electric power station.

(*b*) Brown Coal and Lignite
These have a much higher calorific value than has peat, and occur furthermore in deposits large enough to justify the installation of heavy and specialized equipment to extract and process the coal. They do not, however, occur widely. There are large reserves in the United States, where they are no longer seriously exploited, and in the Soviet Union. The most intensive use is made, however, of the much smaller resources in central Europe and Australia. East Germany and Czechoslovakia in particular make great use of their brown coal and lignite resources. The fuel is extracted, compressed into briquettes to express the moisture and reduce bulk, and used, for the most part, to fuel power stations. The exploitation of these deposits is economic only if the processes are fully

mechanized, and this, as with metalliferous ores (see Unit 7.1) effectively precludes the development of small deposits. Only in remote areas such as parts of the Balkan Peninsula, where transport costs reduce the competitive advantage of bituminous coal, can small reserves of brown coal be used profitably. Reserves are, moreover, much smaller, probably about a fifth of those of bituminous coal, and well over a half are to be found in the United States, principally in the prairies and Rocky Mountains. The United Kingdom has no significant deposits of these low-grade coals.

(c) Bituminous Coal

This is of much greater geological age than lignite, and, although it may outcrop at the earth's surface, it is normally obtained from a much greater depth. Coal is not found in rocks older than the Carboniferous, because, until this period, plants had not attained a sufficient stage of evolution to produce the masses of vegetable matter required for its formation and no coal is therefore found in the great shields of ancient rock which are so abundant a source of metalliferous minerals. The coal measures were folded, faulted and hardened in the course of the earth movements which followed their deposition, and the coal itself underwent a slow chemical change by which the gaseous content was reduced and the proportion of carbon increased. Although coal may occur in Mesozoic and Tertiary beds, the lapse of time has generally not been sufficient to compact the carbonaceous matter into bituminous coal: deposits of this age are more likely to be of sub-bituminous coal or lignite.

A coalfield usually consists of a number of *seams*, which may be anything from a few centimetres to several metres thick, separated by very much greater thicknesses of barren rock. The seams may lie horizontally, but are more often tilted. The gentle flexing of the coal seams may develop into intense folding. This increases the difficulty and cost of mining and may lead to the abandonment of a pit.

In most coalfields the seams reach the surface at some point; very few fields are completely 'hidden'. Near the surface the coal is likely to be of poor quality, soft and rotted by the soil acids. It cannot be mined in the normal way owing to the weakness of the roof and the danger to structures on the surface. If, however, the seams are inclined at only a shallow angle, opencast working may be practicable. The German methods of lignite mining have been to some extent used in Great Britain for the opencast mining of bituminous coal. Proposals for any opencast coal project pose the problem of balancing the value to the nation of the coal produced against the loss of the agricultural land sacrificed. Each case can be considered only on its merits and in relation to the current economic situation. Though authorities often require the topsoil to be replaced after mining, the original conditions can never be fully restored, and drainage and the water-table will inevitably be greatly disturbed.

Besides the inclination of the seams, other physical factors affect the profitability of coal-mining. Thin seams are more difficult to work than thick, as more of the surrounding country rock has to be removed to allow miners and machinery to move through the seam. A weak roof increases the cost of timbering; excessive water, that of pumping; the presence of poisonous or inflammable gas, that of ventilation and of other safety precautions; and excessive dust increases the risk of explosion. These factors vary from pit to pit, almost from seam to seam, so that one pit can make a considerable profit and its neighbour, a heavy loss.

The profitability of mining is further influenced by the age of a mine, the quality of its equipment and the efficiency of its organization. Old mines are likely to be small, the working face far from the shaft and the winding equipment out of date. In Great Britain a large number of such old and inefficient coal-mines have been closed by the National Coal Board (though many still remain), and a small number of very large, highly mechanized and automatically controlled mines opened up in their place. The same has been happening on the Ruhr coalfield, which is, in terms of its resources, the largest in Europe.

(*i*) **Types of coal.** Differences in the original vegetable content of coal and in its geological history are responsible for the many varieties of coal available. These range from the sub-bituminous, with a low carbon content and poor heating power, through 'house' coal which burns well in the fire-place and steam coal which is used for firing boilers, to anthracite, an almost smokeless fuel with a high calorific value. As a general rule the anthracite coals occur near the base of the coal series, and the more gassy coals in the higher and later beds. Most coalfields yield several different coals, and some, including the Ruhr, run the whole gamut of the varieties of bituminous coal.

Coking coal is of particular importance, since it yields a firm, hard coke suited for use in the blast-furnace (a soft coke may be crushed by the weight of the furnace charge, and thus chokes the draught). Though coke can be made from certain other types of coal, coking coal retains its value and importance. It does not, however, occur widely. France is notably short of this quality of coal, whereas the Ruhr is relatively well endowed. The United States formerly had large reserves of the Connellsville coking coal, which supplied the iron-smelting industry of Pittsburgh.

(*ii*) **The world's coal reserves.** The association of coal with a narrow range of geological deposits means inevitably that it is far from evenly distributed. Vast areas of the earth's surface are wholly devoid of coal. Moreover, it is very difficult to estimate the total resources of any coalfield, and impossible to foresee what will be economically workable a generation hence. The effective reserves are constantly being added to, partly by fresh discoveries and partly through the development of new mining techniques that can make possible the working of resources hitherto considered uneconomic. On the other hand, worked coal-fields are being depleted of their better and more easily accessible coal. In the long run the price of coal relative to that of other commodities can be expected to rise.

Coal reserves in Africa, Australia and South America are very small. Almost half the known resources occur in China and the Soviet Union, and more than half of the remainder in the United States. Europe, which is the heaviest user of coal, has little more than one-eighth of known resources (see Table 8.1).

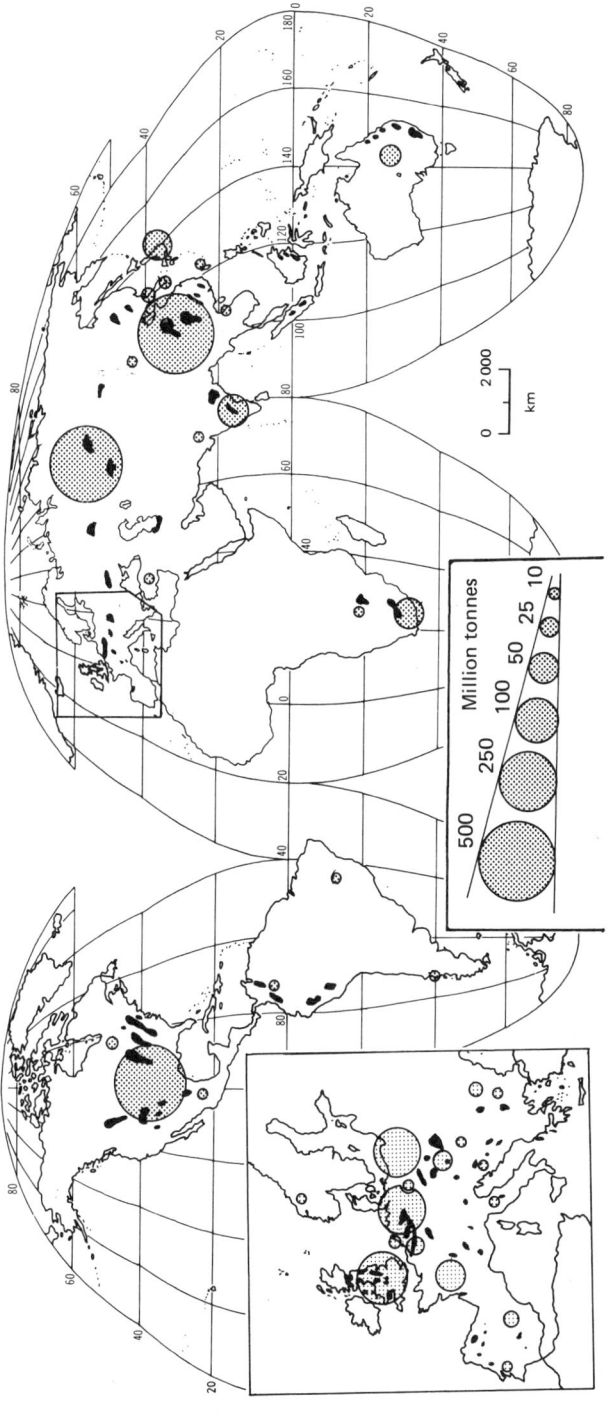

Fig. 8.1 Map of the world's coalfields: the symbols represent production of bituminous coal. Note the poverty in solid fuels of the southern continents

Table 8.1   The world's estimated coal reserves

		Estimated reserves (millions of tonnes)	Percentage
Europe		575 000	13·8
Asia (excluding USSR)		1 097 000	26·4
of which China	1 001 000		(24.1)
USSR		998 000	24·0
North America		1 391 000	33·5
of which United States	1 303 000		(31·3)
Africa		70 000	1·7
South America		14 000	0·3
Australia		14 000	0·3
Total		4 159 000	100·0

Source: UN statistics

About a fifth of Europe's known coal reserves occur in the United Kingdom — around 100 billion tonnes. The coalfields are found in four main groups:

1. in central Scotland, where the Lanarkshire basin to the east of Glasgow is the most important;

2. on the flanks of the Pennines, where the Cumbrian, Lancashire and North Staffordshire coal basins occur along their western margin, and the Northumberland–Durham and Yorkshire, Nottingham and Derby fields lie on the east;

3. the Midlands coalfields, all of them small and of diminishing importance, lying between Shropshire and Leicestershire;

4. an important coal basin extending across South Wales.

Outside these regions there are small coalfields in North Wales, in Kent and near Bristol. There are no significant coalfields in Ireland. Production is now tending to concentrate on the largest and richest coalfields, those of Northumberland–Durham and of West Yorkshire and Nottinghamshire. Here the seams extend eastward towards the North Sea, beneath the Vale of York and the Trent valley, and can be reached by deep mines. New mines are today being sunk in the virgin countryside, far from the grimy industrial regions which were once the source of most of the United Kingdom's coal. This has not happened without vigorous protest from conservationists and agricultural interests.

(*iii*) **World production of coal.** Coal supported the rapid industrial expansion of Europe and North America during the nineteenth century. A century ago more than 80 per cent of the world's coal output was mined in Europe and most of the remainder in the United States. Since then world production has increased almost tenfold, but the European proportion is now less than a third. Production has immensely increased in the Soviet Union, China, India, South Africa and Japan (Fig. 8.1).

The rapid rise in coal production characterizing the nineteenth century continued, though at a diminishing rate, until the Second World War. Since then the worldwide rate of increase has been slight, and in the developed countries coal production has declined (Fig. 8.2). Coal production reached its peak in the

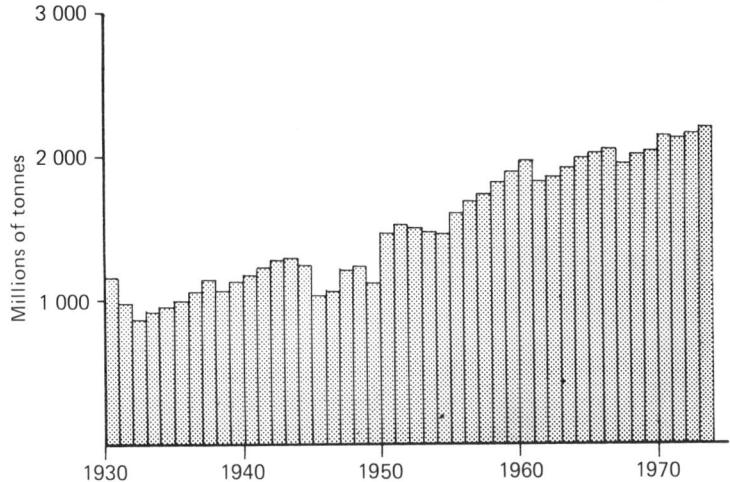

Fig. 8.2 World coal production since 1930; note the stagnation in production since about 1960. Compare with Fig. 8.4

United States in 1948, and in the United Kingdom in 1952; West German output continued to increase until 1956, but has since contracted. By contrast production has continued to rise in both the communist and the developing countries. The reason is clear. The developed countries have found it both economic and convenient to substitute oil for coal in the generation of electricity and the fuelling of locomotives and ships. The communist and developing countries, on the other hand, have lacked the resources to make the conversion and to import oil fuel. Even the Soviet Union, despite its very large oil reserves, still relies very heavily on its coal resources rather than turning to an alternative fuel which, though desirable, would consume its limited supplies of foreign exchange.

(*iv*) **Coal production in the United Kingdom.** The United Kingdom has long been one of the world's leading coal producers. Output expanded continuously throughout the nineteenth century and reached about 280 million tonnes a year before the First World War. The largest production was from South Wales, Northumberland–Durham and Yorkshire. About a quarter of total production was exported, chiefly from the ports of South Wales and the north-east. Production began to decline between the two world wars, in particular during the Great Depression of 1929 and the succeeding years, and continued to fall after 1945; in 1976 it was only about 128 500 000 tonnes, fifth in the world after the United States, the Soviet Union, China and Poland.

There were many reasons for this decline. Foremost was the change from the use of solid fuel to oil as a source of energy. Ships were gradually converted to use oil fuel, the British railways changed to diesel locomotives from about 1960 onwards, while oil came to be used increasingly for the heating of homes and offices and for the energy supply in factories. A second factor was the mounting problems of the British coal-mining industry. Most mines were old and in many the equipment was obsolete, while many of the seams exploited were too thin to allow modern coal-cutting machines to be used. Only the largest mines could show a profit, and most in Great Britain were small.

In 1947 the coal industry was nationalized and has since been managed by the National Coal Board. The Board at once closed down most of the small and unprofitable mines. The Bristol coalfield entirely ceased production. At the same time the bigger and more profitable mines were modernized and made more competitive and several very large mines were opened.

During the 1950s and 1960s the movement of prices favoured the use of oil rather than coal, but since 1974 the price of oil has risen sharply and with it that of natural gas. This will inevitably lead to an increase in the importance of coal. Production may never return to the levels reached at the beginning of this century; for example, ships and railways cannot be expected to return to the use of coal. Nevertheless, increased demand is certain to stimulate production from the most favourably placed coalfields in Yorkshire, Nottinghamshire and the north-east. In particular, new electricity-generating stations are likely to burn coal rather than oil fuel.

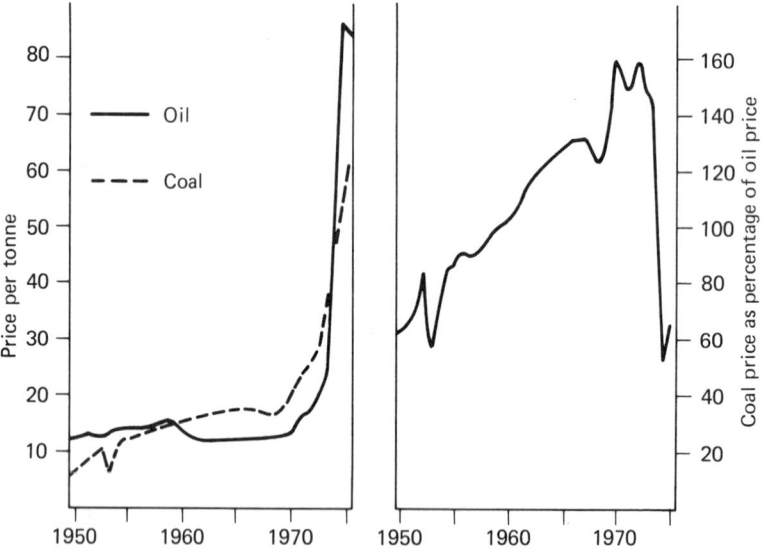

Fig. 8.3 Comparison of the prices of oil and coal since 1950: (left) prices per tonne: (right) coal price as a percentage of oil price

(*v*) **Trade in coal.** There was at one time a vigorous international trade in coal. Great Britain, particularly the Northumbrian and the South Wales coalfields, exported coal to Scandinavia, the Netherlands, France and Spain, and British coal was stored at ports throughout the world for refuelling ships. German coal was exported to Italy where it was met by Welsh coal brought by colliers from Cardiff to the docks of Naples or Genoa. British coal was sold in Brazil and Argentina, and was always available as a return cargo for any ship which had unloaded at a British port. This international trade in coal has almost ceased, except to Scandinavia, and the occasional shipment from the United States port of Newport News; the tanker has replaced the collier, and oil has ousted coal from the furnaces of power stations, factories and ships.

8.4   Oil and Natural Gas

World energy demands have more than trebled since the Second World War, most of this increase being met by oil and natural gas. Fig. 8.4 illustrates the remarkable increase in oil and gas output during the last half-century.

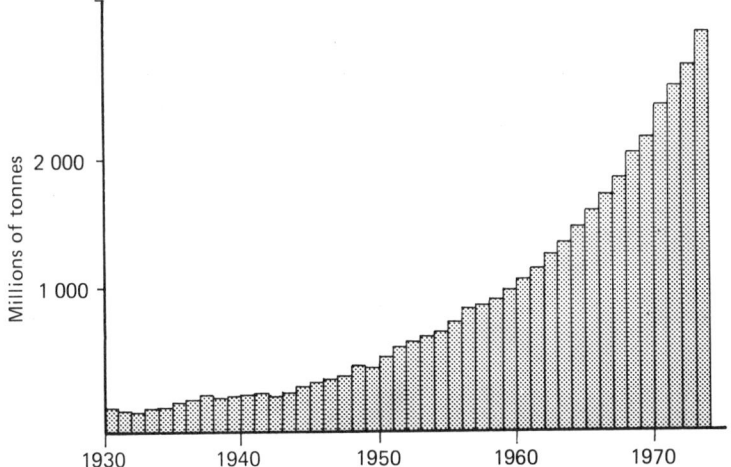

Fig. 8.4 *Production of crude petroleum since 1930; note the accelerating output since the end of the Second World War*

(*a*) Geology and Distribution

Crude oil is similar in its origin to coal. It consists mainly of liquid hydrocarbons, derived ultimately from animal and vegetable organisms. Its fluid nature allows it to move through the interstices of porous rocks such as sandstone, so that it tends to form a pool of oil trapped in sedimentary rocks, often resting on a reservoir of salty water and capped by natural gas. Much, however, depends on the nature of the beds above and below the oil-bearing rocks. Where the original organic material is contained in impervious material, such as clay, the oil particles resulting from its disintegration are unable to flow together to form a pool of oil. Instead they are dispersed through the rock to form *oil-shale*, and can be extracted only by crushing, followed by distillation.

Oil may occur in rocks of a geological age from the Upper Palaeozoic to the Tertiary. Oil-bearing strata may even be older that the earliest coal. Of greater importance than the age of the rocks is the presence of structures that can trap the oil. Gently folded rocks can preserve and concentrate the oil into workable pools, and these are most common near folded mountain ranges, notably those of the Middle East, North America and parts of South America.

It is more difficult to estimate the reserves of oil than those of coal, because oil occurs in a wide range of sedimentary rocks laid down over a longer period of geological time, and also because the oil may be lost through the imperfect seal of the oil-bearing beds. It is unlikely that any significant coal deposits remain undiscovered, but fresh finds of oil and its accompanying natural gas are probable, as the recent development of the resources in the continental shelf and discoveries in southern Mexico have demonstrated. Nevertheless, the oil resources of the world are finite. They will ultimately be exhausted, and before this stage is reached, the price of oil will inevitably rise in response to the greater difficulty and higher cost of extracting it.

Another factor tending to push up the world price of oil is the monopoly position of the major producers. Although there are many small producers, the oil market is dominated by a very small group of countries (see Table 8.2), all of which (except for the Soviet Union and the United States) are members of OPEC—the Organization of Petroleum Exporting Countries.

Table 8.2　World production of crude oil

	Production in 1977 (thousands of tonnes)	Percentage of world production
USSR	545 799	18·3
Saudi Arabia	458 460	15·4
United States	402 489	13·5
Iran	282 608	9·5
Iraq	122 390	4·1
Venezuela	117 007	3·9
Nigeria	102 970	3·4
China	100 000	3·3
Libya	99 503	3·3
Others	754 653	25·3
Total	2 985 879	100·0

Source: *Statistical Yearbook*, UN (1978)

No less than 40 per cent of production, and about 75 per cent of known reserves, are in the Middle East and North Africa. No other raw material has quite the political significance of oil. So many features of twentieth-century civilization depend upon oil that the ensuring of a regular and uninterrupted supply is now a matter of national importance. Aircraft, motor vehicles, nearly all railway locomotives and most ships depend on oil. Modern warfare consumes vast quantities and gives a strategic aspect to the acquisition of oilfields. Lubricating oils and greases for machinery are no less necessary than fuel oils, and petroleum constituents are vital raw materials for the chemical industry. The dependence of *all* developed countries on imported oil inevitably has important political consequences, intensified because no less than four-fifths of the crude oil entering into world trade comes from a narrow group of Arab countries, which have not been reluctant to use their strong position for political purposes.

Coal prices have generally been related closely to production costs, since there is no scarcity of coal today. On the other hand, oil prices are fixed by OPEC at a level far above the prime costs of production. As a consequence, these countries have a highly favourable trade balance and are able to invest their oil income in other parts of the world. Political considerations aside, there is some justification for OPEC pricing policies in that oil reserves will become exhausted within a short and measurable period. Except for the United Kingdom, the oil-exporting nations are very poor apart from their oil reserves, and they do well to sell their product at whatever price the market will bear, and to invest their very considerable profits in projects which will continue to yield an income long after the wells have been pumped dry and the refineries have closed.

(b) Transport and Processing
Crude oil differs from solid fuels in two major respects: it is in many ways easier to transport, and it requires to be processed before it can be used.

(i) Pipelines and tankers.
Being a fluid, crude oil will pass through a pipe, can be stored in a tank and can be pumped into the hold of a ship. This greatly reduces the cost of handling and transport. Networks of pipelines have been built in most areas which produce and some which consume. The United States is criss-crossed by pipelines (Fig. 8.5), so that other means of distribution are used only for the short-distance movement of oil and its products to the retail outlets. Considerable use is also made of pipelines in the Middle East; in western Europe pipelines are used to convey oil from the ports to the refineries, and in eastern Europe they are used by the Soviet Union to supply oil to its satellite countries. Within the United Kingdom, a pipeline is used to move oil from the deep-water port of Milford Haven to the refinery at Llandarcy, near Swansea. Pipelines, however, are inflexible. They represent a very large fixed capital; they cannot be shifted or adapted to other purposes, and they are very vulnerable to sabotage.

Most crude oil reaches its destination by sea. It is, indeed, admirably suited to maritime transport. It can be pumped into and out of the hold of a ship in a very short period of time. Indeed, a tanker need not even dock; frequently it need only tie up at a mooring buoy to load or unload its cargo. Nor is there any practical limit to the size of the vessel used, since it is unlikely to need to navigate narrow and shallow channels. The larger the tanker, the greater are the

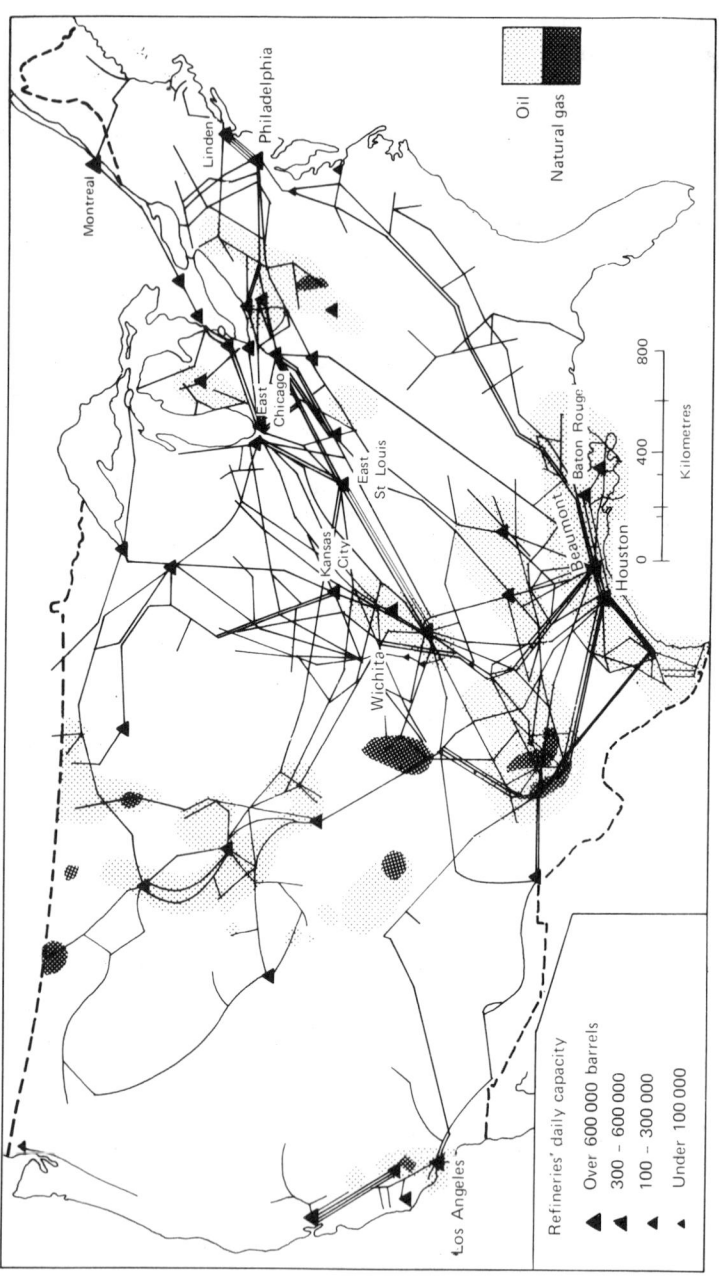

Fig. 8.5 Map of the major pipelines and refineries in the United States

economies of transport, as are also the dangers of accident. Much Middle Eastern oil is now distributed by giant tankers, for which the Suez and Panama canals are far too small. Against the obvious convenience and economy in the use of very large tankers must be set the environmental hazards they pose. The contents of a single tanker, if discharged at sea, can do an incalculable amount of damage to wildlife, fisheries and physical amenities.

(*ii*) **Refining.** Crude oil has little use as such. The process of oil-refining consists in separating the various constituent hydrocarbons from the thick, crude oil obtained from the ground. This is normally performed by *fractional distillation*. The crude oil is heated and the more volatile components, such as benzene, boil off first and are condensed. The less volatile follow in order: petrol, kerosene and paraffin, diesel fuel and lubricating oils, vaseline and grease, until only a wax or asphaltic base remains. In the past, it was impossible to control the proportions in which these fractions were produced, irrespective of the relative demand, and some oils were produced in far larger quantities than the market could absorb. This problem in joint production was solved by the introduction of the *cracking process* by which, under conditions of great heat and pressure, the more complex molecules of the heavier oils can be broken down into the smaller molecules of the lighter oils and motor spirit for which demand is greater. The technique of cracking is now so flexible that the output of the refineries can in large measure be adjusted to the nature of the demand.

Crude oil from different fields varies greatly in composition. North Sea oil is characterized as 'light' and that from the Middle East or Nigeria as 'heavy'. A refinery commonly requires a blend of different oils in order to produce the full range of commercial products. The United Kingdom is thus unlikely ever to become self-sufficing in oil, though it may on balance produce enough oil, and export some.

Oil-refining, like the processing of any other industrial raw material, may be located near the source, near the market or at some intermediate point, though the last would require a break of bulk. Most crude oil is refined near the market so that the products can be distributed conveniently. Refineries are usually situated near the ports through which crude oil is imported; in Great Britain, for example, they are located on the Thames estuary and on Southampton Water, and also in South Wales, where the refinery is linked by pipeline with the oil port of Milford Haven, which is accessible to giant tankers. In western Europe too, much of the crude oil is refined near the ports, such as Genoa, Marseilles and Rotterdam, but pipelines also convey crude oil to a number of inland points where it is refined and from which it is distributed (Fig. 8.6).

(*iii*) **The pattern of trade in crude oil.** Except for the Soviet Union, no developed country can satisfy its needs in crude oil from internal sources. The United States has been the world's biggest consumer since the industry's early days, but until recently could meet its requirements from its once great reserves. But one by one the oilfields have been almost or wholly exhausted. The bulk of American production now comes from the oilfields of the Gulf Coast, Texas and

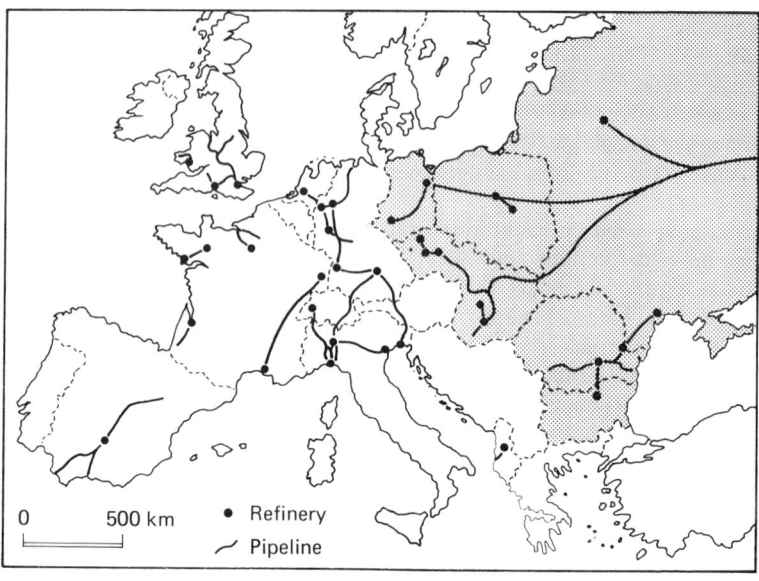

Fig. 8.6 Map of the major pipelines and refineries in Europe; note the two systems dependent respectively on (a) the Atlantic and Mediterranean ports and (b) the Soviet Union

Oklahoma. Much is expected of the field now being developed on the so-called Arctic Slope of Alaska, though environmental problems make this one of the costliest to exploit.

The other major consumers are Europe, especially western Europe, and Japan. The latter has no resources and relies exclusively on oil from the Middle East. Some west European countries, notably France, Italy, West Germany and the Netherlands, have long had a small domestic oil production. Developments in the continental shelf, especially in the North Sea, should greatly increase Europe's internal production, and the United Kingdom hopes for self-sufficiency in the 1980s. Western Europe must, however, continue to depend for the foreseeable future on imported oil; even the North Sea reserves may not outlast the present century.

The developing countries, no less than the industrialized, are interested in the oil supplies essential to their economic development. Most, however, have great difficulty in paying the inflated prices which the OPEC countries now demand. The price which the North American and west European markets can bear is far beyond the reach of most developing countries. In any event, with increasing scarcity, the price for all consumers will rise to a level that will force them to turn to alternative sources of fuel.

Oil, as well as being one of several competing sources of energy, is also an industrial raw material. The manufacture of fertilizers and plastics not only requires energy for its industrial processes, but in many cases uses oil as a starting-point. When governments determine their pricing policies they must therefore consider not only the allocation of oil to various energy consumers, but also its use as a raw material. Oil is thus a far more versatile source of energy than any other currently available, and this is a major reason for the extraordinarily rapid rise in demand during recent years (Fig. 8.4).

(*iv*) **The United Kingdom as an oil-producer.** The United Kingdom, like much of western and central Europe, has long been an oil-producer on a very small scale. Most of the production came from the Trent valley. In the 1960s the existence first of natural gas, and then of oil, was demonstrated beneath the floor of the North Sea, and exploratory work during the ensuing decade proved the existence of very considerable reserves. During these years the United Kingdom negotiated treaties with her partners in north-western Europe by which the floor of the North Sea and the riches it contains were partitioned between them (Fig. 8.7). Fuel resources in the more southerly part of the North Sea consist largely of natural gas, but to the east and north-east of Scotland they are mainly of oil. The sea is relatively shallow over much of this area, but is particularly stormy, so that oil drilling has been fraught with very great risks and is extremely costly. Potentially productive areas of the sea-floor have been divided into concessions, which have been auctioned to oil companies to explore and exploit. The government, however, retains a close control over these operations, and has a financial stake in each enterprise. Oil began to flow in 1977, and production is expected to increase until a peak production is reached in the early 1980s. It is planned to bring most of the oil ashore by pipeline from the oil rigs to storage tanks and refineries located on the east coast of Scotland, near Aberdeen, and at Sullom Voe in the Shetland Islands. Though it is claimed that the United Kingdom may on balance become self-sufficient in oil, this can only be for a relatively short period, and reliance must ultimately be placed on other sources of energy.

It is probable that other parts of the continental shelf may also contain reserves of oil. Exploratory work is taking place to the north-west of Scotland and in the so-called Celtic Sea, between south-western England and Ireland.

(*c*) Natural Gas

Natural gas occurs in most oilfields, and is in fact in joint production with oil. Some fields produce only gas—for example, those in the southern North Sea, Transylvania and the North American prairies—but these are structurally connected with reserves of oil. Natural gas had long been regarded as a by-product of oilfield exploitation, of little value and to be burned off. This arose from technical difficulties in the storage and transport of natural gas—and, indeed, gas continues to be burned off on many oilfields, as their conspicuous flares demonstrate.

Problems have been overcome, however, by the 'pipeline revolution'. In the United States, a dense network of small-gauge pipes has been laid down to distribute the gas from the major centres of production in Kansas and Texas (Fig. 8.5). Natural gas from the field in the northern Netherlands and north-

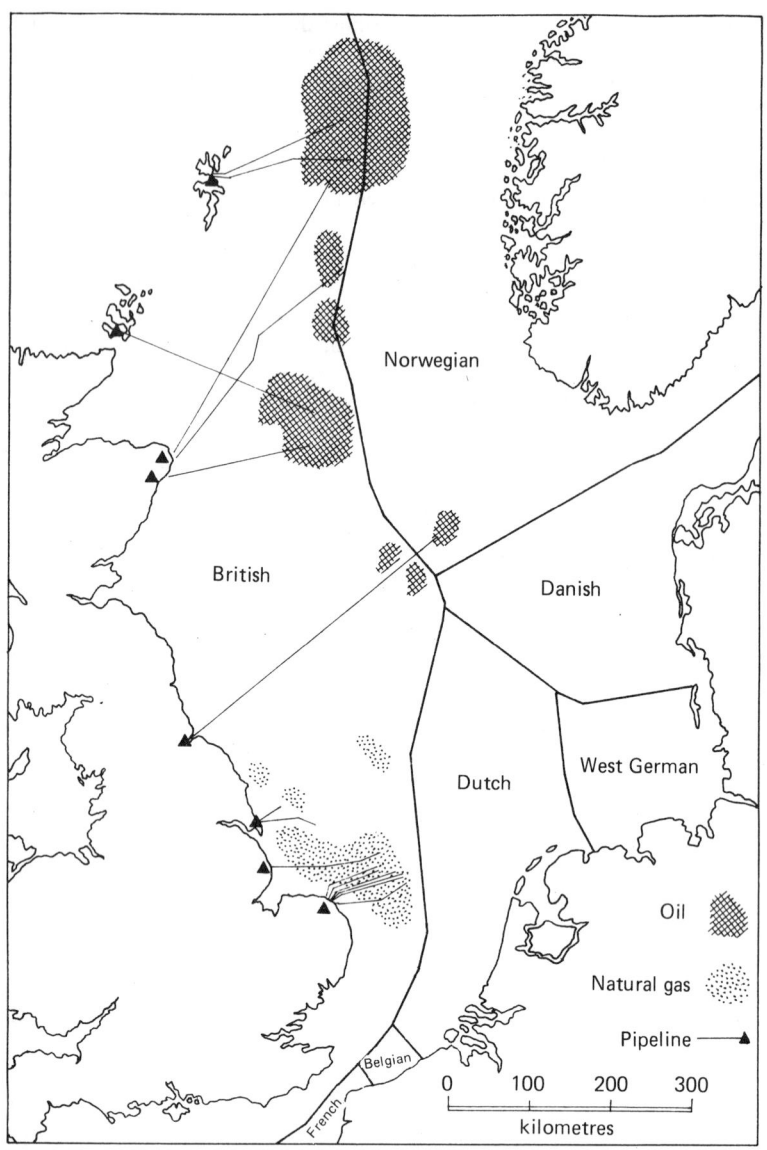

Fig. 8.7 The partitioning of the oil and natural gas resources of the North Sea

western Germany is piped to consumers in this region, and Transylvanian gas is even exported by pipeline to Hungary. The United Kingdom now receives over 95 per cent of its gas supply for domestic and industrial use by pipeline from the North Sea, and today ranks as one of the foremost gas-producing countries after the United States and the Soviet Union. The traditional gas-works, which produced gas from coal, have now disappeared from most of our cities.

Gas pipelines, like those for oil, represent very heavy capital investment, which must be amortized before the field is exhausted. As with almost every form of mineral extraction, it is not economic to exploit any but the larger reserves.

(d) Synthetic Oil

Mineral oil is derived from plant and animal materials, and it might be supposed that oil could be made artificially from its source material without waiting for the slow operation of natural forces. Oil has been produced in the laboratory from fish and from vegetable materials, but no economic process is yet available.

A synthetic oil can be made from coal, but it is relatively expensive, and only political necessity can justify its production. The German production of synthetic petroleum and oil during the Second World War is an outstanding example of the willingness of a government to sacrifice economics for a strategic advantage; synthetic oil is at present important in South Africa.

8.5 Nuclear Energy

Nuclear power is often said to hold the key to the future. But as at present exploited, this too depends on mineral raw materials which could eventually become exhausted. Amounts used are small, however, and reserves of radioactive minerals, though highly localized, are sufficient to last for a very long time. The problems with nuclear energy lie in the immense costs of research and of the construction and maintenance of nuclear plants, and in the environmental risks inherent in the use of radioactive materials and the disposal of radioactive waste. These risks, it has recently been claimed, are a great deal less than had been supposed. The degree of probability of a serious radiation leakage cannot be precisely estimated: though every precaution may be taken at the plant, the possibility still remains, as shown by events at the Three Mile Island plant near Harrisburg, Pennsylvania, in 1979. Nuclear reactors are normally located as far as possible from densely populated areas, but their operation nevertheless leads to 'a range of unquantifiable social and environment costs' which must be set against the undoubted long-term benefits of their use.

At the time of writing, eighteen countries have built nuclear reactors for the commercial generation of power, but in none of these is nuclear energy of more than marginal importance. The United Kingdom has made one of the largest developments of nuclear power relative to its total energy demands: about 7·5 per cent. In the United States the proportion is about 5 per cent. Other countries which have developed nuclear energy are the Soviet Union, France, Japan, Canada and the German Federal Republic. The nuclear-fusion process, which produces the energy of the hydrogen bomb, cannot yet be used to generate power for commercial purposes, though the possibility is being explored experimentally; though the necessary research is enormously costly, the process could open up immense reserves of power, since the basic raw material—water— is found everywhere.

Fig. 8.8 Two approaches to the use of wind power: (a) small windmills used to provide power for irrigation in Greece; (b) a wind-driven turbine generator in the Isle of Man

8.6   Non-exhaustible Sources of Energy

Reserves of coal and petroleum will eventually be exhausted, and the high environmental risks of nuclear fuel are increasingly evident. The alternatives are those sources of energy which derive either from solar radiation or the force of gravity. Many such sources are in theory available, and some have been developed experimentally. The objection to their use is the extremely high cost of many of the necessary installations and in some instances also the environmental damage they may cause.

(a) Wind and Wave Power

The wind has long been used as a source of power for pumping water, crushing seeds and grinding corn, but it has hitherto been harnessed only in very small units, quite inadequate for modern industrial use. It has been claimed that about 1 500 windmills on towers more than 30 m high would have to be built to replace the capacity of a single medium-size power station, and of this there is no conceivable chance.

Wind power is more likely to be exploited through the medium of the waves of seas and oceans which it stimulates. Experimental work has demonstrated the possibility of harnessing the energy of water particles in rotary movement, and the British government is sponsoring work directed to this end. The cost, however, is likely greatly to exceed that of nuclear power, and this work can only be aimed at filling energy shortfalls after the depletion of oil reserves.

(b) Tidal Power

The tides of the sea are an obvious potential source of power. Indeed tide-mills were once not uncommon round the British coasts, each consisting essentially of a waterwheel set in a small dam or barrage built across a tidal creek. Like other forms of watermill, however, they generated only small amounts of power, and probably none now remains in use. A barrage capable of yielding a large supply of power raises immense engineering problems. The much-discussed scheme to built a barrage across the Severn estuary would cost far more than any conceivable benefits that might ensue. At the time of writing, the development of wave power appears more promising than that of the tides.

(c) Solar and Geothermal Power

These represent immense sources of energy, but the problems of concentrating them and of converting them to a transmissible form of power remain unsolved except on a small and local scale.

(d) Hydro-electric Power

The energy of falling water is thus the only non-exhaustible source of power likely to prove economic in the present state of technology.

The motive force of running water has been exploited since early times. During the nineteenth century the efficiency of water-power plants was found to be increased if the water were allowed to fall in a pipe from a considerable height. The success of these experiments, combined with the invention of the water turbine and the introduction of long-distance transmission of electricity, made possible the widespread development of hydro-electric power, in which water under pressure is made to pass through a turbine coupled with a generator. Certain physical factors must be considered in the design of any hydro-electric scheme.

(*i*) **The 'head' of water.** The efficiency of the generating plant depends directly on the pressure exerted by the water on the turbine blades. The *head* is the vertical height of the intake of the pipe above the turbine; the pressure of water at the turbine clearly depends on the height of the pipe. A very small stream dropping through a considerable height can acquire a great motive force. A larger body of water falling a smaller distance might have a similar capacity, but a very large body of water falling a great distance is a potential source of power of considerable importance. In this lies the significance of such waterfalls as Niagara, the Victoria Falls and the Ripon Falls in Uganda. A number of hydro-electric stations make use of falls of water of over 1 000 m. The highest so far developed is a head of 1 750 m at Dixence in Canton Valais, Switzerland.

A head of water can be established artificially by damming a river, and a generating station may be built at the foot of the dam. The resulting fall of water is not likely to be large, but the small head may in some measure be offset by the greater volume of water. Alternatively, water may be allowed to fall through a tunnel or pipeline leading from the dam to a generating station in a valley far below. The courses of certain Alpine rivers, such as the Mur and the Rhine above Basel, have been formed into a series of steps, each bounded by a dam with its appendant hydro-electric station. The Vah river of Slovakia, the upper Danube and the Tennessee and Missouri rivers have been developed in the same way.

(*ii*) **The regime of the river.** Clearly, the generating station should be able to produce electricity throughout the year, not only because electricity is difficult and costly to store, but because the generating station and other plant represent a very large capital investment which must be kept fully employed if the enterprise is to be financially sound. A steady flow is usually achieved in midlatitudes, though winter frosts and summer drought may interrupt discharge. In many instances it is necessary to construct a large storage basin in order to maintain an uninterrupted flow throughout the year.

(*iii*) **The location of the generating stations.** The greatest demand for electricity is in the large towns and on the plains. Hydro-electricity generation, however, is easiest in the mountains and hills, because here the gradient of the streams is

Fig. 8.9 An aerial view of the Cruachan hydro-electric scheme in Argyll. Electricity is produced by allowing water to fall through shafts inside the mountain to underground generators 300 m below the dam; the water escapes into the loch below. When public power demands are low, the turbines are reversed and water is pumped in the opposite direction to replenish the reservoir

steepest. Clearly, either the power must be transmitted to the towns, or industries must move to the mountains.

Electricity can be carried over very serious natural obstacles. Transmission lines cross the high fjelds of Norway, the ranges of the Alps and estuaries like that of the Thames, and cables have been laid across the floor of the Sound from Sweden to Denmark. The use of high voltages has solved some of the problems of long-distance power transmission. The United Kingdom 'Supergrid' operates at up to 400 000 volts, and research is in progress on transmission plant for use at even higher voltages. Even so, there is a wastage, and it is very unusual for power to be transmitted over more than 800 km.

While most power is used in the large cities, one group of industries has migrated to the source of power. These are the electrochemical and electrometallurgical industries, which in general consume relatively small quantities of raw material and make small demands on labour, but need a great deal of electric power. The fjords of Norway and the high, bare valleys of Savoy are now dotted with factories which refine aluminium or make carbide or electrolytic copper.

Hydro-electric power contributes only a small fraction—less than 2 per cent—of the total energy produced in the world today, and this percentage is unlikely to alter greatly, since few large unexploited sources remain. There is still scope for large hydro-electric projects in the Americas, in Africa and in parts of Asia, but there is little further opportunity in Europe; the Iron Gate and the Hungarian Vac projects on the Danube may be the last big European undertakings.

8.7   Conclusion

The world's consumption of energy of all kinds is increasing rapidly; for the past ten years its annual rate of growth has been more than 10 per cent. Expansion in the use of coal and of hydro-electric power has been slight. Nuclear power is likely to become increasingly important, but its production remains small. Growth has been very largely in the use of oil and natural gas (Fig. 8.10).

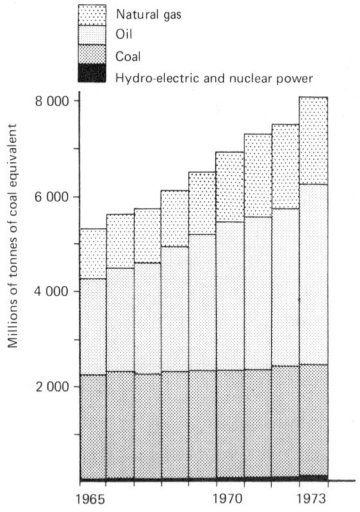

Fig. 8.10 The increase in energy consumption expressed in terms of coal equivalent, 1965–73 (based on United Nations statistics)

Industrial development is based upon the consumption of energy; even agriculture uses increasing quantities either directly in powered machinery or in heating glasshouses, or indirectly in fertilizers, insecticides and other chemicals, some of which are derived from petroleum. All developed countries make heavy demands on energy, and energy consumption per head is a rough measure of development; its average value in the developed market countries is well above that in the developing countries. Fig. 8.11 clearly demonstrates the contrast between the developed countries of Europe and North America on the one hand, and Africa and southern Asia on the other. In Fig. 8.12, energy consumption per head is plotted against *per capita* gross national product; the best-fit regression

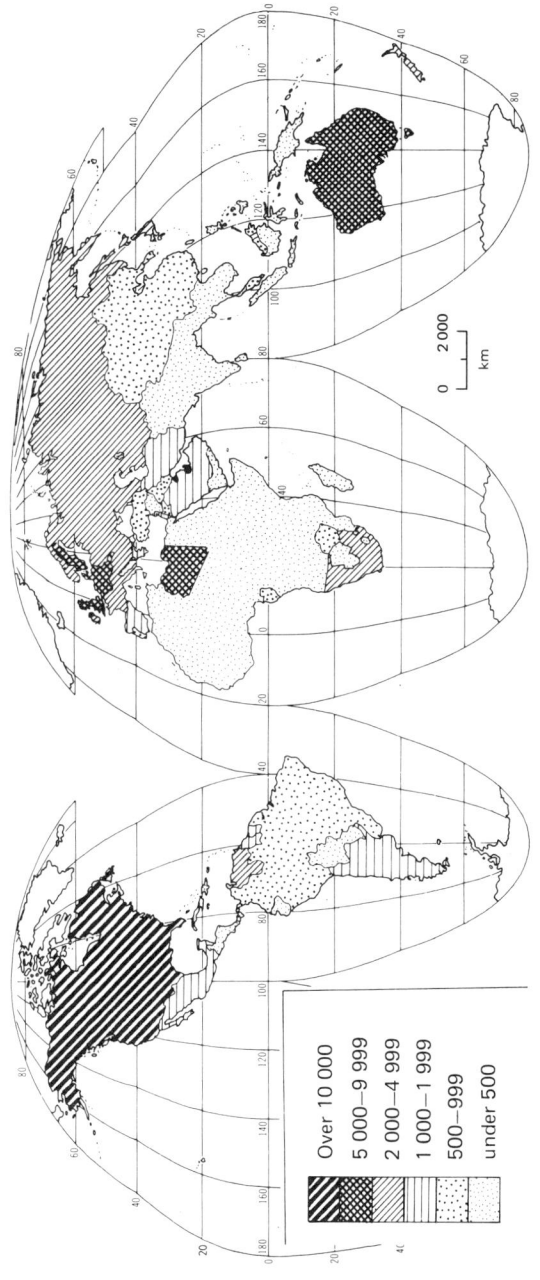

Fig. 8.11 World map showing the consumption of energy per head (in kg of coal equivalent) from all sources

Over 10 000
5 000–9 999
2 000–4 999
1 000–1 999
500–999
under 500

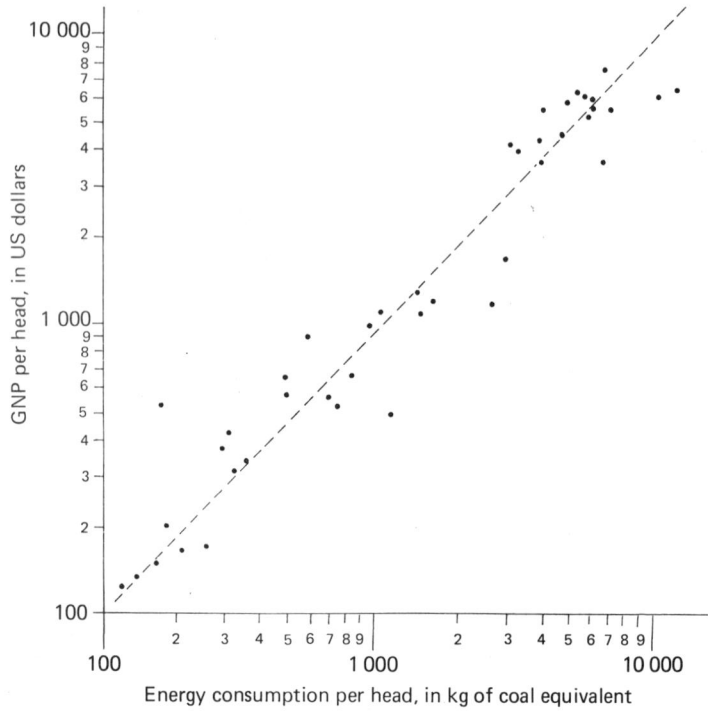

Fig. 8.12 Energy consumption per head plotted against GNP per head, demonstrating the association of high energy consumption with high GNP (based on United Nations statistics)

line indicates the high correlation between them. (This graph uses logarithmic scales on both axes; these scales are explained in Unit 7.3(*b*).)

(*a*) The Future of Fuel Supplies

This raises two problems of world importance: first, the short-term problem of making energy available to the developing countries, and, secondly, the long-term problem of the continuing availability of reserves of fuel. While enough coal remains, even though at increasing prices, for decades or even centuries, most oilfields will become exhausted within a calculable period of time. Their extinction will be hastened by the demands placed on them by the developing countries. It is unlikely that hydro-electric power, although it uses an inexhaustible resource, can make any significant contribution towards filling the gap between the demand for energy and its supply. Nuclear energy may do so, though at a high and probably increasing cost. But at some time in the not-too-distant future the human race, if it survives the other dangers that threaten it, will be forced to turn to the energy inherent in the movements of the earth itself, as manifested in the wind, waves and tides, and to the sun, ultimate source of terrestrial energy. The amounts of energy potentially accessible from these sources are immense, but so too are the probable costs of harnessing them. The resources required to develop and exploit these energy sources will have to be diverted from other purposes; in other words, the world will in real terms become poorer.

(b) Decision-making

It is against this background that decisions must be made which will shape the future energy supply and thus the future wellbeing of mankind. The alternatives to the mineral fuels on which generations have relied require not only a vast capital investment but also a long period of experiment and development. This is proving to be complicated by two considerations. First, governments are reluctant to invest heavily in projects that cannot yield any significant return for many years and will not earn them many votes in the immediate future. Second, the public in the richer countries cannot easily perceive dangers which lie a generation or more ahead, and its lack of enthusiasm for heavy investment in energy research tends to find support among environmentalists.

Most energy production has in the past involved some damage to the environment: deforestation in the distant past, and more recently atmospheric pollution and disfigurement of landscape by opencast mining, spoil heaps and subsidence. In the seventeenth and eighteenth centuries coal-burning was opposed because of the sulphurous fumes emitted, and now a similar opposition is focused on the harm which radioactivity can do to the environment. The choice for posterity may be between a world contaminated by radioactivity and one deprived of energy. It is between these extremes that our decision-makers must chart their policy, weighing energy needs against environmental damage. Above all, they must evaluate the dangers, which *may* be greatly exaggerated, inherent in the use of breeder reactors and nuclear fusion, and take the appropriate decisions on investment in research and development.

Questions

1. Solid and liquid fuels are a rapidly wasting asset. How then should we use them?
2. What have been the implications for Great Britain of the replacement of coal by oil and natural gas?
3. Examine the political consequences of the fact that some 42 per cent of the world's oil is obtained from the Middle East.
4. What are the non-exhaustible sources of energy? What factors influence their development both now and in the future?

Unit Nine

The Structure and Location of Industry

The purpose of manufacturing industries is so to alter and to process materials that they serve new ends and satisfy different requirements. Manufacturing is normally carried on in a factory or workshop and makes use of mechanical power. If machines are not used the activity may be classed as a *handicraft* rather than a manufacturing industry. Building construction is not generally regarded as a manufacturing industry, though it makes use of factory-produced components; nor are operating a laundry or running a garage in this class, even though they may be practised on a large scale and in factory-like buildings, since they do not satisfy the basic criterion of involving the transformation of one substance into another. Mining is similarly excluded from this category, which nevertheless includes the refining and processing of metals.

9.1 The Manufacturing Process

The manufacturing industries have certain features in common which greatly influence their location and development.

(*a*) Value Added
Manufacturing adds value to the raw materials it uses: that is, the manufactured product is worth more than the total value of the materials from which it is derived. Cotton, for example, is spun into thread that is worth more than the raw material; the thread in its turn is woven into a yet more valuable fabric. The latter is finished and finally made up into clothing, gaining value at each stage. A suit costing £100 may incorporate wool, cotton, man-made fibres and other materials which in their unprocessed state might together have cost less than a pound.

The difference between the cost of a manufactured article and that of its raw material is the *value added* in its production. Most of the value added will reflect the cost of labour and management. Part will, however, represent the necessary expenses of maintaining the factory, the cost of fuel and power, insurance and transport, and national and local taxes.

(*b*) Reduction in Bulk
The process of manufacturing is usually accompanied by a *loss of bulk*: the finished product not only costs more but weighs less than the raw materials from which it is derived. There is wastage in all processes, and in some the loss is very great. In iron-smelting, for example, ore, coke and usually limestone are introduced into the blast furnace. The fuel is burned, part of the ore is dissipated

in waste gases, a great deal of slag is produced only to be dumped in a spoil heap, and the iron drawn from the furnace generally represents no more than a fifth of the materials that are put in. In spinning and weaving and in most branches of food-processing the losses consequent on processing are relatively small. Most chemical industries, however, involve a considerable reduction in bulk. Since transport costs are related to the weight and volume of the goods carried, the degree of bulk reduction can be significant in the location of a factory (see also Unit 10.2).

(c) The Use of Mechanical Power

The factory was the creation of the Industrial Revolution, though large numbers of workers were occasionally employed under one roof before this; but the principal purpose was to achieve discipline among them and to secure an adequate standard of work, rather than to make use of mechanical power and to profit from the division of labour.

The factory system was preceded by a system of craft industries pursued by individual workmen, each having perhaps one assistant and an apprentice. Such an organization of production was once widespread in the United Kingdom. Wool was spun into thread by women at home in their kitchens; the thread would be made into cloth by a weaver who sat at his loom in a shed adjoining his house or even at an upstairs window where the light was better—here and there in this country old cottages with broad 'weavers' windows' can still be seen. Metalwork and objects made of wood, basketry or clay were also produced on a small scale.

The domestic system grew out of the craftsman's difficulty in marketing his goods. Sometimes he bought his own raw materials, or he collected or dug them; but frequently raw materials were regularly delivered to his door and the finished goods collected by the merchant or 'putter-out', who in effect controlled the workmen's labour but not their premises. The Spitalfields silk industry of the eighteenth and nineteenth centuries was organized on this basis. In Bethnal Green and Mile End, hundreds of weavers worked at home; and if conditions were bad in the early factories, they were probably much worse in the silk-weavers' dingy, ill-ventilated workrooms, which were rarely seen by the public. The domestic system still survives in the United Kingdom here and there in remote areas and in a few industries which do not lend themselves to mechanical methods and mass production. Even in the 1970s, shoe-buckles, brooches, ornaments, fish-hooks and novelties are still cut and made at home for so much the dozen during the evenings to supplement the family income. 'Harris' tweed, too, continues to be woven in the cottages of the Hebrides.

Domestic or craft industries account for only a minute proportion of total production in the United Kingdom or, indeed, in many other developed areas, although markets remain for craftsman-made products ranging from components of Swiss watches to the toys turned out with limitless patience and skill by the peasants of the Black Forest. In some rural areas, the blacksmith still practises his traditional craft, and high-quality furniture and pottery continue to be made by the 'small' man in his workshop. But the association of craft organization of production with quality workmanship and costly products is itself evidence that it is expensive and has for the general run of goods been replaced by mass-production methods in a factory. In the rest of the world, however, craftsmanship retains much of its importance. In most Third World countries, domestic weaving, potting and wood- and metal-working continue to supply a large part of consumer needs. In much of Africa and southern and south-eastern Asia, factory products have barely begun to cut into the market for the goods produced by local craftsmen. Everywhere, however, the craftsman is at a potential disadvantage, because he controls only one pair of hands, whereas his rival in the factory has a great many mechanical aids at his disposal.

The domestic system of manufacture was undercapitalized. It made little use of mechanical power and, indeed, its units of production were individually too small to be able to profit from it. Moreover, there could be no effective *division of labour*. Two centuries ago Adam Smith in *The Wealth of Nations* described how the making of pins, instead of being accomplished from beginning to end by a single craftsman, was in fact divided among many:

> One man draws out the wire, another straights it, a third cuts it, a fourth points it, a fifth grinds it at the top for receiving the head; to make the head requires two or three distinct operations; to put it on is a peculiar business, to whiten the pins is another; it is even a trade by itself to put them into the paper; and the important business of making a pin is, in this manner, divided into about eighteen distinct operations

If one man accomplished all these operations he could, wrote Smith, scarcely produce twenty pins in a day. But if each worker in a group gave all his attention to a single process, the group could collectively make many hundreds. The division of labour increased production, but at the expense of making people's work more tedious.

The use of mechanical power could still further speed up the industrial process and to some extent make work less laborious, as in the replacement of the hand-quern by the watermill and windmill. The earliest mechanical inventions of the Industrial Revolution aimed to speed up the spinning of thread and later, with the power-loom, the weaving of cloth.

Who, then, profits from these labour-saving innovations? After all allowance is made for the capital cost of machines and buildings, industrialization usually reduces the total unit costs of production. Is the product to be sold more cheaply, is the worker to be paid higher wages, or is the entrepreneur to receive greater profits? All these *may* happen, but in the earlier stages of industrialization wage rates are unlikely to increase substantially. Profits will probably rise, but the most significant short-term result may be a fall in the product's selling price, as industry competes for wider markets.

(d) Labour in Manufacturing

The domestic system of manufacturing used large amounts of labour inefficiently; the factory system uses labour very much more effectively by equipping it with mechanical tools and machines and by organizing it so that each worker achieves more. Modernization and technological advance tend to make labour more efficient—in other words, to reduce the labour input in the industrial process in relation to the total production. Despite this general trend, many industries still employ very large quantities of labour in proportion to their output, especially those in which mechanization offers few advantages. In the Swiss watchmaking industry, for instance, the raw material demands are small; a thousand watches might require less than 10 kg of metal and glass. On the other hand, the minute moving parts can be put together only by hand. The cost of a watch thus incorporates a very large labour component but only a very small raw material component: the industry is *labour-intensive*.

At the opposite extreme are those industries which have largely replaced labour by machines. In a modern steelworks the floor seems almost deserted, and the machines are largely controlled automatically. Though the design and construction of the machines represent a significant labour input, the overall labour component in the production of a tonne of rolled-steel goods is nevertheless very small; the industry is *capital-intensive*. Other capital-intensive industries are power generation, the cement industry and the more modern branches of the textile industry.

In general, value added during manufacture is largest in the labour-intensive industries, since outgoings in wages are large, though this may be offset by the low wage rates in some less-developed countries.

This raises an important consideration: labour is not a uniform commodity. It varies in quality—that is, in skill and efficiency—and in price (that is, in wage rates) from one place to another, and an entrepreneur seeking to establish a factory must balance the efficiency and price of the local labour very carefully against the cost of other factors of production (see Unit 4.3). This question is especially important in the international sphere, since wage rates in countries like Hong Kong, Taiwan or India are considerably less than those in western Europe or North America (see also Unit 15).

Even within a developed country there are variations in wage rates, and the entrepreneur will profit from these if he can. Within the United States, for instance, wages are lower in the South than elsewhere, partly because labour is relatively plentiful, and therefore cheaper, in this region, and partly because the climate is warmer, land more abundant and the cost of living lower. The comparative abundance and cheapness of labour have attracted industries, especially labour-intensive industries, to the South.

This situation is, however, self-correcting in the long run. As more manufacturing industry moves to a region with a labour-cost advantage, the competition for labour increases and its price rises. At the same time wages and working conditions are likely to improve through trades union activity, so that the attractiveness of low labour costs gradually becomes eroded.

Sometimes a particular labour force is said to have special qualities of patience or manual dexterity, and thus to be unusually well suited to a particular task. It is very doubtful whether such claims are valid. Most workers in most parts of the world can acquire the aptitudes necessary for their tasks. The development of special skills through education and training is of increasing importance in the

Fig. 9.1 Construction methods: (a) in China, where labour is plentiful and a great deal of work is done manually—on this site, by women, and

more industrialized countries, however. Automation of manufacturing processes reduces the need for workers whose skills are severely limited, and in some countries, pre-eminently the United States, the unskilled are having increasing difficulty in finding employment; meanwhile there is increased demand for the highly skilled worker who can understand the operation of complex machines, evaluate shop-floor situations and make quick decisions.

On the other hand if, as in many developing countries, semi-skilled and unskilled labour is very abundant and therefore cheap, the entrepreneur may be reluctant to introduce more than a limited degree of mechanization and automation. You may have seen a photograph of large-scale construction works —a dam, perhaps—with hundreds of labourers conveying earth in wheelbarrows and baskets, and it is easy to condemn the gross inefficiency of the system which encouraged such methods. Nevertheless, this may be a cheaper method of construction than to bring in earth-moving equipment, if labour costs are abnormally low and capital expensive.

There is, however, an important distinction to be made between the male and female labour forces. Men can handle tasks requiring great physical strength more easily than women, though this does not totally exclude women from certain forms of heavy work, especially in the developing countries (Fig. 9.1(a)). Women have traditionally commanded lower wage rates than men even for

(b) in a country where labour costs are high and maximum use is made of cranes and other machinery (the construction of a shopping centre in Exeter)

closely comparable work, partly because the supply of female labour was in general larger than the market required. In the United Kingdom, the USA and other developed countries it is now illegal to discriminate against women in this way. Some branches of manufacturing industry nevertheless remain the traditional sphere of women, partly because the differential wage rates have become established by custom, and partly because women are believed to show a greater physical and psychological aptitude for them. For instance, the assembly of radio, television and other electronic equipment requires a finesse which many men do not possess. By contrast, work in a motor-car assembly plant has become essentially men's work, even though women are regularly employed in this way in the Soviet Union and other communist countries. Women have dominated the spinning branch of the textile industry ever since they occupied themselves at home with the distaff and spinning-wheel, though weaving has, from the days of the handloom, been dominated by men.

Given that there exists a rough division of industrial employment by sex, every industrial region should offer factory employment for both women and men. In most regions where mining and the heavy industries predominate there is little employment which can be offered to women, therefore 'light' industries are often attracted to such areas because of the abundance, and probable cheapness, of female labour.

9.2   The Organization of Manufacturing

The factory is a highly complex system, set up in order to transform or process one or more commodities as cheaply as possible and to market the product. Its size, organization, relationship to other branches of industry and linkages with the market are all adjusted to these ends.

(a) Size of Plant

It is commonly said that the larger the plant or factory the more economical its operation since overheads, including managerial costs, can thus be spread over a larger number of units of production. But size is not the only criterion of profitability. The volume of production must be geared to the mechanism for the supply of raw materials and power, to the transport and marketing of finished products, and to the extent of the market.

To take a very simple example: suppose that a power unit supplies a single factory and is fully used. Any increase in the capacity of the factory would require the installation of a second power unit, but this could double or even treble capacity. Even if the market could absorb the increased production, it might still be difficult for financial or technical reasons to extend the floor-space of the factory and to introduce new machinery on a scale that would allow maximum use to be made of the expanded power plant; again, expansion on this scale might call for an impracticably large increase in the transport services or in the supervisory, sales or marketing staff. But the unused capacity of the factory nevertheless remains a loss to the entrepreneur.

Even in the simplest industrial undertaking there must be some sort of balance between its component operations, though perfect adjustment may be unattainable. If the market for the product is expanding it may be cheaper and more profitable to build another factory rather than to undertake the difficult process of enlarging the old. It is the function of management to minimize any lack of adjustment between the several phases in an industry, and in today's competitive conditions the difference between profit and loss can lie in the elimination of underused capacity. Company board rooms are often faced with questions of this kind, and every problem which arises may have several possible solutions. The board's decision is often of great importance to the geography of the industry.

(b) The Structure of Manufacturing

Manufacturing rarely consists merely of the processing of a single raw material and the sale of the product. More often it constitutes a stage in a series of processes, and makes use of the products of other industries. The following is a simple classification of manufacturing industries according to the organization of the processes involved.

(i) **One-stage manufacturing.** At its simplest, a factory uses one or more raw materials to make a product which then enters the market and reaches the consumer (Fig. 9.2(a)). Most food-processing industries are of this kind. The miller grinds corn and markets flour; the meat-packing factory slaughters the

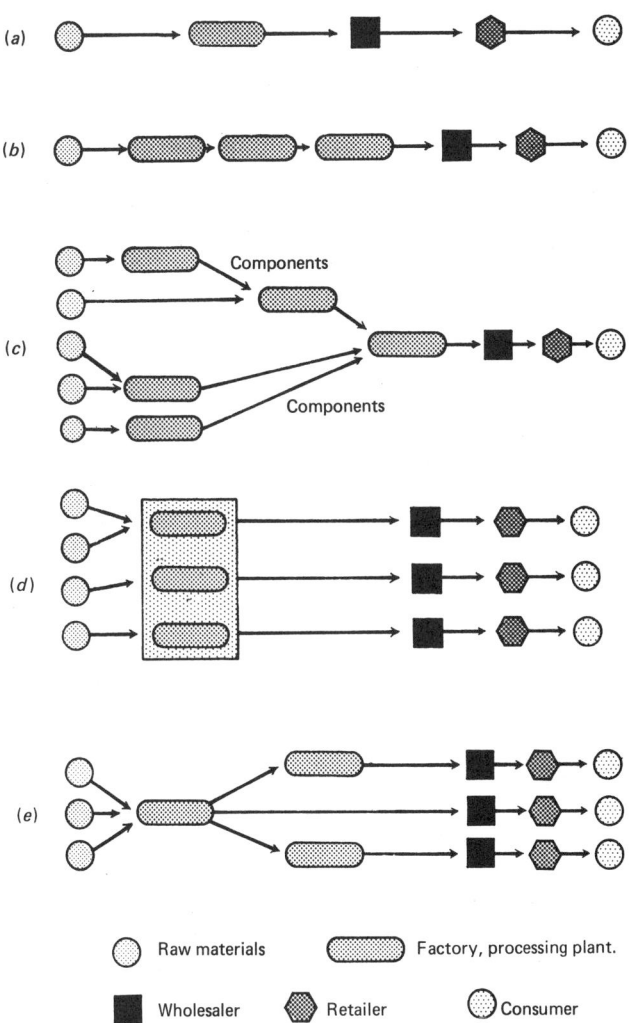

Fig. 9.2 Structures of manufacturing: (a) single-stage manufacturing; (b) multi-stage (vertically organized) manufacturing; (c) parallel or horizontally organized manufacturing; (d) complementary manufacturing (plant used for different purposes in turn, seasonally for example); (e) manufacturing with by-product utilization

animals, cuts up and processes the carcases and delivers meat, hides and other products to the market; the cheese factory receives liquid milk and sells cheese along with certain by-products. Few other industries, however, are so simply structured as these.

(*ii*) **Vertically organized manufacturing.** More commonly, the product of one industry becomes the raw material of another. The tanning industry thus supplies the boot and shoe industry. The spinning industry supplies the weaving, at least in areas like Lancashire where the two are geographically and organizationally distinct, and the weaving supplies the cloth-finishing mills and the latter the clothing industry. This type of manufacturing is described as *vertically organized* because the commodity moves through the branches in sequence before reaching the wholesaler, retailer and market (Fig. 9.2(*b*)).

The several branches of a vertically structured industry tend to be carried on in close proximity; tanning, for example was once important in the East Midlands, the former home of the British footwear industry. The consequent economies, especially those of transport costs, may occasionally be offset by other factors. In the aluminium-smelting industry, the crude bauxite must first be processed to remove impurities and to obtain the pure oxide, alumina. Since this purification involves a very considerable reduction in bulk (nearly half the ore may be discarded) it is usually carried out close to the quarries from which the ore is taken. The final refining, however, is carried out electrolytically, and is extravagant of electric power. The chief aluminium refineries are thus located close to major sources of hydro-electric power, even though this may necessitate a very long haul—from West Africa to the western Highlands of Scotland, for example, or from the West Indies to British Columbia.

(*iii*) **Horizontally organized manufacturing.** Most manufacturing today relies heavily on components which are made elsewhere and delivered to a factory ready to fit or install, so that the final process consists mainly of the assembly of components. Automobile manufacture is pre-eminently an assembly-line industry, with parts brought from a great number of factories to a convenient central point. In many instances—window glass, electrical systems, tyres, for example—one components factory may supply several rival or competing assembly workshops. Fig. 9.2(*c*) represents the structural organization of such an industry, though not its complexity.

(*iv*) **Complementary manufacturing.** A factory may diversify its range of production in order either to employ plant, equipment or labour that might otherwise have been idle, or to use a by-product of its primary manufacturing process.

For instance, suppose a factory is established to make jam. It boils fruit and sugar, bottles the product and markets it. But fruit is in season only for a short period of the year, and it therefore imports oranges to occupy part of the slack season. It is led on to manufacture a variety of foodstuffs having little obvious connection with jam. It grows its own fruit and thus becomes involved in other aspects of farming. It preserves vegetables, makes soups, sells milk and builds up a complex and heterogeneous industrial structure.

This kind of complementary activity, represented in Fig. 9.2(*d*), is now a common feature of the food industries, in which a great range of dissimilar products are associated under one brand name.

Lastly, some industrial processes generate by-products which themselves give rise to subsidiary processing plant (Fig. 9.2(e)). Examples are common in the chemical and petrochemical industries. The old-fashioned gas-works produced coal tar and ammonium sulphate as by-products of coal gas, and these were valuable starting-points for other branches of manufacture, usually at different sites.

(c) Ownership and Control of Manufacturing

The ownership and control of manufacturing parallel in many ways the functional structure described in the last section. In most countries manufacturing industry remains in the private sector of the economy. Only in the communist bloc is it wholly nationalized. In the United Kingdom iron and steel, shipbuilding, aircraft manufacture and part of the automobile industry are in the public sector. In other branches of industry decisions regarding scale and organization are made in the board room, though government can usually influence them if it wishes to do so.

Factories associated with one another in any of the structural patterns already discussed may belong to separate and wholly independent companies. It is unlikely, however, that they will act entirely independently of each other. They may, for instance, have long-term agreements for the supply of materials or components at prearranged prices. There may be some degree of common control, though the arrangement may be disguised: firms may retain their original names for trading purposes, while their managements may be so interlocked that they become in effect one unit. A predominating interest in a group of firms may be in the hands of a single 'holding' company, co-ordinating the activities of the subsidiaries. Or a number of firms, while remaining in most respects distinct, may form a federation known as a *cartel* or *trust*, which may fix prices, check wasteful competition or allocate a production quota to each firm or factory. The extremes of monopoly are rightly condemned, but the formation of such units is sometimes a means of *rationalizing* an industry, that is, of organizing it in a less wasteful and more profitable and efficient manner.

Some manufacturing companies have attempted to protect themselves by extending their control both backwards to the sources of their raw materials and the factories which supply their components, and also forwards to the purchasers of their by-products and the organizations marketing their manufactures. This is known as *vertical integration*. When a company gains control of other companies operating in the same field so that it dominates the market the process is sometimes called *horizontal integration*. Both processes have been very active in recent decades, leading to the creation of giant corporations, such as Unilever and Imperial Chemical Industries in the United Kingdom and US Steel and the Exxon Petroleum Company in the United States.

9.3 Industrial Location.

The manufacturer aims to produce at the lowest cost, to sell as widely as possible, and to make the maximum profit. In this the location of his manufacturing activity is an important factor. Since transport costs form a significant part of his total manufacturing outgoings, the choice of a site which minimizes the expense of moving raw materials, components and finished goods is greatly to his advantage.

Transport costs are not the only factor in the location of industrial activity. Certain material advantages are highly localized, and cannot be transported—a large supply of water, for example—but may be no less necessary. Space for factory development, a plentiful supply of labour, or congenial surroundings which might attract labour, are all important, and the publicity value of a factory site on a well-travelled highway may also confer some advantage. We must, however, distinguish between manufacturing industries which developed many years ago, and those which have been established in recent decades after prolonged and careful examination of the market and of production conditions.

(a) Traditional Industries

Many traditional British industries originated in response to transport and market conditions that have now wholly disappeared: iron-smelting and steelmaking in the Midlands and on the South Wales coalfields, cottons in Lancashire, woollens in Yorkshire and shipbuilding along the banks of the Tyne and Clyde. Often a location was chosen simply because that was where an entrepreneur lived or owned some asset which he could use. He *might* have been more successful on a different site, but only with the benefit of hindsight can this be determined.

Once established, an industry tends to build up an *infrastructure* — means of transport, supply and marketing organizations—to serve its needs. The greater this capital accumulation, the less practicable it is for the industry to change its location, at least until its primary plant becomes obsolescent and can be written off. It is then possible to make a start elsewhere in a new and more carefully considered location. One example of the relocation of a long-established industry is the shift of the United States textile industry, once centred mainly in New England, to the southern States. Another is the closing down of the Welsh iron industry which had been established in the eighteenth century near Merthyr Tydfil, Dowlais and Tredegar, and the creation of a more modern industry on the coast near Port Talbot and Newport.

The more developed countries are strewn with decaying manufacturing centres in which the costs of closing and abandoning old plant are very nearly matched by the economies of building new factories on sites more favourably placed with reference to the factors of production.

(b) New Industries

These may be old manufacturing industries relocated with a view to securing greater economies, but the class also includes new activities brought into being by advancing technology, such as the production of man-made fibres and electronic equipment. Location factors for these industries will have been very carefully considered, though the task of the entrepreneur today is in some respects easier than that of his nineteenth-century predecessor. The latter probably depended on coal-fired steam engines, and would have been concerned to secure easy access to the coalfields. Today's manufacturer is very much more likely to use electric power, which can be brought to his works by overhead cable from very great distances. One important constraint on industrial location has thus largely disappeared, but the entrepreneur must still consider problems of transport, labour supply and—a very recent concept—environmental damage.

9.4   Factors in Industrial Location

(*a*) Transport and Industrial Location

The location of a manufacturing activity is likely to be influenced by the availability of its raw materials, the location of its markets and the presence of means of transport to link them all together.

(*i*) **Raw materials.** The transport costs incurred in acquiring raw materials may be minimized by locating near to the source of the materials. The availability of raw material is, however, less important in locating industry than formerly, because materials are used more efficiently and the real costs of transport have declined with the introduction of improved techniques. Moreover, more than one material is frequently needed, it may cost little more to transport materials over 100 kilometres than over 10 (see Unit 12.1(*b*)), and management is likely to want the option to switch its demands between competing sources. Only where bulk is greatly reduced during processing is manufacturing strongly attracted to the source of raw materials, since in such instances transporting the raw material is more costly than transporting the product.

(*ii*) **Fuel and power.** When factory industry was first introduced, it was strongly attracted to the coalfields. This attraction was reduced by the construction of canals and then of railways, and today no longer exists. Indeed, the opposite is true, and industry is tending to leave the coalfields, because of the introduction of alternative, more mobile sources of power, notably oil and electricity. Electricity has the advantage that it can be used in very large units or very small, and can be transmitted wherever pylons and cables can be erected. The proximity of fuel is in fact really significant only to the power-generating industry and certain energy-intensive metallurgical industries.

This implies, of course, that either mineral fuel or hydro-electric power is available. In some regions of the world these are scarce commodities, and the cost of imported fuel is necessarily high. Here the absence of sources of fuel and power unquestionably discourages industrial development.

(*iii*) **Markets.** There is a strong tendency for manufacturing industries to be drawn towards their market, or at least to the largest sector of their market. This is in part because many consumer goods—furniture, for example—are awkward to package and expensive to transport, in part because the market is likely to be a source of labour, and in part because a conspicuous site in the heart of a consuming area can provide useful publicity. Industries which involve an increase in weight through the addition of a readily available raw material such as water (brewing, for example) are attracted towards the market. Market attraction is also the norm for those industries which involve an increase in volume, such as the production of electrical goods, or which manufacture a perishable product, such as bakeries. Consumer-goods industries which are not closely tied to any particular site tend to be attracted to the large centres of population. London is the largest manufacturing centre in Great Britain, but most of its industries could be carried on as effectively in the Midlands, the North or Scotland. They are attracted to the capital because it represents a significant part of their rather diffused market area.

In Unit 9.2(*b*)(*ii*), we discussed the interdependence of some manufacturing concerns, in which the product of one firm becomes the raw material for another. In such an instance the latter constitutes a market for the former and the two are likely to be relatively close together; this is illustrated by the clustering of car-components factories of the West Midlands where much of the automobile industry is located (cf. Fig. 10.6). This is one example of a group of industries which are usually found close to one another because of their mutual relationship as producers and consumers, and benefit from *agglomeration* or clustering.

(*iv*) **Industrial location theory.** The role of transport costs in industrial location is central to the *theory of industrial location* put forward by Alfred Weber in 1909. Weber assumed that the source of the industrial raw material and the market for the finished product were in different places, as in practice they almost always are. He further assumed that transport costs were directly related to distance and to the weight of the goods being moved. The best location, he claimed, is that which minimizes the costs of transporting goods between the two points. The location of a manufacturing industry in relation to its market and the source of raw materials is thus a function of the extent to which raw materials lose weight during the production process. If there were no change in weight, processing could, in theory, take place at any point on a line between material source and market. If, on the other hand, there was a loss in weight then transport costs would be lowest if the raw material was processed at its source. The converse would be true if the manufacturing processes led to weight gain.

Reality is, however, never as simple as this. There is almost always more than one raw material or component, especially if fuel is included as it must be in any cost analysis. The situation for two raw materials and one market is represented in Fig. 9.3, in which *A* and *B* are the sources of raw materials I and II and *C* is the market. The industry will always locate within the triangle formed by *A*, *B* and *C*. If there is a loss of mass in either or both of the raw materials the optimum location will be nearer *A* and *B* than *C*, but always nearer the source of that material which loses the greater proportion of its mass. Thus if more of material I is required than material II, then the optimum location will be nearer *A* than *B*. The same principles apply for any number of raw material sources and markets — although their application might be a long and complicated business!

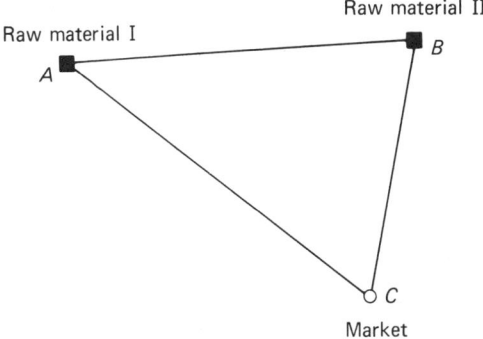

Fig. 9.3 Diagram illustrating Alfred Weber's theory of the location of industry

The importance of Weber's theory lies in the emphasis that it places on the costs of transport. On the assumption (not strictly justifiable) that these are directly related to weight and distance, it should be possible to define the point at which total transport costs are reduced to a minimum. But, like most theories, Weber's is deficient in several ways.

In the first place, many—perhaps most—manufacturing industries derive each of their materials from more than one source, and the relative importance of each source varies with changes in economic conditions. The most desirable location for material from one source might be quite unsatisfactory if material from another source had to be used.

Secondly, the Weber theory assumes that the surface over which goods are moved is isotropic, and that they can move equally easily in all directions. In reality, there already exists a network of roads, railways and canals, and any new manufacturing enterprise must adapt its location to this network.

Thirdly, the market is not a single point, like the factory itself. It is usually widely spread, though there may be within it large and important centres of consumption.

Lastly, freight rates are not a simple function of weight and distance. It is usual for carriers to grant concessionary freight rates, especially when a particular commodity is moved at regular intervals. Nor is weight the only significant characteristic of a raw material or product. Volume, fragility and ease of handling also significantly influence transport costs.

Nevertheless, the Weber model does provide a simple framework for the analysis of industrial location. That transport costs have a role to play is irrefutable and while Weber did not consider the full impact of many other factors that can influence location, he did demonstrate under what circumstances agglomeration economies and labour savings could cause an industry to be deflected from the least-transport-cost location.

(b) Labour

The supply and conditions of labour are increasingly important in the location of industry. Once almost all factory workers were skilled, but today most are at

Fig. 9.4 (a) Nineteenth-century textile mills in Lancashire, surrounded closely by artisans' houses;

best semi-skilled, supported by a very small number of highly trained professionals. Industry no longer has to go in search of 'suitable' labour; usually almost any labour will do provided that it can be given a short course of training.

Labour nowadays is increasingly mobile; workers frequently live at considerable distances from the factory, and also move readily from one job to another. Nineteenth-century factories were often surrounded by the terraced houses of their workers, but today such space is more likely to be given over to car parks. If the worker finds difficulty in selling his home and purchasing another, he can nevertheless 'commute' over large distances, and thus has great flexibility in his choice of employment.

Labour, lastly, is highly unionized in most developed countries. This has had the effect of raising general wage levels and improving working conditions, and also of evening out local variations in rates of pay. But wage differentials are not usually a decisive factor *within* a country, though the American South has lower rates than the northern states, and labour is cheaper in southern Italy than in the north. As between countries, however, the situation is quite different. Such branches of industry as are free to move find the low wages prevailing in Hong Kong, Singapore or Taiwan highly attractive; but only industries which are very labour-intensive and which produce easily and cheaply transported goods such as electronic equipment, embroidery and clothing find it worth their while to set up factories in these areas.

If the employer cannot expect to find cheap labour without going abroad for it, he can at least look for a docile or well-disciplined labour force. Many would

(b) a modern factory in a rural setting in Bedfordshire; extensive car parks are necessary since most employees use their own cars to drive to and from work

willingly sacrifice certain site economies in order to secure freedom from wild-cat and other strikes. Some industries—notably automobile manufacture—have been particularly prone to disastrous interruptions that have cost the industry far more than the most disadvantageous site could have done.

(c) Considerations of Public Policy

When most of our traditional industries were established, it was government policy to remove all obstacles to the freedom of action of industrial firms: the prevailing belief was that what was good for British shipbuilding or British textiles was good for the country. Though the government did enact some social and safety legislation, it did nothing to influence the location or size of plant.

This policy—or lack of it—has changed dramatically, especially since the structural decay of industry became apparent after the First World War. Some branches of industry declined for technical or resource reasons or through changes in popular taste or preference, leaving pools of unemployment in certain regions. The government assumed the necessary though nonetheless unwelcome task of restoring prosperity to these areas by locating suitable industries there. Trading estates were established and certain subsidies were made available to encourage the setting up of new factories in these regions.

The role of government in the location of industry has since grown rather than diminished. The Great Depression in the 1930s led to more strenuous efforts to stimulate industry, especially in the areas where unemployment was at its worst. Sometimes the most elementary principles of industrial location were violated in order to establish a factory in a place where it seemed politically desirable to have one. For example, an integrated iron and steel plant was built at Ebbw Vale in the Welsh mountains, even though the site necessitated transporting iron ore inland from the ports, and the steel products back again to the ports. Not surprisingly the plant has now been closed, and has in effect been replaced by new plant on the South Wales coast.

We have already mentioned the attractive force of Greater London; the government intervened to check the movement of manufacturing industry to the capital by creating a number of 'new' or satellite towns, each separated from London by a 'green belt'. Industries have been encouraged to settle in these new towns, and in similar towns in the West Midlands and in central Scotland.

In addition to locating new industries, governments have sometimes sought to preserve those which have been long established but have declined in importance, usually in order to maintain employment opportunities. While governmental policy on industrial location has been inspired very largely by social considerations, the protection of the environment has more recently become an important influence on policy. Environmental factors include the sterilization of the land by the extraction of minerals, the pollution of the atmosphere, the contamination of rivers and water supply by industrial effluents, the destruction of wildlife and the loss of rural amenities. All must be put into the balance of social gain and loss which results from the location of any industrial activity.

(d) Other Factors

A number of other factors influencing industrial location can be identified. The *cost and availability of capital* varies in different parts of the world and this variability provides a partial explanation of the concentration of manufacturing in the developed, compared with the developing, countries (see Unit 14).

Certain industries have special *site requirements*—perhaps for extensive areas of flat land, as in the case of a modern integrated iron and steel plant. Other industries, such as the nuclear power industry or some chemical industries, may require sites where the controlled disposal of wastes and pollutants is possible. For an industry that is a large user of land, the *cost of land* may play a significant role in the location decision.

In the final analysis the locational decision—that is, the decision where to produce, whether or not it is made rationally—depends on the decision-taker's *perception* of the comparative locational advantages of a large number of possible sites.

(For questions on the material in this Unit, see the end of Unit 10.)

Unit Ten

The Pattern of World Manufacture

Unit 9 discussed, in a very generalized manner, the factors in the location of manufacturing industry, showing how varied and complex they are. On close examination, the geographical pattern of modern manufacturing shows little evidence of logical choice of location on the part of the early entrepreneurs. With the benefits of hindsight, a great many industrial locations can be condemned as irrational and not calculated to maximize profits and minimize costs. Nevertheless the location of manufacturing is not random; certain types of site are selected relatively frequently for certain types of industry, and this unit discusses the principal categories of manufacturing according to the ways in which entrepreneurs have perceived their location requirements.

We must first distinguish between the *site* and the *situation* of an industry or plant. The site represents its positioning in the narrow and local sense, as alongside a railway or canal, or beside a dock; the situation denotes its placing in its broad context—on a coalfield, for instance, or at a port, or close to the market. Site is a matter of local convenience and planning consent; situation is one for careful and detailed consideration.

10.1 The Historical Factor

In all the developed countries, the pattern of manufacturing is strongly influenced by its past. In Europe it evolved among communities which were each self-sufficing in most of the basic necessities of life. Each spun and wove, built huts and made tools, according to the aptitudes of its people and the natural endowment of its territory. During the Middle Ages these simple crafts, universal in their distribution, became more and more highly localized and specialized. This was made possible only by the improvements in the means of exchange; transport became easier and a money economy more general. Slowly and haltingly, locations with the greatest relative advantage increased their share of production and distributed their produce more widely. *A*'s increased activity brought with it a decline in its less favoured neighbour, *B*; meanwhile *C*, on the further side of *B*, benefited from the weakened competition from *B*, until it too met the full blast of *A*'s commercial strength. This is a simple rationalization of the kind of process by which the industries of medieval England came to be distributed. But we cannot precisely know the factors which gave *A* its initial advantage; was it some natural endowment in raw materials, or one enterprising man's initiative, or convenience of transport, or even a miracle wrought by a local saint? We can only consider the early distribution of an industry, and see whether it helps us to understand the present.

Once established, however irrational its situation may subsequently appear to be, an industry tends to remain fixed as long as society has need of it. Its sources of raw materials or power may change completely, while local advantage in soft water or damp atmosphere may become available elsewhere, either naturally or artificially. However, a large volume of capital will have been sunk in the industry's fixed assets of factory buildings, machinery and roads. It will have built up a body of 'goodwill', as well as an infrastructure of transport, insurance, brokerage and the means of supply of subsidiary raw materials and of disposal of by-products, and it will have recruited and trained labour. All these 'inertia' factors act to discourage it from leaving its original situation.

An industry will probably move only if it can be managed more efficiently and more cheaply elsewhere. Such a move is likely to be costly, and the cost will include the sacrifice of some or all of the factors we have mentioned. The additional profit from the new location would have to be sufficient to outweigh the capital loss consequent upon the shift. Examples of such relocation of industries are rare; more often an industry grows, not by additions to plant in an old and no longer favourable site, but rather in the establishment of new units in a situation more favourable in relation to the new balance in the factors of production.

Consider a simple example. The British iron and steel industry was first located close to supplies of iron ore and of charcoal for smelting. With the replacement of charcoal by coke, the smelting processes were transferred to the coalfields, which supplied not only the fuel but a certain quantity of iron ore from the coal measures. But when the local ores began to run out the location became relatively uneconomic. There was an increasing use of lower-grade ores, which because of the high proportion of useless matter were expensive to transport, while improved blast-furnace techniques reduced the amount of fuel required to produce a tonne of metal. Thus new furnaces and steel plants now tend to be built away from the coalfields, either on the iron ore, as in Lincolnshire and Northamptonshire, or on the coast, as at Dagenham and Port Talbot, where the raw materials can be imported relatively easily and cheaply. The older furnaces were not necessarily closed at once. Most remained in use until age, inefficiency or economic depression compelled their abandonment.

Thus the location of an industry cannot be explained wholly in terms of the adequacy of its present factors of production. No industries, not even those created *ab initio* by the planner, are wholly free from the influences of the past; on most of our industries the dead hand of history lies heavily indeed, and may influence their present distribution in any of four ways.

(*a*) An earlier pattern of industry may survive through the influence of the 'inertia' factors we have mentioned.

(*b*) An industry may have grafted on to itself a range of new activities with which it has little in common. The newer occupation may be designed to occupy a slack season, or to give employment to a type of labour which, owing to the demands of the predominant industry, is locally or temporarily abundant. It is thus complementary to the older or *primary* industry and carried on alongside it.

Thus the manufacturers of jam from English fruit turn in winter to making marmalade, jellies and other foods, while coal-mining areas, where female labour is relatively plentiful (see Unit 9.1(*d*)), have recently tended to attract certain clothing industries. Alternatively, the new industry may use a by-product of the primary industry, or furnish one of its essential requirements. It may thus be linked with the primary industry by the complementary nature of their labour needs or by the joint production or consumption of materials. In time, with changes in public demand, the younger industry may develop and eclipse or even exclude the older.

(*c*) An old-established industry may gradually cease to carry on its old manufacture and take on a new. The ancient straw-hat industry of Luton in Bedfordshire, for example, has over many years adapted itself to changing fashions, and felt hats have replaced 'boaters', with which they have nothing in common so far as raw materials are concerned. Similarly, the Oxford motor industry has grown out of a bicycle factory, while Rolls Royce's aircraft-engine manufacture evolved from that of cars; and the factories which once produced railway locomotives have now also turned to radically different forms of engineering.

(*d*) The decline of an industry, from whatever cause, is likely to leave a pool of unemployed labour, as well as assets such as factory buildings, railway facilities and transport nets. In the past this 'structural' unemployment often brought about a fall in wages, by intensifying the competition for fewer and fewer jobs. This in turn encouraged the development of fresh industries that could take advantage of the low labour rates and cheap premises. Though trades unions have been able to check the fall in wages and thus have reduced the mobility of industry, the United Kingdom government's policy towards its depressed and later its development areas is a large-scale example of the location of new industries so that they may take over the abandoned assets of the old (see Unit 13.4).

An example from the past is provided by the eighteenth-century decline of the East Anglian woollen industry, which resulted in an abundance of cheap labour in Norfolk and Suffolk. This in turn encouraged the silk industry to move out from Spitalfields and Bethnal Green, where wages were rising, so that during the nineteenth century a miscellaneous collection of industries came to colonize the area where the 'New Draperies' had once ruled supreme. They were all loosely connected with textile working, which allowed them to benefit from certain surviving skills, but their predominant characteristic was that they took over at second hand and at a knockdown price the derelict assets of an extinguished industry. Fig. 10.1 shows how the old and the new industrial patterns are so closely similar that their history is almost implicit in the maps.

10.2   Raw-materials-oriented Industries

Some manufacturing industries are attracted to the source of their raw materials either because there is a great loss of bulk in processing (see Unit 9.1(*b*)) or

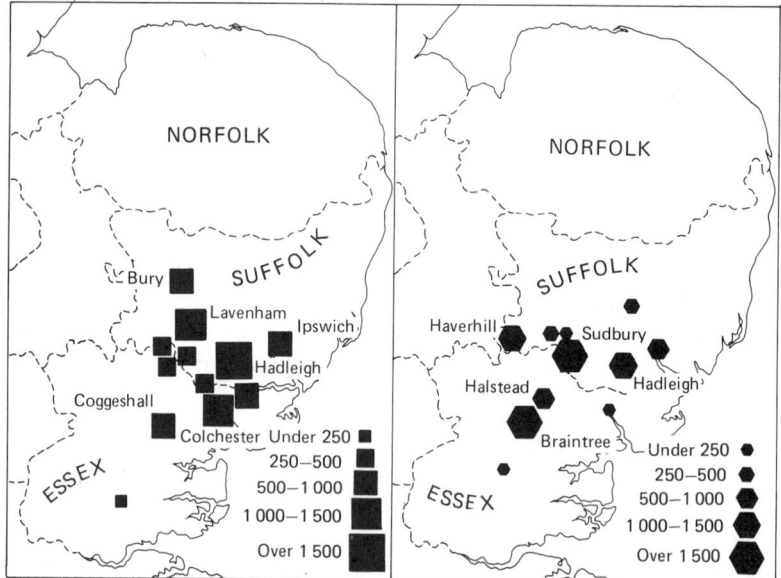

Fig. 10.1 (a) Distribution of East Anglian cloth production in 1468; the key indicates the number of pieces of cloth made (based on figures supplied by Miss J. B. Mitchell from documents in the Public Record Office); (b) present-day textile industries in East Anglia; the key indicates the numbers of people employed

because the materials are difficult or awkward to transport. Most are associated with mineral-processing.

(a) Cement and Bricks

Brick-making consists of digging clay, usually from a shallow pit, shaping it in a mould and firing it in a kiln. There is no significant loss of bulk and there would appear to be no reason why the industry should not be carried on close to the market or at the source of fuel. In fact the kilns are almost always found close to the clay-pit. This is because the unprocessed clay is intractably difficult to handle and transport. Any clay deposit of suitable quality *may*—provided there is a demand for bricks—attract a brick-making industry. In Great Britain the chief sources of bricks are the clays of the East Midlands, especially those found near Bedford and Peterborough.

Cement is now very much more important in building construction than bricks, but its manufacture too is narrowly restricted, in this case to locations where the raw materials—chalk and clay—are both available. In Europe at least, these are often found in the more densely populated areas, along the lower Thames valley, for example, so that the industry is in fact close to its market.

(b) Smelting Industries

Since there is a very great loss in weight during smelting, these industries might be expected to be found close to the orefields, and for many non-ferrous metals

Fig. 10.2 A Yorkshire brickworks, sited very close to the clay-pit that supplies its raw material

this is true. The grade of these ores (see Unit 7.4(*b*)) is so low that long-distance transport becomes impracticably expensive, especially if it involves a break of bulk. On the other hand, very few metalliferous ores occur in close proximity to fuel resources, and smelting at, or close to, the mine may necessitate a costly movement of fuel.

To this dilemma there are several solutions. The first consists in the partial smelting of the ore, which may use much less fuel than would be needed for complete refining. A *matte* containing perhaps 90 per cent metal is thus produced and can be shipped economically for further refining elsewhere. Part of the copper mined in Zaïre and Zambia is marketed in this form. Aluminium too is produced from bauxite by a two-stage process (see Unit 9.2(*b*)(*ii*)) in which the initial step consists only of the concentration of the ore and the elimination of most of the waste. The beneficiation of low-grade iron ore (taconite) in the Upper Great Lakes region of the United States before export to the smelting centres is another example. Much, however, depends on the kind and quality of the ore and the degree to which it can be separated from the unwanted *gangue* materials.

An alternative solution to the problem lies in the use of electric power, which is increasingly important in the metallurgical industries. It is often available in areas—Scandinavia and central Africa, for instance—which are deficient in or even devoid of coal, and it can usually be carried to a smelter more easily than solid fuel. In the electrolytic refining of aluminium, already mentioned, the demand for current is so great—32 000 amperes can be required—that the final process is drawn to major sources of hydro-electric power, such as Norway, the French Alps, British Columbia and the Rocky Mountains of the United States.

(*i*) **Iron industry.** Like other basic metallurgical industries, the iron-smelting industry is attracted to the source of its raw materials. The problem of location is, however, complicated by the varying grade of the ores, and hence the varying reduction of weight in their processing, by the relatively short lifetime of an orefield, and by the dependence of the conventional blast-furnace process on coking coal, together with the tendency for the ratio of available fuel to ore to diminish.

The traditional location of iron-smelting was close to the source of ore, provided there was an abundance of timber for charcoal. The early smelting industry was extravagant of fuel, and with the introduction of coke-smelting, the industry tended to gravitate towards the coalfields. Thus the West Midlands, West Yorkshire and the Glasgow region, the Ruhr, the Saint-Etienne region and Upper Silesia, western Pennsylvania and the Donetz basin all came to the fore during the nineteenth century. The so-called *blackband* ironstone was obtained widely though in small quantities from the coal measures, and the supply of ore from more distant sources was made practicable by the use of canals and—on an increasing scale—of the railways. Until the early twentieth century the iron-smelting industry appeared to be oriented strongly towards its source of fuel rather than that of the ore itself. But this orientation has now changed. In the first place the introduction of fuel economies, including the adoption of the continuous process which reduced heat loss, has diminished the attractiveness of the coalfields. Secondly, the exhaustion of domestic sources of ore in the developed countries has necessitated the import of ore from overseas. Lastly, the diseconomies of a coalfield site, where there is usually little scope for a modern, planned layout, have all tended to drive the industry to locate itself elsewhere.

To some extent there was a return to the orefields, in particular to the low-grade deposits of phosphoric ore of the scarplands of western and central Europe. Corby and Scunthorpe in England, the Salzgitter area of Lower Saxony and, above all, Lorraine and Luxembourg all became centres of the smelting industry with the works located on the orefields. The crucial factor was the low grade of the ore—from 25 to 35 per cent—so that there was a reluctance to transport it further than was absolutely necessary. The rest of Europe's ore supply came increasingly from overseas, including that from northern Sweden. Since this ore had to be unloaded from oceanic ore-carriers to barges or freight-cars at the docks, the most suitable location for the smelting industry appeared to be the docks themselves, especially as this allowed for great flexibility in the supply of ore. Iron-smelting thus joined the growing number of 'port industries' (see Unit 10.3).

In recent years, most new plants have been located on the coast (Fig. 10.3). Teesside and South Wales, along with Scunthorpe on the scarplands orefield,

Fig. 10.3 Ore is brought by sea-going carriers direct to Port Talbot steelworks on the South Wales coast

have become the principal British centres of the industry. Coastal sites are increasingly important in continental Europe, especially in Italy, and in North America most recent developments have been either on the tidewater, as near Baltimore and Philadelphia, or on the shores of the Great Lakes, where they are accessible to sea-going ore-carriers. Coastal locations are also usual in Japan, which has to rely on imported ore, and in Australia where domestic ore is largely moved by sea-going carrier. Most of the locational patterns conform with one of the models represented in Fig. 10.4, which illustrates the varying relationships of smelting, refining and fabricating, from a traditional charcoal–iron industry, located beside a river in order to use water power, to a modern works sited on the coast.

(*ii*) **Steel industry.** The steel industry consumes almost all of the crude iron produced. Traditionally, the two branches of the industry were geographically separate. At one time smelting remained close to the source of ore, while refin-ing—mainly by the notoriously fuel-extravagant puddling process—moved to the coalfields. Then, in the later nineteenth century, the introduction of the new open-hearth and converter methods of refining made it practicable, even desirable, to economize in fuel, and smelting and refining processes thenceforward tended to be merged at a single site. Molten iron could thus be introduced directly or by way of a 'mixer' from the furnace into the steel-making plant. Further economies in fuel were achieved by passing the white-hot ingots from the steel-making works direct to the rolling mill. As the rolling process became 'continuous', as opposed to the older reversing rolls, it became quicker, and could be completed without the need to reheat the metal. Thus the fully integrated iron and steelworks emerged during the present century. To be

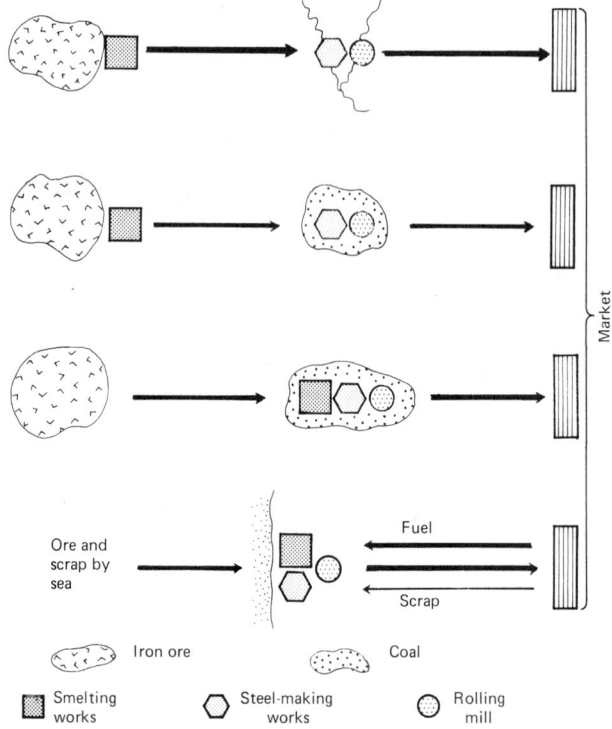

Fig. 10.4 Models representing typical locations of iron and steel production in relation to ore, to fuel and power, and to the market

economic it had to be large, with an annual capacity of 2 to 3 million tonnes of ingot steel. It was relatively less fuel-dependent than earlier forms of organization had been, and any necessary reheating of metal could usually be done with natural gas piped to the site, or with coal gas, a by-product of the local coke-ovens. An enormous site is needed for plant layout; Llanwern covers 200 hectares, far more than could be found within the part-congested, part-derelict area of the coalfields.

Almost 30 per cent of the world's steel production derives from the scrap generated by a wasteful modern society, which can be re-refined with relatively little fuel and re-rolled into half-finished steel goods. A steel industry may thus be located with reference primarily to the supply of scrap metal. A developed society generates a great deal of scrap metal, and some countries—Japan is the foremost example—find it expedient to import scrap, much of it in the form of derelict ships to be broken up.

(c) Other Branches of Manufacturing
Not all those industries which can be described as in some way raw-materials-oriented are concerned with mineral-processing. Many industries which use raw

materials of vegetable origin have been attracted to their source. Jute-processing, for instance, is heavily concentrated in Bengal (India) and Bangladesh, where the jute is grown. Most of the United States textile industry has been attracted to the south, though other factors besides the supply of raw cotton are also involved. The wood-pulp industry is found almost exclusively on the fringes of the softwood forests which supply the logs.

Food-processing industries are even more strongly drawn to the source of their raw materials, many of which are liable to perish quickly after harvesting. Fruit- and vegetable-preserving must be carried on close to the farms, and flour-milling is often found near the cornfields. Meat-packing is located where live animals can be driven into the plant, and the tanning and sometimes the leather-using industries are to be found near the slaughter-houses which supply the skins and hides.

10.3   Port Industries

These might well be called the 'break-of-bulk' industries. They consist essentially in the processing of raw materials imported by sea, mainly from tropical or equatorial regions where for a variety of reasons it is not practicable to establish their manufacture; some derived their raw materials mainly from the former colonial empires of the United Kingdom and France. Most are capital-intensive.

Some of these industries are concerned with processing vegetable oils and oil-seeds, usually of equatorial origin; they produce margarine and other edible fats, soap, cattle cake and other forms of animal feedstuffs. Others refine cane sugar, or roast and prepare coffee; some mill cereals, or smelt metalliferous ores. Added to these is a branch of industry which can be carried on nowhere else — shipbuilding and ship-repairing.

Oil-refining, too, tends to be drawn to a break-of-bulk location, generally a coastal one. Crude oil is transported most easily and safely by tanker, and the larger the tanker the smaller are transport costs as a proportion of total costs. Immense quantities of crude oil are therefore discharged at the terminal ports where storage facilities are to be found, and this point is thus often the best location for the refinery (Fig. 10.5). The use of pipelines, however, may make it possible to locate the refinery at some distance from the tanker port; for instance, Milford Haven, the most suitable port in South Wales for giant tankers, was not at first acceptable as the site of a refinery, and pipelines were built to carry the oil to be refined 100 km away at Llandarcy, near Swansea. Nevertheless most of the major refineries established by the consuming countries are coastal; Thameshaven, Shellhaven and Fawley in Great Britain are examples.

10.4   Other Factors in Location

A few industries, including some associated with food-processing, are drawn towards their market. The baking of bread continues to be carried on close to the

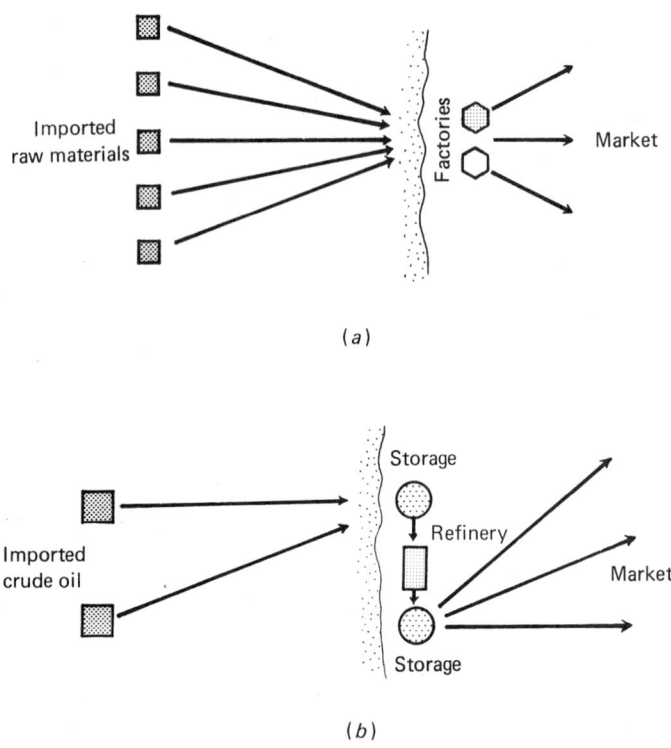

Fig. 10.5 Models representing typical port industries: (a) manufacture of commodities such as soap; (b) oil-refining

consuming centres. This was once true also of the brewing of beer, though modern preserving and packaging methods now enable this to be centred mainly in a small number of very large breweries.

A great many industries gravitate towards the market with the aim of thereby reducing their total transport costs. It is far from certain that they are doing so. Most are 'footloose' industries, with no strong attraction to any particular location. They commonly require good means of transport by road or rail. Such industries include the manufacture of clothing and of furniture, printing, light engineering, die-stamping and the assembly of electrical and electronic equipment, and the making of domestic and kitchen equipment. This is a very wide range of industries, but everything in it will be found in Greater London, or indeed in any major conurbation. A market-oriented location for these industries is appropriate because they use relatively little raw material and produce goods which are sometimes bulky, even clumsy to transport. Many are labour-intensive, requiring deft but only semi-skilled and often female labour, which the larger consuming areas can generally supply.

Four highly important categories of manufacturing have so far been omitted from this discussion, because they are too complex to lend themselves to a simple classification according to factors of production. They are the textile, chemical, heavy engineering and automobile industries.

(a) Textile Industries

The textile industries are as universal as the food industries and almost as varied. They draw upon materials of vegetable origin (cotton, flax, hemp, jute), of animal origin (wool, mohair, silk) and even of chemical origin (man-made fibres like nylon and Terylene). All, however, have certain processes in common: the production of a thread, either by spinning or extrusion, and the weaving or knitting of a fabric. They usually require certain finishing processes, such as bleaching, dyeing and printing. The similarity of the techniques employed in most branches of the textile industries has meant that they have tended to be closely associated spatially. The same place may produce two or more kinds of textile fabric, and there are even mills that make both woollens and cottons. The degree of separation to be found in the United Kingdom between woollens, cottons, linen, jute and the synthetic fibres is quite unusual amongst the developed countries, in most of which the individual branches are closely linked. There are numerous areas that have changed their emphasis from, say, linen to cotton, or from cottons to woollens, in response to market demand.

The textile industries are to be found almost everywhere, so that the location process has consisted less in choosing a place where cloth could be made than in eliminating places which were unsuitable for the industry on a large-scale or a factory basis. In Europe, at least, local advantage in the textile industry consisted in the possession of good-quality raw materials and the entrepreneurial skills to use them to advantage. The industry was carried on domestically, and the supply of power, even of water power, was not at first important. Certain cloth-working regions emerged: East Anglia, the west of England, the Low Countries, especially Flanders, northern France, and northern Italy and Florence. All these had some small advantage in the supply of raw materials, but this was probably of less importance than the initiative of the leaders of the industry.

In the eighteenth and early nineteenth centuries the European industry began to be mechanized. Although water power was at first the source of energy, the steam engine quickly replaced it, and many branches of the textile industry came to be anchored to the coalfields. The progression from hand-spinning and the hand-loom to machine-spinning and the power-loom was neither simple nor inevitable. Many people strenuously resisted mechanization, believing that it would lead to a loss in quality, and the introduction of new textile materials, such as cotton, was also opposed. The result was that the diffusion of innovation was strongly influenced by the attitudes both of entrepreneurs and of the ordinary spinners and weavers. Cotton-working spread in Lancashire largely because the woollen industry there was not highly developed and could not offer serious resistance. The East Anglian woollen industry decayed in part because it clung to traditional methods, in part also because it catered in the main for a luxury market at a time when coarser and cheaper fabrics were in greater demand. The expansion of the industry in the West Riding (now West Yorkshire) was, in the words of the Barlow Report on the distribution of the industrial population, 'the ordinary case of a pushing, hardworking locality with certain slight advantages attacking the lower grades of an expanding industry'.

In continental Europe also the spatial pattern of the textile industry changed radically during the late eighteenth and nineteenth centuries, in response far more to the initiative of local entrepreneurs than to the intrinsic merits and disadvantages of particular locations. The only nineteenth-century instance of the creation of a textile *ab initio* was at Łódź, now in Poland; the German entrepreneurs chose the situation because it lay just within the tariff boundary of the Russian Empire, so that their produce could be sold freely throughout Russia. The site was, in terms of accepted factors of location, entirely unsatisfactory.

The geographical pattern of the textile industry is changing, like that of all other branches of industry. The traditional industry is in decline in much of the developed world, and from Lancashire to New England mills are closing, as demand shifts from wool and cotton to man-made fibres. To some extent the manufacture of man-made fibres has moved to old-established centres of the textile industry, such as East Anglia and Lancashire, but like other light consumer goods industries it is likely to be found in any densely peopled region.

(b) Chemical Industries

The earliest modern chemical industries consisted of the manufacture of a few common acids and alkalis and their use in the production of equally simple materials, such as glass and fertilizer. They tended to use cheap and bulky raw materials, and were thus oriented towards them. The chemical industries have since developed so immense a range and variety of products, from dyestuffs to pharmaceuticals, that it is impossible to generalize regarding their location. Some are produced in such small amounts and at so high a price that they can be made wherever labour is available and transport facilities are good. Oil-refining and the petrochemical industries are attracted to break-of-bulk points. Fuel continues to be important in the production of many chemicals, and for some constitutes a raw material

The production of plastics and synthetic fibres has become a major branch of the chemical industry. Most are made by polymerization, the process of building up very large molecules. Wood pulp is an important raw material for the production of rayon, and many plastics and man-made fibres are derived from petroleum. The whole complex of the plastics industries characterizes the developed countries which have evolved the elaborate technology and the mass demand for such goods.

(c) Engineering Industries

The heavy engineering industries must necessarily be closely connected with the iron and steelworks which supply their basic raw materials. Steel-making, however, has proved remarkably mobile, so that the engineering industries are more closely related to a former pattern of the iron and steel industry than to today's. This is clearly demonstrated by the importance of the engineering industries in the West Midlands, in central France and in parts of West Germany, where the smelting industries are now of negligible importance.

Transport can present problems, owing to the awkward and bulky shapes of some of the products. The West Midlands have thus tended to specialize in the lighter and more easily transported engineering products. Heavy steel constructions, of which drilling platforms for the oil industry represent the largest, most recent and most sophisticated form, are commonly made near the coast. Steel 'shapes', pipes and tubes are usually produced at the steel-making works, though steel ingots are often reheated for pressing and rolling, notably in the Birmingham–Wolverhampton region.

Light and electrical engineering are most often market-oriented. Prominent in their output are components for use in other industries, particularly the automobile industry. They are highly specialized and tend to be one another's best customers. In consequence they cluster in heavily industrialized regions, such as the West Midlands, West Yorkshire and Lancashire, and, in continental Europe, in northern France, central Belgium and the northern Rhineland. Some branches of the metal-using industries are also highly localized. The tinplate industry is associated with the western part of the South Wales coalfield, for no better reason than that the tin was formerly obtained from Cornwall. The British shipbuilding industry—or what remains of it—is located on the Tyne, the Clyde and at Belfast, all, except Belfast, close to sources of steel.

(d) Automobile Industries

Motor and aircraft manufacture make perhaps the widest demands on the products of other industries; both consist essentially of the assembly of a vast number of components. Since the structure of freight rates usually favours the shipment of components rather than that of finished goods, automobile companies have several assembly plants, each located with reference to a particular market.

In Great Britain the chief centres of the motor industry are in the West Midlands, particularly Birmingham and Coventry, with lesser nuclei at Oxford, Luton and Dagenham. In France much of the car industry is in Greater Paris, in Italy it lies in the populous and industrialized region between Turin and Milan, and in Germany, between Frankfurt and Stuttgart. The United States industry is dominated by Detroit, though component and assembly plants are found throughout the country. It is difficult to find any common factor in these locations, except that all lie in densely populated regions with a high consuming power.

The effect of modern technological development is to liberate manufacturing industry, or at least most branches of it, from close dependence on any narrowly circumscribed set of factors. Very few branches are strictly 'determined' in their location. For most, any losses incurred on the transport side in choosing a particular site are offset by gains in labour and amenities. The present industrial pattern is a heritage from the past, slowly being modified as obsolescent plants close and new works are opened. In locating these, social and political considerations are probably at least as important as the narrowly economic. The ideal location may still, in Dennison's words, be 'that which gives the lowest cost for a given output under given technical considerations'. But the 'cost' should be understood to include the unemployment and environmental damage which might ensue if the industry were moved.

10.5 Manufacturing Regions

We have emphasized that manufacturing industries are highly aggregative: that is, they tend to form clusters. At one time this arose because of their common dependence on a source of fuel. More recently it has been either because they depend on certain services—transport, commercial or technical—or, more often, because they constitute collectively each other's chief market. Such clusters are commonly termed *industrial regions*, though they may be difficult to define. Fig. 10.6 shows how the engineering and related industries in the English Midlands are distributed in a number of clusters centred on Manchester, Birmingham and other large cities. In each the frequency of industrial works diminishes with increasing distance from the urban centres, and the intervening areas have only a thin scatter of industry. Yet the Midlands are quite clearly distinguishable from the relatively unindustrialized regions of the Welsh Border, of Lincolnshire and East Anglia, and of southern England.

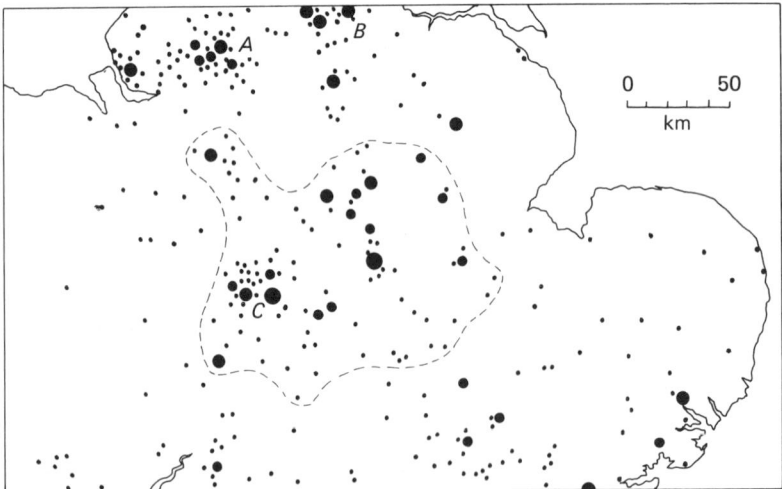

Fig. 10.6 Location of engineering and related industries in the English Midlands; the dotted line represents a suggested limit for the industrial region. The letters represent the following clusters: A, Manchester; B, Leeds; C, Birmingham

Fig. 10.7 shows the distribution of the American automobile industry, including assembly and components factories; this also appears as a cluster, with diminishing density as the distance increases from Detroit. If we were to superimpose on this map the patterns of other forms of industrial activity, with foci elsewhere than in Detroit—the steel industry, for example, with its nucleus in Pittsburgh—we should blur the pattern to some extent, but the result would be a number of overlapping clusters in the north-east of the United States. Similarly, we could build up a picture of clusters of industrial activity in the

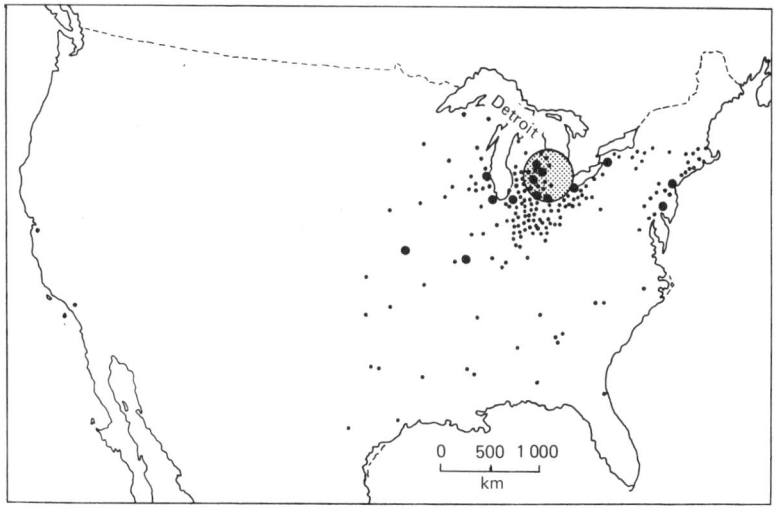

Fig. 10.7 The United States automobile industry: the largest proportion of employment is in Detroit. Note the clustering of factories in Michigan, Indiana and Ohio, and the 'distance-decay' from this area

United Kingdom, encroaching on one another to some extent, and extending from London to Lancashire, with outlying clusters in central Scotland, Tyneside, Cleveland, South Wales, Avon and Belfast. The optimum location appears to be at the centre of the cluster, where, however, land values, rates and other overhead costs are likely to be highest. Many enterprises are therefore driven away from the centre, some to the periphery where certain diseconomies, including perhaps higher transport charges, may be partially offset by lower overheads.

An industrial region is a grouping of such clusters. A line can be drawn around them, and the area enclosed can be described as the Midland, or central Belgian, or the Ruhr industrial region. Such a line has, however, to be drawn with care. It is unlikely to embrace all the manufacturing industry which looks to or is dependent upon a particular nucleus, and unless the geographer is fully conscious of the criteria he is adopting, the cartographic expression of industrial regions will have little meaning. In Fig. 10.6, for example, no less than a quarter of Midlands manufacturing industry is excluded from the region as shown, because it is scattered too thinly.

It is useful also to study the *degree of diversity* of industrial function within an industrial region. It is often said that the industrial base of the South Wales region is too narrow, that it relies too heavily on the steel and engineering industries and would suffer exceptionally if these were to become depressed. A similar degree of specialization marks Lancashire and West Yorkshire, the Ruhr, central Belgium and Upper Silesia. The Midlands and London, northern France and northern Italy are, on the other hand, relatively diversified. Government has sometimes attempted to remedy an overgreat specialization in a particular area by inducing other branches of industry to locate there.

It is possible to measure and compare the degrees of diversification in different regions, and even to represent this graphically. It is necessary first to define the region and the only practicable source is the census. These should then be arranged in ascending rank-order, as in Table 10.1.

Table 10.1   Percentage distribution of workers in 23 major industrial categories, in South Wales

		Per cent of workforce	Cumulative percentage
1	Leather and furs	0·2	0·2
2	Woodworking	0·7	0·9
3	Agriculture	0·8	1·7
4	Mining, other than coal	1·0	2·7
5	Printing and paper	1·0	3·7
6	Textiles	1·3	5·0
7	Insurance, banking	1·4	6·4
8	Other manufactures	1·5	7·9
9	Clothing	1·7	9·6
10	Gas, water, electricity	2·0	11·6
11	Food, drink, tobacco	2·5	14·1
12	Chemicals	2·7	16·8
13	Metal goods	2·9	19·7
14	Vehicles	3·4	23·1
15	Miscellaneous services	5·0	28·1
16	Public administration	5·4	33·5
17	Engineering	5·9	39·4
18	Building	7·1	46·5
19	Professions	7·8	54·3
20	Transport and communications	8·9	63·2
21	Metalworking	10·3	73·5
22	Distributive trades	10·5	84·0
23	Mining (coal)	16·0	100·0

Based on Conkling, E. C.: *A Geographical Analysis of Diversification in South Wales*, Northwestern University, Evanston, Illinois (1962)

In a region with a maximum degree of diversification, there would be an equal number of employees in each employment category. This is, however, unlikely in practice, as there is always one branch of industry which is well ahead of all others.

There are several ways of manipulating these data in order to measure and compare degrees of diversification. One way is to plot the successive cumulative percentages shown in the last column of Table 10.1 against the number of the industrial groups (Fig. 10.8), to produce a *Lorenz curve* (see Unit 1.8(e)). A

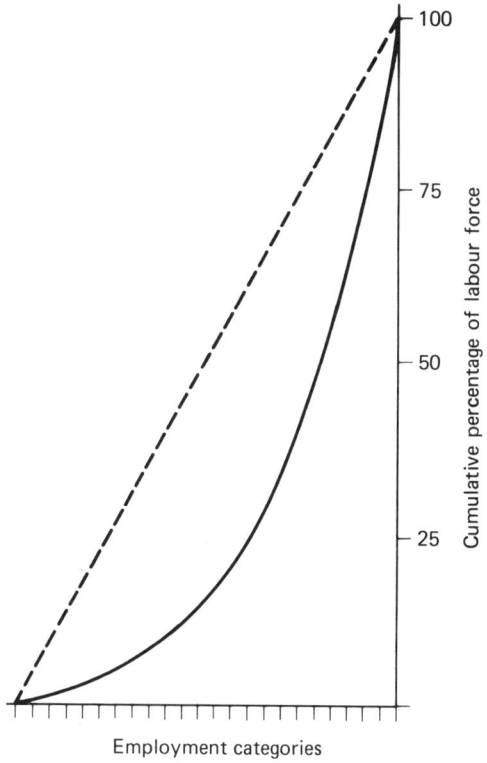

Fig. 10.8 A Lorenz curve, showing the level of diversification of manufacturing in a city

straight line represents the maximum degree of diversification; a very markedly concave curve shows that employment is highly concentrated in a few occupational categories. From the 1930s onwards, attempts have been made to diversify the economy of South Wales (as well as those of other traditional manufacturing areas). The Lorenz curves for employment in the region drawn for 1931, 1949 and 1959 are shown in Fig. 10.9: they make it clear that these efforts have met with only limited success.

Curves like these can be used for comparison with other regions or countries. It is essential, of course, to use the same occupational categories, such as those in the *Standard Industrial Classification* used by the United Kingdom government, for all the units being compared.

Table 10.2 presents the percentage employment in each of the seven categories used by the British government in its *Regional Statistics*. The data therein are weakened by the large number of occupational categories included among 'others'. Nevertheless Lorenz curves based on these statistics would show little variation between the regions—far less, in fact, than one's preconceived ideas

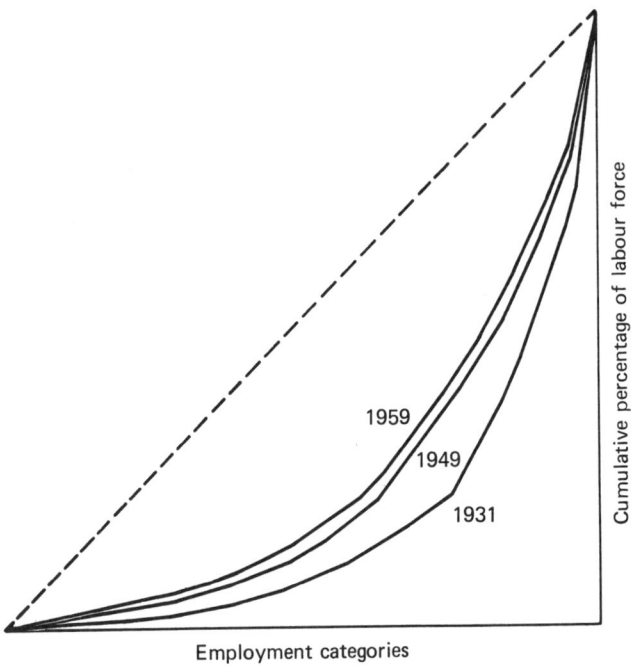

Fig. 10.9 Diversification of manufacturing in South Wales (after E. C. Conkling)

of where particular manufacturing industries are carried on might lead one to suppose.

10.6   Industrialization and Standards of Living

The mechanization of industrial processes allows a single worker to produce far more than he could ever have done manually. After all allowances have been made for the cost and maintenance of his mechanical equipment, he is still incomparably more effective. This means that a country in which manufacturing

Table 10.2   Employment in England (percentages)

	Yorkshire and Humberside	East Anglia	North-west	South-west	West Midlands	East Midlands	South-east	All England
Agriculture, forestry, fisheries	1·8	6·9	0·7	3·4	1·5	2·6	1·2	1·7
Manufacturing	38·4	30·8	40·3	29·5	48·1	41·6	27·4	34·8
Construction	5·7	6·8	5·4	6·4	4·8	5·2	5·0	5·5
Mining and quarrying	5·7	1·8	2·0	2·6	2·4	6·3	1·6	3·4
Distribution	11·4	12·6	12·1	13·8	10·5	10·7	13·3	12·3
Professional and scientific	14·6	15·8	13·8	15·7	12·3	12·5	16·0	14·6
Others	22·5	25·1	25·7	28·6	20·4	21·0	35·4	28·1

Source: *Regional Statistics*, No. 11, 1975, Central Statistical Office, HMSO

is highly mechanized produces more and has a higher gross national product per head than one which lacks modern factory industry. The increased industrial production does not necessarily result in a higher level of welfare. The surplus might be drained away in military expenditure or it might be re-invested in plant and equipment. It is likely, however, that some part of the increase will be passed on to the general body of the population in the form of a higher standard of living. In general, therefore, an industrialized country enjoys a higher living standard than a non-industrialized country, and the higher the level of industrialization the better will be living conditions.

As we saw in Unit 4.2, there is no satisfactory measure of living standards, nor of the level of industrialization, and in every country, including those which

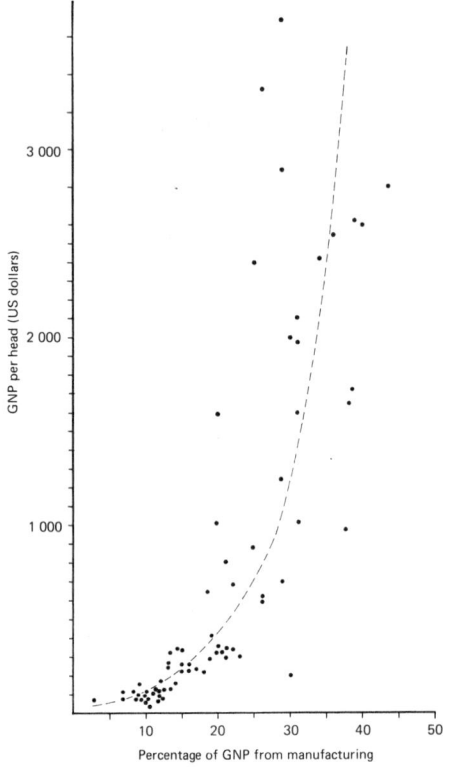

Fig. 10.10 The percentage of GNP from manufacturing, plotted against the GNP per head

make a parade of their equality, there are rich and poor. For purposes of comparison we must take *average* levels of welfare, and for this the only handy measure is gross national product (GNP) per head. As a measure of the level of manufacturing industry we can use the amount of energy consumed per head. How then does the level of manufacturing relate to the general level of

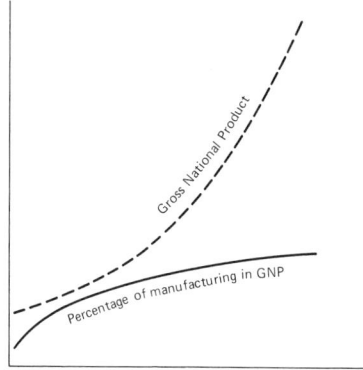

Fig. 10.11 Model to show the share of manufacturing in GNP with increasing GNP per head

production? Fig. 10.10 plots the one against the other, and shows that there is no simple relationship between them. The poorer countries derive very little of their GNP from manufacturing; increasing wealth is linked with a rising proportion of the GNP from this source, but above a level of about $1 500 per head there is little change. The richer countries rarely derive more than about 40 per cent of their GNP from manufacturing; with increasing wealth, a sharply increasing fraction of the GNP comes from tertiary activities such as transport and the provision of services (Fig. 10.11). Nevertheless, in the eyes of the poorer nations what divides them from the richer is, above all, their relative lack of manufacturing industries, and most of them pin their hopes for the future on remedying this deficiency. For this reason the industrialization of the developing world is discussed separately in the last unit of the book.

Questions

1. Under what conditions can domestic manufacturing be economically successful?
2. Why are the textile industries among the first to be adopted in a newly industrializing country?
3. Mechanization does not necessarily lower production costs. Discuss, with examples.
4. Explain what you understand by 'footloose' industries.
5. What are the chief factors to be considered in the location of (*a*) a new steel works, (*b*) an oil refinery, (*c*) a factory for the production of electronic components?
6. Some manufacturing industries can be described as gregarious. Explain why, citing examples.
7. Explain, with examples, what you understand by 'industrial inertia'.
8. Choose any important industrial region; examine the range of manufacturing carried on there, and the stages by which the region developed.

Unit Eleven

Trade and Service Functions

We have so far discussed only *primary* and *secondary* economic activities (see Unit 1.6). These however could not be carried on without *tertiary* activities, which are sometimes regarded as unproductive, and for this reason are omitted from the calculation of the GNP in most communist countries. They do not, it is true, yield tangible products, and some of their achievements are impossible to measure and difficult to put a price upon. Yet these tertiary activities are essential for the production processes.

11.1 Tertiary Activities

Tertiary activities include transport and trade, banking, finance and commercial organization, educational, cultural, medical and defence services, and indeed the whole apparatus of government. They are employing an ever-expanding proportion of the total population and contribute an increasing share of the GNP. In the United Kingdom, about 58 per cent of total employment is in this sector, and in the United States the proportion is similar.

The chief categories of tertiary or service activities can be summarized as follows:

(a) Government, Defence and National Security

This includes the personnel in both central and local government, the police and people serving in defence establishments. The largest concentration is likely to be found in the national capital, where its presence by a kind of multiplier effect increases the size of all other branches of service activity. There is nothing new in this; as far back as the sixteenth century the Italian political scientist Giovanni Botero wrote that 'the greatest means to make a city populous and great is to have supreme authority and power; for that draweth dependency with it, and dependency concourse, and concourse greatness.' The same is true, though in lesser degree, of local government. Every county hall and local government office provides services and creates employment, and thus has an important geographical dimension. Defence establishments, usually fewer and more concentrated than those in public administration, have nevertheless the same effect of bringing about large groupings of population and service industries. Any threat to the future of a military or naval base at once arouses howls of protest from shop-keepers and a host of non-military services whose prosperity is thereby endangered.

Fig. 11.1 A commodity market at work in the City of London; the coffee that is bought and sold here is not physically present and may not yet even have been harvested

(b) Transport

The movement of goods from one point to another is linked intimately with the production and manufacturing processes, whose location depends primarily on the provision of transport. However close these links may be, transport is nevertheless a tertiary activity or service; but because of its immense importance it is discussed separately in Unit 12.

(c) Wholesale and Retail Marketing

Goods produced in the factory or on the farm have to be made available to the consumer, and this is generally done in two stages. A wholesaler assembles, sorts, packs and transmits to the retail outlet, usually a shop, where the customer makes his purchase. The process is sometimes shortened; large chain stores, for example, combine the wholesaling and retailing functions. There may even be an additional stage in the process, as when a local wholesaler comes between the retail shop and the primary wholesaler.

The geographer is concerned primarily with the location of these activities. The siting of a retail shop must be closely related to the distribution of the consuming public, and the geography of market and shopping centres is discussed in Unit 11.4. The wholesaler requires storage space as his chief fixed asset, but is also heavily dependent on transport facilities, primarily by road. Depending on the range of goods in which he deals, he is likely to draw from a number of varied and widely separated sources. He will certainly deliver to a very much greater number of shops, which his vehicles will probably visit in turn to deliver small consignments of merchandise. The wholesale warehouse or storage depot is likely to be located as near as practicable to the largest number of retail outlets, and is thus consumer-oriented.

(d) Banking and Financial Institutions

The services these provide range from simple banking, mortgage and insurance transactions to merchant banking and security and commodity exchanges. Most of these call for 'face-to-face' transactions, at least in their initial stages. They must therefore be carried on where their customers are to be found. The small town will have one or two banks, a few house agents, and offices of a handful of mortgage and loan companies. There is also likely to be a stock-broker or two and representatives of some insurance firms. The number of such services is probably related to the size and also to the degree of affluence of the local population upon which they depend. Sometimes several of these functions are combined in a single person or office. All will, however, be linked with a branch or head office, according to the hierarchy of their particular organization, probably in a 'regional' or national capital. Here 'face-to-face' transactions are less important, and business consists rather of overall administrative control and judgment on cases submitted from the local branches.

Such activities call for good communications, but are otherwise not highly localized. Their higher-level activities, however, are closely interconnected, and their head offices therefore tend to cluster. The most familiar such cluster of banking and other financial houses is in the City of London. The Wall Street area of New York City is closely comparable, and all major capitals have such groups of financial institutions.

(e) Commodity Markets

These are the places where certain types of goods—ranging from stocks and bonds to tea, grain and non-ferrous metals—are bought and sold. The commodities need not be, and in fact very rarely are, physically present. Only the evidence of ownership is transferred from one company or one individual to another. Like the financial institutions, such markets primarily require excellent worldwide communications; they show a strong aggregative tendency, however, and are always found closely associated with the central banking and related institutions.

(f) Communications

Communications are the means whereby messages are transmitted and received. Some, such as the mail, depend on means of transport, but most rely increasingly on telecommunications, which have become a service industry of great size and complexity. Within a single country or group of contiguous countries land lines are used, but in trans-oceanic communication radio links are replacing the older cables. The exchanges, and with them a large part of the technical personnel, must be located near the large centres of population which generate most of the traffic. Any weakness in the system of telephone communications can have very serious consequences for industry and commerce.

(g) Education

In any developed country the provision of schools is directly related to the density and distribution of the population. Nevertheless the location of a school is not necessarily a simple matter. In few human activities is it more desirable to minimize the journey to work, especially to schools designed for younger children. The location of a new school calls for an intensive investigation of both the pattern of housing and the traffic flow.

Institutions of higher education are more narrowly concentrated. In their location they show two conflicting tendencies. The first is to establish themselves within or very close to the largest centres of population: there is thus at least one university in every big city in the United Kingdom. Schools of art, drama, medicine and other professional activities tend to adopt a similar distribution, encouraged by an aggregative tendency arising from joint use of resources such as libraries and research laboratories.

On the other hand, modern universities and polytechnics tend to be established away from large conurbations, in the open country where land is more readily available and there is space for more generous planning. In terms of amenities there is much to be said for this trend, but many would question the wisdom of divorcing higher education and research from the social milieu of the great cities.

Educational levels are an important measure of development, and there is a direct relationship between the extent of literacy and the numbers of graduates and of those in higher education on the one hand, and national income on the other. It is sufficient here to emphasize that in all developed countries education is a very important component of tertiary activities.

(h) Culture and Entertainment

These, like teaching, have traditionally been regarded as face-to-face activities; the audience must be in the presence of the entertainer, and this has in turn led to the growth of an entertainment industry with its theatres and cinemas. Similarly, museums and art galleries also require the physical presence of those who would profit from them.

Nowadays, however, the electronics industry is engaged in destroying the significance of location. Concerts can be fixed on records or tapes, or they can be broadcast, while television has brought into the home entertainment of a kind which could once be seen only in the theatre. A geographer can perceive the significance of this in the cinemas which have been closed or converted into bingo halls, and in the large areas of the United Kingdom and other developed countries which are totally without a 'live' theatre or concert orchestra.

Sport—that is, spectator sport—is a form of live entertainment which has largely maintained its position despite television and radio. Professional sportsmen, from footballers to jockeys, today constitute a small but important and relatively highly paid service group. Like other entertainers, they depend upon their public's affluence and leisure, neither of which is permanent or dependable. The 'migration' of league football teams in the United States is a response to the increasing wealth and prosperity of the southern and western parts of the country. In Great Britain a comparison of league football clubs today with those of half a century ago reflects the decline of the traditional northern industrial centres and the development of newer centres of population in the south and south-east of the country (Fig. 11.2).

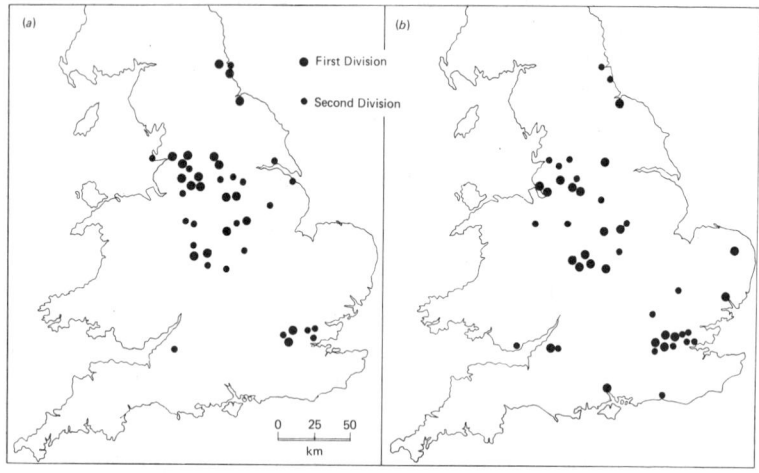

Fig. 11.2 The clubs of the Football League (a) in the 1919–20 season, (b) in 1978–79; the southward movement reflects the changing economic levels of northern and southern England

(i) Tourism and Vacation Industries

The recreation and vacation industries are no less a response to increasing wealth. It is the function of countless towns, coastal and inland, to provide tourist accommodation and a concentrated form of entertainment. But their activity is seasonal: climatic reasons ensure that in most there is a part of the year when their attractiveness is diminished. In Cornwall, for example, the 'high season' lasts less than ten weeks, and for much of the remainder of the year the beaches are deserted. Shops and hotels are closed: their 'take' during a short season of feverish activity must be made to cover expenses during the ensuing slack period. Summer employees must find winter employment elsewhere: waiters and hotel staff who work on the French Riviera in summer may go to the Alpine ski resorts for the winter—a contemporary form of transhumance. Some relief can be afforded if off-peak visitors can be attracted by reduced rates, but there is no real solution to this problem of seasonally underused resources, an important factor in the high cost of holiday accommodation. Only the staff can move to complementary employment elsewhere; the fixed assets of hoteliers must remain, shuttered and unused, beside the cold grey sea.

For this reason, while most governments and public authorities adopt measures designed to exploit the tourist advantages of such regions, they are more interested in encouraging the development of sources of permanent employment, especially manufacturing. For example, major policy instruments of the Italian government's attempt to raise living standards in the *Mezzogiorno* are the provision of incentives to new manufacturing industry and the establishment of large industrial plants to act as foci for growth. These include the integrated iron and steel works at Taranto and the Alfasud car factory in Naples, which in fact generates substantially more employment in supporting industries in the region than it provides directly.

Complementary to the provision of hotels and the means of amusement and entertainment at coastal and inland resorts is the organization of tours and packaged holidays. These are based on the principle that if facilities are fully used the cost per person can be greatly reduced (see Unit 12.1(*e*)). Fully booked planes result in fully occupied hotels and densely packed beaches on the Costa Brava, the Algarve or Corfu. Distant travel and foreign holidays are thus brought within the financial reach of people who a generation ago would have regarded Cornwall or North Wales as their ultimate holiday objective. The result has been on the one hand the construction of resort hotels on a lavish scale and on the other the rise of tour operators whose primary objective is to keep them full for as long a period of the year as possible.

On a smaller and more local scale, the provision of parks, picnic areas and trails for walking or horse-riding is a matter of great importance to the geographer. With greater leisure and a car in many families, large numbers of people are now able to use such facilities. Their location in relation both to centres of population and areas of natural beauty is important. All large urban areas must have public parks, not only for the recreation of man and dog, but also for their environmental effects on atmospheric quality and temperature. In the country at large, the creation of national parks and the protection of areas of great scenic beauty from intrusion by industry or housing development, or even by electricity pylons, is a matter of importance and sometimes even of urgency.

On the other hand, the environmentalists' desire to preserve much of the countryside inviolate is neither logical nor practicable. The landscape of this country is itself the product of an evolutionary process extending over thousands of years, during which countless generations have in various ways changed or modified the environment. Even the hedgerows, against whose destruction so many protest, are a product of only the last few centuries. Moreover, some intrusion of urban settlement and urban pursuits into the countryside is necessary if a growing population is to be better housed, and if manufacturing, whose importance none could deny, is to be restructured and developed.

(*j*) Personal Services
The dominant feature of these occupations is that they serve people directly. No communications or electronic device can intervene between the barber and his client, or the dentist and his patient. The relationship is direct, and if the service is not provided close to a person's home, then he must travel in search of it. The services in question can be grouped as (*i*) medical and welfare, (*ii*) religious ministration, (*iii*) personal, such as hairdressing and tailoring, (*iv*) legal and financial and (*v*) educational (discussed separately in 11.1(*g*)).

These services are characterized by a tendency for units to increase in size. Doctors and dentists, for example, tend to form group practices, and lawyers and accountants to merge into partnerships. Most of these services possess a hierarchical organization: the family doctor can refer his patient to a specialist, or a lawyer may seek the advice of counsel. These features are reflected in the geography of personal services. Those who provide them tend to form clusters, particularly conspicuous in the medical field. Since fewer people perform the higher-level services than the lower—there are fewer barristers than solicitors, fewer consultants than general practitioners—these services are likely to be concentrated in the larger centres of population, thus reinforcing their hierarchical tendency. It is essential, however, that people should be able to reach them, since unlike the central banking, financial and commercial services, they cannot (or should not) do their business by telephone, but depend upon personal contact.

Hospitals and clinics are large units, each representing a vast fixed investment and catering for the medical needs of many thousands of people. Each serves a well-defined geographical area and, since ease and speed of access to it are of the utmost importance, it should be located with careful reference to roads and transport facilities. Like other forms of personal service, hospitals have a distinctly hierarchical organization, with small local hospitals with restricted equipment and capabilities, larger district hospitals, and hospitals which are able to offer certain highly specialized services.

11.2   Distribution of Services

It is tempting to assume that the distribution of personal services is determined by that of the population. If, for example, one general practitioner can attend to the health needs of, say, 2 500 people and must be available to them, it should be easy to predict within a few streets roughly where these doctors will be found. Reality, however, may be quite different. The provision of many personal services is dependent on the ability to pay for them.

Even within a single society fewer such services are, as a general rule, available in a poor or working-class area than in one which is more affluent. Even services which are paid for by the state may be less abundant in a poor district—as are the health services in the United Kingdom, partly because such a district is an inherently unattractive place for a doctor to choose to live. In the United States, where there is no national health service and the patient has at most a group insurance scheme to cover medical expenses, the poorer quarters of the large cities are notoriously lacking in medical services. The geography of service industries, especially that of personal, medical and educational services, offers great scope for study and research.

While the differences in such provision within a developed country are significant, the contrast between the developed and the developing countries is immense. Services make a relatively small contribution to the GNP of poor countries; in the United States they account for about a third. In the less-developed societies, however, there is a higher level of mutual self-help than in the more developed and, in consequence, some services are available without ever appearing in the national accounts. Nevertheless, an important difference between the developed and the developing countries lies in the very much greater expenditure by the developed countries on service industries. This is illustrated in Fig. 11.3 in which the ratio of hospital beds to population is mapped for much of the world. The correlation between the provision of medical services and GNP per head is a very close one; Table 11.1 presents data for countries near the top and the bottom of the scale of wealth.

Table 11.1   Medical services and GNP per head

	GNP per head ($)	Population per hospital bed	Population per doctor	Population per dentist
United States	4 289	138	621	1 969
Switzerland	2 963	88	615	2 469
West Germany	2 752	88	543	1 908
United Kingdom	1 990	116	787	4 158
India	93	1 571	4 795	40 078
Pakistan	164	4 015	9 014	140 584
Afghanistan	83	7 051	18 655	102 934
Niger	135	1 796	43 000	669 333

Source: *Statistical Yearbook*, UN (1974)

A complete correlation between these medical parameters and national wealth is possible on the basis of statistical data published by the United Nations. Comparisons can furthermore be made between the provision of educational institutions and such factors as GNP per head and urbanization, and these emphasize yet more the gulf between the rich nations and the poor. A more general comparison of total employment in tertiary occupations (or of the proportion of the GNP deriving from them) is no less desirable but incomparably more difficult, because of the inadequacy and unreliability of many national statistics.

11.3   Building and Construction Industries

This group of industries is intermediate between manufacturing and service industries. Like the manufacturing industry, it creates a product; but this is not under normal conditions transportable, and it has value only where it has been built. It is an assembly industry, putting together components—bricks and blocks, pipes and plumbing—which have been manufactured elsewhere. Building is thus, in a certain sense, a service which has been brought to the people who need it.

But the immobility of its product differentiates the construction industry from all others. Components have to be brought to the construction site, so that the range of materials available is sometimes restricted by costs of transport. There is a tendency to use building substances of local origin, and, since the medium

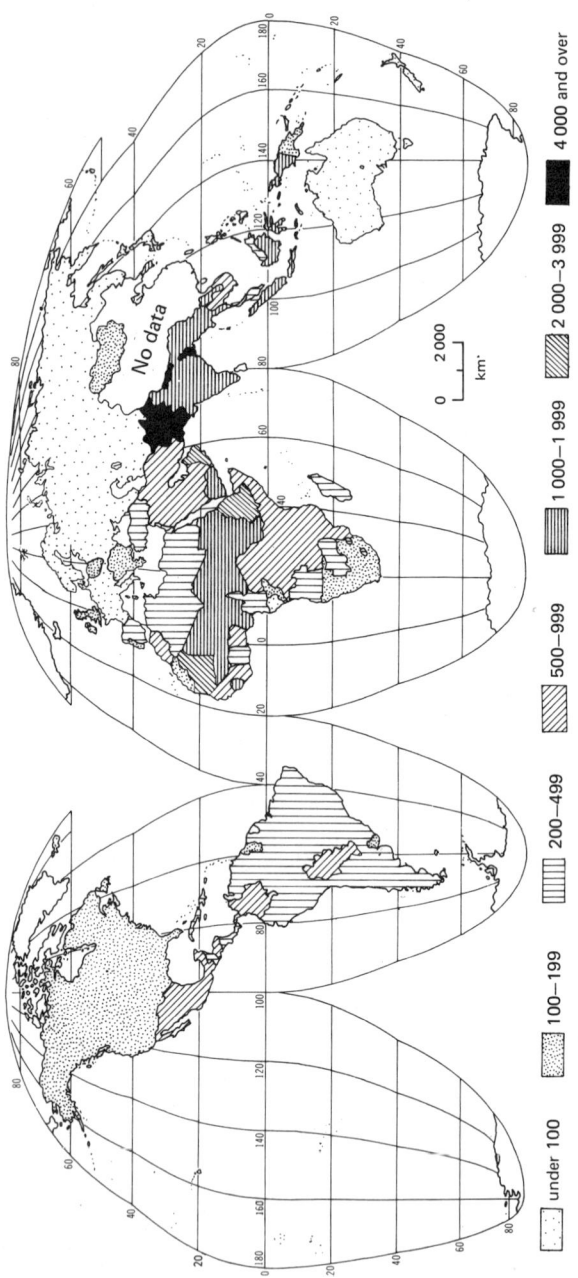

Fig. 11.3 World map showing the population per hospital bed

strongly influences the form of the product, a rich variety of local styles arises, especially in domestic architecture. Nowadays the relative cheapness of mass-produced building materials tends to offset greater transport charges, and the use of traditional and local materials is thus of diminishing importance. The styles of factory buildings and of office and tower blocks are today almost uniform throughout much of the world, and call mainly for structural steel, concrete and glass for their construction.

The quality of building construction is closely related to the living standards and relative wealth of those who commission it. It ought to be possible by comparing and mapping the style and size of domestic housing to arrive at a certain measure of affluence, and to correlate this with other parameters, such as the availability of personal services. The task, however, is complicated by the age of houses, their tendency, with increasing age, to go 'downhill' socially, and the converse practice of rescuing and reconditioning old houses, often at great expense. Nevertheless, a survey of domestic architecture can often provide a valuable supplement to other forms of geographical data; in this field a useful textbook is Toyne and Newby's *Techniques in Human Geography* (Macmillan, London).

In most countries of the world, the building and construction industry accounts for from 3 to 10 per cent of the gross national product. This figure varies greatly, however, and is subject to sudden fluctuations. It appears to be very high in the communist countries, at least partly because of their methods of national accounting. It is also abnormally high in many of the West Indian islands, where it is inflated by the current boom in the construction of hotels and office blocks.

11.4 Shopping and Retail Services

The service which most people require most frequently is that provided by retail shops. An absence of shops presupposes a self-sufficiency which is rare in the modern world and certainly is not found in the developed societies. In Great Britain there is one shop for (very approximately) every 150 of the population, and between 1 and 2 per cent of employed persons work in retail outlets of one kind or another. In all except the least developed countries, both the function and the spatial pattern of retail services are changing. There is a trend away from specialized shops towards those that carry a very wide range of goods. The 'store' now sells meat as well as groceries, and often stocks a range of goods extending from stationery to packaged clothing. A corresponding trend has been the disappearance of the small shop, often family-run, and its replacement by the large store, which usually forms part of a chain.

The greatest changes have been made in the United States, where supermarkets and hypermarkets controlled by chains such as Standard, Kroger and A and P, dominate the trade in 'convenience' goods (see Unit 2.3(c)). In Europe the chain stores dominate the food and convenience trade to a lesser degree, as Table 11.2 demonstrates.

Table 11.2   Population and shopping services

	Inhabitants per food-shop	Average turnover, 1974 (£)	Share of chain stores and co-operatives (per cent)
France	475	87 000	67
Great Britain	350	59 000	62
West Germany	475	96 000	42
Italy	310	28 000	17

Source: *Annual Abstract of Statistics* (HMSO, 1976)

The small shop is much more significant in Italy than in France, as any tourist will appreciate. Throughout Europe, however, the significance of the supermarket is increasing. Its advantages include the more effective use of floorspace, lower labour costs and a wider range of goods. The disadvantages are the smaller number and wider spacing of outlets and their diminishing ratio to population. The average journey to shop is increased, and the burden on those who do not use cars is greater. It is not surprising that the small 'corner shop' is most important wherever the ratio of cars to population is lowest. On the other hand, the hypermarket, built on the periphery of a town where land values are lower, can usually afford to lay out its own large car park.

The department store is the equivalent outlet for durable goods, such as clothing, furniture and household equipment. Electrical and electronic goods have tended to have their own specialized outlets, though they are increasingly sold in department stores. The department store is visited much less frequently than the convenience store, but purchases there are on average considerably larger. This conditions the distances which people are prepared to travel to visit department stores, and hence the location of the latter.

11.5   Service Industries and Central Place Theory

In Unit 2, we said that a major function of towns is the provision of services for the population of the surrounding area. Although many towns have acquired other functions, their role as central places is still an important factor in influencing settlement patterns, especially in more rural areas.

The structure of service industries, particularly those requiring personal contact with their consumers such as retailing, is hierarchical and reflects different ranges and thresholds for different goods and services. The multitude of retail outlets, such as newsagents or bakers, offering low-order functions are widely distributed in low-order central places. High-order functions provided from larger or more specialized establishments are normally concentrated in high-order central places. The hierarchical organization and distribution of service activities are closely linked with the hierarchical structure and locational pattern of central places. Christaller's central place theory (see Unit 2.1), which is an attempt at a theoretical explanation of settlement patterns, is based on this connection.

Questions

1. 'A large tertiary employment is a mark of a high standard of living.' Discuss.
2. Compare the location of a supermarket with that of a 'convenience' shop.
3. Choose any medium-sized city (population 100 000 to 200 000) and discuss the range and importance of its tertiary activities.
4. 'Tourism is today's boom industry.' Discuss.
5. 'Primary occupations dominate in the developing countries; tertiary in the developed.' Do you agree?

Unit Twelve

Transport and Trade

Transport and trade are inseparably linked: trade between producers and consumers in different areas requires the existence of transport systems to connect them, and the existence of transport systems facilitates trade. For this reason, these two complementary topics are discussed together in this Unit.

Transport is part of the production process, since a commodity cannot be used or consumed until it has been delivered to the purchase or consumer. As we saw in Unit 9.4(*a*), transport costs are an important factor in the competition between the producers of marketable commodities. The geography of agriculture and of manufacturing can only be studied in relation to the available means of transport. The transport of goods and the movement of people on the land surface of the earth follows certain pre-established lines formed by roads, railways and canals. Movement off these lines may be difficult or dangerous, and for practical purposes can be disregarded here. These means of transport and communication form a *network*.

A payment must be made in order to use any part of a network. Such payment may take the form of toll, fare or freight charge, or of road tax and cost or rental of a vehicle. Even the use of a pipeline must be paid for and its capital cost must be covered as well as pumping charges, rents and way-leaves. The price of using air or water transport must cover operating costs as well as capital charges on ships and docks, planes and airports. There is, of course, an inducement to secure the cheapest form of transport consistent with the commodity being moved.

12.1 Characteristics of Transport Systems

All systems of transport, whatever means they use, have certain features in common.

(*a*) Transport Networks and Economic Development

The density of a transport network can be measured most easily in terms of an *index of density*, defined as the length (in km) of road, railway or other medium of transport per 100 sq km of network area. These data are commonly published in national statistical year-books. In general, the network is densest where the level of economic development is highest, and least dense where the economy is more nearly self-sufficing. The most primitive economies have little need for a transport net. A companion volume (*Success in Geography: Human and Regional*, page 110) has compared the railway nets in France and West Africa. France is found by whatever criteria we use to be the more highly developed, and its railway net far denser, with an index of 7·33 as against values of 0·48 for Ghana, 0·33 for Nigeria and even lower figures for the rest of West Africa.

In Fig. 12.1, the index of railway density is plotted against gross national product per head (the most convenient measure available of wealth and the level of development). The correlation between these two parameters is fairly high. Some countries (*residuals*, see Unit 1.8(*d*)) lie at a distance from the regression line in the graph, however. We must consider why these should not conform to the general pattern.

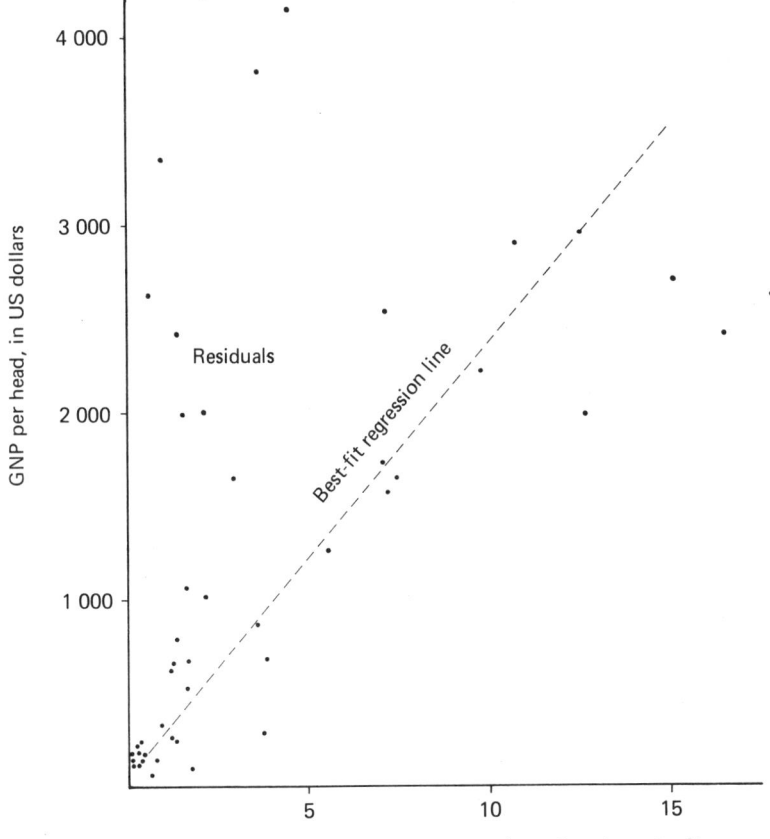

Fig. 12.1 The index of railway development plotted against GNP per head

Two reasons at once suggest themselves. Some countries have a low network density because, though highly developed as a whole, they embrace vast areas which can support only a very small population and a low level of economic development; Australia, Canada and Saudi Arabia are examples. In others, such as the United States, the low network density is due to the strong development of alternative forms of transport, notably road and air, which has restricted the further expansion of the rail system.

Within a *developed* country the density of the transport network is likely to vary with that of the population. This is apparent in the United States, where the density is much greater to the east of the Mississippi river than to the west. Similarly, in the Soviet Union there is a very much greater density in European Russia than in Asiatic Russia, where lines are totally lacking over most of Siberia.

(b) Transport Costs and Distance

In general, the cost of any transport increases with distance. Yet there is no simple relationship between the two. Transport costs are made up of two elements: *terminal costs*—the costs of loading and unloading freight and the maintenance of terminal facilities at origin and destination—and *running costs*, the costs of actually moving or running the transport vehicle. Terminal costs are constant however long the intervening journey; they form a decreasing proportion of total costs as distance increases. In addition, longer journeys offer economies in running costs. Thus transport costs per tonne/kilometre may be expected to diminish with increasing distance, as shown in Fig. 12.2.

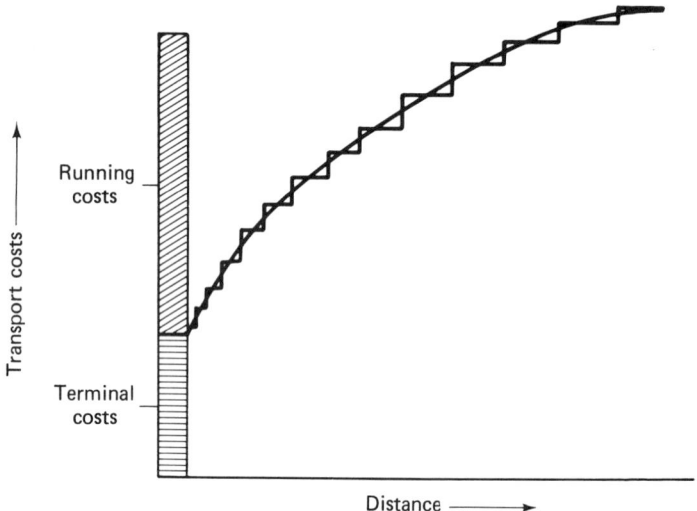

Fig. 12.2 Transport costs: the relationship with distance, and the structure of stepped fares

Furthermore, although the costs to carriers may be continuously variable with distance, they are rarely so to users. This is because carriers simplify fare schedules and discriminate in favour of longer hauls by grouping destinations and charging accordingly, so that transport rates typically rise in a series of stages or steps (Fig. 12.2). Thus transport costs are not only related to distance but also to the pricing policy of the carrier. Policies are rarely uniform and are often adapted to the intensity of use or the availability of alternative routes and methods (see also Unit 12.1(*e*)).

(*c*) Transport Costs and Different Media

Different transport media are characterized by different cost structures, as terminal and running costs are of varying relative importance. Typical cost curves for road, rail and ocean transport are shown in Fig. 12.3. Road transport has very low terminal costs, reflecting its flexibility and ease of loading and unloading, whereas its running costs are high because of the limited capacity of individual vehicles.

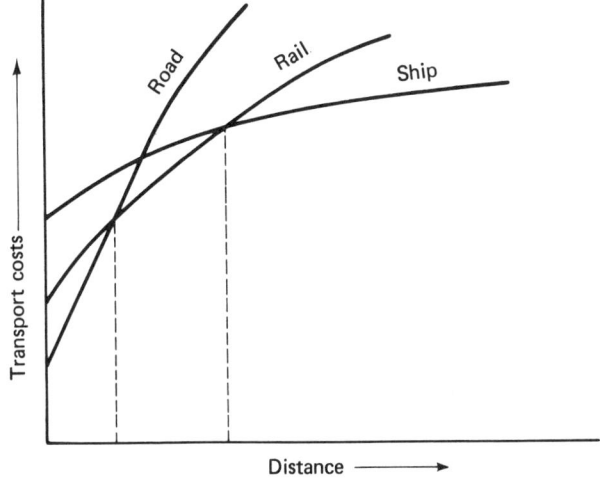

Fig. 12.3 Structures of transport costs for road, rail and ocean transport

Rail transport has higher terminal costs but lower running costs; it is less flexible and requires more specialized handling facilities but has to overcome less frictional resistance to movement and each train has much greater capacity. Ocean transport has the highest terminal costs as terminal installations are necessarily large and costly; running costs are, however, very low as friction between the ship's hull and water is minimal and goods can be moved in very large quantities by each vessel. Different media are discussed in greater detail later in this Unit, but it is clear that the distance over which goods are to be moved is an important factor in the selection of the transport mode, since different modes have cost advantages over different distances. Fig. 12.3 shows that road transport is more suited to short-distance movements, rail to middle distances and ocean transport to long distances.

In practice, however, the situation is more complicated than this, as the flexibility of road transport precludes the necessity to incur *transshipment charges*—the costs of transferring goods from one medium to another. Thus road transport usually has a cost advantage over greater distances than indicated by Fig. 12.3. This is one factor explaining the importance of road transport in the economies of many countries, especially the smaller countries of western Europe where average lengths of haul tend to be short.

(d) Transport Costs and Commodities

The cost of moving goods varies also with the weight of commodities, and freight rates are generally quoted per tonne/kilometre or per tonne/mile. But rates depend very much on the nature of the commodity to be carried, some of which need more care and attention than others. They may be fragile (like china and glass) or perishable (like meat and fresh fruit) or they may be liable to injury by rain or by a salt-laden atmosphere. The transport of such goods causes extra work or demands special packaging, and the cost of moving them at once rises. In the last resort, all carriers tend to charge the maximum rate the traffic will bear. Regular shippers, however, can sometimes negotiate special rates for large volumes of freight, especially if its movement is known well in advance and can be planned for.

(e) Unused Transport Capacity

A characteristic of many transport systems is that their capacity is only fully used during short periods of the day, week or year. The London Underground is crowded only at the morning and evening rush hours, and some motorways only at the peak of holiday travel. Airlines are more fully booked and intercity trains more fully used at certain seasons than at others. While most passengers eventually return to their starting point so that in the long run capacity is likely to be used equally in both directions, this does not apply to freight, which rarely makes a return journey. Freight-cars delivering coal or iron ore, or refrigerated lorries carrying foodstuffs, must return empty to their point of departure and some ships, especially tankers, are obliged to sail 'in ballast' for part of their time at sea.

This underuse of capacity is a major source of financial loss to transport systems. The London Underground and other suburban transport services are subsidized from public funds but must still charge high fares because their equipment is fully employed for only four hours or so each day, while for the rest of the time part of it is standing idle. Freight rates on bulk commodities could be reduced if a load could be found for the returning freight-cars or lorries. Ships, especially the so-called tramp vessels, will exercise considerable ingenuity in picking up cargoes or part-cargoes, so as to avoid sailing 'in ballast'.

Often reduced or concessionary rates or fares are made available during off-peak periods, and thus traffic is attracted away from the peak times. Since capacity is probably fully used during the peak, any increase in the off-peak load will represent a gain for the carrier. Such concessions are most familiar in passenger travel: reduced rates at midweek, for instance, or for elderly and retired people who seldom need to travel at peak hours. Though these measures, together with similar practices by the freight-handlers, may help to iron out sharp fluctuations in the volume of passengers and freight carried, much of the capacity remains underused much of the time. Coal and iron-ore trucks and refrigerated cars returning empty illustrate the basic inefficiency of all transport systems, and the more specialized a carrier the more will its level of use fall short of the maximum possible.

12.2   Networks

Every transport system consists of a network, whether of railways, roads, pipelines or some other medium. Those who develop and maintain the system aim to serve as many points as possible while keeping the network as simple and short as practicable. As an example of a network we shall consider part of the English railway system.

Fig. 12.4 shows the railway network in East Anglia. It is, since the closure of a number of lines, a comparatively simple system. This system can be simplified and represented by Fig. 12.5 which is made up of a series of straight lines, known as *edges*, and of intersections or junctions called *vertices* or *nodes*. Such a representation of a network is termed a *topological map*. There are 11 nodes in the present-day rail network, and 15 edges. A network may be as simple as Fig. 12.6, or as complex as the network of 'A' roads in the English Midlands. The more complex the network, the higher its degree of *connectivity* and, generally speaking, the better it serves the area over which it extends. Network connectivity can be measured by the ratio of the number of edges to the number of vertices, defined as the Beta (β) Index:

$$\beta = \frac{\text{Number of edges}}{\text{Number of vertices}}$$

For the network in Fig. 12.6, β is $\frac{3}{4} = 0.75$; for all the East Anglian railways it is $\frac{15}{11} = 1.36$. A value of β calculated for the Midlands would be found to be considerably higher since that system comprises a great many more edges binding together the vertices. The β-index was formerly a great deal higher in East Anglia, before the Beeching plan closed many of its railways. In Fig. 12.4 these abandoned tracks are represented by light lines; in the days before their closure there were 39 edges and 27 vertices. The β-index was than $\frac{39}{27} = 1.44$. The network was clearly more complex before the secondary lines were closed.

You will find it easy, using OS maps or an atlas, to draw a skeleton network of any transport system in any country. You can thus compare the networks of different countries, or of different regions of any one country. You can thus measure the effect of closing 'edges' within a system or of opening new ones, and you will find that the higher β-indices—those which are over, say, 1·2— characterize the more developed countries and that indices of less than about 1·0 are a mark of the developing countries.

There are, however, anomalies. If the β-indices were plotted against GNP per head, residuals would emerge, requiring separate examination. Reasons for such departures from the expected values might include:

(*i*) the competition of other forms of transport, since the β-index cannot tell us whether the network is fully or only partially used;

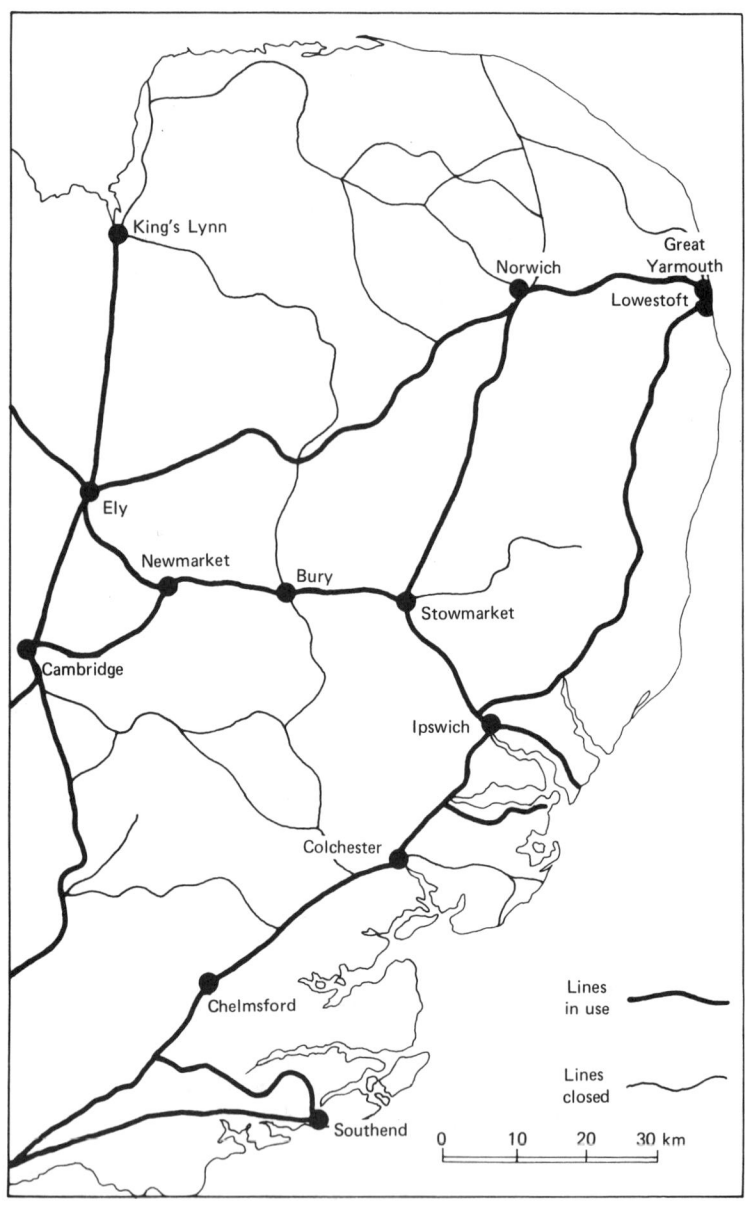

Fig. 12.4 Map of the East Anglian railway net, including lines closed since 1960

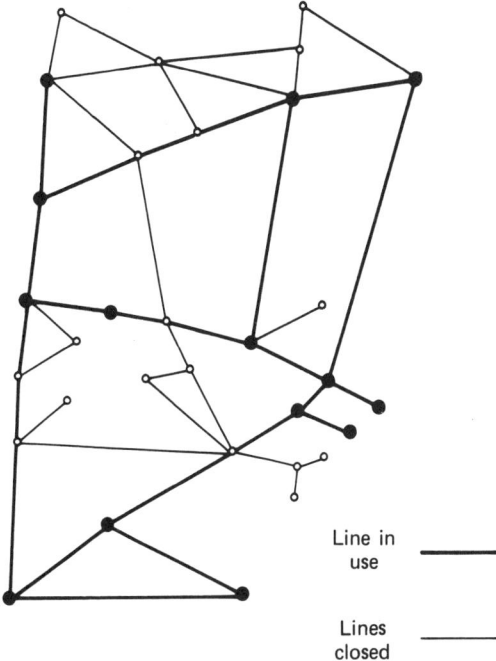

Fig. 12.5 Diagram of the East Anglian railway net in simplified forms

(*ii*) the existence of areas of low population and slight economic development, calling for only rudimentary networks;

(*iii*) the shape of the country, which might place constraints on the complexity of the network, as for example in Chile or Norway;

(*iv*) the relief of the area, which might set a limit to railway construction and severely hinder that of roads.

(*a*) Accessibility

The vertices in Fig. 12.4 are not necessarily large towns. Some are merely junctions whose location was chosen wholly for technical reasons. We also need

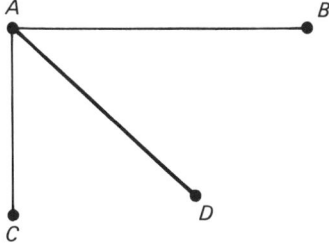

Fig. 12.6 A simple form of network

a measure of the ease with which access can be gained to the more important places, one which will take distance, and hence travelling time, into consideration. Such a measure would be of vital significance in the selection of an administrative capital for a 'county' of East Anglia (which happily is not yet required), or for the location of regional services such as hospitals or planning or taxation authorities or of a factory producing a simple consumer good. Suppose that we have eight candidates for this central role, including the major cities of the region as well as two smaller but centrally placed towns, Ely and Bury St Edmunds.

First, a table should be prepared showing the distance from each of the eight towns to every other in the list (Table 12.1). Road distances, read off from an ordinary road map, have been used since we can assume that most of the travel would be by road.

Table 12.1   Distance between East Anglian towns

	Bury St Edmunds	Cambridge	Chelmsford	Colchester	Ely	Ipswich	Lowestoft–Yarmouth	Norwich	Total
Bury St Edmunds	—	27	42	30	28	31	57	42	257
Cambridge	27	—	45	47	16	53	79	60	327
Chelmsford	42	45	—	22	61	40	50	102	362
Colchester	30	47	22	—	63	18	80	61	321
Ely	28	16	61	63	—	54	80	61	363
Ipswich	31	53	40	18	54	—	62	43	301
Lowestoft–Yarmouth	57	79	50	80	80	62	—	19	427
Norwich	42	60	102	61	61	43	19	—	388

The last column in Table 12.1 shows the aggregate distance from each town to every other in the list. Clearly, if the number of journeys made to and from the regional 'capital' were the same to each of the remaining seven towns, Bury St Edmunds would be the most favourably placed, followed by Ipswich, Colchester and Cambridge. This, however, is not borne out by the evidence. The large centres do more business with other large centres than with small; moreover, Bury St Edmunds, with a population of 26 000, will offer less attraction to most people than Norwich with 122 000, Ipswich with 123 000 or Cambridge with 99 000. The total in the last column should be modified or *weighted* to take this into consideration. (Methods of measuring the probable attractiveness of towns and thus their catchment areas are discussed in Unit 2.5.)

A table similar to Table 12.1 could be prepared to measure the accessibility of East Anglian towns in terms of the number of edges linking them. Such a table is termed a *shortest-path matrix*—a *path* being a number of consecutive edges linking two vertices. The most accessible vertex will be that which requires the least number of edges to connect with all other vertices in the network and may be determined, as in Table 12.1, by calculating the row totals for each vertex and finding the one with the lowest total. Row totals in shortest-path matrices are known as *Shimbel numbers*; they are measures of the accessibility of each vertex. Table 12.2 shows that A is the most accessible vertex in the simple network shown in Fig. 12.6; it has the lowest Shimbel number.

Table 12.2   Shortest-path matrix for the network shown in Fig. 12.6

	A	B	C	D	Row total (Shimbel number)
A	—	1	1	1	**3**
B	1	—	2	2	5
C	1	2	—	2	5
D	1	2	2	—	5

In East Anglia, where the land is fairly flat, there are few physical barriers to communications; the road network is quite dense and most road links are fairly direct. Measures of accessibility derived from a distance matrix are unlikely to lead to different conclusions from those derived from a shortest-path matrix. If, however, similar exercises were carried out for Wales, the Scottish Highlands and Cumbria, the differences might be significant, as the actual distance to be travelled between vertices may be twice as much as the straight-line distance, because of the tortuousness of some of the routes.

(b) Intensity of Network Use

Figs. 12.4 and 12.5 show only the physical pattern of the network. They tell us nothing about the intensity of its use: nothing about the number of trains or passengers or the volume of freight carried each day or week. These data can sometimes be obtained; for instance, the number of passenger trains can be found from the published timetable, though it must be remembered that an intercity train is likely to carry far more passengers without counting any more heavily than a two-coach train on a branch line, and it is almost impossible to obtain the numbers of passengers using any given British Rail service. It is, however, an interesting if time-consuming exercise to represent by various thicknesses of line the number of trains on each route, and in this way underused sections of the network can be identified. Since the whole track has to be maintained and the costs per kilometre of maintaining a branch line and a main line are not significantly different, it is clearly the branch lines of the system which might become a financial liability to the railway management. Branch lines, however, usually serve as 'feeders' to the main line, and the closure of the branch line would probably diminish traffic on the main line. A further consideration is that closure of a branch line would deprive a number of people of their only means of reaching the nearest city or market centre. The social importance of a branch railway or of a bus route cannot be measured wholly in terms of its profitability or of the number of people who use it.

Similar studies can be made of road traffic, though the raw statistical data are

Fig. 12.7 Taking a traffic census: drivers are likely to be asked their starting point and destination, so as to ascertain the intensity of use of different parts of the road network

in this instance harder to obtain. They are, however, a necessary prelude to improving the layout of the road network: for example, the planners need to know how much of the traffic in a congested town centre is merely passing through it and how much will end its journey in the town (Fig. 12.7). If the latter proportion is large, then better parking facilities rather than a by-pass are probably needed. A by-pass, in fact, increases the ß-index of the network (Fig. 11.6).

(c) Boundaries and Networks
Physical obstacles and political frontiers can both restrict the spread of a network. Most networks show a degree of discontinuity as they approach an

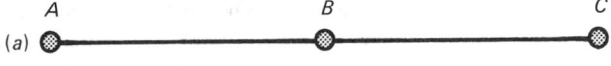

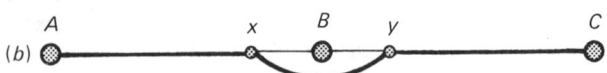

Fig. 12.8 The effect of constructing a by-pass around a town B: (a) β = 0·66; (b) β = 1·0

international boundary, and there are likely to be fewer crossing points on a boundary than on any comparable line drawn at random *within* any country. This is partly because frontier posts are expensive to maintain and their number is kept to a minimum, but also, and probably more significantly, because settlements on each side of a boundary are oriented towards the interior of their respective countries. Fig. 12.9 shows the railway net close to the Canada–United

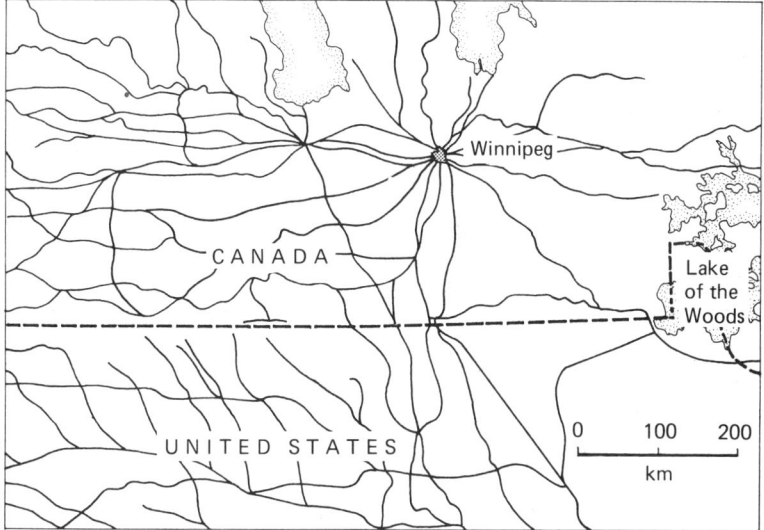

Fig. 12.9 Railway construction near the Canada–United States boundary, illustrating the barrier nature of the latter

States boundary. It forms in effect two networks tenuously linked together by only four international lines.

Physical obstacles such as mountain ranges play a similar role. Roads and railways tend to be spurs probing their way into the barrier region, and if the roads do in fact link up to form a system, their quality deteriorates and this in turn diminishes their usefulness.

(*d*) Networks and Population

The evolution of a network is a response to the demand for transport of goods and movement of people. It is likely to develop fastest and to become most dense where the population is greatest, but, in its turn, a developed transport net itself attracts population. Many governments have sponsored railway development— in the Canadian prairies, for example—*in order to* encourage settlement and the growth of population.

The development of a network of transport and communication follows a distinct pattern. In much of the world—Africa, Asia, Australia and the Americas—the road or rail system originated on the coast and extended inland, linking up centres of population and mining and farming areas. The stages in its growth are summarized by a model derived from the work of Taaffe, Morrill and Gould (Fig. 12.10).

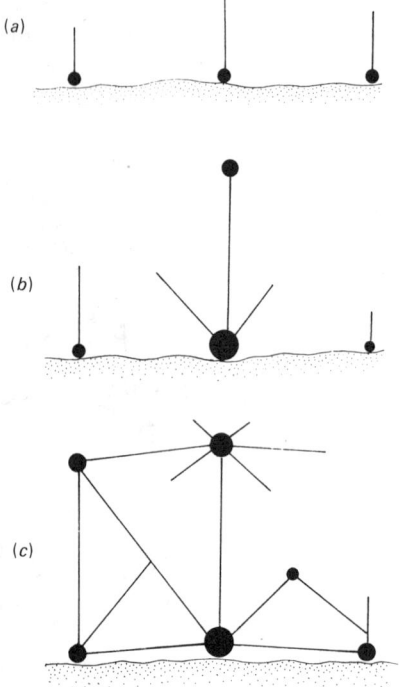

Fig. 12.10 Model representing the development of a transport net: (a) initial phase, with a series of ports; (b) penetration of the interior; (c) the filling out of the net (based on Taaffe, Morrill and Gould)

(*i*) *Initial phase.* There is a series of ports and coastal settlements, chosen usually for the convenience of their sites, carrying on a restricted trade with their immediate hinterlands.

(*ii*) *Penetration of the interior.* Railways and roads are then built from one or a few of these coastal sites, leading to the growth of the ports at their seaward termini and the emergence of nodes along the routes and at their inland terminations. At the same time those coastal settlements not favoured by the new communications network tend to decay.

(*iii*) *Thickening of the net.* Branch routes are built and links established between nodes, some of which are thereby encouraged to develop into major commercial centres.

The transport net thus established is unlikely to remain stable for long. Changes in population and in the level of economic development—the exhaustion of minerals, for example—may lead to shifts of emphasis within the system. The

growth of major inland concentrations of population and economic development will contribute to the emergence of trunk or 'Inter-City' routes with a very
high level of use. Lastly, roads and motor transport, at first developed to
supplement the railways, are likely to take over from them. Most transport nets
being developed today are made up of roads rather than of railways.

This model can be used to interpret the transport system in most of the world.
The exception is Europe, where the network of roads and railways did not
originate on the coast but in its capital cities and major resource areas such as
coalfields; otherwise, however, its development followed very similar lines.

12.3   Modes of Transport

Our discussion must now be related to the specific ways in which goods and
people are moved from one place to another, and the conditions and constraints
which these impose.

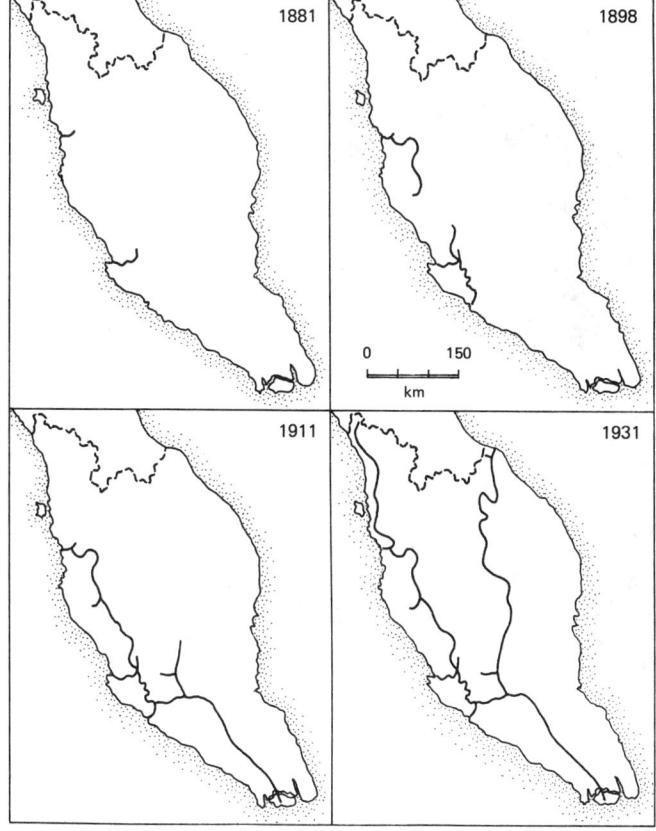

Fig. 12.11 Evolution of the rail network in Malaya (after Leinbach)

(a) Human Porterage and Animal Transport

These are the oldest means of transport, and the everyday spectacle of the housewife returning from the shops shows that it is far from obsolete. They call for less capital investment than any other mode of transport and are the most flexible. They remain significant in areas of rugged terrain and where living standards, and thus the ability to afford other methods, are low. Elsewhere they are supplemented or replaced by more developed means of transport. Even the housewife usually carries her purchases only to the nearest car park or bus-stop, and countless urban studies have shown that she parks her car as close as possible to the shops and does her utmost to minimize her journey on foot.

Fig. 12.12 Animal transport: a caravan crossing a bridge in Isfahan. The camel has been the mainstay of desert transport for many centuries

(b) Transport by Road Vehicles

The significance of vehicular transport lies in the fact that the use of wheels allows greater loads to be moved than by any other form of land transport. Carts and waggons are still extensively used in the less-developed countries, especially for short journeys to the market, but elsewhere have been largely replaced by cars and lorries.

In recent years, motor transport has become immensely important in all the more developed countries. Wherever suitable roads exist, motor-driven vans and lorries are used, and even in roadless areas such as grassland and semi-desert and desert regions, the internal-combustion engine is still the most convenient and efficient source of motive power. The automobile is the most flexible,

Fig. 12.13 The LandRover can travel wherever roads exist, and in many places where they do not

serviceable and economic means of transport ever created by man. Roads adequate for heavy lorries can be constructed comparatively cheaply; rivers can be crossed by ferry, and very steep inclines, up to 25 per cent, can be negotiated. The automobile has played a vital role in the opening up of new lands; it is of no less importance in the economies of the old.

In the developed countries the lorry has brought about a revolution in land transport. It can go from the factory direct to the consumer, it can deliver goods where there is neither railway nor canal, and it allows such journeys to be made without expensive break-of-bulk. Road haulage is unsuited for the bulk movement of goods of relatively low value, such as coal or ores, though it has sometimes to be used for the final delivery of such commodities to the consumer. It is admirably adapted to moving small consignments of goods of higher value, and in this field has made drastic inroads into the business formerly controlled by the railways.

The expansion of road transport of both passengers and freight has revolutionized the design and construction of highways, beginning with the building of the German *Autobahnen*, designed as much for strategic as for economic purposes. The development of the motorway system marks the triumph of the long-distance lorry and automobile. Even the most highly developed motorway systems, those of the United States and Germany for example, are designed to interconnect only the major centres of population on the well-founded assumption that most of the traffic flow is between large centres. Everyone has been inconvenienced by a motorway that misses a particular town by a few kilometres, and most of us must have claimed that we could devise a more flexible system. The connectivity of the British motorway system is low ($\beta = 1.19$), and this reflects its recent development and very high construction costs. You may wish to work out for yourself the β-index for the Interstate road network of the United States (Fig. 12.14) where there has been much greater investment by a more vehicle-dependent society than ours.

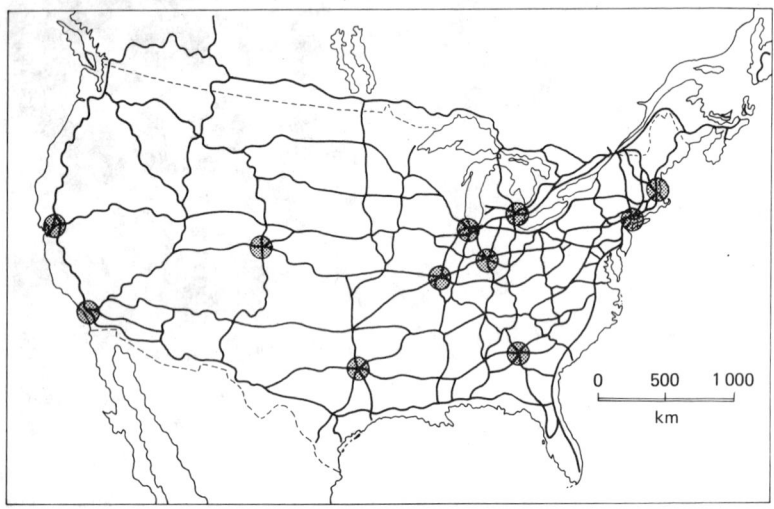

Fig. 12.14 The Interstate road network of the United States

(c) Inland Waterways

(*i*) **Rivers.** The use of rivers is one of the oldest means of transport, and from quite early times rivers have been supplemented by canals. Most rivers have certain natural disadvantages: during the dry season they may be too shallow for navigation, in winter they may be frozen, and at other times too swift and dangerous. The upstream voyage is always more difficult and costly than the downstream; the floating of timber down a river from forests surrounding its headwaters provides an instance of the use of rivers for downstream traffic only.

In the Middle Ages goods were usually sent down the Rhine in roughly made wooden boats, which were broken up on reaching their destination for sale for building or as firewood, so difficult was it for a vessel to move upstream against the current; similarly, on the Tigris and the Euphrates inflated skins were used, which on completion of the downstream voyage were deflated and carried upstream again on a pack-animal.

In very few rivers is the bed naturally even. In almost all there are shallows and narrows, where the river is constricted between its banks or flows swiftly over partially submerged rocks. The rocky bar across the Rhine at Bingen was for a long time a serious obstacle to traffic further upstream; the 'Iron Gate' gorge and rapids on the Danube were made navigable in modern times only with great difficulty, and the construction of a dam at the lower end of the gorge has proved necessary in order to remove remaining obstructions to shipping. The same is true of the Yangtse gorges in central China. Large rivers, moreover, particularly in their lower courses, deposit silt and form shifting, treacherous mudbanks, which are a constant danger to shipping and must be frequently surveyed and marked by buoys if the river is to be made safe for traffic. A great many physical obstacles in the world's rivers have not yet been either circumvented or removed: the St Anthony Falls on the Mississippi, the Stanley Falls on the Congo and the cataracts of the Nile are formidable examples.

Rivers do not always flow in the direction in which man might wish. Some of the biggest and most easily navigable discharge into the frozen Arctic Ocean — the Mackenzie, the Pechora, the Ob, the Yenisei and the Lena. The Volga flows into an inland sea; the Murray and the Darling flow away from the more densely settled and more effectively developed regions of Australia towards the less populous interior. On the other hand, some rivers have been and remain of limitless value and importance in opening up new countries and in transporting heavy merchandise. The Amazon is navigable for some 3 200 km upstream from the sea. The Rio de la Plata and its affluents are shorter but scarcely less significant, and the great rivers of Africa, Asia and North America — the Congo, Niger, Yangtse, Ganges, St Lawrence and Mississippi — have all been of incalculable importance. In Europe, the Seine and its tributaries, the Rhine, Elba, Oder, Vistula, Danube and Po have played varying but vital roles in the continent's history and commerce. But while rivers have provided an all-important means of opening up new countries, their functions were taken over by roads and railways as their shortcomings and inadequacies came to be recognized.

(*ii*) **Canals.** Canals supplement the natural communications provided by rivers, and follow routes along which their builders could expect a movement of goods. They suffer from certain disadvantages: while they are usually constant in depth and free from current, they tend to freeze more readily than flowing water, and the maintenance of their water supply often constitutes a severe problem, especially over high ground. Further, while they can be carried over hills by means of locks, these works are costly and can render a canal scheme prohibitively expensive. Canal boats may be fitted with engines, or they may be towed by tug, man or animal or by a stationary engine on the bank. On some rivers and many canals, particularly in England, France and the Low Countries, the horse-drawn barge is still seen, though it is no longer economically significant. Most barges are hauled by tugs, usually diesel-driven.

Fig. 12.15 Barges carrying coal on a Buckinghamshire canal

Intermediate, as it were, between rivers and canals are those natural waterways which have been so straightened, deepened, regulated and equipped that they have become, in effect, canals. Most navigable rivers have in some measure been modified to make them more suitable for navigation. They have been dredged, their banks straightened and levees or groins constructed, but the canalized river is more than this. The Moselle (Mosel), the Main and the Austrian Mur rise in a series of giant steps; their discharge is controlled, and they are made to combine the advantage of both river and canal.

Water transport is slow, and rivers and canals often follow courses which are far from direct. They are seldom employed to carry goods which are perishable or urgently required; they are best suited for the conveyance of heavy and bulky goods for which there is a sustained and predictable demand. Bricks, cement, gravel, coal, iron ore and timber are the life-blood of inland water transport; oil and petroleum are carried on the Rhine and the Seine, grain on the St Lawrence, and cotton on the Mississippi. In the region of the Amazon and of many other tropical rivers, almost everything that is transported must be carried by water in the absence of any alternative.

Though canals are still being built, notably the Rhine–Main–Danube in south Germany, the use of inland waterways is declining. The networks they form are in general too simple, and for technical reasons it has often proved to be too costly to interconnect some important centres of population. In Great Britain, much of continental Europe and the United States, inland navigation systems were very largely replaced by railways.

(d) Railway Transport

During the nineteenth century the railways became, after ocean shipping, by far the most important carrier. The railway is more adaptable than the canal. It can mount inclines of up to about 1 in 50; by zigzagging, as in the Western Ghats, or

Fig. 12.16 The Landwasser viaduct, Grisons, Switzerland. Railways can be carried by means of tunnels and bridges across some of the world's most difficult terrain

by circling in the thickness of the hill, as on the St Gotthard line at Göschenen and in the Canadian Rockies at Mount Robson, it can climb very steep hills indeed. A railway is, in general, easier to engineer than a canal. It may require embankments and cuttings, viaducts and tunnels, but can be laid quickly and cheaply on flat land—and the greater part of the earth's surface is flat, or nearly so. The course of a railway can be diverted to take in a town; branch lines can be constructed to places off the main route. Above all, railway transport is swift, faster indeed than any except air transport; freight trains can travel 1 600 km in a day, and passenger trains even more. American trans-continental expresses used to travel from New York to San Francisco (5 075 km) in 66 hours, though this service has now been suspended.

Railways are used for the transport of both bulk goods and of smaller, more valuable commodities, for moving mail and for bringing milk and vegetables to the towns. Rail-cars can be air-conditioned for the transport of perishable goods, and refrigerated cars can be used for meat. The rail-car is less well adapted than the barge to bulk-handling; it is generally smaller, and comparatively awkward to load and unload. In North America, however, large rail-cars have been introduced for the bulk-handling of grain, iron ore and coal, and in both North America and Europe the practice is growing of using containers which can be transported by rail and, if required, be transferred directly to a lorry or a ship.

The world's rail network is spread as unevenly as is its population, but does not precisely reflect the population distribution. Of the major regions of dense population only two, north-eastern USA and western Europe, have dense railway networks; the others in general have not. There are railway nets of comparable density over the La Plata region of Argentina, in the hinterland of Rio de Janeiro and in south-eastern Australia. In general, a highly developed railway system goes with a high degree of industrialization rather than with a dense population; but it may also be found in an area of agricultural production which has, as a result of a high degree of specialization, a considerable transport requirement.

The United States railways are slowly but surely modifying their role, since the transport of passengers has largely been taken over by aircraft and the automobile. This trend may be repeated in Australia and other large high-income areas. It is less likely to become important in western Europe, where journey distances are generally too small to give any great advantage to aircraft.

(e) Pipelines

Pipeline transport has been developed during the twentieth century for the transport of gases or liquids, or of slurries, semi-fluid mixtures of solids with water. China clay, for example, is carried in this form over short distances in Cornwall. Long-distance pipelines are, however, used exclusively for crude oil and petroleum products, fuel gas and water.

Pipelines are costly to install, but relatively cheap to operate, though they must be operated at or near capacity. In general, they cannot transport any commodity other than that for which they have been built, and a pipeline, especially if it is linked directly with a refinery, is accordingly likely to 'fix' or stereotype the pattern of oil supply. Poland and East Germany are thus indissolubly linked with the Soviet Union by the Friendship Pipeline. On the other hand, a pipeline is particularly vulnerable to sabotage. A pipeline is not necessarily hindered by mountains, rough terrain or even by rivers and shallow seas, and can be built where it might be impracticable to construct a railway or even an all-weather road. A pipeline is proving to be the only practicable means of bringing out the crude oil of the Arctic Slope of Alaska (Fig. 12.17).

Fig. 12.17 The Trans-Alaska oil pipeline

Pipelines are most used in western Europe, North America and the Middle East. In the United States they form a complex system (Fig. 8.5), but elsewhere their connectivity is low, most consisting merely of links between an oilfield or refinery and a dock.

The United Kingdom has now a primary network of pipelines for the supply of gas from the points on the North Sea coast, where it is brought ashore, to most parts of the country (Fig. 13.15), and there are short pipelines for the movement of crude oil to refineries, such as that from Milford Haven to Llandarcy. The distribution of oil within the United Kingdom is, however, mainly by road tanker and small ships in the coastal trade.

(f) Air Transport

Aircraft are becoming an increasingly important form of transport, and have in North America largely replaced the long-distance train. They have the incontrovertible advantage that they are not restricted, except at their terminal points, by any physical obstacles. No mountain range offers the barrier to flight that it does to land transport.

This freedom of the air is, however, limited. The movement of aircraft is controlled by international agreement. They may not overfly certain areas, and they must keep to certain 'air corridors' and fly at altitudes predetermined by air traffic controllers. But the greatest restraints on the freedom to fly are found in the location and maintenance of the termini of air travel, the airstrips and airports.

Airports, especially if they are designed to receive the heaviest modern aircraft, must be very large; London Airport (Heathrow) covers an area of nearly 15 sq km. They are also extremely costly to administer and maintain. The

Fig. 12.18 Concorde: the fastest form of civil passenger transport yet developed

fuel cost, furthermore, of taking a large plane off the ground is so high that intermediate stops in any flight must be kept to a minimum. As a result, only a minority of cities, even of large cities, are able to maintain their own airports, and, even then, long-distance hauls predominate over short.

In air travel, as in all other forms of movement, the greatest part of the total transport is between the large centres of population. The traffic, however, is not directly related to the population of these centres. The population of Greater London is about four times that of the West Midlands conurbation, but the ratio between the volumes of movement through the London and Birmingham airports is far greater, even if the transit traffic at Heathrow is ignored. This is due to the so-called *traffic shadow* cast by an airport: it attracts traffic from a very large surrounding area and inhibits the development of rival airports within this area.

The pattern of air travel thus tends to be a fairly simple network linking a small number of large and widely spaced urban centres. The vast intermediate areas are served, if at all, by 'feeder' lines which operate lighter aircraft able to

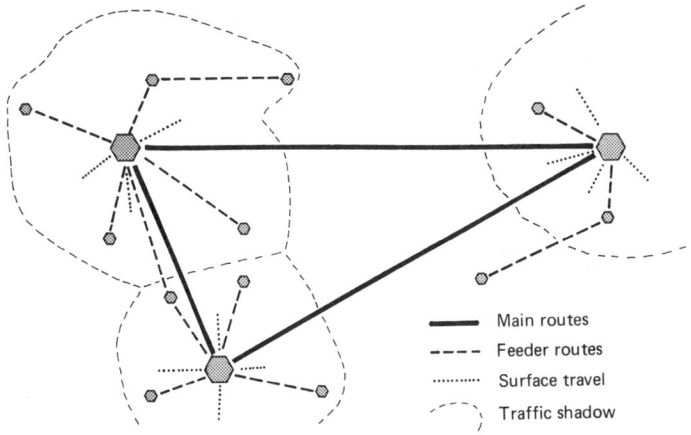

——————	Main routes
– – – –	Feeder routes
··········	Surface travel
⌒⌒⌒	Traffic shadow

Fig. 12.19 Model representing air travel and movement to and from airports

use small airfields and make more frequent stops. The quality of the road and rail links between a major airport and the area it serves is of very great importance. In this respect Heathrow is well served, especially since the London Underground system was extended into the terminal buildings. It would be very costly, even if it were practicable, to establish similar linkages between Greater London and the alternative sites that have been suggested for an additional major airport.

Air transport is generally thought of as catering primarily for the needs of passenger travel, but it is becoming increasingly important for the movement of freight, especially mail and lightweight goods of high value. Freight is mostly carried on specially adapted planes which can usually fly at off-peak times, thus helping to reduce airport congestion.

(g) Ocean Transport

Most of the world's intercontinental trade is carried on by ship. Freight-carrying ships vary in size from a few hundred to over 2 000 000 tonnes, and range from those designed for general cargo to those built to carry oil or perishable foodstuffs. Ships can move freely upon the seas and oceans, restrained only by ice and weather conditions. But the need for docks and harbours imposes on

Fig. 12.20 Freight containers are equally suitable for transporting goods by rail, road or ship

shipping the same sort of constraint as the need for airfields imposes on aerial communications, and, just as there are many areas without the possibility of a landing strip, so great stretches of coast are virtually harbourless.

Terminal charges are especially high in ocean shipping owing to the costs of removing goods from land transport and loading them on a ship, and vice versa. Furthermore, dockworkers have tended to resist the introduction of schemes to mechanize and simplify transfer operations. Though bulk cargoes can usually be loaded and unloaded mechanically, the mixed cargoes which most ships carry are more difficult to handle. In recent years a revolution has been effected by the introduction of containers: large, box-like structures which, once filled at the factory, can be conveyed by rail-car or lorry to the dock and taken on to and off the ship by a crane quickly and very cheaply. If built to a standard size, containers can be stowed in a ship's hold with a minimum of wasted space, and there are now both docks and ships that have been especially designed and built to handle containers. Their use has speeded up the turn-around of ships and reduced dock charges, at the expense, however, of making a great deal of dock labour redundant.

The world's shipping may, for convenience, be classified into four groups.

(*i*) **Liners.** These are ships which carry some cargo, but are mainly engaged in the transport of passengers, sometimes in conditions of considerable luxury. In their sailings they keep to regular routes, hence their name. They are among the largest, the swiftest, the best advertised and most widely known of all sea-going ships. But they have for many years faced the mounting competition of the airlines. Very few liners today remain in service, and these are used for much of the time for holiday cruises. Their significance in the international carrying trade is negligible.

(*ii*) **Cargo liners.** These are concerned mainly with freight transport, though many have cabin space for a few passengers. Like passenger liners, they keep to regular routes. Examples are the Australian and New Zealand meat boats, the oil tankers which sail regularly to the Persian Gulf, the grain ships of the St Lawrence trade, and the iron-ore carriers which travel between South America and the United States east coast and between African and British ports.

(*iii*) **Tramp shipping.** Tramp shipping adheres to no regular route. It carries odd cargoes hither and thither; when it has finished one task the tramp steamer looks for another. It may well be away from its home port for two or three years at a time. It may carry coal from Cardiff to South America and thence a cargo of hides to New Orleans; there it may load cotton for carriage to Genoa and then sail in ballast to North Africa to pick up iron ore, directed in all its wanderings by radio or cable from its home port.

(*iv*) **Coastal shipping.** These vessels are of small tonnage. They keep to inshore waters, and can ascend the estuaries of rivers sometimes to the tide limit. They carry bulk cargoes such as coal, timber and building materials in competition with road and rail transport, and their commerce belongs to their country's internal rather than international trade. The coasts of western Europe are dotted with small estuarine ports, few taking ships of over 1 000 tonnes and some of them visited only infrequently.

Most good atlases give maps of world shipping routes, and on some of these the intensity of traffic is represented by lines of varying thickness. These show an immense volume of traffic crossing the Atlantic via the busiest sea lane in the world, that between the ports of north-western Europe and those of the north-eastern USA. Next come the routes from north-western Europe to the South American ports, through the Suez Canal (at least under normal conditions) to India, the Far East and Australia, and to South Africa. The volume of trade in the Pacific is very small compared to that of the Atlantic. This is largely because of the relatively small volume of exports and imports of the east Asiatic countries resulting from their low standards of living and small degrees of industrialization. The conspicuous exception is Japan, however. Japan's flourishing trade with Australia and North America is large and growing.

The pattern of shipping routes has twice been revolutionized by the cutting of canals. The Suez Canal was opened in 1869. It greatly shortened the sea route to India and turned the Mediterranean from a cul-de-sac into one of the most heavily used shipping routes. The Panama Canal was opened in 1914, and for the first time put the Atlantic Ocean into effective contact with the Pacific.

Maritime canals are highly vulnerable. The Panama Canal, with its numerous locks, is the more susceptible to damage and obstruction, but the Suez Canal has suffered the more severely, having been blocked twice in its history.

So important have maritime canals become that the commercial nations of the world demanded some assurance that these waterways would remain open, without discrimination, to the peaceful shipping of all peoples. International treaties exist guaranteeing this right. Nevertheless, for twenty years the United Arab Republic (Egypt) excluded Israeli vessels from the Suez Canal, and this was a major cause of the military campaigns which twice in eleven years led to the closing of the canal. When it was first blocked in 1956 the world's shipping was disorganized until the canal was reopened in 1957, and in Great Britain there was rationing of motor fuel, much of which came through the canal from the Persian Gulf. In 1967 the canal was again closed, but this time there were fewer repercussions. It was almost as if it had been anticipated and other plans made. The reason was that large supertankers had been developed that could carry fuel to Europe by way of the route around the south of Africa.

A major extension of oceanic shipping routes in recent years has been the advance of shipping into seas normally icebound for the larger part of the year, a development made possible by the use of icebreakers (Fig. 12.21). Several ports of the Baltic Sea are thus accessible to shipping for a much longer season or even for the entire year. Besides such developments as these, the two great Arctic routes, so long sought by Elizabethan sailors, have been in greater or lesser measure opened to trade. The Hudson Bay, which approaches so close to the prairie provinces of Canada, is now reached by grain ships, during the short summer. The difficulty of this route lies in the very short period during which the Hudson Strait is open to shipping. The Russians have similarly opened up what used to be called the North-east Passage. There are regular sailings along the Arctic coast of the USSR. Igarka has been made into a timber port, and the routes are kept open by icebreakers for much of, if not all, the year. It is

Fig. 12.21 An icebreaker clearing a way for a trapped freighter through the ice of the Gulf of St Lawrence

doubtful, though, whether such undertakings are wholly practicable on economic grounds, whatever their political or strategic implications. More recently, the development of the vast oil and gas reserves in northern Alaska has stimulated interest in the American Arctic sea route, and in 1969 a specially equipped giant tanker sailed from the Atlantic to the northern coast of Alaska, demonstrating that the export of oil from the new field by sea was technically possible, if not economically feasible. Since then, however, a pipeline across Alaska has proved to be a more practical means of exporting oil from the 'Northern Slope'.

(*h*) **Ports and Harbours**

We have said that ocean navigation depends upon the availability of ports and harbours. A *port* is a place where ships may tie up and discharge their cargoes; a *harbour* is a stretch of water protected by man or by nature from the open sea beyond, in which ships may lie at anchor in safety. Not all harbours need be ports of Trieste or Genoa, with their indifferent harbours, with Kotor (Cattaro) more than a sheltered stretch of water. The goods which are loaded or unloaded there must be collected from or distributed over the hinterland, so that without a network of communications it cannot grow as a commercial port. Compare the ports of Trieste or Genoa with their indifferent harbours, with Kotor (Cattaro) and Falmouth, both having deep, spacious, protected harbours and very little trade. Trieste is a port of European importance, while Kotor is merely visited by Mediterranean cruises. Falmouth has perhaps the finest natural harbour in the British Isles, but the docks there have recently closed. On the other hand, Liverpool and London lie on shallow, muddy estuaries and are among the foremost ports of Europe in the volume of shipping. Clearly situation is more important than site in the development of a port, though development can be helped if basins are excavated from soft sediments (as along the lower Thames and lower Rhine), if tides are helpful in allowing large ships to dock, and if the depth of water is adequate at all times.

Ports may be divided, according to the functions which they perform, into *terminal ports* and *ports-of-call*; these do not constitute exclusive categories, however, since there are few terminal ports which do not sometimes serve as ports-of-call, and vice versa.

(*i*) **Terminal ports.** These are large ports, commanding a wide and varied hinterland. They are the ultimate destination of ships which will as a general rule expect to take on full cargoes. London and Liverpool, Rotterdam and Hamburg, New York and San Francisco are all terminal ports. They may be equipped with facilities for the overhaul and repair of ships—dry dock, for example.

(*ii*) **Ports-of-call.** Ships sailing between terminal ports may pause at ports-of-call to unload or take on part-cargoes. These ports may be of great importance to the countries in which they lie but then make little difference to the operations or the profits of the shipping companies. Many specialized ships—ore-carriers and oil-tankers, for example—make no such intermediate calls between their terminal ports.

The *outport* is a particular kind of port-of-call designed to save a ship from a slow and perhaps costly voyage up an estuary to take on only a small part-cargo. It is like the letter-box affixed to the garden gate to save the postman the walk up a long driveway to deliver a single piece of second-class mail. A ship sailing from the terminal port of Hamburg might thus call at Bremerhaven to pick up goods brought down from Bremen by barge or lighter.

Many other large ports also have an outport between themselves and the ocean. Thus Rouen has Le Havre, Hamburg has Cuxhaven, Nantes has St Nazaire, Bristol has Avonmouth and London has Tilbury. Some outports even outgrow the ports they were originally created to serve.

An *entrepôt* is another specialized port-of-call, a port that serves as a collecting centre. At Mayaguez in Puerto Rico, for example, small cargoes are collected from the many small islands of the West Indies, none of which would be likely to be visited by a large ship. Here they are held for loading. Similarly, goods from Europe or other distant points can be brought here for distribution. Hong Kong and Singapore perform the same function in eastern Asia.

This entrepôt function has been assisted and encouraged in many instances by the creation of either *free ports* or *free zones* within ports. Normally the goods collected at an entrepôt are subject to customs examination, as are also those brought to it for distribution. But if the port, or some zone within it, is placed outside the customs boundary of its own country, these small cargoes are not subjected to inspection and duty, and the port's entrepôt function is greatly assisted. Many large ports—New York, San Francisco and Hamburg, for example—have free zones. It is even possible for goods to be brought overland in transit and in bond to such ports. In this way the port of New York may serve the needs of Canada; Trieste serves Hungary, Yugoslavia and Italy; and Thessaloníki serves Yugoslavia and Greece. Free zones are now to be found at railway junctions of international importance, such as Innsbrück, and at major international airports.

(i) A Model of International Shipping

Fig. 12.22 represents diagrammatically the movement of ocean shipping between major ports. Large ships are more economic to operate than small, but for technical reasons they can only sail between the larger and better equipped ports. They require therefore the services of many small vessels which are able to ascend estuaries to the inland ports at their heads (*a* in Fig. 12.22), and to concentrate freight at the entrepôts (*b* in Fig. 12.22). The resulting model bears a close similarity to that of long-distance and international air traffic (Fig.12.19), with its linkages by way of feeder lines to the major airports. It seems inevitable that the network of transport by ship, as also by air and rail, will be reduced

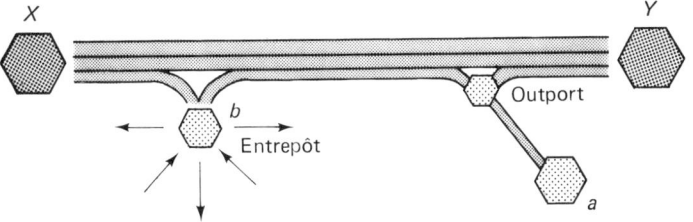

Fig. 12.22 Model representing ocean shipping

more and more to a skeleton of major linkages with, at each of its nodes, a complex pattern of road, rail or air feeders.

Although we have discussed the various modes of transport separately, they rarely if ever operate in isolation, and usually they are mutually dependent. Air transport, which has competed so successfully with sea, road and rail transport, cannot function effectively without them, since the service area of a major airport must embrace tens of thousands of square kilometres with a population of many millions. Advertised passenger fares and freight rates may incorporate the cost of travel by as many as three or even more modes. Rail transport is usually supplemented by road, especially since the density of the rail net and the frequency of stations have been reduced.

Usually, however, these modes of transport are in competition. Ocean transport, especially passenger movement, has suffered very greatly from the competition of air transport since 1945. During the nineteenth century the more flexible railway system put most of the canals in Great Britain out of business, and in continental Europe greatly reduced their range of traffic. In the last three decades the railways' predominance in both passenger and freight transport has been undermined by the road vehicle. It would be socially desirable to restore some of this traffic to the railways which can operate much more cheaply on a tonne/kilometre basis. The convenience and flexibility of road transport, coupled with its ability to avoid costly break-of-bulk, have won the day for the lorry, at least for the immediate future. Whether in the long run any small country can afford the traffic congestion, the pollution of its atmosphere and the high cost of fuel—all features of road transport—is a question for the rising generation to answer.

It may happen that a new form of transport will one day be developed that will replace conventional road transport. If so, then road transport will simply have followed the pattern, established by canals and railways, of initial development, expansion, retrenchment and decline in the face of competition from a newer mode. All transport innovations represent attempts to reduce movement costs and so more successfully overcome the barriers imposed by distance. Their application and development facilitate, and sometimes actually engender, interregional and international trade which themselves increase the economic welfare of participating producers and consumers.

12.4 International Trade and Specialization

Trade is the result of specialization. Ideally, each region or country produces the commodities which it considers itself best suited to produce, and exchanges its surplus for those goods which it does not produce. A century and a half ago Adam Smith set out the theoretical basis of international trade in words which cannot be bettered and which are equally applicable to inter-regional trade within a country:

> The natural advantages which one country has over another in producing particular commodities are sometimes so great that it is acknowledged by all

the world to be in vain to struggle with them. By means of glasshouses, hot-beds and hot-walls, very good grapes can be raised in Scotland, and very good wine can be made of them at about thirty times the expense for which at least equally good can be brought from foreign countries. Would it be a reasonable law to prohibit the importation of all foreign wines merely to encourage the manufacture of claret and burgundy in Scotland? But if there would be a manifest absurdity in turning towards any employment thirty times more of the capital and industry of the country than would be necessary to purchase from foreign countries an equal quantity of the commodities wanted, there must be an absurdity, though not altogether so glaring, yet exactly of the same kind, in turning towards any such employment a thirtieth, or even a three-hundredth part more of either. (*Wealth of Nations*, chapter 1)

Clearly, if each country grows or makes that which it can grow or make most easily and cheaply, the total world production of all commodities will be greater than if each tries to make a large variety of goods, not all of which it can make cheaply or well. For instance, if the climate and soil of the United States and Egypt enable them to grow enough high-quality cotton to supply their customers, there is little sense in, say, East Africa producing an inferior fibre more expensively. Similarly, Great Britain has the coal and iron needed for steelmaking, while Canada and Argentina can produce meat and wheat on a vast scale. It would be as idle for Great Britain to try to feed herself as it would be for Argentina to produce her own iron and steel. Such was the doctrine of *comparative advantage* that was evolved in the nineteenth century to explain the development and direction of production and trade. Its instrument was free trade, and its bible Adam Smith's *Wealth of Nations*. It encouraged each country to carry on whatever productive activities it could practise most cheaply.

During the nineteenth century restrictions on trade gradually disappeared, and traffic passed with less and less hindrance from one country to another. Conditions favoured international specialization, and the world's trade system became characterized by the division of countries into the primary producers of foodstuffs and industrial raw materials on the one hand, and manufacturing countries on the other. A greater degree of international specialization was probably achieved in the closing years of the century than has been known before or since. This does not mean that there were no artificial restrictions on trade, or that people always evaluated correctly the advantages of soil and climate, labour and transport in deciding what to grow or to produce or where to do it. Often enough, no attempt was made to evaluate them at all. Nevertheless, in general it was the cost of production that determined what goods should be made or grown, and manufacturing was carried on wherever the greatest chance of profit could be found.

Since then, the trend has been away from international specialization, despite its revival in the current objectives of COMECON (the Council of Mutual Economic Assistance). Many countries have increased the variety of their products and now make goods whose manufacture would once have been thought economically unwise or technically impossible. Technical development has tended to diminish the relative advantages of the older producing areas. It has reduced the premium on highly skilled labour and, in some cases, has cut an industry clean away from its old reliance upon some quality of water, convenient feature of transport or climatic characteristic. It has also made possible the manufacture of synthetic or imitation goods. Something approximating to silk, for instance, can now be spun through fine glass tubes from a cellulose solution derived from wood, cotton linters or other organic waste: the 'silk' industry no longer depends on the mulberry tree. Rubber, once the monopoly of the tropical forest, can be produced from synthetic chemicals or squeezed from the stalks of the guayole plant in Mexico.

Some countries have thought the development of a wider range of industries to be desirable in the interests of their national security—for example, that the possession of a steel or a chemical industry is essential for survival. Thus a factory is established or a crop grown at the order of a government, and its higher cost is borne by the community.

In this century of fluctuating trade, the country with a varied and comprehensive industrial establishment, able to produce much of the raw materials and foodstuffs it needs and having a small volume of trade in relation to its population, is in a sounder economic position than one more specialized in its development. Such a many-sided development has become a sort of insurance against depression. In contrast with the relative freedom of nineteenth-century trade from obstacles and restrictions, that of today has been greatly narrowed in its range and variety.

12.5   Multilateral Trade

Before 1914, and to some extent thereafter, world trade followed a *multilateral* pattern. The trade between country *A* and country *B* did not necessarily balance. Neither made any attempt to restrict its buying from the other to the value of the goods it sold there. Great Britain did not balance her sales of factory goods to Malaya or the Gold Coast (Ghana) against her purchases of rubber, palm oil and cocoa. This would have given her far more of these commodities than she could have consumed. Instead, these countries sent their products to many other countries, some of which sold more goods to Great Britain than Great Britain could pay for directly. The transaction was completed by the export of manufactured goods from Europe to tropical countries.

This multilateral pattern of trade was made possible by the interchangeability of the currencies of the countries concerned. All were based on gold, which prevented any great fluctuations in the value of any one currency in terms of another. In effect gold and, to a very small extent, silver made up a common currency, known and accepted throughout the world, and such a system obviously encouraged that international specialization which, as we have seen, makes for a greater volume of production and a higher level of welfare. The system broke down during the First World War; it was re-established and achieved a measure of success in the twenties, but it collapsed again in the aftermath of the Great Depression. Attempts have been made to revive it since the Second World War, and it may be said to operate once more in a somewhat restricted fashion over part of the world.

12.6 Bilateral Trade

Bilateral trade is the exchange of commodities between two countries; *A* buys from *B* to the same value as *B* buys of *A*. Thus the Soviet Union's exports to Hungary balance precisely Hungary's exports to the Soviet Union; Poland buys only a small quantity of Swedish manufactures, though she wants more and Sweden has it to spare, because she pays in coal for which there is now only a limited demand in Sweden.

Within the older system of multilateral trade there was always, of course, a considerable element of bilateral trade. Great Britain bought from and sold to all countries in the world, but the imports from these countries did not—except accidentally—balance the exports to them. Multilateral trade filled the gap. The change from a multilateral to a predominantly bilateral pattern was one of several tragic consequences of the Depression. For reasons we need not examine here, the volume of world trade contracted. One by one, each country tried to salvage what it could from the wreck. A sort of 'musical chairs' followed, one country after another, and one producer after another, finding itself the odd man out.

By about 1935, a large part of the world's trade was of necessity running through bilateral channels. The departure of one country after another from the gold standard was a factor preventing restoration of the free pattern of multilateral trade. The folly of this trend was self-evident, but none could afford to be left out in the scramble for markets. All paid lip-service to the ideal of free and unrestricted trade, and turned at once to the task of safeguarding the remaining markets by means of bilateral trading agreements. Germany's agreements with the Danubian countries are perhaps the most familiar example: Germany bought the grain surplus of these countries, and paid them in whatever commodities she had to spare. Rather earlier, the Dominions, who were competing with the South American countries, Denmark and the Netherlands and others to dominate what was left of the British market, succeeded in substantially increasing the amount of their mutual trade at the expense of their rivals by the Ottawa Agreement of 1931. The industrial development of Argentina was in part a result of her loss of British markets and her consequent inability to buy British manufactured goods.

Many countries which had hitherto been large exporters of primary products—cotton, sugar and rice, for instance—began to diversify their economy, producing less of these commodities and more goods for their own consumption. The diminution in the volume of trade and in international specialization was altering the worldwide pattern of production. A new economic geography was being written.

To the United States, beyond any other country, this contraction and canalization of trade was a misfortune of the gravest order. Her immense productive capacity could supply to all parts of the world not only primary produce like wheat and cotton, but a vast range of manufactured goods; but her imports came very largely from tropical territories. If European countries no longer imported her manufactures, she would find it less easy to import the tropical goods she required. Her industrial machine would be inadequately used and unemployment would rise to unacceptable levels. This was the lesson of the Depression to the USA, and it was the background of the American Secretary of State Cordell Hull's attempts to widen the basis of trade by clearing away restrictions. In a series of trading agreements in the 1930s, Cordell Hull persuaded one country after another to offer to everyone the benefits which it accorded to its most favoured trading partner. The result was to broaden the effect of the 'most favoured nation clause', and thus to reduce the obstacles to trade. But by 1939, when the outbreak of war put an end to any orderly system of trade, little impression had been made on the vast structure of exchange agreements. Only after the Second World War could the American government revive its efforts to lower tariffs and liberalize trade.

12.7   Free Trade Areas and Common Markets

Since 1945 many attempts have been made to free trade from bilateral, quota and other restrictions. The acceptance by 37 states of the General Agreement on Tariffs and Trade (GATT), negotiated in 1948, is helping very greatly to liberalize trade, and subsequent negotiations such as the so-called 'Kennedy Round' have further lowered tariffs. The same period has seen the formation of several free trade areas—groups of countries, usually contiguous, that have removed the tariffs, quotas and other restrictions on their mutual trade. First came the Benelux union (Belgium, the Netherlands and Luxembourg), then the European Coal and Steel Community, and, most recently, the European Common Market and the European Free Trade Association (see Unit 14.3). Other similar groups have been formed in central and South America and in West and East Africa. Within each of these groups freedom of trade will contribute to localizing economic activities in the areas best suited to them—the ideal of Adam Smith.

There is an important difference between a free trade area and a common market. In both, the participating countries have agreed to lower or abolish all tariffs, quotas and preferences on goods moving between them. Members of a *free trade area*, however, maintain their individual tariffs and restraints on trade with the rest of the world. A given industry may thus be more highly protected in one part of the area than in another, and this in turn may reduce the effectiveness of the free trade area itself. Moreover, goods can enter the area by way of one of its members with low tariffs, and then be sold freely into a high-tariff country. A *common market*, by contrast, establishes a uniform tariff wall around all its members. In this way a more nearly perfect competition is achieved within the market and Adam Smith's ideal—production at the site which minimizes total costs—is more likely to be achieved. The difference between the two kinds of groups is illustrated diagrammatically in Fig. 12.23.

The only effective common market in the world today is that which embraces

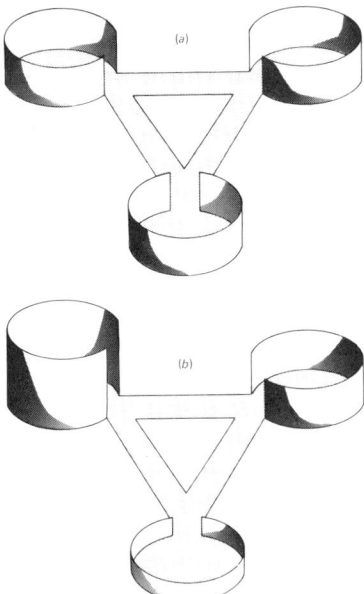

Fig. 12.23 Diagram illustrating (a) a common market and (b) a free trade area; while neither has tariff barriers between its members, the common market has uniform tariffs against all other countries, and the free trade area variable tariffs

the 'nine' of western Europe. The European Free Trade Association (EFTA) collapsed in effect when three of its members including the United Kingdom, commercially the most powerful of them, deserted it to join the European Economic Community. The effectiveness of the free trade areas in West Africa and central America is small, because their member states produce similar rather than complementary products, and trade between them is therefore slight.

12.8   Balance of Trade

It is not essential, nor is it necessarily advantageous, that the trade of any two countries should balance. It is, however, desirable that there should be some regular relationship between the total volume of exports and the total volume of imports of any single country. We hear frequently of a 'balance of trade', but this is a misnomer. It very rarely happens that the physical, visible trade of a country does balance; exports are seldom if ever equivalent in value to imports. There is almost always an overplus of one or the other.

The reasons for the lack of balance may be summarized as follows:

(a) Cost of Transport
The exporting country receives payment for goods delivered to the dockside, 'free-on-board' (*fob*) as it is usually expressed, while the importing country pays

'cost-insurance-freight' (*cif*). The difference is, of course, the cost of the transport and insurance across the oceans. The total value of the world's imports thus exceeds the total value of the world's exports. There can be no balance, except by chance.

(b) Services

Very considerable sums are earned for insuring and transporting merchandise. Some countries have developed this into a major industry, and own large merchant fleets that serve their own commercial interests and those of other countries by carrying goods. Among these are Greece, Norway and of course the United Kingdom: a British tramp steamer might carry Swedish timber to the Netherlands or Spanish iron ore to Germany, earning payments for the United Kingdom from Germany and the Netherlands. Where a country renders the services of shipping companies, insurance agents, brokers, ship chandlers and repair yards and is paid for these services in foreign currencies, it is clearly able to purchase goods from other countries.

There is a distinction between a ship's country of ownership and its country of registration. A very large number of merchant ships are owned in the United States but are registered in Liberia or Panama, and fly the colours of their country of registration as a 'flag of convenience', thus enabling them to escape the strict American maritime jurisdiction. The profits of their operations nonetheless go to their American owners.

(c) Tourist Traffic and the Remittances of Emigrants

The English traveller in, say, Switzerland buys goods and services from the Swiss, who can use the sterling they receive to import goods from the United Kingdom. In certain countries—Switzerland, Italy and France in particular—tourists' purchases pay for imports of foodstuffs and raw materials. Tourism is an 'industry' to be encouraged as much as possible (see Unit 11.1(*i*)). On the other hand, the money spent by tourists while abroad may cause a serious drain on their country's resources and gravely complicate its balance of payments (see Unit 12.8(*e*)). The United Kingdom, like many other countries, once found itself in this situation and took steps to limit tourist expenditure.

The remittances sent home by emigrants may have similar effects. In the past

Table 12.2   Balance of trade (in millions of US dollars)

	Imports (cif)	Exports (fob)	Excess of imports over exports
Developed countries	795 700	730 300	65 400
Developing countries	243 709	285 800	−42 091
Planned economies	115 200	149 100	−33 900
World	1 154 600	1 124 500	−10 591

Source: *Statistical Yearbook*, UN (1978)

the many small sums sent from the United States by Italian, Greek and Polish emigrants to their relatives at home have been quite important in enabling these countries to purchase their necessary imports.

(d) Investments

The assets owned abroad by governments or their nationals have in the past formed a most fruitful source of income. The investments made by Britain in South America, by France in eastern Europe, by Germany in the Danubian countries and now by America in many parts of the world have yielded to these countries a steady and valuable income. At one time the United Kingdom was able to receive interest in kind on the loans she made—in the form of meat or wheat, for instance. On the other hand, a borrowing country may wish to pay off a loan, and the United Kingdom has herself sold many assets in order to balance her payments in time of emergency. Overseas investments may, however, be liable to nationalization, as the British found in Egypt and the Americans in Mexico and Peru.

(e) Balance of Payments

In contrast with the 'balance of trade', a nation's *balance of payments* is always complete. It is its audited accounts, in which income from all sources is set against outgoings. A balance in hand at the end of the year must represent lending to another country: a deficit represents borrowings from elsewhere.

Before 1939, the United Kingdom's balance sheet did not look unfavourable, but in the course of the war which followed much of her assets were either lost or sacrificed in order to secure some immediate advantage; in 1947 there was a deficit of £655 million, though this was greatly reduced during the following years.

12.9   Terms of Trade

One factor that exacerbated Britain's position in this respect was the change in the *terms of trade*, that is, the terms on which her imported goods were exchanged for those which she exported. At one time Britain could export, say, 100 pieces of cotton cloth and obtain for them enough dollars or rupees to buy 20 bales of raw cotton. During and since the war years the prices of all commodities has risen, but the price of certain raw materials has gone up faster and further than the price of most manufactured goods: an outstanding example was crude oil, the price of which was multiplied several times during the 1970s. More manufactured goods have to be exported to pay for the *same* quantity of imported raw materials—maybe 130 pieces of cloth for 20 bales of cotton; alternatively, fewer materials are imported in exchange for the same export. If, however, the volume (not the value) of both exports and imports changes little or not at all, then the importing country will not be able to pay for all its raw materials as it has in the past. It is in debt to some other country.

It is no new thing for terms of trade to fluctuate, in favour now of industrial countries, now of primary producers. During the Great Depression, the price of agricultural produce in general fell much more sharply than that of manufactured goods, and though the industrialist may have had a smaller market, he at least had the advantage of cheaper raw materials. During the nineteenth century, too, the terms of trade generally favoured the producers of manufactured goods, and the United Kingdom was enabled to make immense investments abroad.

(a) Variations in Terms of Trade

Variations in terms of trade may be due to the overproduction, and hence cheapening, of certain commodities or to a sudden increase in the industrial demand for raw materials. Another reason may be an alteration in the rates at which currencies exchange with one another: for instance, in the early 1920s the United Kingdom's iron and steel exports fell off while those of Germany and France increased, despite the damage and dislocation of the war. One cause was the devaluation of the German Reichsmark and the French franc, while the pound sterling was overvalued. Before the war the franc had exchanged at the rate of about 25 to the pound, but by 1920 its value had fallen very sharply. The pound had also fallen but was brought back to its old level in 1925, when it was worth about 125 francs. Wages and prices had risen in France in the meantime, but not sufficiently to restore the pre-war ratio of the values of English-made and French-made goods. French goods therefore appeared cheap in the English market and English goods dear in the French. A broadly similar relation existed between the pound and the mark. In Italy, the lira was overvalued, and Italy's export trade suffered in consequence.

During the early phase of the Depression this adverse ratio of the prices of British exports to those of other countries' exports to Britain brought about a strong movement of goods to the United Kingdom. They could not be paid for by the currently low volume of exports, which were too dear to secure a ready sale. A movement of gold took place to rectify the strongly adverse 'balance of trade', until in October 1931 the United Kingdom was forced to refuse any longer to convert currency into gold. The effect was to alter drastically and suddenly the terms of trade. The franc's rate of exchange changed from about 123 to 90 francs to the pound. The United Kingdom began to enjoy the advantage possessed only a few months before by France, and her exports increased as those of France declined.

(b) Devaluation

Similar circumstances have arisen twice since the Second World War. In 1949 the adverse balance of trade of the post-war years led to the *devaluation* of the pound, in other words to a restatement in lower terms of its gold value. The effect was to make British products cheaper in her overseas markets and, conversely, to make foreign goods more expensive in the British market: in short, to encourage exports and discourage imports.

The effects of devaluation may not be long-lasting. It may set off a round of competitive devaluation, at the end of which things are no better than before. In 1967, the United Kingdom found it necessary to devalue again so that, in terms of dollars, the pound sterling had less than half its value before the Second World War. Moreover, the value of the pound in terms of the stronger currencies, such as the German mark, has fallen since the middle 1970s in consequence of domestic inflation. This has again made British goods appear to be cheap in foreign markets and foreign goods expensive in the United Kingdom.

This consideration of the economic conditions of international trade is a necessary introduction to the study of the present-day pattern of trade. Trade patterns change slowly as countries develop their industries, exhaust their mineral resources or intensify their farming. They are also subject to smaller, short-term changes resulting from currency and payment problems, from changes in national policy and from the cycle of economic expansion and depression.

12.10   The Pattern of Trade

The immense complexity of world trade is difficult to reduce to an easily comprehended pattern or model. Nevertheless, there are certain durable features beneath the ever-changing detail of the overall pattern.

(a) Trade and National Wealth

Fig. 12.24 shows the volume of international trade of the countries of the world per head of their population. Clearly, commerce is far more significant to the countries of western Europe than to any other parts of the world except entrepôt ports like Singapore and Hong Kong (see Unit 12.3(h)) and the oil-exporting countries of the Middle East. Can we generalize and say that the volume of a country's foreign trade per head of its population is directly related to its level of economic development? Such a generalization can be made only with reservation, since some developed countries carry on only a relatively small volume of international trade per head.

(b) Trade and Territorial Size

Foremost among these developed countries is the United States. This is because the United States is territorially a very large country, with a great range of resources and contrasted environments. Much of its trade might be termed inter-regional, and takes place within its own boundaries and is not therefore recorded in the statistics of foreign trade. Thus when Lancashire takes cotton from the Sudan or India, this counts as international trade; the mills of South Carolina, however, obtain their cotton from Mississippi, and this does not appear in trade figures. The very size of the USA and the USSR, and the range of their resources, tend to diminish the volume of their international trade. Other things being equal, we may expect a small country to have a higher *per capita* volume of trade than a large one. At the same time, a high standard of living and a high degree of specialization in production are likely to increase the volume of a country's trade.

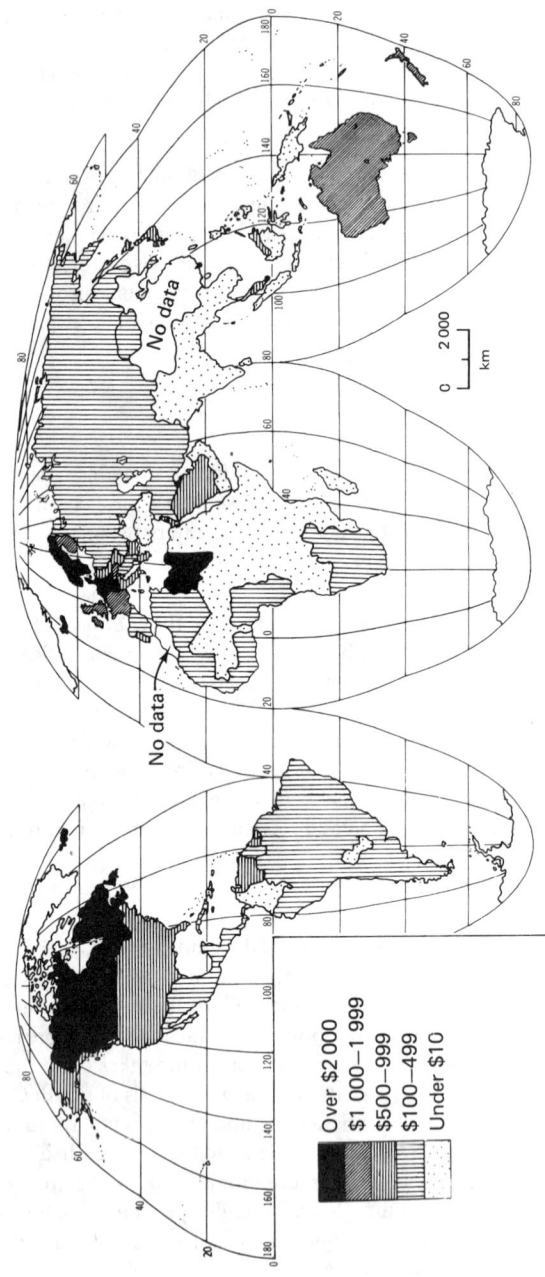

Fig. 12.24 World map showing the volume of foreign trade per head of population

(c) **Trading Partners**

We suggested earlier that the United Kingdom and other western European countries developed an export trade in manufactured goods which were paid for by the import of foodstuffs and industrial raw materials. Even in the nineteenth century, however, this was an oversimplification and it is certainly no longer true today. Table 12.3 shows the volume of trade between and within the three groups of countries into which the world is customarily divided. It demonstrates that the developed countries conduct no less than 75 per cent of their total foreign trade between themselves, and only about 20 per cent with the developing world. Moreover, the communist bloc carries on almost two-thirds of its international commerce between its own members. Only the category of developing countries is concerned primarily with trade outside its own group.

Table 12.3 Generalized pattern of world trade (in millions of dollars)

Exports to from ↓	Countries of Economic class 1	Countries of Economic class 2	Countries of Economic class 3
Economic class 1[1]: Developed countries	575 590	199 980	90 830
Economic class 2[2]: Developing countries	402 820	138 290	33 440
Economic class 3[3]: Soviet–east European Chinese bloc	23 060	13 320	47 570
Total	1 001 470	351 590	171 840

[1]United States, Canada, western Europe, Japan, Australia, New Zealand and South Africa
[2]Rest of the world, except Classes 1 and 3
[3]USSR, east European countries, China (mainland), Mongolia, North Korea, North Vietnam

Source: *Statistical Yearbook*, UN (1975)

Questions

1. Why are railways being closed in many developed countries?
2. 'What makes transport expensive is the fact that transport systems are scarcely ever used to capacity.' Discuss.
3. What factors have to be considered in planning a bypass for a small town?
4. Illustrate the stages in the development of a transport net in a newly developing country.
5. Examine the transport net (road, rail, air and river navigation) in *either* Africa *or* Australia.

6. What is the importance of (*a*) multilateral trade and of (*b*) bilateral trade in the modern world?
7. Why has the European Economic Community become the only successful common market in the modern world?
8. Explain the importance in international trade of (*a*) emigrants' remittances and (*b*) the tourist industry.
9. Why is Great Britain able to maintain a deficit on visible trade?
10. Why do developed countries carry on most of their foreign trade with other developed countries?

Unit Thirteen
The United Kingdom

The United Kingdom was the first truly developed nation. During the eighteenth century and the early years of the nineteenth, a revolution occurred in both agriculture and manufacturing. The land began to be used more intensively and the production of foodstuffs was greatly increased. At the same time manufacturing became organized more and more in factories, mechanical power was increasingly used, and output was immensely expanded in relation to labour. The United Kingdom had conspicuous advantages for agriculture and manufacturing: large areas of good soil, abundant reserves of coal and, at this date, reserves of the ores of iron and of certain non-ferrous metals. Population was increasing; there were few restrictions on its mobility, and much of it was equipped with the elementary skills in weaving and metal-working.

It was not, however, on account of these advantages that the revolutions in agriculture and manufacturing first took place in the United Kingdom. The British were already a commercial nation, carrying on trade with much of the Old World, as well as with parts of the New. Merchants wanted cloth and metal goods to export to North America, India and elsewhere. Not only was the manufacturer attracted by the market which was thus created; the merchants themselves made large profits, part of which they invested in land and in manufacturing. At the same time the growing population created an ever-expanding market for the products of both the factory and the farm. Thus two of the most important factors in development, whether industrial or agricultural, were present: *investment capital* and a *market for the products.* A third factor was the presence of a social and intellectual climate that encouraged and rewarded both the entrepreneur who established new industrial works and the innovator who developed new processes in manufacturing and farming.

Many other countries—France, the Low Countries, Germany, the newly independent United States—possessed physical advantages similar, or indeed superior, to those of Great Britain, but during the period of the Industrial Revolution, no other nation combined physical and human resources with capital for investment and a market for the products.

In continental Europe comparable developments had, by and large, to wait until the nineteenth century, when social conditions had changed and innovations, developed and perfected in Great Britain, could be adopted. Both industrial technology and scientific agriculture, which largely originated in Great Britain, were thus diffused (see Unit 14) to western and central Europe, to the United States and then to Russia and Japan. More recently these innovations have spread to Australia, China and India, and are today being adopted throughout the Third World.

The United Kingdom has paid dearly for being the first developed nation. The processes of invention were slow and costly. Decades of experiment preceded each important innovation, but once achieved, it could be borrowed, copied or imitated by any entrepreneur in any country. We can, for example, trace the rapid diffusion of the railway, the steam engine, the power-loom or the puddling furnace over much of the world from the British birthplace of these inventions. Only thus can we explain the rapid industrialization of Japan, or the equally rapid spread of railways across the North American continent.

Far from the United Kingdom deriving profit from this achievement, the effect has been to create competitors within its own markets, to the point at which cotton cloth from Pakistan, for instance, sells more cheaply in Britain than that woven in Lancashire or Lanarkshire. It can, of course, be said that the United Kingdom should have maintained the technological lead it had established by the late eighteenth century, by continuing to innovate and to produce machines and goods of ever-increasing sophistication and refinement. This has happened to some degree: synthetic fibres have in some measure replaced natural ones, and advanced technologies have been developed in power-generation, electronics and computer-based industries. But nevertheless the gap between Great Britain and other industrial countries narrowed during the nineteenth century, and in the twentieth many of them have overtaken the first industrial nation in technological proficiency. Even Third World countries are today adopting modern industrial technologies, and are in some respects far better equipped in the supply of raw materials to pursue them than Great Britain herself.

Lastly, the 'age of manufacturing' in Great Britain's history is itself a handicap. Many factories are now old, and industrial sites are cluttered with the debris of a century or more of manufacturing activity. The older mines are relatively small and inefficient. The transport system was developed to meet needs that no longer exist, and can be adapted to modern requirements only at a high cost. In many ways, the legacy of its early industrial enterprise lies heavily on British industry today, restricting and inhibiting its advance in ways unknown in countries that have developed more recently.

13.1   The Physical Conditions

British development took place in a small island. The surrounding sea gave it protection and at the same time provided the means for its precocious commercial development. No point lies much more than 100 kilometres from the coast and the many estuaries have facilitated the development of ports. The British Isles can be roughly divided into two zones by a line running from south Devon to Teesside (Fig. 13.1). The more westerly zone of mountains and hills, which includes Scotland and the Pennines, Wales, the south-western peninsula and Ireland, is made up of hard, old rock, which yields in general only a poor soil, and has a higher rainfall than the rest—850 millimetres or more, sufficient to reduce the soil in large areas to an infertile podsol. Lowland Britain is made up of younger, softer rocks that give rise to a gentler landscape of rounded hills,

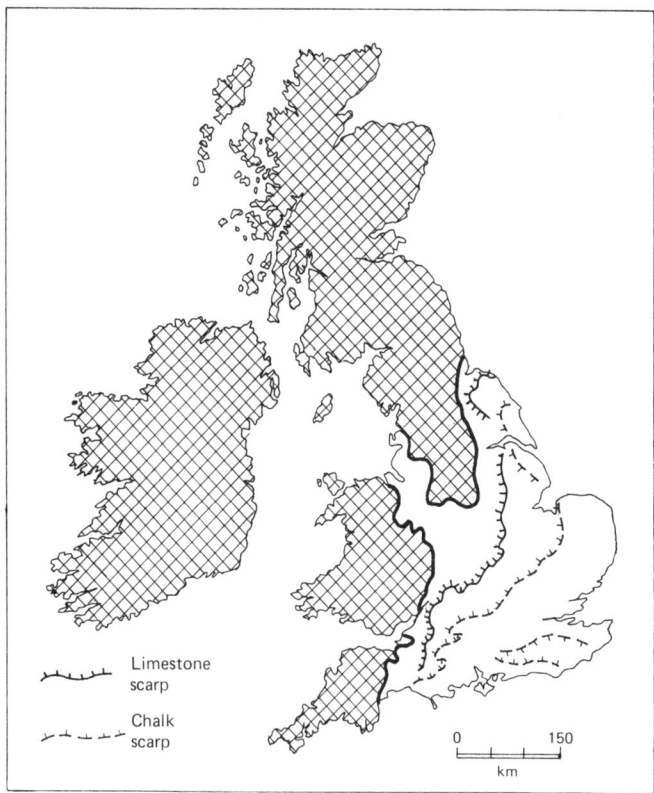

Fig. 13.1 The British Isles: the Highland (shaded) and the Lowland Zones

mostly of limestone or chalk, and low-lying vales floored with clay. Resulting soils are good, except over the restricted sandy areas, and in contrast with the prevalence of pastoral farming in the Highland Zone, the land here is given over mainly to arable farming.

The coal resources, on which Great Britain's industrial primacy was originally founded, are associated with the older rocks of the Highland Zone. They are preserved in the coal basins of central Scotland. Very small reserves are known in Ireland, but most are found, as a result of the accidents of geological history, close to the border between the Highland and Lowland Zones. Coalfields flank the Pennines, in Lancashire and Cumbria to the west, and from Northumberland southward to Nottingham in the east. Small pockets of coal are found throughout the Welsh Border country, and one of the richest and most extensive of British coalfields lies in south Wales. The older, coal-bearing rocks underlie the plain of the English Midlands, rising in places to the surface and creating islands of old rock amid a sea of younger limestones and clays (Fig. 13.2). Coal is also associated with these islands, and this gives rise to the cluster

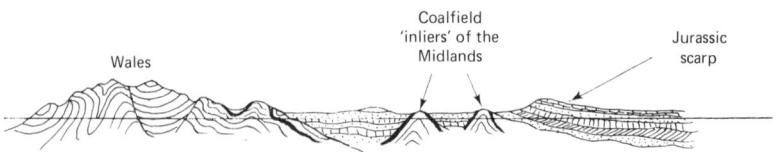

Fig. 13.2 Diagrammatic section across England from South Wales to East Anglia: coal shown in black

of Midland coalfields, a kind of outlier of which lies as far from the Highland Zone as east Kent.

These coalfields vary greatly in their resources, also in the quality of coal and the ease with which it can be extracted (see also Unit 12.6(b)). Today the emphasis is on large seams suitable for the installation of mechanical equipment, and these are most numerous and most extensive in Nottinghamshire and West Yorkshire, where thick seams extend eastward beneath the Vales of Trent and York. The map (Fig. 13.3) shows the extent of the coalfields and the present output of coal according to the districts established by the National Coal Board.

The metalliferous ores that once supported major smelting industries are now of little importance. Iron ore was once widespread, but most of the deposits were small and many are now exhausted. The most substantial of them—those of the Cleveland Hills, the West Midlands and south Wales—have, for practical purposes, been worked out, and the ironworks they formerly supplied are either closed down or forced to use imported ore (see Unit 7.2(a)). The bedded ores of the East Midlands are of low grade and thus costly to smelt. They are still worked near Corby in Northamptonshire, but may soon be abandoned. Non-ferrous ores, once important in many parts of the Highland Zone, are so no longer. Today's production of lead and tin is very small, though it might be expanded if metal prices were to increase sharply.

The British Isles are surrounded by a continental shelf whose greatest depths do not exceed 100 fathoms (about 200 metres). The shelf has long been important for its fisheries, especially shoal fish like the herring and mackerel. It was, indeed, a major source of food, especially to Great Britain and the Low Countries. However, fish stocks have been seriously depleted, and at the time of writing herring-fishing has been temporarily halted. The British fishing fleet was formerly active in Norwegian and Arctic waters, as well as the Iceland seas from which it has now been excluded, as the Icelandic government has asserted its control over fishing up to 200 nautical miles (371 kilometres) from shore.

The chief wealth of the continental shelf is now its oil and natural gas (see also Unit 13.6(a)). These large resources were discovered in the 1960s, and further finds in the northern part of the North Sea have greatly extended the known reserves. Oil reserves, which may be large enough to exploit, have also been located to the north-west of Scotland and in the Celtic Sea, between south-west England and Ireland, and in the Western Approaches to the English Channel. Natural gas fields occur mainly off the Lincolnshire and Norfolk coasts; the oilfields so far developed lie to the east and north-east of Scotland. The true

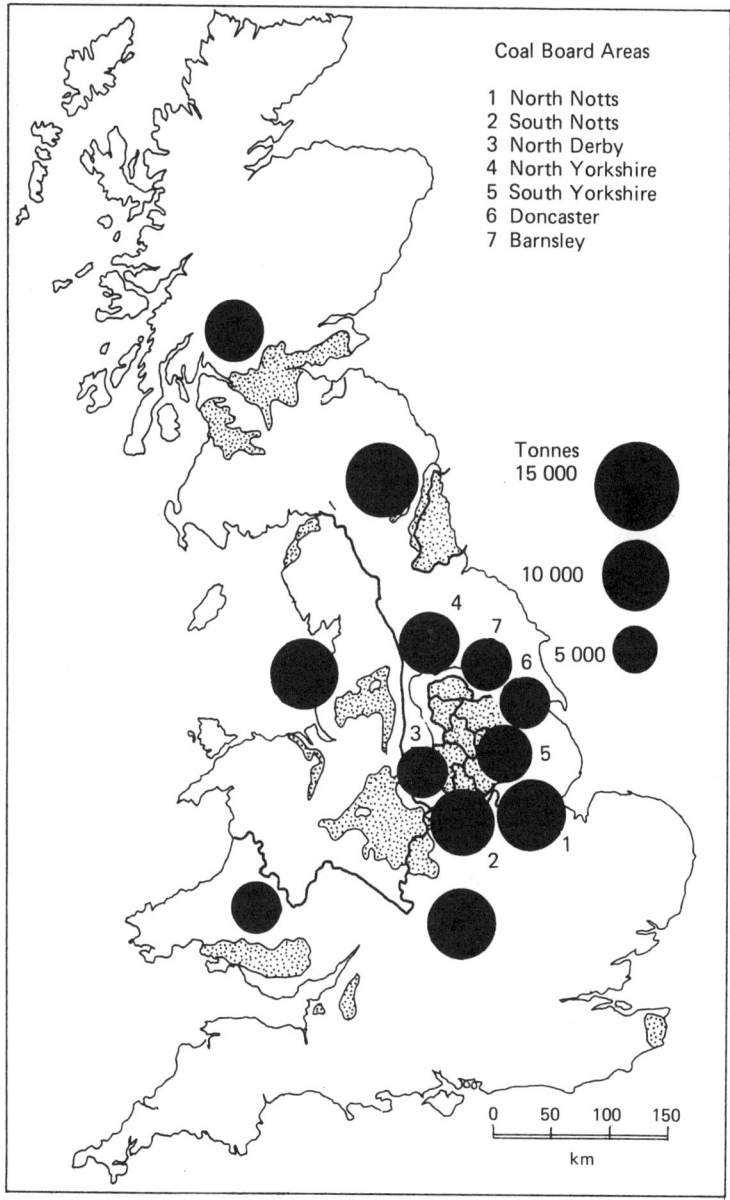

Coal Board Areas

1 North Notts
2 South Notts
3 North Derby
4 North Yorkshire
5 South Yorkshire
6 Doncaster
7 Barnsley

Tonnes
15 000

10 000

5 000

0   50   100   150
km

Fig. 13.3 The coalfields of Britain: output is represented by the sizes of the circles (1977 figures; for statistical purposes the East Kent coalfield is included with that of the East Midlands)

Fig. 13.4 Aerial view of the Sullom Voe terminal on Calback Ness in the Shetland Islands, where oil from the North Sea is brought ashore

extent of these oil and gas reserves are far from clear, owing to the difficulty of exploratory work beneath the sea. At the time of writing, the British government speaks in terms of self-sufficiency by the early 1980s, but there is no assurance that reserves will outlast the present century.

13.2   The Human Resources

The population of Great Britain has increased from about 6 500 000 three centuries ago to about 54 000 000 at the present time: one of the fastest rates of growth known. Three hundred years ago this population was preponderantly rural and engaged in agriculture. Apart from London, which at this time must have had nearly half a million people, there were few cities with more than about 25 000 inhabitants. The density of population was adjusted to agricultural rather than mineral and industrial resources. Most densely peopled were the Home Counties, where soils were good and London provided a market for agricultural produce. The west country and south Midlands were well populated, but the north Midlands and the whole of northern England, as well as Wales and Scotland, had only a sparse population, relieved by somewhat higher densities in Lancashire, Nottinghamshire and central Scotland.

By the time of the first census in 1801, the map of population was changing. Industrial regions were beginning to develop in Lancashire and West Yorkshire, in Tyne and Wear, and near the coalfields of the Midlands. The south-east was starting to lose its economic and demographic dominance, and the northern industrial cities—Manchester, Leeds and Sheffield, as well as the urbanized Birmingham region—had begun to challenge London's supremacy. This trend continued through the nineteenth century, and by its end the pre-industrial pattern of population had been almost reversed. London aside, the greatest densities were to be found in the Midlands, northern England and South Wales. The south and south-east, once the most populous and developed parts of the country, remained mainly agricultural and relatively thinly peopled.

The chief factor in this reversal of the population pattern was the coalfields, which attracted manufacturing industry in the nineteenth century like a magnet. The industrial cities of the north of England, the Midlands and central Scotland grew rapidly (Fig. 13.5). The quality of building was often poor, homes and

Fig. 13.5 Housing of the Industrial Revolution: thousands of streets like this one, photographed in Leeds at the turn of the century, were built in the industrial towns of the north. The crowding together of factories with poor-quality houses led to problems of air pollution and lack of sunlight and people's health inevitably suffered

factories were crowded together and amenities were neglected, resulting in the creation of vast areas of urban blight that constitute one of the most serious problems of our cities today.

The present century has witnessed, if not a reversal of the nineteenth-century trend, at least a change in emphasis. One reason is the decline—relative or absolute—in the traditional British industries: cotton and woollen textiles, iron and steel, shipbuilding; another is the shift in their raw material base. Coal-mining in the United Kingdom reached its peak in the 1930s, but since then oil and natural gas have gone far to replace coal as a source of energy (see Unit 8.6). New industries have therefore found a coalfield site less desirable; indeed, the litter and congestion left behind by earlier industrial growth have tended to repel developers. Instead, port and coastal sites have proved attractive. London's vast market has drawn manufacturing to its suburbs, and this has in turn added to its capacity to attract yet more people and industries.

The overall birth rate is low—about 12 per thousand—and currently only a very small rise is projected before the end of the century. Out-migration has exceeded in-migration by a relatively small margin in recent years. The age-structure of the population can be expected to alter to some extent in the years to come: the proportion of retired elderly people is likely to increase, thus adding to the burden on the health services. At the same time, the numbers of school-age children may decrease, leaving school capacity unused.

There has been in recent years a very considerable internal mobility within the United Kingdom. Since the Second World War there has been a large out-migration from much of the Highland Zone, more especially from the Scottish Highlands and islands, the Southern Uplands and Cheviots, and from much of Wales and south-west England. But even within these regions that on balance lost population, there are small areas of growth around the larger towns and where government-sponsored industry has been established. Growth areas are by and large the south and south-east, and that of strongest growth—more than 30 per cent over twenty years—extends from Greater London north-westward to the West Midlands. Here, between London at one extreme and Birmingham, Manchester, Leeds and Nottingham at the other, a demographic and industrial axis has formed, containing some of the highest population densities to be found anywhere in the United Kingdom. It is here that much of the new manufacturing industry has developed and that most of the mobile sector of the population has settled. Unemployment here is relatively low, though areas of acute umemployment nevertheless remain in the inner cities, such as London and Birmingham.

This migration from the Highland Zone has been due in large measure to the decline of traditional industries and occupations, including crofting and hill-farming, with the resulting high level of unemployment. Despite the out-migration from these areas, unemployment remains very considerably higher in Scotland, northern England and Wales than in the rest of Great Britain (Fig. 13.6). Of course, there are employment black spots in the Midlands, the extreme south-west, the south and the east, and especially in the West Midlands, but the most serious employment problems are found in central Scotland, the north-east, Lancashire and south Wales, all of which are to be related to the decline in the traditional industries (see Unit 13.4(a)).

A significant change in the distribution and composition of the population has resulted from immigration from the New Commonwealth, in particular from the West Indies and the Indian subcontinent. The exact size of this inflow of population is uncertain, since part of it entered the country illegally, but the

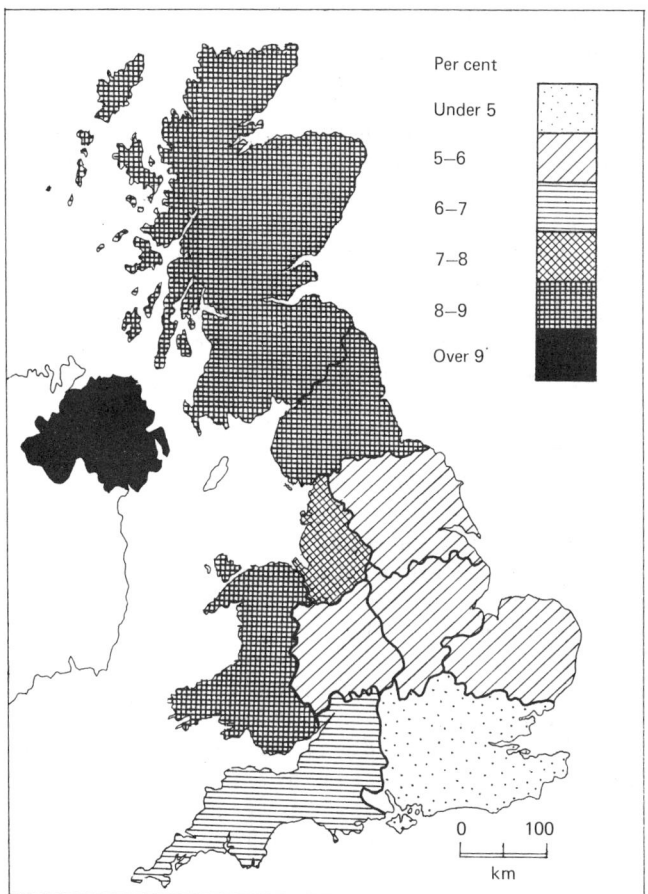

Fig. 13.6 Percentage unemployment in the planning regions of the United Kingdom in 1978

total immigrant population from these sources was estimated to have reached about 1·6 million in 1978, of whom about two-thirds came originally from Pakistan, India and Bangladesh. Legal immigration has now been reduced to a trickle; most of these immigrant communities have a high birth rate, however, and according to whether or not this high level is maintained, their numbers are expected to rise to 2·1 to 2·4 million by the mid-1980s. Even more significant than the numbers of these immigrants is their tendency to concentrate in closely-knit communities in a relatively small number of cities. Over 40 per cent are now settled in Greater London, and no less than two-thirds in the great conurbations of London, the Midlands and the north. In general, immigrants tend to seek the cheap housing available in the decaying inner city districts of the larger conurbations. The Bayswater, Notting Hill and Brixton districts of London have become significant centres of immigrant communities, and a similar development characterizes the blighted area which rings the city of Birmingham.

The population map of the United Kingdom shows a low density—40 or less per square kilometre—over most of the Highland Zone, and a relatively high density—80 or more—in much of the Lowland Zone. Superimposed upon this simple pattern, however, are areas of high density—160 or more. Most of these—central Scotland, the north-east, Lancashire, West Yorkshire and Nottinghamshire, the West Midlands and South Wales—are the areas where traditional industries developed on the basis of coalfields; most of these are of declining importance, and some are the source of a large out-migration. Another region of high density covers the growth area of Greater London and the Home Counties, and the lands to the north-west of London into the Midlands and southward to the coast.

13.3   British Agriculture

The structure of British farming is shaped on the one hand by the physical constraints of climate, relief and soil and, on the other, by the needs of the large urban and industrial population. There is a need to restrict food imports as far as possible, and thus to concentrate on producing those which are least easily transported. For the past two centuries agriculture has employed a steadily diminishing proportion of the total population. Today it is less than 3 per cent, one of the lowest in the world, and the numbers employed are only between a quarter and a third of those so engaged in the late eighteenth century. During this period the volume of foodstuffs produced has roughly doubled. This greatly increased productivity was achieved despite the abandonment of much marginal land, especially in the Highland Zone. It has been made possible by the widespread mechanization of agriculture, by the absorption of small subsistence farms into larger units capable of achieving economies of scale, by specializing in those commodities which the land is most capable of producing, and by the adoption of scientific methods of cultivating the soil and of breeding livestock and seed.

Except in a few small and highly specialized areas, British farming combines the cultivation of field crops in rotation with the rearing of animals (Unit 5.4 (*b*)). Part of the crop provides feed for stock, which in turn supplies manure to the land. This is a traditional pattern of farming, yet one which provides immense scope for variation and adaptation to local conditions of climate, soil and market. There is, in fact, a spectrum in British agriculture from the farm which consists almost wholly of grazing land and that which is made up almost entirely of cropland. At one extreme is the Welsh hill-farm, which embraces many hundreds of hectares of rough pasture grazed by sheep, and no more than a paddock or two of improved land. Near this pastoral extreme is also the West Country dairy farm, on which most of the land is improved pasture, some of it cut each summer for hay which, supplemented by foodstuffs bought in the market, is fed to the cattle. At the opposite extreme is the arable farm in East Anglia or the Fenland of Cambridgeshire and Lincolnshire. Here most of the land is sown in rotation with wheat, barley, sugar-beet (in districts relatively close to a beet-processing factory), potatoes and, more recently, oil-seed rape. The actual rotation used varies with soil and market conditions. Animals are not important to the arable farmer and on many farms none are kept. All crops have therefore to be sold off the land. At this arable end of the spectrum is also the intensively cultivated market garden in which heavily fertilized land is used to produce vegetables and fruit.

Between these pastoral and arable extremes lie the great majority of British farms, in which crops, including fodder crops, are integrated with animal-rearing in proportions which vary from one part of the country to another, and even from farm to farm.

The spatial distribution of these farming types is determined largely by conditions of climate and soil. Hill-farming is restricted to the mountainous regions of the west, where rainfall is heavy and the soil is usually too poor to be worth cultivating. Exclusively arable farming, apart from specialized fruit and vegetable farming which is found close to every large urban centre, occurs only in the dry regions of eastern England, where grass does not grow well and the soil is too valuable to be used in any less intensive way. Very approximately the Lowland Zone, together with the eastern part of the Scottish Lowlands and much of Northern Ireland, is predominantly an arable region, though it includes many areas, notably the clays of southern Essex and the poor sandy soils of the Weald, where pastoralism predominates, partly on account of the soil.

Table 13.1   The overall pattern of land use in the United Kingdom

	Thousand hectare	Per cent
Crops and grass	11 990	63·7
Rough grazing	6 400	33·9
Other (including forestry)	451	2·4
Total agricultural land	18 841	100·0

Table 13.2   The crops of the United Kingdom

	Area (thousand hectare)	Harvested (thousand tonnes)	Yield per hectare (tonnes)
Barley	2 400	10 738	4·5
Wheat	1 076	5 244	4·9
Sugar-beet	202	6 382	31·6
Potatoes	233	6 622	28·4
Oats	195	778	4·0
Kale, etc	55	2 450	44·6
Turnips, swedes	97	5 869	60·5

Fig. 13.7 shows in simplified fashion the distribution of the chief farming types. Reality is a great deal more complex. The generalization that the east is arable and the west pastoral hides the fact that dairy farms and market gardens are found in the outskirts of every city and town, irrespective of soil and climate, and that everywhere the blend of animals and crops varies according to the perception of the individual farmers when deciding how to use their land.

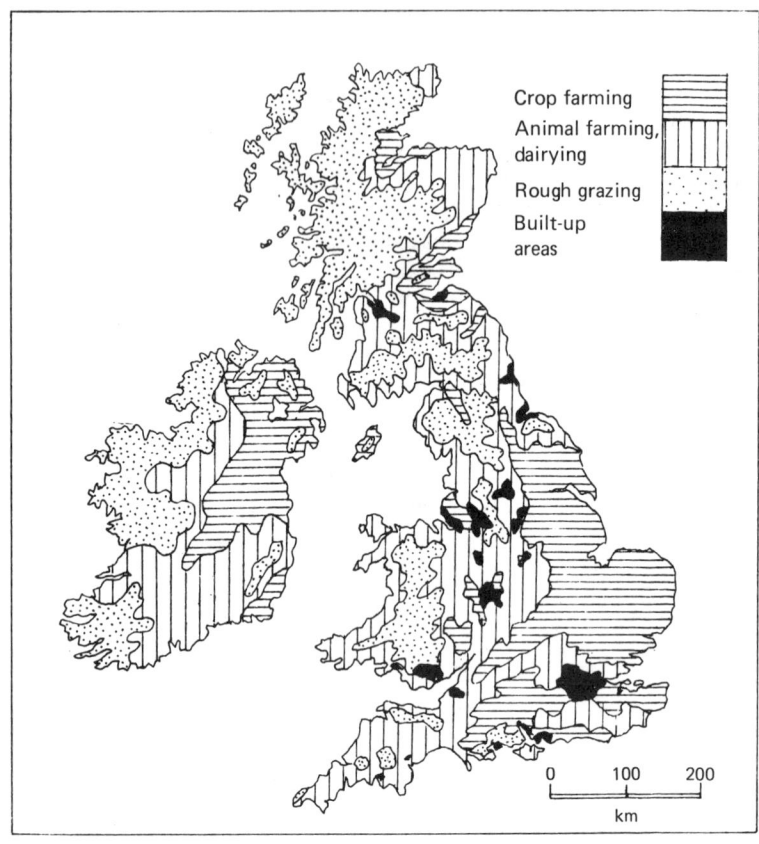

Crop farming
Animal farming, dairying
Rough grazing
Built-up areas

0   100   200
km

Fig. 13.7 The principal types of farming in the British Isles

Agriculture within the United Kingdom supplies about half the country's total food supply. This is made up very largely of meat, milk and other animal products, fruit and vegetables, and sugar. The country could be made more nearly self-sufficing by substituting the production of bread grains for animal products, but only at the expense of living standards and of a severe strain on the land. While the good soils of the drier east can stand continuous cropping, provided that a rotation is used and sufficient carefully selected fertilizer is applied, soils in the moister west will not readily stand cropping for long periods. Such lands must be grassed down under 'long leys' at frequent intervals if they are to maintain their fertility. It is clearly best to devote as much land as possible to the production of high-value foodstuffs like milk, meat, fruit and vegetables, and to rely on imports to supply bread grains and even some fodder crops, except on land to which they are unusually well suited.

In recent years, British agriculture has become a highly organized and very efficient business. The average size of farms has greatly increased. Although two-thirds of all farms are still of less than 40 ha (100 acres), well over 60 per cent of agricultural land is in farms of 60 ha (150 acres) or more, and the number of farms of over 200 ha (500 acres) is tending to rise. These large farms are highly capitalized and mechanized, and most are very efficient units of production. But some of the smaller farms, especially those in marginal areas and in particular in parts of the Highland Zone, still retain a considerable subsistence element. They cannot compete with more efficient and more highly capitalized farms, and they afford only a poor livelihood to their farmers. Many receive some form of government assistance and are eligible for help from the Common Agricultural Policy of the European Community; but many such marginal units may be forced to cease production.

Traditionally, the land of Britain was held in estates, part of which was cultivated by the owner as the 'home' or manor farm, and the rest leased to tenant farmers. During the present century this pattern has undergone profound changes. Inheritance laws have led to the break-up and sale of many estates. Much of the land has passed into the hands of corporations, including insurance companies and pension funds. This land is invariably rented to farmers and, since good land management is in the best interests of the corporation that owns it, it is usually leased in large units that can be managed efficiently. At the time of writing a little over half the farmland of Britain is owned by the farmers who work it. The rest is rented. The tendency is for the amount of rented land to increase, as land passes increasingly into the hands of absentee owners. The questions must be asked: is this a good thing for British farming? Should the government take steps to protect the owner-farmer, who might be expected to show a deeper concern for the long-term interests of his land?

Food Supply and the Common Agricultural Policy
Throughout the nineteenth century and indeed until the United Kingdom's admission to the Common Market in 1973, foodstuffs were imported from all parts of the world and especially from the Commonwealth countries, where grain, meat, vegetable oils and many other agricultural goods could be produced more cheaply than in the United Kingdom. New Zealand butter, cheese and lamb and Australian and Canadian wheat sold below the British costs of production, so the British farmer was subsidized by the government to make him competitive. The taxpayer paid the subsidy, but in return obtained cheap food. This simple system, which benefited both producer and consumer, has now been abandoned in favour of the Common Agricultural Policy (CAP) of the European Community (see Unit 14.3(c)). The Community aims to satisfy its food requirements insofar as this is climatically possible. Most imports from outside the Community are penalized, and have to be replaced by goods from

within—usually at a higher price. Since the system of selective food subsidies has been abandoned, prices to the British consumer have increased.

The CAP was designed for countries with a much higher level of agricultural self-sufficiency than that in the United Kingdom. Three of its members— Ireland, the Netherlands and Denmark—are in fact net exporters of foodstuffs, and they see the United Kingdom as an opportune market for their exportable surplus. Indeed, it might be said that the CAP was conceived for countries in which agriculture employed a much higher proportion of the population than in the United Kingdom. Furthermore, since the Community penalizes imports from outside its borders and stimulates production and sale between its members, food imports into Britain from the Commonwealth are subject to a levy, while those from, say, Denmark are subsidized.

13.4   Manufacturing Industries

The United Kingdom has undergone two Industrial Revolutions. The earlier and more spectacular consisted of the application of mechanical power to industrial processes and of the development of the factory system. It occurred before the introduction of the railway, when bulky, low-value goods like coal could be transported only by river, canal and sea. Under these conditions manufacturing was attracted to the coalfields, leading to the development of industrial regions which, blackened, decaying and often derelict, constitute one of the major economic and social problems of this country today.

The second Industrial Revolution has come in the present century. Its energy base is electricity brought to the factory by the grid system, and the manufactures to which it contributed have in general been of light and consumer-oriented goods. They are mostly labour-intensive; the value added (see Unit 9.1(a)) is usually high and the loss of bulk in manufacturing rarely large. These manufactures include plastics, pharmaceutical and chemical goods, electrical and electronic equipment, light engineering and the manufacture of automobile components and their assembly. They are all, in a sense, footloose industries without rigorous locational requirements and they can be carried on more or less profitably wherever transport is good and labour of sufficient quality is available.

The new industries could have been located in the older and traditional centres of manufacturing. Some, in fact, were so located under the stimulus of government pressure or subsidy. But most sought new areas, uncluttered by the debris of decaying manufacturing, and all looked for good road and rail systems. Most were attracted to Greater London and to the routes that radiate from the capital. They are the chief reason why the Midlands and south-east constitute a region of in-migration and of low unemployment, compared with the traditional industrial regions (see also Unit 13.5(h)).

(a)   Traditional Industrial Regions

There has thus been a relative and in many instances an absolute decline in the importance of the traditional industries of the United Kingdom. Few ships are now built along the Clyde, Tyne and Wear. Most of the cotton mills of Lancashire have ceased production and their buildings have been either demolished or converted to some other use. Not a single blast furnace is now active in the Black Country of the Midlands or in West Yorkshire, where they were once numerous and important, and the last ironworks on the South Wales coalfields has now closed. All these industries had their origins in the eighteenth century. Their decline and even disappearance has left large areas almost derelict and tens of thousands unemployed in cities which once hummed with the activities of the traditional industries.

The decline of these older industries has been to some extent balanced by the development of new, some of which belong to the advanced technologies and call for more sophisticated skills than old-fashioned machine-minding. None of these new industries use energy directly: they were never attracted to the old industrial regions which developed on the coalfields, though some firms have been directed to such sites by the government, anxious to provide employment and to use an existing infrastructure of roads and services. They use electric power from the grid, and are thus not anchored to any one place. Their labour supply is rarely drawn from the older manufacturing regions, and their markets are more likely to be found in Greater London, the south of England and continental Europe than in the industrial north and Scotland.

It would not be true to say that industry has, during the second Industrial Revolution, moved south. Rather, the industries in the traditional manufacturing regions of northern England have declined, and new branches of industry have been established in the Midlands and south-east. The 'new towns' founded within the last thirty years beyond London's 'Green Belt' (see Unit 13.4(b)) have had no difficulty in attracting new industries, and the vigour with which the Milton Keynes project is being pursued shows how great is the continuing demand for industrial sites in this region. The newly industrializing region of Britain is made up of the Midlands, particularly the East Midlands, Greater London and the south-east.

The advantages of these areas are as conspicuous today as those of the coalfields were a century or two ago. They have access to electric power, they are served by the network of roads and railways that radiates from London and they are close to the ports of south-eastern England and easily accessible to continental Europe which provides a market for many of the products of their industries.

(b) Regional Development

The United Kingdom has its share of problem regions in which income levels are low, industry or agriculture declining, and unemployment high. Some are areas from which the life blood has been drained away with the migration of people, especially younger people, to regions where manufacturing was developing. Others are regions where initial advantages have been lost and local industries have been destroyed by the competition of more favoured areas. The existence of such 'depressed' areas has long been recognized. Even before the Second World War attempts were made, through the creation of trading estates, to develop new industries in areas where traditional industries had declined. After 1945 the planning of economic growth assumed a greater importance.

A series of Royal Commissions and legislative enactments attempted to establish a policy towards industrial location and resource use. The nationalization of the coal-mines, the energy-generating system and the railways gave the government direct control over important aspects of the economy. At the same time, the Town and Country Planning Act (1947) endowed it with wide powers over land and resources, and established the fact that social factors are no less important than economic in locating industry, using land and developing towns.

A number of *development areas* was defined, including much of central Scotland, the industrial north-east and Cumbria, Merseyside and south Wales — very broadly, the areas formerly characterized by the coal-based traditional industries. It was the government's intention to encourage the establishment of new industries in these areas and thus to absorb the large pools of unemployment they contained. In 1962 a new scheme of *development districts* was proposed. Within these, points of potential growth were selected and heavy investments made in factories, transport and housing, in the hope that their new prosperity would communicate itself to surrounding areas and the prosperity of the whole region be raised.

The development districts included much of the Scottish Highlands as well as of central Scotland, scattered areas in the north-east, Cumbria, Lancashire and Wales and parts of the extreme south-west. Various government subsidies were offered to firms which located in these districts, which had been defined wholly in terms of their level of unemployment. As development took place in them and the unemployed were gradually absorbed into jobs, so the depressed nature of neighbouring areas which had not previously been classified for development became apparent. These included industrial Lancashire and West Yorkshire, as well as other parts of Scotland and the north of England. The problem of depressed areas, it seemed, could not be tackled on a merely local scale.

In 1964, therefore, the United Kingdom was divided for purposes of planning and economic development into eleven large *economic planning regions*, and these have since remained the basis for the publication of economic statistics, as well as for the implementation of economic policy (see also Unit 13.5). In a further revision of its planning policy in 1972, the government sought to spread its support for development very much more widely. It recognized the existence of *special development areas*, which included most of those designated earlier, and an extensive *development area*, which included the whole of Scotland and the north of England, Wales and much of the south-west (Fig. 13.8). In addition, much of Lancashire and Yorkshire were declared to be *intermediate areas*, less in need of help than the development areas themselves. (The Government abolished this classification in 1979.)

In the course of these changes of policy, south and south-east England and the Midlands were consistently excluded from direct government aid. Unemployment here was low, and average incomes were above the national level. Indeed, new firms were seeking to locate there, and there was even a

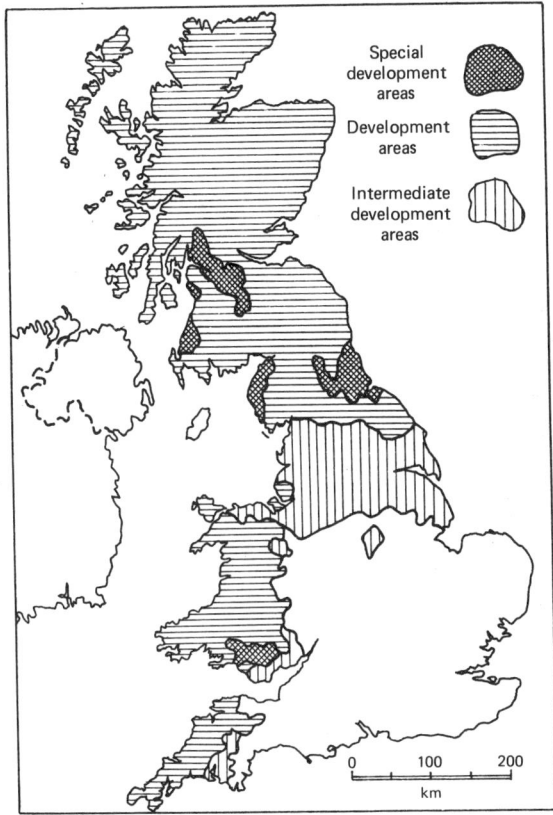

Special development areas

Development areas

Intermediate development areas

0 100 200
km

Fig. 13.8 The development areas of Britain (before 1979)

shortage of some types of labour. The in-migration from other parts of the United Kingdom was directed primarily toward London, which was becoming dangerously extended. The remedy was to enclose London with a *Green Belt*, within which development was thenceforward to be tightly controlled, and at the same time to establish *new towns* close enough to London to benefit from the services which it could offer and yet separated from it by at least the breadth of the Green Belt. Such towns were Harlow, Stevenage and Bracknell. Certain designated older towns were also expanded as 'overspill' centres, where population from congested or redeveloped areas of London might be settled. The concept of the Green Belt and of new towns beyond its limit was applied also in Birmingham and in south Lancashire. Thus governments have, since 1945, pursued the conflicting policies of stimulating industrial growth in the formerly depressed areas and, simultaneously, creating new industrial centres in the relatively prosperous areas of the south and south-east.

Meanwhile, the government was also attempting to protect the natural beauty and rural amenities of much of the country from intrusion by manufacturing

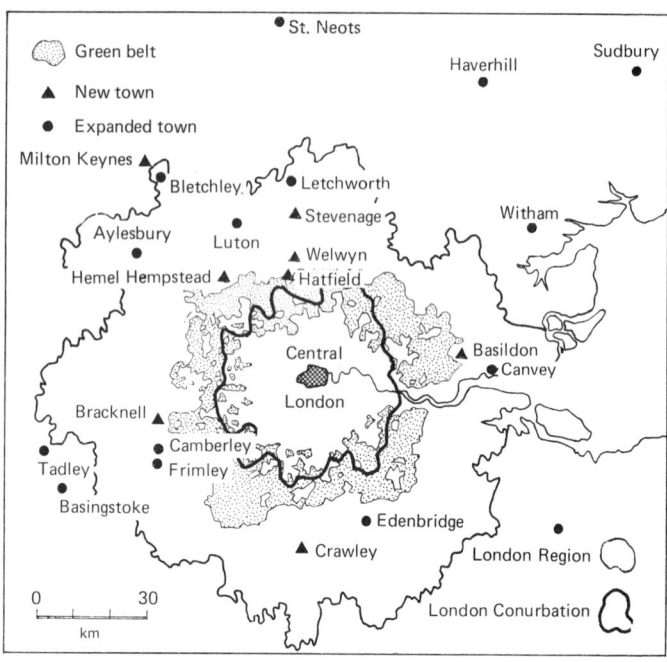

Fig. 13.9 Greater London and the 'Green Belt', showing also the new towns and the expanded ('overspill') towns

industry and housing developments. In fact almost 15 per cent of the area of England and Wales has been designated as *national parks* or as *areas of outstanding natural beauty*. National parks include the Lake District, the Yorkshire Moors and much of the Pennines, the mountains of Wales and, in the south-west, Exmoor and Dartmoor. Areas of outstanding natural beauty include much of the British coast as well as the Cotswolds, the Chilterns and the North and South Downs.

No attempt is made to restrict farming activities in these areas, or to interfere with traditional developments. Fortunately, most would be highly unattractive to the industrialist and developer. Many, however, serve as water catchment areas, and some have great potential for summer or holiday homes. Mineral development is even possible in some, and china clay working has recently been expanded in Dartmoor National Park. There are clearly great difficulties in pursuing a policy of restricting economic development in such areas, and the government has not yet succeeded in reconciling its policies of development on the one hand and environmental conservation on the other.

13.5   Planning Regions

The needs of the planners brought about the division of the United Kingdom into regions for purposes of defining problems, gathering statistics and planning the strategy of economic growth during the rest of this century. A new set of economic regions was defined in 1964, and these were considerably modified in the light of experience in 1974. Eleven were defined, in each of which there was some common factor. Criteria, however, were not wholly economic. Three regions—*Wales, Scotland* and *Northern Ireland*—were political. One of them, Northern Ireland, had enjoyed since 1922 a degree of 'devolved' government (terminated in 1972), and the other two had their respective Secretaries of State, charged with the supervision of their local affairs, in the British government.

England is itself divided into eight regions (Fig. 13.10):

Fig. 13.10 The planning regions of the United Kingdom

(*a*) *northern England*, made up of Northumberland, Tyne and Wear, Durham, Cleveland and Cumbria;

(*b*) the *north-west*, basically Lancashire and Cheshire;

(*c*) *Yorkshire and Humberside*;

(d) *West Midlands*;

(e) *East Midlands*;

(f) *East Anglia*;

(g) the *south-west*, from Wiltshire and Dorset to Cornwall; and

(h) *south-eastern England*, including Greater London.

None of these eleven planning regions can be regarded as a homogeneous 'region'. The least varied is East Anglia; the most diverse is probably Scotland, which is in area by far the largest. Each, however, has in common certain dominant characteristics in terms of economic development, resources and employment.

(a) Northern England

The Northern Planning Region is the only one in England which is wholly classed as a development area. It spans the Pennines and extends from the Irish Sea to the North Sea, including the Lake District and Cheviot Hills as well as the coalfields of Cumbria and Northumberland–Durham. It combines a low agricultural potential with a narrowly based and, in some respects, obsolete industrial development. The Cumbrian coalfield, always small, is now of only minor significance and supports little industry. The coalfield of Northumberland–Durham, on the other hand, is large and important, yielding about 12 per cent of the United Kingdom's coal production. It was at one time the most productive in the country, and played an important role in the early years of industrial growth.

The most important industries in the region, apart from the mining and export of coal, have been traditionally iron-smelting, steel-making and shipbuilding. To these has been added during the present century the manufacture of basic chemicals at Billingham. The older industries have declined disastrously, while the chemical industry remains capital- rather than labour-intensive and, in terms of employment, cannot compensate for the decline of traditional industries. Despite attempts to develop new industries and the creation of modern trading estates, the unemployment level remains consistently the highest in England.

The chief urban and industrial concentrations are in Tyne and Wear (Newcastle and Sunderland) and in Cleveland (Middlesbrough). The former was the chief centre of the shipbuilding industry, now almost reduced to insignificance; the latter now contains all of the diminishing iron and steel industry of the region. North of the Tees is the very large, important and expanding chemical industry of Billingham. Attempts have been made to attract new industries both to the older centres and to such 'new' towns as Peterlee and Washington, but a major problem is the remoteness of northern England from the major consuming centres of the Midlands and south-east.

(b) The North-west Region

This is essentially made up of Lancashire and neighbouring Cheshire. Its chief urban centres are Manchester with its ring of satellite towns, the port city of Liverpool, and a line of industrial towns, including Preston and Blackburn, in the Ribble valley. It is primarily a manufacturing region and agriculture is of minor significance, though dairying and intensive market gardening are carried on on the Lancashire plain. Industry is far more diversified here than in the Northern Region. There are nevertheless a number of single-industry towns, mainly founded on cotton-spinning or cotton-weaving, to the north of Manchester and in the Ribble valley. With the decline of traditional industries these have experienced an acute depression. The larger conurbations of Manchester and Liverpool have a more broadly based economic structure, and this has protected them from the worst consequences of economic decline. Nevertheless, the region as a whole suffers from severe unemployment, from the out-migration of the more energetic elements of the population, and from widespread urban blight. New and 'overspill' towns have been designated in the more open country between Greater Manchester and Liverpool, and new industries, in particular the manufacture of cars, have been located there. Development in the north-west is greatly encouraged by the road and rail net linking it with the Midlands and south-east and by the presence of the ports of Liverpool and Manchester, together with intermediate shipping points along the Manchester Ship Canal.

(c) Yorkshire and Humberside

This, like the north-west, is a well-diversified region, but within it are areas of intensive local specialization. To the west, close to the Pennines, are the woollen- and worsted-weaving districts centred in Leeds, Bradford and Huddersfield, and the steel-making area of Sheffield and Rotherham. In the centre, the Vale of York is an important agricultural region and also contains the most productive areas of the Yorkshire coalfield, where new reserves are being reached at ever-increasing depth. Lastly, the eastern part of the region, with the exception of Humberside, is little developed industrially and over the Yorkshire Wolds and Moors has small agricultural potential.

Present plans call for some diversification of manufacturing in the more specialized regions of the west, and a considerable development near Selby, where large new coal reserves are being exploited. The M1 and A1 motorways form an axis through the area of most vigorous growth, linking it with the East Midlands and the south-east. Humberside presents a special case. There has been some industrial development near Hull, and at Scunthorpe in South Humberside is the only iron and steel production site away from tidewater that is destined to expand. Nevertheless, the industrial potential of this estuarine region has not been realized, and there is unlikely to be any significant growth in the near future. The reason probably lies in the weakness of its transport links with the Midlands and south. It lies apart from the north–south axis, and Hull has been regarded—not altogether fairly—as one of the less accessible of English cities. The completion of the new bridge across the Humber to the west of the city will do something to correct this isolation.

(d) The South-west Region

This diverse region extends from Wiltshire and Gloucestershire to Cornwall. It includes the important growth area around Bristol and Bath, the mainly agricultural lands of Somerset, Dorset and east Devon, and the relatively depressed south-western peninsula. Few factors are common to the whole region. The Bristol area, including the port of Avonmouth, is a growth point, integrated increasingly with London and the Home Counties, but its weakness is its dependence on the aircraft industry. Little growth is anticipated in the rural areas to the south, though the development of light industry is being encouraged near Taunton and Exeter. The far south-west faces more intractable problems. The traditional industries in western Devon and Cornwall are mining, fishing, the repair and outfitting of ships, and agriculture, but only the last has retained its earlier importance. The fishing industry has collapsed, ship-repairing is being run down, and only two tin-mines remain active in the whole region. Despite the creation of new industries, especially in Plymouth and west Cornwall, the level of unemployment is very high and there seems little prospect of any significant economic growth.

On the other hand, the whole of the south-west has become a resort area, and catering for summer tourists is now the most important industry in many coastal districts. The holiday season is, however, short—not more than three months— and attempts to develop a winter season have not been successful. An urgent problem is to develop employment opportunities in the off-season (see Unit 11.7(*i*)). There is, furthermore, a limit to the capacity of the region to absorb tourists. Already most resorts are far too crowded during the season, roads are congested and environmental damage close to the coast is considerable.

Fig. 13.11 The tourist season: inadequate roads are choked with traffic carrying thousands of holiday-makers towards the sea

(e) East Anglia

This is one of the smallest and most homogeneous of the planning regions of the United Kingdom. It is furthermore one of the least industrialized and agriculturally among the most important, with one of the finest areas of arable farming in the Fenland. The region is dominated by four widely spaced urban centres—Ipswich, Norwich, Cambridge and Peterborough—all of which have a variety of light and food-processing industries.

East Anglia is relatively close to Greater London, and, like the Bristol region, is steadily becoming more intimately linked with south-east England. A number of towns in the southern part of the region have become overspill centres, notably Haverhill, Bury St Edmunds, Thetford and Huntingdon, while there are major industrial developments at Ipswich and Peterborough.

The coastal region, including the Norfolk Broads, is a major resort area, with its attendant problems of summer congestion, environmental damage and winter unemployment. On the other hand, the ports of Harwich and Felixstowe have achieved major importance in the United Kingdom's foreign trade. They already have good links with Greater London, and further improvements in the road from the East Midlands must bring about an increase in container traffic. Indeed, there is a possibility that the Ipswich–Bury St Edmunds–Cambridge–Peterborough route will develop as a kind of industrial axis.

The last three planning regions of England are classed as 'growth' regions. Despite the existence of a few depressed areas with high unemployment, largely as a consequence of overconcentration on traditional industries, the economy is expanding and there is in-migration of population.

(f) West Midlands

At the heart of the West Midlands region lies the conurbation of Greater Birmingham, with almost half the region's population. To the east lies the industrial concentration centred on Coventry and to the north the specialized industrial development of Stoke-on-Trent. The western half of the region, embracing the counties of Shropshire and Hereford and Worcester, is more hilly and less populous and urbanized.

The Birmingham region developed during the eighteenth and nineteenth centuries on the basis of the metal industries. Iron-smelting and fabrication were its life blood. Smelting has long been in decline, and the last furnaces have now closed. Metal-fabricating, however, remains the dominant industry, making up no less than 70 per cent of the total manufacturing output of the region. The metal industries are dominated by automobile and other forms of engineering and by the production of electrical goods. A heavy reliance on an uncertain car industry casts a shadow over the region.

The vast Birmingham conurbation, which has more than its share of derelict housing and industrial premises, is enclosed within a Green Belt that checks its growth. Nevertheless, little progress has been made with the creation of 'new' and 'overspill' towns within the region.

The West Midlands region lies at the focus of the motorway system of Great

Britain, and its excellent transport system is without question a major factor in its continued vitality. Nevertheless, both a greater diversification in its economic activities and also the movement of population from its central conurbation to new urban communities within the region seem to be desirable.

(g) East Midlands

In contrast, the East Midlands is not dominated by a single conurbation. It has a number of widely spaced urban centres, each having a distinctive range of economic activities and its own dependent local district. Most lie towards the west of the region, where there is no clear boundary between the East and the West Midlands. On the south, Northampton and neighbouring towns seem to have more in common with Bedford and Milton Keynes, within the south-east region, than with the derelict industrial areas near Chesterfield in the north. This merely emphasizes the impossibility of defining homogeneous planning regions.

Despite some black spots, the East Midlands present a general picture of prosperity and growth. Engineering, electrical and electronic industries are expanding, and service industries are increasingly important. Derby, Nottingham, Leicester and Northampton are major growth points, and the southern part of the region is now receiving a considerable 'overspill' population from Greater London. There are, however, several problem areas, including the long-exploited coal-mining districts to the north-west of Nottingham, the footwear industry of Kettering, Wellingborough and Northampton, and the hosiery and knitwear manufactures of Nottingham and Hinkley. To these may shortly be added Corby in Northamptonshire, where steel-making, the only significant local industry, has now ceased.

Transport and communications are, as we have seen, a more important factor in economic prosperity than the possession of industrial resources. In this respect the East Midlands are well served, with excellent road and rail links with Greater London and the south-east and improving connections across East Anglia to the east coast ports.

(h) South-east England

This is one of the largest regions in terms of area and by far the biggest in population. It also has the fastest rate of economic growth. Its population of about 17 million (1975 estimate) may soon rise to 20 million. There has been a movement of population to the Greater London area during most of the present century, and the problems this created were recognized at least forty years ago. By 1939, the population of the London conurbation had risen to about 8·7 million. This created immense social, economic and environmental problems. The Greater London Plan, published in 1945, aimed to control the population of Greater London by (a) enclosing it within a Green Belt, and (b) absorbing the population increase, as well as part of that from derelict areas, into 'new' and 'overspill' towns in other parts of the south-east region (see Unit 13.4) and even intruding into the neighbouring East Anglia and East Midlands planning regions. In consequence, London's population is showing a decline, while some of the 'new' and 'overspill' towns continue to grow.

Fig. 13.12 Aerial view of a new town (Milton Keynes) in the early stages of the construction of roads, houses and factories in the Buckinghamshire countryside

The growth of the south-east region is self-perpetuating; the more it develops, the greater the incentive for industrial and service enterprises to locate there. But the physical and environmental advantages of the region are immense. It is the only planning region in Great Britain with a fast road and rail link with every other. Though the docks along the Thames downstream from the City are of diminishing importance, the region is served by a succession of ports from Felixstowe to Southampton, and has quick and frequent links with continental Europe. From the point of view of transport, the most serious shortcoming is the lack of a completed ring road to enable traffic to avoid the congestion of Greater London.

Few branches of manufacturing have not been attracted to the south-east, and in particular to Greater London. Its activities range from iron-smelting (at Dagenham) and car manufacture to the lightest of consumer goods industries. Textiles and heavy chemicals are under-represented, but service industries are more strongly developed than in any other region. The range and variety of industries established in a 'new' town such as Harlow or Stevenage is such as to defy any quick or easy description. Furthermore, the size of the population—about a third of that of the whole United Kingdom—necessitates a developed food industry and system of food marketing. London contains commodity markets, especially in fruit, vegetables and meat, which supply a large part of the British population.

Service industries are especially important in Greater London, particularly the financial, insurance and educational services; but London also contains the headquarters of a great many firms whose manufacturing activities are carried on elsewhere. Such concerns necessitate the daily movement of a very large workforce into and out of London, in particular 'inner' London. Around one-third of a million people commute into and out of the City of London every day, and this traffic is drawn from the whole area to the south and south-east of London and, in the north, from as far afield as Oxford, Luton and Cambridge. A movement on this scale is possible only with a highly developed system of transport, but the fact that it is fully used only at peak hours in the morning and late afternoon tends to make it relatively expensive. Partly for this reason, some business houses have moved out of Greater London to other sites in south-east England where problems of congestion and travel are less conspicuous.

The chief problems in south-east England are those of controlling growth and directing it into courses which are economically and socially the most desirable. By contrast those of northern England and of the three regions yet to be described consist largely of arresting economic decline and of ameliorating its socially destructive consequences.

Wales, Scotland and Northern Ireland have each been constituted separate planning regions. This may be a concession to the strength of local feeling and it would be sensible if some form of 'devolved' government were established in these regions. Each is very far from homogeneous, however, and parts of Wales and Scotland could more realistically have been linked for planning purposes with neighbouring areas of England.

(*i*) Wales

The planning region conforms with the extent of the historic Principality, and embraces three distinct and contrasted subregions. Two of these, north and mid-Wales, are mountainous and lack resources for either agriculture or industry; their population is sparse, declining and in some parts insufficient to support the basic social services. Though there is an industrial development in the north-east, the steelworks at Shotton on the Dee estuary has closed; there is little scope elsewhere for manufacturing, and even this development belongs economically more to Lancashire and Cheshire than to Wales. Much of north Wales has been constituted a national park and is an important tourist area, with all the resulting environmental and social problems.

South Wales, by contrast, is one of Britain's traditional, coal-based industrial regions. Its nineteenth-century prosperity was based upon coal, much of which was exported, and on iron and steel production. The latter, located originally *on* the coalfield, provided metal for the tinplate and engineering industries which lay closer to the south coast of Wales. Coal-mining has declined and the coal export has ceased. The last integrated iron and steel works on the coalfields, located there in the 1930s in an attempt to rescue the area from economic decline, has been closed, and the industry is now concentrated at two giant coastal sites, Port Talbot and Llanwern, near Newport. The tinplate industry, once the principal manufacture in the Llanelli–Swansea region, is now reduced to only two factories.

The economy of south Wales was always more narrowly based than that of any other of the traditional industrial regions, and it has suffered proportionately. The decline of coal-mining and iron-working in the mountain valleys has been disastrous, and even in the 1930s the British government attempted to stimulate new industries in the region. Since the end of the Second World War, new towns have been developed at Cwmbran and Llantrisant and major expansion has taken place at Newport, Cardiff, Bridgend, Swansea, Llanelli and elsewhere; the Royal Mint was moved to Llantrisant, and the Department of Vehicle Licensing and Control was established at Swansea. This new growth is largely on the Glamorgan plain. Nothing, however, can be done to arrest the economic decline of the mining valleys of the interior.

The future of south Wales is closely bound up with its transport links with the Midlands and south-east. The M4 motorway, the Severn bridge and the improved roads through the Glamorgan plain, as well as the Head of the Valleys Road across the northern end of the mining valleys, are having the effect of making south Wales more accessible and encouraging to the location of new industries.

(j) Scotland

Like Wales, Scotland consists of a traditional, coal-based industrial region set in a region of infertile mountains and hills with a small and diminishing population. Most of the Scottish population—no less than 66 per cent—are found in the central Lowlands, and a large proportion of these live in the congested Glasgow conurbation. To the south are the thinly peopled Southern Uplands, and to the north the even less populous Highlands. These two areas have long been losing population, both to the more highly urbanized central Lowlands and to England. In southern Scotland there are minor growth centres in the Tweed valley, once important for its textiles. In the Highlands and islands crofting and fishing, the former mainstays of the population, are disappearing. Hydro-electric power has done something to revivify some areas, notably near Inverness and Fort William. The sparse population of some coastal areas has encouraged the location of nuclear reactors, but the only significant developments in the foreseeable future are likely to be associated with North Sea oil. This has, indeed, set off dynamic changes in the region of Aberdeen, where much of the oil is brought ashore, and in the Shetland Islands, where it poses the big question of whether the economic advantages accruing from the oil outweigh the environmental damage resulting from its exploitation.

The dominant problem in Scotland is the highly urbanized western central Lowlands. The traditional industries were iron and steel, shipbuilding and textiles, particularly cottons and linen. All were carried on in a very congested urban area. Iron and steel remain important and, indeed, the British Steel Corporation has recently modernized and extended its Ravenscraig works. Shipbuilding on the Clyde, once a major user of steel, has declined almost to the point of extinction, and the textile industries of Paisley and Motherwell have suffered the same fate as those of Lancashire. The problems have been to attract new industries, to disperse part of the population of the conurbation to new and overspill towns, and to redevelop the congested and decayed areas of the inner cities.

New towns have been established close to the Glasgow conurbation at Cumbernauld, East Kilbride and Irvine, and, farther to the east, at Livingston and Glenrothes; a new industrial complex is also being planned for the Tay valley, near Perth. Dundee, traditionally a centre for the manufacture of jute and marmalade, is diversifying and expanding its industrial production.

Attempts to arrest the economic decline of Scotland and the out-migration of its younger and more vigorous population are linked closely with, first, the spin-off effects of the oil and petrochemical industries and, second, the improvement of communications with southern England. The construction of motorways has made relatively little progress, though the Forth and Tay road bridges have provided an essential link between Tayside and the south. But although emphasis has hitherto been on the north–south linkages with England, it is possible that routes across the central Lowlands from the Firth of Clyde on the west to the Firths of Forth and Tay on the east might become part of a routeway between the Atlantic and continental Europe, with beneficial effects on the Scottish economy.

(k) Northern Ireland

The six counties of Northern Ireland were not only separated from the rest of the United Kingdom by the Irish Sea and North Channel, but also, until 1972, by a separate, devolved government at Stormont. Economic growth has been hindered by the difficulties engendered by this separation: the high cost of energy and transport and problems of break-of-bulk. Northern Ireland has always been poorer than the rest of the United Kingdom; personal incomes are lower and capital available for development very much smaller. The province is, indeed, being subsidized by Great Britain.

The region is dominated by the Belfast conurbation, which contains about 27 per cent of the population. Its traditional industries of linen-weaving and shipbuilding are all in decline, and political unrest and the high cost of all inputs except labour do nothing to encourage new industries. The rural areas, which make up most of Northern Ireland, are poorer even than the urban. Farms are small and inadequately capitalized and part of their potential market lies on the far side of the Irish Sea.

There is a movement of labour from rural areas to Greater Belfast, and from here to other parts of the United Kingdom. Nevertheless, very high levels of underemployment and unemployment remain in both rural and urban areas. Plans for redevelopment are bedevilled by political unrest and uncertainty. It is proposed, however, to limit the growth of Belfast, to establish new and overspill towns, especially in the counties of Antrim and Down, and to establish light industries in various parts of the province in order to provide employment. Redevelopment of substandard areas of Greater Belfast is also planned. Development is, however, complicated by the sectarian issue. The highest levels of unemployment are found in the predominantly Roman Catholic areas, and it is in these that much of the investment would have to be made.

13.6   Energy Supply

The United Kingdom, whose industrial prosperity was first established on the basis of coal, now derives scarcely more than a third of its energy from this source, as Table 13.3 shows.

Petroleum and natural gas have come to dominate the energy supply. The power used in transport, whether by rail, road or ship, is derived almost exclusively from oil, and since the 1960s natural gas from the North Sea has almost wholly replaced the town gas previously made from coal (Fig. 13.13). Hydro-electric power, mainly from the rivers of the Scottish Highlands, is of trifling importance. The amount of electricity produced by nuclear-powered generators is still small but is likely to increase in importance with the completion of projected plans. Almost all nuclear reactors are located on the coast (Trawsfynydd in Wales, sited beside a large reservoir, is the only

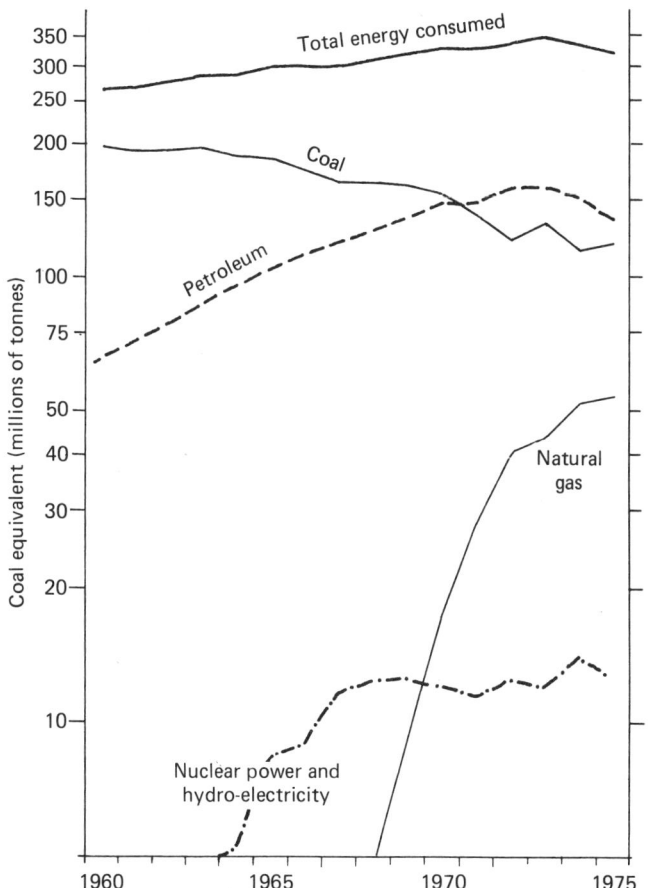

Fig. 13.13 Changes in the consumption of primary fuels in the United Kingdom

Table 13.3   United Kingdom sources of energy, 1977 (per cent)

Coal	36·3
Petroleum	40·4
Natural gas	18·5
Nuclear electricity ⎱ Hydro-electricity ⎰	4·8

Source: *Digest of United Kingdom Energy Statistics* (HMSO, 1978)

exception), both to obtain the great quantities of cooling water they need and also to restrict the danger of radioactive contamination. There has been vigorous opposition to the nuclear energy programme from environmentalists, but it should be said in reply that there is not a single energy source whose development does not present risks. The dangers inherent in the further development of coal resources may well be much greater than those resulting from the use of nuclear reactors.

Energy requirements are likely to continue to increase throughout the rest of

Fig. 13.14 Trawsfynydd nuclear power station in Gwynedd

this century. During this period the North Sea reserves of oil will be greatly reduced if not exhausted, and amounts available from the Middle East and elsewhere are likely to be small. The United Kingdom will be obliged to turn to other energy sources. Aside from the unlikely contingency that solar, tidal and geothermal power may be greatly developed, reliance must be placed on coal and nuclear power. Coal reserves, as we have already seen (Unit 8.3(c)), are large, though technical problems will make mining expensive in most coalfields. Nuclear power can be expected to become a great deal more important, though any decision to invest in reactors is a political one, and the environmentalists' lobby may succeed in restricting developments.

(a) Oil and Natural Gas

Natural gas from the North Sea field was first brought ashore in significant quantities about 1970. Most is found off the coasts of Norfolk, Lincolnshire and Yorkshire, though there is reason to anticipate further finds off the southern and south-western coasts, as well as in the main oilfields off Scotland. Pipeline networks radiate from the Norfolk coast, near Happisburgh, and from the Humber (Fig. 13.15). There are few parts of this country that are not now accessible to the gas net.

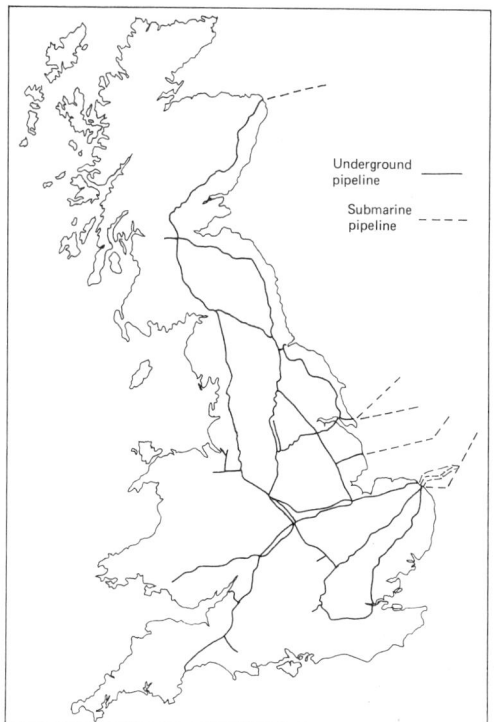

Underground pipeline ——

Submarine pipeline – – – –

Fig. 13.15 The natural gas transmission system in Britain

Oil has been of increasing importance as an energy source (see Unit 8.4), though until the later 1970s it was imported mainly from Nigeria and the Persian Gulf. The oil crisis of 1973 led to a decline in consumption, but with the growing supply of oil from the North Sea, demand is likely to increase. The most abundant reserves lie to the east of the Shetland and Orkney Islands, and most of the oil brought ashore by pipeline at Sullam Voe (Shetland), Flotta (Orkney) and at St Fergus and Cruden Bay in north-eastern Scotland. Oil from the Norwegian 'Ekofisk' field is piped to Teesside owing to the deep submarine canyon which separates it from the Norwegian coast. Other overseas oil, which until very recently supplied the whole of the United Kingdom's requirements, is imported through a small number of ports, most of which also have refineries and plant for manufacturing petrochemicals.

(b) Coal

Only coal appears to offer a long-term source of energy for this country. Reserves are large, considerably more than half of the exploitable resources of the European Community. Most of the more easily worked seams have been exhausted, and some of the older mines are too small to be worked economically. Some coalfields, notably those of the Welsh Border and of the Bristol region, have ceased production; others, like the Scottish, Cumbrian and East Midland fields, are of diminishing importance, and production is tending more and more to concentrate on a few areas with thick, level seams of good-quality coal. Foremost among these are Yorkshire and Nottinghamshire, where Selby and the Vale of Belvoir are now the scene of highly important developments.

Coal production reached its highest level—about 258 million tonnes—on the eve of the Great Depression. Since then there has been a steady decline as, first, weakening demand and more recently the competition of other sources of energy cut back on production. By 1972 the total annual output had fallen to 122 million tonnes. The following year, however, saw the Middle East oil crisis. Attention was again turned to coal as a source of energy. Its decline was arrested, and within a few years demand, and hence production, began to increase. Output for 1977 was 122 100 000 tonnes. About 80 per cent of the coal produced is converted into 'secondary fuels' by way of the steam generator, and this proportion is likely to grow. A very much smaller proportion of oil and natural gas is used in this way.

13.7   Transport in Britain

The national electricity grid (Fig. 13.16), which has made possible the wide dispersion of manufacturing of recent years, is a form of transport insofar as it allows energy to be moved from generating stations to consumers. No less important, however, is the movement of more tangible commodities: raw materials, components and finished goods. If the newer manufacturing industries were to be located away from the traditional industrial centres, they had to choose areas well served by transport, and, in the circumstances of the late twentieth century, good roads are far more essential than railways.

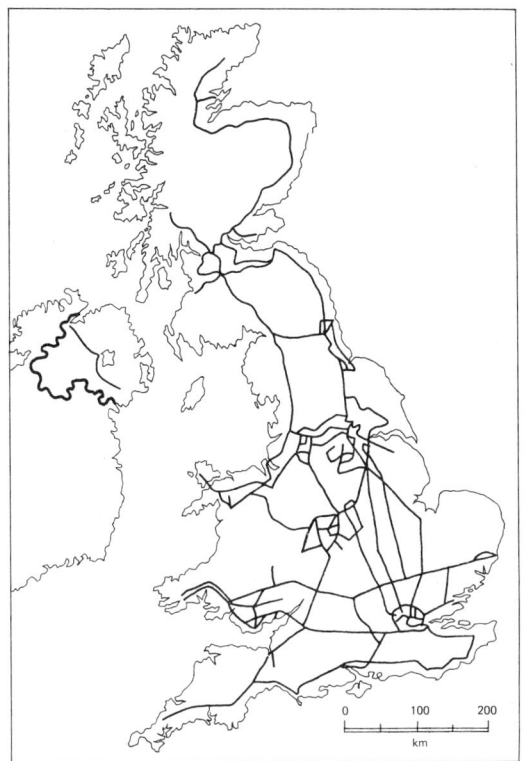

Fig. 13.16 The principal transmission lines of the electricity grid system of the United Kingdom

In the eighteenth and early nineteenth centuries, rivers were made navigable and canals were built to convey goods which could not easily be carried over the rough roads. Internal navigation was then replaced by the railway system which, built by a number of competing companies, spread over the country until it linked every significant centre of population; indeed, it was perhaps overdeveloped, with too many competing lines on the main routes and too many branch lines carrying too little traffic.

The development of road transport between the two world wars began to cut into the use of the railways. There was a degree of unification and rationalization of the railway system in the 1920s, and in 1947 it was nationalized. As time went by, much underused capacity was eliminated: between 1950 and 1974, the total length of the railway system was reduced from 31 690 kilometres to 18 532, the number of passenger stations was reduced by 60 per cent and that of freight-handling stations by over 90 per cent. The number of passenger-kilometres travelled has increased slightly, a result of the greater use of the long-distance 'Inter-City' trains, but the movement of freight, measured in tonne/kilometres, has fallen by a third.

Fig. 13.17 shows the changes in the pattern of passenger travel on British Rail. The movement of both passengers and freight is today overwhelmingly between London and the south-east, the Midlands, Yorkshire and the north-west. The railway lines from London toward Lancashire and Yorkshire form a kind of axis along which much of the new industrial development has been located. All the 'new towns' in south-east England have been established on these major routes.

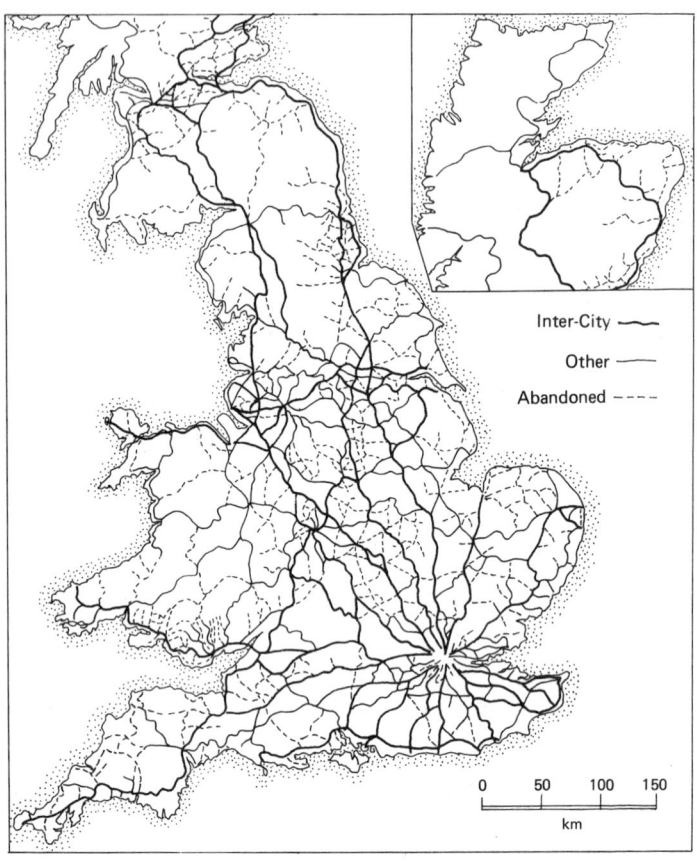

Inter-City ——
Other ——
Abandoned ----

0   50   100   150
km

Fig. 13.17 The railway network of Great Britain; the closure of hundreds of miles of track during the 1950s and 1960s left a drastically slimmed-down, streamlined system

The contraction of the railway network has been due chiefly to the competition of road transport. Between 1951 and 1975 the number of passenger cars on the roads increased almost sixfold, from 2·4 million to 14·1 million, and that of freight vehicles doubled, from 0·9 to 1·8 million. At the same time the network of trunk roads increased by only 16 per cent, from 13 829 kilometres to 16 032 kilometres. The closure of the less-used railways placed a burden on road transport. The private car and public bus gained an added importance, even though in many parts of the country the road network, and also the public transport system which uses it are totally inadequate. One of the most serious social problems resulting from these changes in the transport system is the growing isolation of small rural communities and the consequent decay of village life as the villagers move increasingly to the towns.

The effect of recent developments in the road network, especially the construction of motorways, has been to reinforce the axial pattern of transport which radiates from London to the Midlands and north. Trunk roads closely parallel the railways and are an important—perhaps the most important—factor in attracting manufacturing to the south-east. Road vehicles now account for about two-thirds of the freight movement in the United Kingdom, as against only 17·5 per cent by rail. Their predominance in passenger travel is overwhelming: about 80 per cent is by private car, 12 per cent by bus, and only 8 per cent by rail. Dependence on road transport is overwhelming, and the Midlands and south-east have by far the best road network.

The closure of many branch railways, together with the failure to modernize or improve the roads, has left many parts of this country relatively isolated. Among them are much of Scotland and Wales, as well as parts of East Anglia and Lincolnshire and of the south-west. The effect has been to deter the location of new industry in these areas and to hasten the out-migration from them towards the south-east.

Domestic air travel plays only a small role in the United Kingdom. It is practicable only between major urban centres, and here it has to compete with 'Inter-City' rail services. Only where a sea-crossing is involved, as with Northern Ireland and the Channel Islands, is the saving in time considerable, and the only heavily used routes are those between London and Edinburgh, Glasgow, Belfast and the Channel Islands.

13.8   Seaports and International Trade

The United Kingdom is a commercial nation. Overseas trade provided both capital and incentive for the Industrial Revolution. It continues to furnish today about a half of the domestic food supply, most of the metals used, part of the oil supply and much of the raw materials of industry. These imports have to be paid for: they are paid for in part by services provided for other countries in banking, insurance and shipping, in part by the diminishing and now very small income from overseas investments and in part by tourist expenditure, but mainly by the export of the products of British industry. Some of the 'invisible' sources of income, such as that from tourism, must be set against the corresponding payments made by British tourists abroad.

The United Kingdom's visible trade is almost never in balance. The value of imports regularly exceeds that of exports, and the 'invisibles' are used to rectify the balance of payments. Even so, the balance is sometimes adverse, and the United Kingdom is left owing money to its creditors abroad. Nevertheless, over the long term, payments are approximately in balance.

Table 13.4   Visible and invisible elements in the United Kingdom Balance of Payments, 1977 (£ million)

Visible trade:		
exports	32 182	
imports	33 891	
balance		−1 709
Invisible trade:		
services and transfers	1 560	
interest, profits, dividends	438	
total		1 998
Overall balance		289

Source: *Annual Abstract of Statistics,* HMSO (1979)

(a) Commodities in British Trade

The foreign trade of the United Kingdom consists, as we might expect, very largely of the import of foodstuffs and industrial raw materials, and the export of manufactured goods (Table 13.5). This is, however, an oversimplification of the situation. There is, in fact, a small export of foodstuffs, and a large import of manufactured goods. It is a feature of all developed, industrial nations that they sell a large volume of manufactured goods to one another (see Unit 12.10(*c*)).

Table 13.5   The foreign trade of the United Kingdom, 1976 ($ million)

	Total imports	Percentage of total	Total exports	Percentage of total
Food and live animals	8 078	13·7	1 859	3·2
Beverages and tobacco	876	1·5	1 181	2·0
Crude materials	5 420	9·2	13 270	22·9
Fuel	10 137	17·2	2 252	3·9
Animal and vegetable oils and fats	360	5·7	none	—
Chemicals	3 588	6·1	5 468	9·5
Manufactures, basic	10 891	18·5	10 396	17·9
Machinery and transport equipment	11 459	19·4	18 175	31·4
Other manufactured goods	4 431	7·5	4 275	7·4
Others	708	1·2	1 032	1·8
Total	58 948	100	57 908	100

Source: *Yearbook of International Trade Statistics 1976* (UN, 1977)

This results both from international specialization in manufacturing and also from the high purchasing power of these nations. About 75 per cent of exports, however, are of manufactured goods.

(b) Direction of British Trade

The high importance of manufactured goods in both the import and export trades means that it is carried on predominantly with developed, industrial countries, as Table 13.6 indicates. Trade with the communist countries is small, though that with China may be expected to grow. Only about 22 per cent of total trade is with the developing nations, and most of the remainder, more than two-thirds of the whole, is with the developed world. Much of this is with the countries of the European Economic Community (see Unit 14).

Table 13.6   The direction of United Kingdom trade, 1976 ($ million)

	Imports from	Exports to
Developed countries (including EEC)	39 972	32 995
EEC countries	20 438	16 431
Developing countries	13 477	11 488
Communist countries	2 033	1 304

Source: *Yearbook of International Trade Statistics 1976* (UN, 1977)

(c) Ports and Shipping

Almost all the United Kingdom's foreign trade is seaborne; the amount that travels by air is negligible in terms of both volume and value. Most of it—no less than about 87 per cent—is handled by the fifteen leading ports. Their rank-order has been subject to many changes with the shift in the location of manufacturing and the introduction of new types of ship and methods of freight-handling. Among significant developments of recent years have been the emergence of specialized ports designed to handle a single product, usually oil or iron ore, or to handle containers and heavy lorries. The port of Milford Haven, for instance, handles only oil fuel, and oil also makes up most of the freight in Southampton, the Medway ports, Liverpool, Manchester and Clydeside. Port Talbot (Glamorgan) and Newport (Gwent) are dominated by the import of iron ore for the ironworks of Port Talbot and Llanwern respectively. Iron ore is also very important at Cardiff, the Tees ports and Immingham (Lincolnshire).

The use of the container has brought about a revolution in ocean shipping (see Unit 12.3(g)). At the same time the use of ships designed to take lorries and other wheeled vehicles is increasing. The time may not be far distant when all of the United Kingdom's trade, except only the bulk handling of fuels, timber, grain and ores, is carried in containers or on 'roll-on/roll-off' vehicles. The increase in the volume of trade with Ireland and with the other Common Market countries, both of which call for only short sea voyages, has led to the expansion of roll-on/roll-off facilities in the ports of south-east England; indeed most ports of the United Kingdom are now adapted to handling both this type of freight and also containers. British industrial development has always been closely related to ports, since from its beginning much of it has been oriented toward the export trade. With the exception only of the Midlands, all the industrial regions that evolved on the coalfields lay close to the sea, and for each there developed its appropriate port. Central Scotland was served by Glasgow and Leith, and the northern industrial regions of England by Liverpool, Hull and Newcastle. Cardiff and Bristol were accessible to the South Wales region, Bristol, Hull and Liverpool were all within reach of the Midlands, while Belfast served Northern Ireland. But from the earliest times London was the premier British port. It remains so, with about 30 per cent (by value) of Britain's foreign trade. Most ships are no longer handled at the cluster of docks below Tower Bridge, however. Much of the trade has moved downstream to Tilbury, which has been equipped to handle large ships as well as container and roll-on/roll-off traffic.

The movement of manufacturing to the south-east, together with the expansion of trade with the Common Market, has led to the growth of other ports in this region; the two Channel ports of Dover and Southampton now handle 8·5 per cent of all the United Kingdom's foreign trade. The northern ports of Liverpool, Manchester, Hull, Middlesborough and Newcastle are proportionately less active. Before the Second World War they handled more than a third of British trade; their share today is little more than a quarter. This reflects the decline of the traditional industries and the development of newer industries based on London and the south-east.

Questions

1. Write an essay on the decline and rise of the coal-mining industry in the United Kingdom.
2. Explain the position of British agriculture in the context of the European Economic Community.
3. Why have the traditional industries—textiles, iron and steel manufacture, shipbuilding—declined in Great Britain?
4. Why have 'new' and 'overspill' towns been established in south-eastern Britain?
5. Discuss the regional distribution of unemployment in Great Britain.
6. Examine the importance for the economic geography of Great Britain of (a) the use of containers for transport, (b) the building of motorways, (c) the possible construction of a Channel tunnel.

Unit Fourteen

The Developed World

Great Britain was the first developed nation. The inventions and discoveries made here in the eighteenth and nineteenth centuries led to an increased production both of foodstuffs and manufactures. Total output grew faster than the population; the average level of welfare improved, and each year a part of the increased production could be—and commonly was—ploughed back into agriculture or manufacturing or into the infrastructure on which both depended. In this way, continued growth and development was, so to speak, built into the system.

Development is not a peak of achievement to which all countries aspire and which some have reached; it is rather a continuing process. The so-called developed countries are themselves still developing, though at varying rates. Growth has been faster in the United States during the present century than in the countries of western Europe, and more recently has been far more rapid in West Germany and Japan than in the United Kingdom and Italy. Yet all these countries form part of the developed world.

Nor is there any clear line of division between the developed and the underdeveloped or developing countries. In most of the latter there is growth. Their GNP is increasing; some branches of modern manufacturing have been adopted, and agricultural innovations are contributing to increased food production. Brazil, Argentina and Mexico are not now generally regarded as developed countries, but within a decade or two they may all have become part of the developed world, while others, like Nigeria, India and the oil-producing countries of the Middle East, may already be crossing the threshold which separates the developed from the underdeveloped nations.

Development is difficult to define and to measure. At present, a GNP per head of about $3 000 (£1 500) or more *seems* to distinguish the developed countries from the rest. But the fact that Libya and some Middle Eastern countries have *per capita* GNPs greatly in excess of this figure shows how misleading this can be as a measure of development. The essential feature of a developed country is that it possesses a large capital stock, to which it can add regularly and continuously. This stock normally consists of factories, energy sources and the infrastructure of modern commerce and industry. But it also includes a technically trained labour force and a large investment in education. A purely exploitative development, such as that of oil in the Middle East, may give rise to a high GNP, but is not itself a measure of development. If, however, the profits of mining or mineral exploitation are invested in other forms of development, such as factories, energy sources, or even irrigation or other agricultural projects, a development process may be initiated, leading to continuous growth.

This process requires two conditions: the availability of resources, of which energy sources are probably the most important, and, secondly, a socio-economic milieu which encourages, protects and rewards the entrepreneur. Great Britain possessed both when modern economic development began in the eighteenth century. Other countries in western Europe were no less well endowed with resources, but social conditions were less conducive to development. On the other hand, Japan was able to compensate for its poverty in industrial raw materials and energy resources by means of its managerial skills and the determination of its government to develop. North America, Australia and New Zealand rank among the developed countries largely because they were settled by peoples from north-western Europe, who took with them a western attitude to development and progress.

The most successful instances of economic development have been broadly based, and have included both manufacturing and agriculture, as well as transportation, education and service industries. Such a balance has been achieved in most western European countries, though in West Germany agriculture is a great deal less efficient than manufacturing. The United States is the supreme example of balanced development of agricultural and industrial resources, though in some more recently developed countries, like Australia and New Zealand, the emphasis has been heavily on agriculture.

Development necessarily takes place through time, but it is also a spatial process. It is *diffused* from the foci or centres where it first takes place: for example, innovations such as the steam-engine, technical processes in iron and steelworking and the adoption of mechanical spinning and weaving originated in Great Britain and thence spread first to France and the Low Countries, then to central and parts of eastern Europe, and lastly to the New World and Japan. The outward spread of innovations was not regular or easily predictable. They were adopted as and when a need for them appeared, and in many areas they were stubbornly opposed by those who believed themselves threatened by their introduction. Diffusion has a strongly random or stochastic element, and much depends on human perception of a situation. For instance, iron was first smelted with coke fuel in Great Britain about 1709. Subsequent experiments in France and the Low Countries failed, however, and coke was not used successfully in continental Europe until the late eighteenth century in Silesia. It was not used in the Ruhr, which has the most abundant reserves of coking coal, until 1849.

14.1   The Preconditions of Development

It is commonly accepted that fundamental changes in the practice of agriculture are a necessary prelude to developments in manufacturing. Labour has to be diverted from the land, and the output of those who remain must be sufficient to supply industrial workers as well as themselves. The Industrial Revolution in Great Britain was preceded and accompanied by radical changes in agriculture, which eliminated the open fields and the practice of fallowing, and also initiated the selective breeding of livestock. France, after 1815, underwent important changes in agriculture, and more recently the industrial developments of the

Soviet Union and eastern Europe went ahead together with the collectivization of farms. In modern China, drastic changes in the organization and management of the land preceded a programme of vigorous industrial growth.

In most countries development has been accompanied by a sharp growth in population. Opinion is divided on whether this is a precondition or a consequence of industrial growth. In some instances a labour shortage developed in the course of industrialization; some contemporary observers, indeed, regard industrial growth as one way of mopping up surplus labour. Too rapid a growth of population, on the other hand, eats up any increase in total production, and makes continuing investment impossible. At the same time the development of manufacturing may itself contribute to an increase in population by providing jobs and encouraging early marriage.

The availability of energy sources and of industrial raw materials is always an important factor in industrialization and economic growth. In earlier developments it was essential: one could not conceive of modern industry developing except in a country which, like Great Britain, possessed large reserves of coal and at least some other materials, and before 1850 no truly significant industrial development occurred more than a few kilometres from a coalfield. But this close dependence on local energy and raw material supplies no longer prevails. The nineteenth-century development of canals and railways permitted manufacturing to be established at a distance from the coalfields, especially in West Germany, where most of the modern industrial development took place after the construction of the railway network. Today, thanks to high-voltage transmission of electric power, energy supply is far less significant in the location of manufacturing, and in many of the developing countries the most important energy source is imported oil. Although certain industries such as iron-smelting remain closely linked with the sources of their chief materials (see Unit 10.2(*b*)), these are increasingly in the minority.

The effect of this is to spread modern manufacturing more widely, and to permit its establishment in countries which have hitherto been little developed. Environmental constraints on development have been reduced. Transport costs remain important, although decreasingly so with contemporary developments in shipping (Unit 12.3(*g*)) and power transmission (Unit 8.6(*d*)).

Why, then, is there no prospect of a wide-scale diffusion of modern industrial technology to central Africa or south-east Asia? The answer is unlikely to lie in any relative poverty of energy sources or raw materials, some of which are present in great abundance, or in any climatic disadvantage, or in the genetic inheritance of their peoples. The roots of backwardness are more likely to be found in the social order than in physical conditions or racial origins. Development springs from human initiative, whether in innovation or in the acceptance of innovation.

14.2   The Developed Countries

In its collection and compilation of statistics the United Nations defines the developed world as the whole of Europe, Anglo-America, Israel, Japan, South

Africa, Australia and New Zealand, and presents in a separate category the statistics of the centrally planned or communist countries—in effect, the Soviet Union, eastern Europe, China and Mongolia. All these countries, except only Albania in Europe and China and Mongolia in Asia, are in effect developed countries, even though their GNP per head is below that of most other advanced nations. It is impossible within the space of this book to examine all those countries which can in any way be called either developed or developing: we can discuss only some selected countries and areas. In this Unit, therefore, we examine the main features of the economic geography of the Common Market countries (which, with the addition of Sweden, constitute the most developed part of Europe) and of the United States, while in Unit 15 we shall consider the problems of the developing world with, again, emphasis on specific examples.

14.3   The Common Market and its Neighbours

In March, 1957, six countries of western Europe—Belgium, France, Italy, Luxembourg, the Netherlands and West Germany—joined in signing the Treaty of Rome. By this they undertook to form a common market (see Unit 12.7) with no barriers to trade among themselves and a common tariff against the rest of the world. Competition was to be encouraged within the Community, the weakest economic undertakings in agriculture and manufacturing were gradually to be eliminated, and new undertakings were to be located in the most favourable places from the point of view of the Community as a whole.

The treaty became operative at the beginning of 1959, when the first reductions were made in tariffs on goods passing between member states. The economic union was completed in 1968, and at the same time the Common Agricultural Policy (CAP) was adopted. The Community had in some respects been anticipated by the economic union of Belgium and Luxembourg in 1921, by the formation of the Benelux union (Belgium, the Netherlands and Luxembourg) in 1947, and by the common market for coal, iron ore and part-finished steel goods in 1953. It was the success of these associations in stimulating and cheapening production that led to the formation of the Common Market itself.

The United Kingdom declined the initial invitation to participate, but a change of heart led to an application for membership in 1963 and another in 1967, but both were vetoed by France. In 1970, negotiations were opened between the Community and the United Kingdom, Denmark, Ireland and Norway. Norway subsequently withdrew, but the other three nations became members of the Community in January 1972. Greece, too, has recently signed the Treaty of Rome, and the possibility of admitting Spain and Portugal is under consideration (see Unit 14.3(g)).

Meanwhile, the objectives of some members of the Community have gone beyond those of an economic union. They look for a closer political union—a federation, perhaps. This, however, is premature. There remain many economic problems—agriculture, fisheries, a common currency, and the less developed areas of the Community among them—which must be settled before political union is contemplated.

(a) Mineral and Energy Resources

Western Europe was endowed with a wide range of mineral deposits, but many of these have been exhausted. Non-ferrous metals are now worked on a significant scale only in the Iberian peninsula and in Scandinavia. Reserves of iron ore, on the other hand, are large, and include the extensive reserves of high-grade haematite in northern Sweden, and of low-grade bedded ores in Lorraine (eastern France) and the North German plain. The Lorraine ores are adequate for the local iron industry and also supply ore to Germany and Belgium, but the west European industry, including that of the United Kingdom, is heavily dependent upon ore imported from Africa and South America.

(*i*) **Coal.** Energy resources, on the other hand, are considerable. The coal reserves of West Germany and the United Kingdom are very large, amounting perhaps to 15 per cent of the world's total. Those of the United Kingdom have already been discussed (Unit 13.1). The coal resources of West Germany occur mostly in the Ruhr coalfields, which dips beneath the northern plain, east of the lower Rhine. It contains thick, level seams, easily exploited and containing every kind of coal from anthracite to long-flame coal, including rich reserves of the valuable coking coal. The coalfield of central Belgium and northern France is historically of great importance, having served to locate large steel and textile industries, but reserves are relatively small, and very many mines have closed in recent years. To the north a richer and more extensive field underlies the Kempenland (Campine) and extends into the southern Netherlands. Of the many small coal basins scattered over France, however, few are now in production, and none has any long-term importance.

In addition to its rich resources in bituminous coal, West Germany has large reserves of brown coal and lignite. Most occur to the west of the Rhine, near Cologne, at a depth shallow enough to permit opencast working. But brown coal is low-grade fuel. It cannot bear the cost of transport, and most is burned on site in electricity-generating plants.

(*ii*) **Oil and natural gas.** Apart from the reserves underlying the North Sea, western Europe has little oil and no great reserves of natural gas. West Germany, the Netherlands, France, Italy and Denmark each produce a small amount of oil, quite insufficient for domestic needs, and West Germany and the Netherlands each has a large production of natural gas from a gas field close to the North Sea.

The oil and gas potential of the continental shelf is very large. The North Sea has been partitioned among the surrounding states on the 'median line' principle (Fig. 7.5). The lion's share falls within the British sphere, but very large reserves are held by Norway, even though its oil is brought ashore in north-east England. Only the United Kingdom and Norway are likely to meet their oil needs. All other countries are dependent to varying degrees on imports. For this reason the shores of western Europe are dotted with oil terminals and refineries, most numerous near the Rhine mouth, near Hamburg, along the lower Seine and in southern France and northern Italy. From these points pipelines carry both crude oil and its refined derivatives to the interior of western Europe. West Germany is largely dependent on oil brought from Dutch, French and Italian ports and refineries. Though we may anticipate a further extension of the oil pipeline network, the overall pattern of oil imports is unlikely to change.

(*iii*) **Electricity.** At the present time about 81 per cent of electric power used within the Common Market is derived from fossil fuel—rather more than half of it from oil and natural gas. About 12 per cent is generated by hydro-electric stations, and the rest, about 6 per cent, is derived from nuclear reactors.

Hydro-electric power can be produced only where rivers, dropping steeply from the mountains, provide a head of water, and within the limits of the Community it is significant only in the French and Italian Alps, where it is an important factor in locating electrochemical industries. Nuclear power has a far

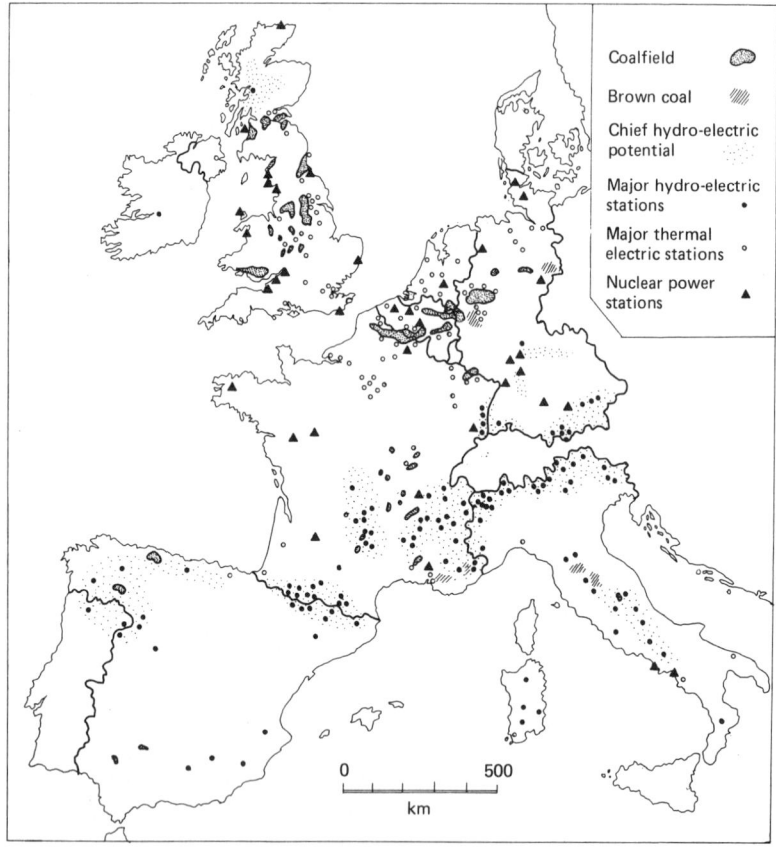

Fig. 14.1 Energy sources in western Europe, other than oil and natural gas

greater potential, and there are plans to expand its production. Euratom, the Community organization entrusted with its development, is planning the location of new reactors within the Community.

Most of the larger generators—thermal, hydro- and nuclear—are linked to a grid system which now covers much of the area of the community.

Table 14.1 Installed generating capacity in the European Economic Community

	Total capacity (thousand kw)	Hydro-electric (thousand kw)	(per cent)
Belgium	11 127	503	4·5
Denmark	6 273	9	—
France	49 200	17 574	35·7
Ireland	1 986	531	26·7
Italy	43 305	16 995	39·2
Luxembourg	1 157	—	—
Netherlands	13 982	—	—
United Kingdom	78 911	2 456	3·1
West Germany	74 356	5 573	7·5
Greece	4 868	1 416	29·1
Portugal	3 149	1 954	62·1
Spain	24 534	11 955	48·7

(b) Population in the Common Market

The diffusion of the Industrial Revolution within continental Europe was accompanied and followed by a sharp rise in population. In general, the pattern followed that set within the United Kingdom, with only two exceptions. The rate of growth in France was very much less than elsewhere, and the population of Ireland suffered a reverse in the 'potato famine' of the 1840s from which it has never recovered. As in the United Kingdom, the past two centuries have been characterized by out-migration from marginal agricultural lands and a sharp increase in the population of coalfield and other industrializing areas. Population increased within the countries of the present Community—making allowance for German boundary changes—from about 83 million in 1800 to 165 million a century later. By 1978 this had reached 260 million.

Until the early twentieth century the rate of growth of population was extremely high, higher indeed than in some Third World countries today. The demographic transition (see Unit 3.4) did not become apparent in much of western Europe, France excepted, until late in the nineteenth century. Then the birth rate fell sharply, and today the overall rate of natural increase is no more than 0·1 per cent a year: the steep rise in West Germany in recent years has been due mainly to in-migration from East Germany and eastern Europe. Unless the pattern of birth rates—at present about 12 per thousand per year—changes greatly, western Europe can expect to have a stable population, or only a very slight increase, in the foreseeable future.

Table 14.2   Populations of the countries of the European Economic Community

	Total population (millions)	Density per sq km	Percent-age urban	Rate of increase (per cent)	Birth rate (per thousand per year)	Estimated population in 2000 (millions)
Belgium	9·9	324	66	—	12	10·7
Denmark	5·1	118	74	0·2	13	5·4
France	53·4	97	63	0·3	14	61·2
Ireland	3·2	45	44	1·1	22	4·0
Italy	56·7	187	45	0·4	14	61·8
Luxembourg	0·4	138	62	0·2	11	0·4
Netherlands	13·9	337	80	0·5	13	16·0
United Kingdom	56·0	229	80	—	12	61·6
West Germany	61·3	247	78	−0·2	10	65·6
Greece	9·3	71	65	0·8	16	9·9
Portugal	9·7	94	26	0·9	19	10·8
Spain	36·8	69	61	1·0	18	45·3

As a result of differential growth and migration, a belt of dense population has arisen, extending from northern England through Belgium, the Netherlands and the extreme north of France to the Rhineland and northern Switzerland. Beyond the barrier of the Alps, it is continued in the Lombardy plain of northern Italy and peripheral areas of the Italian peninsula. Part of this area has been relatively populous ever since the Middle Ages, so that to some extent this dense population is an inheritance from pre-industrial conditions. Density has, however, been increased immeasurably by industrial development, focused at first on the coalfields of central Belgium, northern France and north-west Germany (the Ruhr). But these regions had inherited a network of transport and communications: rivers, canals and railways (see Unit 14.3(e)) permitted the distribution of coal and industrial raw materials over the whole of the Rhineland and north-west Europe, and the traditional industries—the metal, chemical and textile industries—spread far beyond the coalfield areas themselves. The development of manufacturing in this region and the resulting dense population has been due even more to the excellence of the means of transport and communications and to the presence of ocean ports than to the resource base, important though this is.

Other smaller centres of population lie at a distance from this axis of population, loosely referred to as the Manchester–Milan axis: central Scotland, Greater Paris and the areas around Hamburg, Hanover and Kassel in West Germany, together with the Rome–Naples area, Apulia, Calabria and much of Sicily in the Italian peninsula and the coastal region of Portugal and north-western Spain. Lower but nonetheless high densities are found around the rest of the Spanish coast, in Brittany and Provence, near Bordeaux and Lyons–St Etienne, in north Germany and Bavaria and in much of southern Italy.

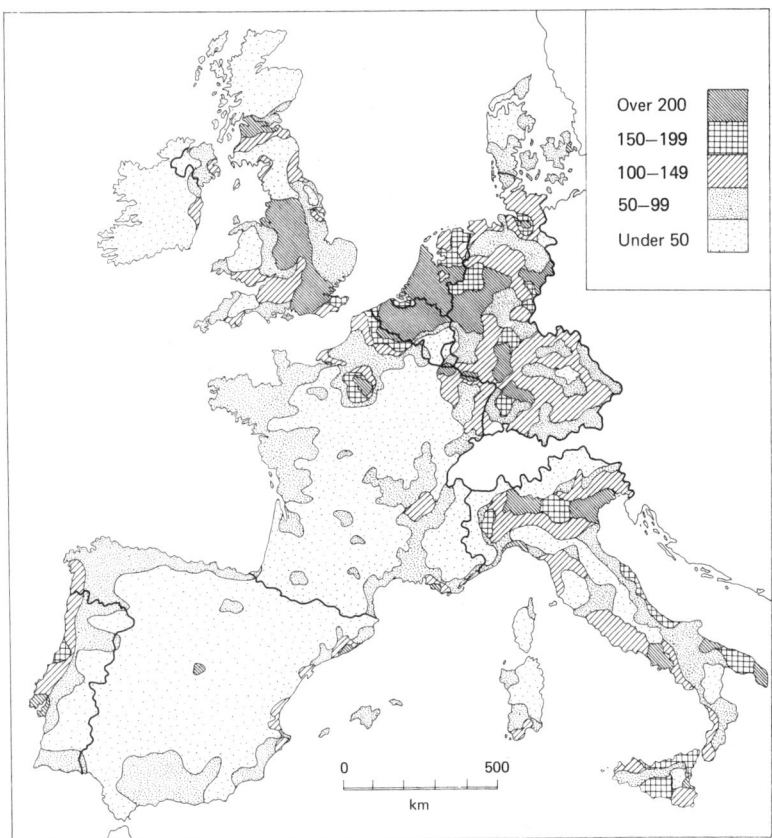

Fig. 14.2 Population densities (per square kilometre) in the countries of western Europe

Here we must recall the distinction, between dense urban-industrial and dense rural populations (see Unit 3.5). The latter are found in most Third World countries, always associated with uneconomically small and undercapitalized farm holdings and severe rural poverty. Such areas within the Community, like southern Italy, Brittany, central France and parts of the Highland Zone of the British Isles, are no exception. Incomes here are well below average for the Community; there is a persistent out-migration from these areas, and they qualify for help under the Community's regional policy.

The European Community is very highly urbanized. In the Netherlands and the United Kingdom, urban population is at least 80 per cent of the total, and in France and Denmark nearly as high. Only in Italy and Ireland does urban population make up less than half the total. Most of the larger cities and conurbations are to be found within the Manchester–Milan axis. Apart from London, the West Midlands, West Yorkshire and Lancashire–Cheshire, the largest are the so-called 'Randstad' in the Netherlands, the Rhine–Ruhr complex in West Germany, central Belgium and the Middle Rhineland. The largest of these is Greater London, closely followed by the Rhine–Ruhr complex with a population of over 10 million and the Randstad with about 4·5 million. In addition there are clusters of large cities, including Frankfurt and Mannheim, in the Middle Rhineland and also in the Lombardy plain, where Milan and Turin each lie at the centre of a cluster of industrial towns. Outside this zone, only the Paris region with a population of nearly 8·5 million compares with the large urban regions inside it.

The conurbations and larger urban centres within the Community can be expected to continue to grow as people migrate from marginal rural areas, such as Brittany, central France, southern Italy and Sicily, into the main industrial belt (see also Unit 13.5(*h*)). Manufacturing, too, is expanding, as is the associated infrastructure—ports, transport networks and service industries.

(*c*) **Agriculture in the European Community**
Agriculture is important in all countries of the Community. All, except the United Kingdom, are able to satisfy a large proportion of their food requirements, and in all except the United Kingdom and Belgium agriculture claims considerably more than 5 per cent of the workforce—in France, Ireland and Italy, more than 10 per cent. Denmark, Ireland and the Netherlands are, in fact, exporters of foodstuffs.

Table 14.3   Agriculture in the European Economic Community

	Agriculture as percentage of GNP	Agriculture as percentage of total employment	Ratio of employment to output
Belgium	3	5	1·7
Denmark	7	12	1·7
France	5	14	2·8
Ireland	14	27	1·9
Italy	8	21	2·6
Luxembourg	3	9	3·0
Netherlands	6	6	1·0
United Kingdom	3	3	1·0
West Germany	3	10	3·3
Greece	17	46	2·7
Portugal	14	37	2·6
Spain	9	34	3·8

Throughout the Community, the greater part of the land is used agriculturally. The extent of cropland varies greatly between countries; it is greatest in Denmark, and least in Ireland and the United Kingdom, where the proportion of the land under permanent grass is highest. Except in the United

Kingdom and Ireland, there are extensive areas under forest—up to a third in the Netherlands, and more than a quarter in Belgium and Ireland; but in no country is this sufficient to make a large import of timber unnecessary. In all Community countries good arable land is concentrated in relatively few areas: the eastern part of the United Kingdom, the Paris basin and the region extending south-westward into the Loire valley and Aquitaine, central Belgium, the southern margin of the North German plain, and the Lombardy plain of northern Italy. This results from a combination of relief, climate and soil. These regions are relatively dry, with less than 870 mm of rainfall a year. Though interrupted by hills, they are in general regions of gentle relief, and soils, though of uneven quality, are mostly deep and fertile.

These areas are characterized by high land values and relatively large and profitable farms, scientifically managed and equipped with labour-saving machines and equipment. Most farming is geared to satisfying the needs of the large urban and industrial population. Dairy farming and the intensive cultivation of vegetables and fruit are important. Farm incomes are relatively high, and this is reflected in the generally high level of prosperity in market towns and service centres.

By contrast the areas of predominantly pastoral and hill farming are less prosperous, and some are made up of marginal land which yields only a very poor livelihood. The reasons are complex: hilly terrain, poor soil, lack of capital, an inadequate network of transport to the large consuming centres, and the generally high cost of farming such land. Such regions bring down the average farm income, and it is one of the declared objectives of the Community to eradicate such anomalies. Table 14.3 shows the percentage of the active population employed in agriculture, together with the proportion of the GNP derived from agriculture. Only in the United Kingdom and the Netherlands do these two figures match, indicating that only here is agriculture as efficient as the rest of the economy. In Italy, France and West Germany, agriculture is notably less efficient, as it is also in Greece, Portugal and Spain.

One of the assumptions underlying the creation of the Common Market was that it is potentially self-sufficing in foodstuffs, except those of tropical and subtropical origin. In fact it is, on balance, self-sufficing in bread grains, potatoes, butter and cheese, and almost so in sugar and vegetables. There is only a small import of meat. The only foodstuffs the production of which is far from adequate, are fats and oils of tropical origin, most kinds of fruit, and such crops as rice and maize for which the climate of much of Europe is not really suited. Self-sufficiency in those foodstuffs for which the Community is suited is, it was thought, possible only if each region concentrated on the production of those commodities for which it was particularly suited: dairy produce in the moist Atlantic region, bread grains and other field crops throughout the great plains of north Europe and of northern Italy, vegetables close to the big city markets, and fruit where climatic and soil conditions made this desirable.

For this, however, two things were essential. The first was complete freedom of movement throughout the lands of the Community: the dairy produce of Ireland, the Netherlands and Denmark was to become available in the industrial regions of the United Kingdom, Belgium and West Germany, and the vegetables, fruit and wine of Italy throughout north-western Europe. This implied not only an absence of restraints on trade in agricultural produce but also marketing organizations and means of transport. A second requirement was the levelling up of the standards of farming and volume of output in marginal and other less productive lands, both by investment of Community funds and by securing an adequate standard of life for farmers in such areas.

The *Common Agricultural Policy* (CAP) was adopted in 1962, and was applied progressively to each of those commodities in which the Community might hope to become self-sufficing. The method was to adopt from year to year a target price for each commodity, fixed so as to yield a fair return to the moderately

Fig. 14.3 The grape harvest in Burgundy: the theory behind the Common Agricultural Policy is that specialized agricultural products, such as French wines, should have complete freedom of movement throughout the Community while the farmers' standard of living is protected even at the cost of production in excess of the Community's needs

efficient farmer. This protected the farming community as a whole against the extreme price fluctuations which had previously bedevilled agriculture. If prices fell below an arbitrarily fixed 'intervention' price, the Community intervened and bought up the surplus. The effect has been to encourage efficient, low-cost producers to expand their production, secure in the knowledge that they have a guaranteed price for their output, resulting in the accumulation of butter and dried milk 'mountains' and of a 'lake' of wine.

Production of many commodities is cheaper in other parts of the world than within the Community countries. Their products can be admitted, however, only on payment of a levy which will bring their price up to the Community's target price. If, on the other hand, prices within the Community should rise above the target level, farm produce from outside would help to bring down the price for the consumer.

The productivity and efficiency of West European agriculture have greatly improved since the formation of the Community, in keeping with its aim of achieving as high a level of self-sufficiency as is possible within the constraints imposed by physical conditions. Use of fertilizer and of mechanical equipment has greatly increased. There has been a sharp rise in yields of bread grains per hectare and of milk per cow. At the same time, labour inputs have been reduced by almost a half over the Community as a whole. There nevertheless remains an immense difference between the levels of efficiency and profitability on a small family holding in, let us say, the Central Massif of France or the Eifel Plateau of West Germany, and those on one of the large farms that are found in East Anglia or on the good soils of the Paris basin.

The CAP was devised in the light of the needs of the original six members of the Community. In each the agricultural sector was large and politically important. In France the Monnet Plan had already done much to improve the standard of farming, but in Italy and West Germany agriculture was notably inefficient. Modernization of farming would lead inevitably to surpluses. There can be no doubt that an important reason why the Community welcomed the admission of the United Kingdom was because it needed a market for part of its farm produce. This it has, indeed, achieved, though at the expense of denying the British market to traditional suppliers like Canada and New Zealand.

(d) Manufacturing Industry

The technical innovations adopted in the United Kingdom in the eighteenth and early nineteenth centuries spread to continental Europe after peace had returned in 1815. The new technologies in the metal industries were first employed in Belgium and those in the textile industries in France. Germany adopted the new technology relatively late, but made up for this by the efficiency with which technical education and industrial research were developed and organized. This, rather than the abundance of raw materials and fuel, explains why Germany made such rapid advances in the chemical industries during the nineteenth and early twentieth centuries.

Western Europe had a long tradition of craft industries, but the Industrial Revolution led to the mechanization of many of these branches of manufacturing and to their concentration in a few well-favoured locations. Among these were the coalfields. After 1815 the iron and textile industries were attracted to their chief source of energy, though excellent means of waterborne transport, together with the rapid expansion of the railway net during the mid-nineteenth century, prevented the emergence of industrial concentrations such as those in the United Kingdom. Nevertheless, most of the early developments in modern manufacturing in western Europe occurred at no great distance from the belt of coalfields which extends from northern France to the Ruhr.

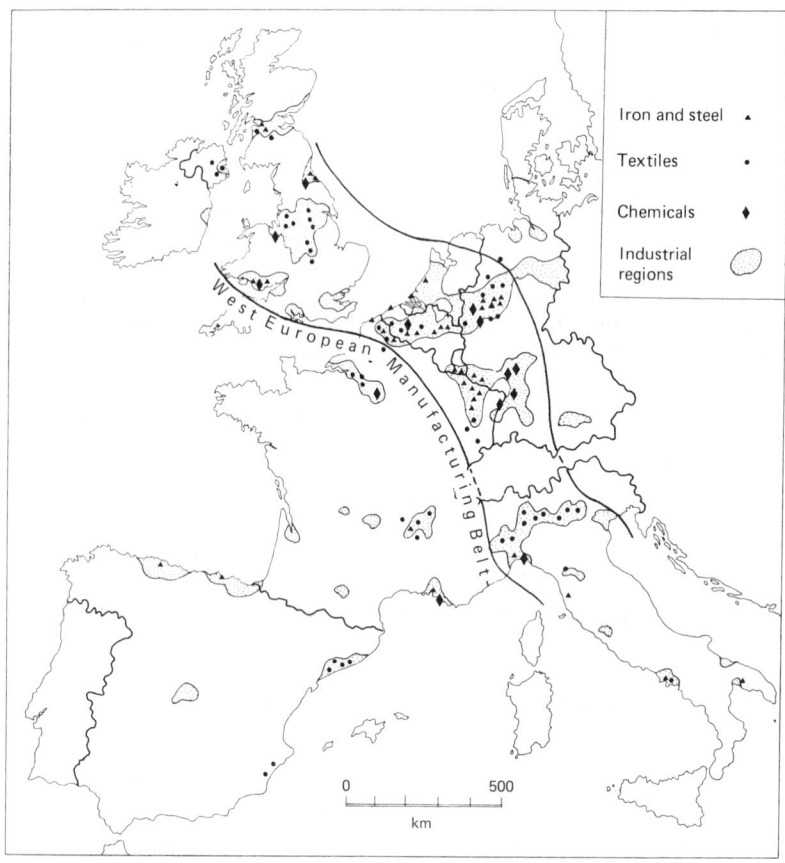

Fig. 14.4 The chief centres of manufacturing in western Europe

The iron-smelting and refining industries, most demanding in their needs for fuel, gradually abandoned the forested hills for the coalfields. The earliest modern ironworks were established on the coalfield of central Belgium, near Liège and Charleroi, whence the industry spread westward into northern France. The development of iron-working on the Ruhr was delayed by technical problems in the use of local coal. But by 1850 these had been solved, and the iron-smelting and steel-making industry began to grow rapidly. An innovation of immense importance was the basic process for making steel from ores rich in phosphorus (1877). These had hitherto yielded only a brittle and useless metal, but were abundant in eastern France and north Germany, as well as in eastern England (Unit 13.1). From the 1870s and 1880s they began to be used on a large scale, and, since their grade was low, the smelting and steel-making works were located close to the orefield in Lorraine and Luxembourg and near Hanover.

The manufacture of textiles in western Europe also derived from an earlier craft industry. There were few areas where a rough cloth—woollen or linen— was not woven for local use, and in some, cloth of better quality was made for sale in the cities or for export. The introduction of machine-powered spinning machines and looms led to the expansion of some of these centres and to the decline and disappearance of others. A new textile industry, making both woollens and cottons, developed in Catalonia in the hinterland of Barcelona, but the old cottage industry disappeared from Languedoc, Brittany and north Germany. A feature of the textile industry in continental Europe was its lack of any sharp spatial distinction between the several branches—woollens, linen, cottons and silk, as well as lace and knitwear. All might be carried on in the same city, and there were examples of factories actually changing from woollens or linen to cotton and vice versa.

The chief concentrations of the continental textile industry lie along the lower river Seine, near Rouen, through which raw cotton was imported, in a broad belt which extends through northern France and neighbouring Flanders, especially at Lille, Roubaix and Ghent, in the Lower Rhineland at Elberfeld and Barmen (now known collectively as Wuppertal) and around Mönchen Gladbach, and in the Westphalian plain near Münster, extending across the Dutch border to the Twente district of the Netherlands. Other concentrations of the textile industry lie in the valleys of the Vosges mountains of eastern France, around Milan in northern Italy, in the Lyons–St Etienne region of France, where silks, ribbons and velvet-making became the dominant branches, and in the Barcelona region of Spain.

The chemical industry, the third major branch of manufacturing in western Europe, grew up in the nineteenth century. It owed much to the discoveries and innovations made by German scientists, and, unlike the iron and textile industries, derived nothing from any pre-industrial pattern of production. The chief centres of production of the primary chemicals—the common acids and alkalis, fertilizers and dyestuffs—were in Saxony, now in the German Democratic Republic (East Germany) and in Leverkusen, Düsseldorf, Mannheim, Ludwigshaven and the Frankfurt region, where the river Rhine offered cheap waterborne transport from the Ruhr coalfield. Chemical industries have also developed near Paris, Lyons and in the industrial regions of northern France, Belgium and the Ruhr.

The processing of imported fats and oils and the manufacture of soaps, margarine and related substances is associated particularly with the ports, and is carried on near Marseilles, Rouen, Hamburg and the ports of the Low

Countries, especially Amsterdam, Rotterdam and Antwerp. Petrochemicals production forms one of the newest branches of the chemical industry. It is closely associated with oil-refining and plants are mostly found near the great oil ports: Le Havre, Marseilles and Rotterdam. They are also carried on close to inland refineries, linked by pipeline with the ports.

Related industries, such as glass, ceramics and plastics manufacture, have tended to locate in the large centres of population that constitute their principal markets. They are particularly important in the Paris region and the Lower and Middle Rhineland. The manufacture of cement, bricks, tiles and coarse earthenware is mainly carried on close to the sources of the clay and limestone that are their raw materials. North-eastern France and north-west Germany are particularly important, but small ceramic industries are widely scattered throughout western Europe. The rubber industry has a similar distribution, though one of the largest producers, the Michelin works at Clermont Ferrand in France, lies in a thinly peopled district remote from other centres of manufacturing.

The steel industry supplies the raw material for an engineering and metal-using industry of immense breadth and variety. Heavy engineering—the rolling of girders for construction, plates for ships and the making of pipes for water and oil—is carried on mainly close to the centres of iron and steel manufacture: the Ruhr, central Belgium and northern France. Light engineering is very much more widespread, since it is in general far more labour-intensive and represents a far greater value added (see Unit 9.1(a)). The highly important automobile industry is today largely a matter of assembling components made elsewhere. Its primary requirement, apart from labour, is a well-developed means of transport, and the largest centres of industry are Paris, Turin and, in West Germany, near Hanover, Stuttgart and Frankfurt. Automobile engineering is a 'footloose' industry, and there is a tendency to locate new branches in areas of severe unemployment—not only at Liverpool and near Glasgow, but also in the Ruhr and northern France. Shipbuilding also uses the products of the steel mills, but is necessarily more restricted in its location. It has long been declining throughout the Community, but remains of some importance in Hamburg, the ports of the Low Countries and at St Nazaire.

The electrical engineering and electronics industries are among the newest. They call for advanced technology and are labour-intensive. They tend to be attracted towards the market and are mostly found in developing industrial regions such as central and south-eastern England, the Paris region and the Rhineland and south Germany. Many consumer goods industries are similarly attracted to the larger centres of population: paper and printing, for instance, clothing and fancy goods, carpets, linoleum and floor coverings, toys and domestic appliances. Of the food industries, some are located in rural areas, as close as possible to the sources of their raw materials—sugar-beet, liquid milk for butter and cheese, grapes for wine, fruit and vegetables for canning and preserving. Others, including the baking of bread, cakes and biscuits, brewing and the production of chocolate and confectionery, are attracted to the market and are characteristic of large urban areas. Still others have developed at the ports through which their raw materials are imported; these include flour-milling and oil-seed crushing and the manufacture of margarine and vegetable fats.

(*i*) **The Coal and Steel Community.** The formation of the Community was preceded by that of the European Coal and Steel Community (ECSC). In the years following the Second World War recovery was hindered by a shortage of steel, partly because of the difficulties in getting access to iron ore, coking coal and steel scrap. In 1953 a common market in these commodities was established by the same six countries that later formed the European Economic Community. Among them, West Germany held a near-monopoly of good-quality coking coal; France and Luxembourg had an abundance of ore and Italy and the Netherlands possessed neither, but relied heavily on scrap metal to supply their steel industry. The ECSC did much to smooth out the supply of raw materials to its member states and thus to facilitate the rapid economic recovery which followed; indeed, it provided a model for the Common Market itself.

The iron and steel industry of the Six has expanded rapidly since 1952: total output of steel has trebled from about 42 million tonnes in 1952 to 125 million in 1975. This has been accompanied by radical changes in technology and location. Immediately after the Second World War the industry was dominated by the converter and the open-hearth furnace, which both used the basic process for refining high-phosphorus iron. Domestic reserves of basic ores remain abundant, especially in Lorraine, Luxembourg, north Germany and eastern England, but they are of low grade, and it has proved in many instances to be more economic to import higher-grade ore. On the other hand, the introduction of the oxygen or Linz–Donawitz (LD) process has permitted a better-quality metal to be obtained from the basic converter.

The effect of recent changes has been to eliminate many small and relatively inefficient iron and steel works and to increase the importance of a few well-favoured areas. Lorraine and Luxembourg, with an abundance of both local ore and coking coal are increasing in importance. The Ruhr, with its excellent coal resources, a developed transport system and a long tradition of iron-working, has enhanced its position, but most other centres, including northern France and central Belgium, without a local source of iron ore and with coal reserves that are difficult to mine and of indifferent quality, have declined and some have ceased production. On the other hand, coastal iron and steel works have become increasingly important. Where imported ore is used, a furnace and related steel works can operate most economically at the chief break-of-bulk point, the port. This type of location is not new; iron works were being established on coastal sites in the nineteenth century, but they have in recent years become very much more important (see Unit 10.2(*b*)). Coastal works produce most of Great Britain's iron and steel. In France, a large plant at Dunkerque is replacing the older works on the northern coalfields, and another coastal plant has been built at Fos, near Marseilles. Similar works have been built near Ghent in Belgium, at Rotterdam (Maas Vlakke) and Amsterdam (Ijmuiden) in the Netherlands, and at Bremen in West Germany. But the most significant development has been in

Italy, where all the fuel and most of the ore have to be imported. Works have been built near Genoa, on the Tuscan coast and at Taranto and near Naples in the south, where it was thought that the presence of major steelworks would be a stimulus to the local economy.

(*ii*) **The Community's industrial axis.** Current trends in the Community as a whole are similar to those in the United Kingdom. In the latter, manufacturing industry is concentrated within a belt which extends from the northern Midlands to London. In continental Europe the comparable belt extends from the North Sea coast between Calais and Hamburg, southwards to the Swiss border, and beyond the Alps to the plain of Lombardy. It includes the coalfields of the Ruhr, Saar and northern France–central Belgium, as well as the iron ore of Luxembourg and Lorraine and the hydro-electric potential of the Alps. To the west lie the separate industrial regions of Greater Paris and of Lyons–St Etienne, and to the east those of Bremen–Hamburg and Hanover–Brunswick.

The main industrial belt of the Community is more broadly based than that of the United Kingdom, because it includes its own energy resources as well as the traditional textile and steel industries. Like south-eastern England, it is attracting new industries, as well as labour both from within and outside the Community. It contains most of the main urban agglomerations, including the Rhine–Ruhr conurbation, itself almost as large as Greater London, the Randstad Netherlands, central Belgium–northern France and the Middle Rhineland from Frankfurt to Stuttgart. It embraces no less than 60 per cent of the population of the whole Community apart from the United Kingdom and Ireland.

(*e*) Transport and Communications

Without a highly developed system of transport and communications the Community could not operate, for local specialization and exchange are basic to the Common Market concept. The network of road and rail communications is well developed and intensively used, and is supplemented with a system of navigable rivers and canals which is more fully developed and better used than any other in the world.

(*i*) **Inland waterways.** Much of Europe's medieval commerce was conducted by river, and the Rhine became an essential part of the commercial axis that linked Italy with north-western Europe. Other rivers, including the Seine, Meuse and Rhône, were also used, and during the eighteenth and early nineteenth centuries these river systems were interlinked by canal. During the present century, despite the competition of railway and road, the canal network has been extended, especially in the Lower Rhineland and North German plain. Most recently the River Moselle has been canalized from its junction with the Rhine at Coblenz upstream to the iron orefield of Lorraine.

At the centre of this system is the Rhine, navigable from the sea to Basel in Switzerland—a distance of 885 kilometres—though this has been made possible only by extensive and costly engineering work on the upper river. By way of both the Meuse and Moselle the Rhine is linked with the canals of eastern France, and with the Seine and Rhône. To the east the Mittelland Canal joins the Rhine with the Elbe and provides an essential link in the communications system of Berlin. Canals are under construction to connect the Main and Neckar, both right-bank tributaries of the Rhine, with the Danube, thus providing a route from the Rhine to the Black Sea. The canal system is heavily used, in part because the extensive, integrated networks allow very long hauls to be made, as from the Rhine to Berlin and from Basel in Switzerland to Rotterdam.

(*ii*) **Railway system.** The west European railway network began to be built in the 1830s, and almost from the first transcontinental routes were planned. Insofar as there is a focus to the system this is Paris, from which there are direct links with most parts of the Community, including train ferries to England. The rail net is densest in the Low Countries and north-western Germany, very roughly the region of greatest industrial growth, and is least developed in southern and western France and in Italy. The railway system is well used both for passengers and freight in France and Belgium, but in the Netherlands and Germany the competition of river and canal transport has reduced its importance for transporting bulk goods. The Alpine system interposes a serious barrier between the railway systems of north-western Europe and that of Italy. A trans-Alpine tunnel links France with Italy, and two routes burrow beneath the Swiss Alps to provide a route from the Rhineland to the plain of Lombardy. Nevertheless, the linkages between Italy and the rest of the Community are among the weakest within the Common Market. The admission of Greece, Portugal and Spain are likely to present even greater logistic problems. Spain has railway links with France, primarily around the ends of the Pyrenean range, but Greece has only the most tenuous links with western Europe.

(*iii*) **Road system.** The basic network of roads in all Community countries developed to meet the needs of earlier societies: in some, roads originally laid out by the Romans are still in use. In all countries a high proportion of both passenger and freight traffic is by road. Inevitably, road traffic has outgrown the capacity of the original road system, and throughout the Community this has been modified by the construction of by-pass and ring roads and supplemented by a system of motorways.

The motorway system was initiated by the German *Autobahnen*, first built before the Second World War for military purposes and since greatly extended. There have been similar developments in other member states, though much less progress in this field has been made by the three potential members of the Community. There is a high degree of integration between the various national motorway networks; they have been constructed to varying standards, however, and their ability to take large vehicles and heavy traffic differs greatly. There are differences also in the standards set by the Community for vehicles; the United Kingdom, for example, has a lower size limit than the continental members of the Community. The larger continental lorries could cause havoc on some British roads.

'Roll-on/roll-off' ferries link Ireland with Great Britain, and the latter with many ports in north-western Europe. Other routes are likely to be introduced, and the number of sailings increased as the volume of commercial and passenger movement rises, though the growing use of these ferries, and also that of containers, has had the effect of increasing the volume of heavy traffic on the roads, as any observer of the British scene will be aware. The construction of a Channel Tunnel would remove many of the existing hindrances at the Channel ports. The Alpine system was once a serious barrier to movement by road, as well as by rail, between Italy and her partners in the Community, but the problems it presents have been greatly reduced by the construction of road tunnels as part of the European motorway system.

(*iv*) **Air transport.** Each member of the Community has at least one large international airport used by intercontinental air traffic, as well as a network of domestic and intra-European routes. Most European countries are, however, so small that internal air services offer little time advantage over road and rail, and are furthermore liable to more frequent interruption by bad weather. Only where a sea-crossing intervenes, as between Great Britain and Northern Ireland, does air travel offer any conspicuous advantage. Air travel is more important between Community countries, since the distances involved are much greater.

(*v*) **Transport by sea.** Most intra-Community transport is over land, though coastal shipping is important in north-western Europe. Only the United Kingdom and Ireland are wholly dependent on maritime trade. The dependence of the Community on sea-borne commerce is likely to increase when Greece, Portugal and Spain are admitted. The Community, before the admission of the United Kingdom, had only a relatively small merchant fleet. In 1976, the United Kingdom had almost 45 per cent of the registered shipping owned within the

Table 14.4   The Community's merchant fleet, 1976

| | Thousands of gross registered tonnes | | |
	Total	Oil tankers	Per cent
Belgium	1 499	303	20·2
Denmark	5 143	2 485	48·3
France	11 278	7 406	65·7
Italy	11 078	4 728	42·7
Ireland	202	—	—
Netherlands	5 920	2 845	48·1
United Kingdom	32 923	16 147	49·0
West Germany	9 265	3 306	35·7
Greece	25 035	8 910	35·6
Portugal	1 174	503	42·8
Spain	6 028	3 029	50·2

Source: *UN Statistical Yearbook* (1977)

Community. The addition of Greece has since increased the merchant fleet by about a·third. These figures reflect both the very large volume of intercontinental trade carried on by the United Kingdom and the important service function performed by Greece (Table 14.4).

(*vi*) **The ports of the Community.** The greatest volume of seaborne trade is carried on by the United Kingdom, whose ports are discussed in Unit 13.8. Much of the seaborne trade of the continental members of the Community is carried on through the ports of north-western Europe from Le Havre and Hamburg. Nowhere else in the world can so many large and important ports be met with along so short a stretch of coast. This is, of course, because they lie close to Europe's most highly industrialized region, and are linked with it by a very dense and efficient transport net. At the heart of this system of ports are Antwerp, Rotterdam and Amsterdam. Of these, Rotterdam, together with its extension, Europoort, has the best communication with its hinterland, and has become the largest port in Europe, even in the world (Fig.14.5). Hamburg grew up as the

Fig. 14.5 An aerial view of part of the port of Rotterdam

port for the Elbe basin, much of which now lies in East Germany, very little of whose trade passes by this route. While it remains a large and well-equipped port, its growth is restricted by the small extent of its hinterland. The same is true of the other north German ports, Bremen and Emden. The highly industrialized Rhineland lies within the hinterland of Rotterdam, linked with the port by a barge traffic that makes the Rhine one of the most heavily used rivers in the world. Belgium is served by the port of Antwerp, linked by the Albert Canal with industrialized central Belgium, and northern France by Dunkerque. Le Havre, the largest port in northern France, serves the needs of the Paris basin, and Marseilles those of much of southern France.

The long coastline of Italy has many ports. The largest is Genoa, which serves as an outlet for the industrial region of Turin and Milan. The other important port of northern Italy, Trieste, also handles part of the overseas trade of the Danube basin. Southern Italy and Sicily, in the past among the least developed regions of Europe, carry on a relatively small amount of foreign trade: the chief ports are Naples, Taranto and Catania.

The expansion of trade between the British Isles and continental Europe has led to growth in the Channel and North Sea ports. The traditional ferry ports of Boulogne, Calais, Dunkerque and the Hook of Holland retain their importance, but the increase in the supply of farm produce to the United Kingdom has led to the expansion of trade between Plymouth and the Brittany ports of St Malo and Roscoff. The movement of goods from the Danish port of Esbjerg and the British east coast ports has also increased.

(f) The Trade of the Community

The Community today constitutes by far the largest trading block in the world, greatly exceeding in the volume of its commerce both the developed countries of North America and Japan, and also the communist bloc. It carries on approximately a third of the world's trade, of which roughly a half is intra-Community trade. A small fraction is with other countries of western Europe, trade with the United States, Japan and the Soviet bloc is even less, and the remainder—only about 30 per cent of the total—is with the rest of the world.

Table 14.5   The direction of the Community's trade (millions of tonnes)

	Imports from	Exports to
Community	297 850	294 960
USA	102 984	106 157
Japan	57 881	55 844
Communist bloc	92 070	78 340
Developing countries	189 300	207 200

The proportion of intra-Community trade varies from country to country. It is very high for Ireland, whose small volume of trade is mainly with the United Kingdom, and also for Belgium, Luxembourg and the Netherlands. It is least for the United Kingdom, which retains strong commercial links with the Commonwealth and the rest of the world. These ties are, however, weakening. In 1970 only 28 per cent of the United Kingdom's trade was with the six members of the Community. The inclusion of Denmark and Ireland, both of them important sources of food for the British market, at once raised this proportion which by 1977 amounted to 37 per cent. This was accompanied by a proportionate, if not also an absolute, decline in trade with Commonwealth and Third World countries. Moreover, the volume of the United Kingdom's intra-

Community trade is continuing to increase. Foodstuffs make up about 18 per cent of imports from the rest of the Community, while most of the remainder consists of manufactured goods. This illustrates the extent to which international specialization in industrial products has gone.

Table 14.6 shows the volume of the intra-Community trade of each of the member states.

Table 14.6   Intra-Community trade of the member states as a percentage of total trade

	Imports	Exports
United Kingdom	37	36
Belgium/Luxembourg	68	74
Netherlands	55	72
France	50	51
West Germany	48	46
Ireland	69	76
Denmark	10	12
Italy	44	48

(g) The Twelve?

Greece, Portugal and Spain have applied for membership of the European Community. Greece has already signed the Treaty of Rome, and the other two countries are likely to follow. They will together add 727 000 square kilometres to the Community's area and about 55·8 million to its population. But these three countries are poorer than the present members, and their GNP per head is much lower; manufacturing is less developed and employment in agriculture proportionately greater. Their membership will present the Community with problems which may be more difficult than any it has yet had to face.

Each of these three countries has an agriculture which is in many respects backward and is enabled to compete in the European market only because the rewards for labour are low. One of the first objectives of the Community must be to inject enough capital to modernize and re-equip these agricultural systems. Much help has already been given for the development of *il Mezzogiorno*, and similar programmes are needed in the other two Mediterranean peninsulas, which have much in common with southern Italy. Development in these lands also requires the building up of an infrastructure of roads, railways, ports, generators and electricity supply networks, without which manufacturing cannot be expanded nor agricultural produce marketed.

14.4   Anglo-America

The chief beneficiary of the technological developments and innovations of the first Industrial Revolution has been the United States of America, where they were accepted more rapidly and refined to a higher degree than anywhere else. America has immense agricultural and industrial resources; but their sheer abundance has provoked a profligacy in their use that has showed itself in the erosion and loss of carelessly managed soil over vast tracts of agricultural land and in the extravagant use of fuel resources with a wanton disregard of the needs of the future. Some of today's most recalcitrant American problems spring from this rash exploitation in the past.

(a) Agriculture

North America is self-sufficing in foodstuffs, apart from coffee and other tropical commodities, and there are large exports of wheat and fruit. Agricultural systems are determined by the climatic conditions. Dairy and mixed farming, including vegetable-growing, predominate in the densely populated north-east, and maize is grown as fodder for cattle in the Corn Belt of the Midwest, together with cereals and tobacco further south. Yet further south lies the Cotton Belt, which once stretched with scarcely a break from the Carolinas almost to the Gulf of Mexico. Today, however, because of the exhaustion of the land and the disastrous depredations of the boll-weevil pest, coupled with competition from man-made fibres, one may drive across Georgia or Alabama without seeing a single cotton-field: most cotton is now grown on the drier lands of Texas and the south-west, where the pest is less active. Vegetables and fruit, especially citrus fruit, are grown in Florida and along the Gulf coast. Over the mountains and plateaux of the west there is at best only very rough grazing, and at worst scrub desert except where irrigation is practised. The valleys and plains of the Pacific coastlands are intensively used: for dairying in the north, where there is year-round rainfall, and for growing fruit and irrigated crops in the region of Mediterranean climate in the south.

(b) Resources for Industry

The coal resources of North America are immense: proved reserves amount to more than a third of the world's total. Oil has been worked for more than a century, and though many oilfields are exhausted, no less than 15 per cent of the world's crude oil still comes from the United States and 3 per cent from Canada. Natural gas output in America is by far the largest in the world, roughly 40 per cent of the total, though proved resources still remaining amount to little more than a tenth. Hydro-electricity is of importance: about 13 per cent of energy generated in the United States comes from this source, and more than 60 per cent in Canada.

Iron ore is abundant; the richest ore-bodies have been depleted but large deposits of low-grade ore (taconite) are being exploited, and the vast reserves of the Laurentian Shield are now being worked in Labrador. Copper, lead and zinc and most of the lesser metals are mined; only tin, cobalt and manganese have not been discovered in quantity. Bauxite is worked, but has to be supplemented by imports.

(c) The Pattern of Manufacturing

Manufacturing industries first developed close to the east coast, and are still densest and most widely diversified in that region; even today, the western edge of industrialized America is very roughly defined by a north–south line passing through Winnipeg, Minneapolis, Kansas City and San Antonio (Texas). Iron and steel manufacture was originally centred on the coalfield of Pittsburgh in Pennsylvania, but as reliance came to be placed increasingly on ore from Lake Superior, new works were established at Buffalo, Cleveland and Detroit, and above all at the head of Lake Michigan, in South Chicago (Fig. 14.6) and

Fig. 14.6 The United States Steel Corporation works at South Chicago on the shores of Lake Michigan. Ore-carriers unload directly into the works and the ore is smelted in the adjacent blast-furnaces (lying behind the ore heaps in the middle distance)

northern Indiana. Automobile manufacture originated in the production at Detroit of waggons for the westward journeys of the pioneer settlers; Henry Ford's genius developed this early involvement with transport into one of the major industries of the Midwest. Food-processing—flour-milling, meat-packing, whisky-distilling and so on—spread throughout the agricultural regions of the Midwest, but has now moved on to St Louis, Kansas City and Omaha.

In recent years the southern United States has become a major growth area. The region has much in its favour: iron, coal, oil and natural gas, cotton and softwood, together with a warm climate, cheap labour and lower social overhead costs. These resources have attracted manufacture to the region—textile mills, petrochemical plants and associated technologies. At the same time labour-intensive manufacturing has been drawn to the Pacific coast, such as the aircraft industry at Seattle and Los Angeles and many electronic and computer-based industries. The advantages of this region include the pleasant climate, which has the effect of reducing overhead costs and of attracting labour, and ease of access to markets throughout the Pacific sphere.

(d) Transport

The structure of North American agriculture and industry depends upon a highly developed system of transport and communications. Rail transport,

Fig. 14.7 Heavy traffic on the Long Island Expressway, New York; the high dependence of Americans on the private car has led to problems of traffic congestion and urban pollution and to immense demands upon the country's oil reserves

however, only retains importance for the carriage of bulky freight like coal and ore. Two transcontinental rail routes still remain in Canada, but the once highly complex American railroad system has now been rationalized, with the closure of many branch lines and stations. Road transport has largely replaced the railways: there are more freight vehicles in the United States than in any other country—no less than 19·7 million—and a car for every two people. Dependence on the car is complete. Public transport within the cities is minimal, and serves largely the needs of those who are too poor or too old to drive a car. The system of motorways and associated main roads is, however, unequalled in the world.

Road travel is supplemented by air. All the major North American cities are linked by direct routes, and even the small towns are connected with the major airports by feeder lines. As a result it is possible to travel between almost any two points in North America (excluding Alaska) within a few hours at most.

The price of this excessive reliance on the car and the aeroplane is high: heavy dependence on imported oil, grave problems of urban pollution and an automobile industry that has become the most important single branch of manufacturing, but which is vulnerable to every fluctuation of the economy and vagary of fashion.

(e) Productivity and Trade

The United States has long been the richest and most productive country in the world, and it has achieved a level of mass-consumption unequalled elsewhere, though closely approached in Canada. Both countries enjoy the advantages of ample space, abundant energy and immense resources, yet Canada remains the more important primary producer. Its principal exports are wheat, iron ore and lumber, whereas the United States exports mainly manufactured goods.

Considering its wealth and large population, the United States foreign trade is not large. The country relies substantially on imports of iron ore, bauxite and some other non-ferrous metals; far more serious, however, is its excessive dependence on oil. Domestic resources are diminishing and demand—and hence imports—are increasing; but since 1974 oil prices have risen very sharply and the world depression has cut the volume of exports. The American economy has been in consequence under great strain and is unlikely to recover without radical changes in energy policy, and the development of new and advanced technologies to replace the old.

14.5   Other Developed Countries

Lack of space prevents full discussion of other developed countries, but brief mention at least must be made of the Soviet Union and the communist countries of eastern Europe, and also of Japan. These, in their very different ways, provide models for development elsewhere.

The communist countries have developed during the past half-century according to government-constructed plans. Most had considerable resources of coal and other fuels, metalliferous ores and agricultural land. Capital for industrialization and development were largely generated by forced savings and the cutting back of consumer production, and it appears that the Soviet–east European bloc could achieve a high level of economic self-sufficiency.

Japan's industrialization and development, by contrast, was achieved in the face of an almost complete lack of energy resources (apart from hydro-electric power), a grave shortage of most industrial raw materials and a serious shortfall in food production. It was achieved, furthermore, under a system of private enterprise, though with government backing and guidance. The Japanese success owes much to their hard-working and well-disciplined workforce and to their skilful and enterprising management. Wage levels are, in real terms, lower than in western Europe, and this has allowed the Japanese to produce their goods more cheaply. A notable feature of Japanese industry is the relative absence of labour disputes, and the extent to which the workers identify with the fortunes of the company that they serve.

Questions

1. Is GNP per head an adequate measure of development?
2. Can the latest countries to be admitted to the European Economic Community (Spain, Portugal, Greece) be considered developed?
3. Examine the role of agricultural production in (a) France, (b) the United States, (c) New Zealand.
4. Examine the energy sources and supply of the countries of the Common Market (the United Kingdom excepted).
5. What effect has the creation of the Coal and Steel Community and of the Common Market had on the location of manufacturing?
6. How important are internal waterways in the transport system of the European Community?
7. How self-sufficing are the United States and Canada, (a) separately, (b) taken together?
8. Examine the importance in the context of the European Community of (a) Europort, (b) hydro-electric power, (c) Euratom, (d) the Regional Development Fund.

Unit Fifteen

The Developing World

Development is difficult to define and measure. The richest countries—some twenty of them—are unquestionably developed, but behind them come countries like South Africa, Argentina and Brazil, which are also, in many respects, developed. Treading hard on their heels is the broad mass of the developing countries and the rear of the procession is brought up by a few very poor countries where one looks in vain for signs of real progress in modernization and economic improvement. But how can we measure development? What are the objective criteria, and what changes when a country 'develops'?

So far we have used as an index of development the GNP per head (see Unit 4.2(*a*)), but there are others. Since development is closely associated with industrial growth, the consumption of energy is one useful measure, and, since development is normally accompanied by a movement of labour from agriculture to manufacturing and tertiary activities, the proportion of the population employed in each sector is another. Developed countries are likely to have a denser network of transport and communication than the less developed, a larger urban population and a larger expenditure on health and education.

But to most people in the developing world the most significant measure of development and the most important factor in economic growth is *industrialization*. Machines increase the effectiveness of labour; they permit higher wages to be paid; and, by the provision which they make possible of tools and fertilizers and the means of transport, they increase the output of agriculture. It is not surprising that the hopes of many poor and backward societies have come to be centred in the building of an industrial society.

Industrialization is thought to have other advantages. Manufacturing industry tends to be regarded almost as a hallmark of progressive nationhood, and those countries which have achieved political independence in recent years look to the planned development of industries to set, as it were, a seal on their new status. Apart from this slight political advantage, industrialization can offer substantial economic benefits. The country which can hold anything like a balance between industry and agriculture is less exposed to today's violent fluctuations in trade. Manufacturing industries, moreover, can confer a measure of political security—most industries can be used for some military purpose.

15.1 The Process of Industrialization

Great Britain was the first industrial nation. From the mid-eighteenth century onwards, technological innovations were made, industrial processes were reorganized, capital was accumulated and labour was redeployed. Slowly, and for many sectors of society painfully, Great Britain emerged from it as a wealthy country with, on average, a greatly improved standard of living.

But British industrialization was unplanned. Those who participated in the process knew only in very general terms the direction in which they were moving. Their objectives were not specific; they were not expressed in terms of units of production. The government's role was permissive. It removed obstacles to growth, but it formulated no plans and provided no leadership in this the most important economic movement of modern times. Industrial growth in the developing world today is very different in character. It is sponsored without exception by the government which defines the objectives. It is expected to be rapid, and its driving force is supplied by considerations which had little or no significance in the British Industrial Revolution: national pride, military preparedness and, above all, demographic pressure.

Fig. 15.1 Rapid industrialization in a developing country: the oil-rich sheikdom of Dubai has invested huge sums in the development of port facilities

(a) Population Pressure and Industrialization

Many developing countries are overpopulated in that the rural population is greater than can be employed by agriculture alone, with its present tools, methods and equipment. Returns from the land have very nearly diminished to the point at which an increase in the labour force brings about no increase at all in food production. The marginal unit of labour thus achieves nothing, and its transfer from the land to some manufacturing activity would be accompanied by an increase in *total* production. The additional production might take the form of chemicals, fertilizers, or tools and equipment for agriculture and transport, which in turn would increase the efficiency of those remaining on the land. The process of industrialization would be 'planned' to ensure that the best use was made of the available labour and raw materials.

It is difficult to quarrel with this simple argument, set out in countless books and papers concerned with the less-developed countries. But its simplicity should not lead us to suppose that industrial development is equally uncomplicated or that planning can always bring about an improvement in living standards. Great Britain used the products of its factories to purchase foodstuffs and raw materials from other parts of the world. The developing nations of today, such as those of the Indian subcontinent or of sub-Saharan Africa, may find this much harder to do. Foodstuffs and raw materials are increasingly scarce, their prices are rising, and a small amount of manufactures can no longer be exchanged for a large volume of primary products. Industrialization may not in the long run be the means of providing food for an increasing population.

(b) Accumulation of Capital

The process of industrialization calls for the replacement of manual dexterity by machines, of the simple workshop by the factory, and of primitive means of transport by freight trains and lorries.

There are two principal ways in which a country may accumulate the tools it needs to increase its productive effort. It may do so by *internal saving*, or by *external borrowing*.

By the former process, which Great Britain employed in the nineteenth century and the USSR in the twentieth, the people consume less than they might have done had there been no process of industrialization. The difference between total production and total consumption is 'saved' and the productive effort goes to the construction of railways and machines, buildings and canals (see Fig. 11.1). Clearly a people near the borderline of starvation cannot save in this way, as their whole effort is required to maintain their existence. The lower the standard of living of a people, the less likely is it to be able to 'save'.

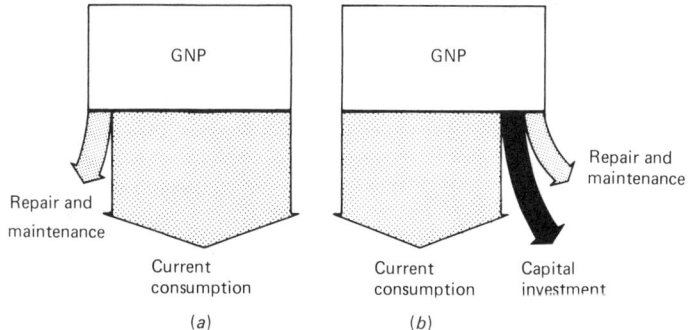

Fig. 15.2 Models illustrating national investment: (a) no capital investment; (b) capital investment at the expense of current consumption

The second method is to borrow abroad. The 'tools' are borrowed from (or occasionally given by) another and more developed state. The industrializing country can then greatly expand its productive power and, out of its added production, can pay an interest to the country which made the loan. During the past century a few countries have been blessed with a productive capacity greater than they need to satisfy their internal requirements, and can thus become capital-exporters (see Unit 15.3(*b*)). The United States is the most important of these, but the United Kingdom, the Soviet Union and France have also made significant contributions. The World Bank canalizes the contributions of many countries into useful development projects.

We have implied that a period of industrialization may be a time of hardship and suffering, especially if the initial development is low, since resources are being diverted from the production of consumer to that of capital goods. This need not be so, at least for more than a short, initial period. If the productivity of the marginal unit of labour on the land is close to zero, its diversion to other purposes can lead to little loss of production. Furthermore, the employment of such labour in manufacturing may bring about an almost immediate increase in industrial production. Much, however, will depend on whether this new capacity is used for the production of capital or investment goods, consumer goods, or some combination of the two. Industrialization in the Soviet Union was focused for a long period on the production of capital goods, whereas the Industrial Revolution in Great Britain emphasized the cheap production of consumer goods, especially textiles. If the objective is rapid growth, as it has been in the planned economies of the communist countries, a large part of new industry must be allocated to the production of capital goods.

The cost of industrialization is high. If the 'new' country is to compete in the world market it needs up-to-date machines and skilled operatives to handle them. Alan Mountjoy has pointed out that the cost 'to train, equip and absorb one individual into non-agricultural employment in Asia has been estimated at $1 500, and this sum is in close accord with the estimated capital figure per new worker in India's second Five Year Plan.' This amount is some 20 times the average annual *per capita* GNP in the countries of southern Asia and much of West Africa. Clearly, no such country could industrialize, except on a very small scale, without help from outside.

(*c*) Labour Supply

Any industrial society, as it evolves, develops a body of skilled labour adequate for the performance of its manufacturing processes. But an undeveloped or agricultural country cannot do this overnight. Skills and aptitudes must be acquired gradually. Some peoples, usually as a result of their social organization, make poor industrial labour, being slow, inefficient, undisciplined and unadaptable. The Japanese have shown themselves outstandingly adaptable; the Indians have been less so, and their industry, quite apart from its smaller size, is less efficient and less ready to innovate. Generalizations, however, are unwise; some Indian peoples, particularly the Parsees, show all the qualities necessary in an industrial people. In terms of crude numbers every developing

Fig. 15.3 A Cree Indian woman of Central Manitoba making moosehide moccasins, while another moosehide is being smoked on a tripod over a smudge-pot; craftworkers like this would find it hard, if not impossible, to adapt to work in factory conditions

country has plenty of labour for any project it might wish to undertake. It may however take a very long time, generations perhaps, to overcome ingrained attitudes to work and to factory-type organization.

(d) Supply of Raw Materials

No manufacturing industry is likely to be established without an assured supply of the necessary energy and raw materials. A country is likely to turn first to the processing of local materials: the manufacture of cotton and jute fabrics in India, of cotton textiles and iron goods in China and of various food products in South America. The cost of transporting raw materials is often exaggerated, however (see Unit 12.1); a large proportion of the industrial raw materials of Japan, for instance, has to be imported, and Italy is an example of an industrial country in which there are almost no industrial raw materials. There are relatively few industries that cannot be operated profitably near their market or wherever labour is abundant.

The developing countries are establishing manufacturing industries at a time of rising real costs of energy and raw materials; west European countries and the United States, on the other hand, undertook their industrialization at a time when these were relatively cheap. The price of exhaustible materials, such as minerals and fuels, must inevitably rise relative to those of labour and of materials of plant origin (see Units 7 and 8). Development of non-exhaustible forms of energy require a capital investment and a level of scientific skill which are likely to be beyond the reach of Third World countries for a long time to come.

Most developing countries rely heavily on oil fuel, especially as few of them are well endowed with coal. The sharp rises in the cost of oil during the early 1970s, which the developed countries sustained only with some difficulty and dislocation, were quite unbearable to many developing countries, and must inevitably have postponed plans to expand manufacturing. The price of ores and metals will increase, and the greater demand for raw materials of vegetable origin can be satisfied only by diverting land now used for food production to the growing of industrial crops, such as cotton, oil-seeds and softwood timber. Long-term prospects for industrialization are thus bedevilled by the growing scarcity and rising price of materials. Prospects of a higher GNP through the development of manufacturing are in many developing countries remote, if not illusory.

(e) The Market

Industries established in the developing countries must be able to dispose of their products. This they may do either internally, to their own domestic consumers, or externally, by exporting them to other countries. Both courses raise problems.

If the market is an *internal* one, then the people must have the purchasing power; they must, in other words, earn sufficient money by their own efforts to be able to buy the goods. This clearly limits the range of appropriate industries. Silks and satins would not find a ready market among the toiling masses of China, nor printed books among the South American peasantry. During the late eighteenth century, Great Britain had the advantage of being able to develop the production of goods in mass demand, whereas France and Germany, which at that time were also attempting to stimulate manufacturing industries, did so by stressing the manufacture of luxury goods such as porcelain and silks. The lack of adjustment between the agricultural and the industrial sections of the community may be so severe that the former has not the purchasing power to absorb the surplus products of the latter.

The market, on the other hand, may be *external*; the products of the new industrial country are then competing with those of older and possibly more efficient centres of production. The 'new' country is unlikely to be able to to produce simple goods very cheaply indeed. This, briefly, is the secret of Japan's early triumphs in her export trade, and is an advantage from which Pakistan and India now profit in developing their own external markets.

Fig. 15.4 Japanese cars on the dockside at Yokohama, ready for loading on to specially built ships for the overseas markets; Japan has been brilliantly successful in penetrating the markets in countries whose industrialization is far older than her own

compete in point of quality, but it may, in virtue of its lower wage levels, be able

During the present century, governmental foresight and planning have assisted developing industries by protecting them from outside competition. Government can encourage one section of the economy by taxing others, or it can protect a branch of industry by taxing heavily all competing imports. The choice of the industries to be thus encouraged, however, may not always be the result of careful consideration of what is best for the welfare of the world, or even of one particular nation. Strategic industries, such as the manufacture of chemicals or steel, may be encouraged even though the country cannot hope to produce such goods at a competitive price; an example of this might be the development of an iron and steel industry in Egypt. If the cost of production is high, as is that of synthetic oil or of sugar from beet the United Kingdom or Germany, then the whole community must pay a higher price for the commodity in one way or another. The difference in price between the domestic, protected commodity and that which might have been imported from a cheaper producer is the cost to the consumer of the added security or satisfaction conferred by its manufacture at home. The government must judge the wisdom of such protection, though the wisdom of its judgment rarely passes unchallenged.

This question of governmental assistance in the location and development of industry is of the greatest importance to the economic geographer. Slowly, under the influence of bonuses, tariffs and planning, the pattern of the world's industrial activity is changing. There may never have been a completely 'natural' distribution of industry, in which all goods were manufactured in the places where this could be done most cheaply. Nevertheless we appear to be moving towards an increasingly artificial distribution of industry, in which a factory is established not because it can satisfy a human want cheaply and easily, but because some other benefit can be derived from its location. We thus have industrialization for prestige or protection or political advantage, not necessarily for greater efficiency and higher standards or living.

15.2   The Spatial Pattern of Development

We discussed some of the parameters of development in Unit 4, and they are illustrated there in maps. There is a high level of correlation between GNP per head, consumption of energy, employment in manufacturing and in tertiary activities, and even birth rate and population increase. However we measure development, most of Africa and Latin America, south, south-east and east Asia must be reckoned to be among the less-developed part of the world. The Middle East, however, presents a special problem. As measured by GNP per head, Kuwait, the United Arab Emirates, Qatar and Saudi Arabia must rank among the richest countries of the world; in three of them, the GNP per head is considerably in excess of that of the United States. This wealth is due almost entirely to the exploitation of particularly rich reserves of oil. Within a measurable period of time these reserves will be exhausted and their wealth will disappear. They are, to this extent, living on capital. Their problem is to invest part of their current income from oil in undertakings—factories, desalination and irrigation schemes—which will continue to provide employment and yield an income long after the oil has run out. Only when this has been done can these countries be considered to be developed.

The Soviet example of rapid growth aroused the envy and admiration of the underdeveloped world, but no country was prepared to accept this model in its entirety. Indeed, none, with the exception of China, had resources comparable with those of the Soviet Union, and nowhere was there a government as autocratic, powerful and ruthless as that of Stalin and his successors.

The Soviet Union had a further advantage. It was not plagued by a too-large population expanding faster than its food supply; there was in fact a labour shortage in the earlier stages of industrial growth. By contrast many Third World countries today are burdened with very dense populations; even more are experiencing rapid population growth—some at the rate of more than 2 per cent a year. Their economic growth can thus be expected to do little more than keep abreast of the rising demand for foodstuffs and other essentials.

It is impossible to offer any meaningful discussion of the developing world within the limits of a single Unit. Instead, we have chosen three examples of developing regions for discussion, in order to highlight some of the varied problems they face and the programmes that they have undertaken: West Africa, India and China.

(a) West Africa

Most of West Africa was once fragmented between the empires of France and Great Britain. Economic development under imperial rule was piecemeal but nonetheless greater than in Liberia which never passed under European control. As West Africa gained independence in the 1950s and 1960s, the internal boundaries of the French and British empires hardened into international boundaries, so that West Africa is today made up of no less than sixteen separate and sovereign states. Many of these are too small and poorly endowed for planned economic growth to be practicable. Others are obstructed in their access to the coast and to sources of industrial power.

The West African environment presents serious obstacles to development. Physical conditions make the construction and maintenance of a transport net both costly and difficult. Apart from Nigerian oil, reserves of mineral fuel are small and metalliferous minerals other than bauxite are scarce, while the soil of much of the region is lateritic and poor; moreover, insects and insect-borne diseases present serious problems in large areas, and much of the interior has a small and uncertain rainfall.

Nevertheless, a number of states formulated development plans shortly after they had gained independence, including the formerly British territories of Ghana and Nigeria, and also Dahomey, Ivory Coast, Mali, Niger, Senegal and Togo, all members of the French Community. Each drew up plans to cover a specified number of years. Most were overambitious, and called for quite unrealistic rates of economic growth—Togo's plan required an annual growth rate of almost 5·5 per cent, and Ghana set itself an even higher goal. In consequence the plans had to be drastically pruned or even abandoned.

Financial resources for development in the formerly French territories were provided in the main by France, the development fund of the European Community and the World Bank. Ghana, however, produced about 27 per cent of the world's cocoa, and its export yielded the equivalent of £240 000 000 a year in foreign currencies. An export tax on cocoa beans provided further sums for capital development. Nigeria has considerable reserves of tin and one of the largest oilfields in Africa. Although both have received aid on a generous scale, each is able to finance from its internal resources part at least of its development programme.

Not surprisingly the development plans of most West African states have concentrated on agriculture. Farming methods have been improved, cropping systems diversified, and marketing organizations established. It was hoped not only to increase the exportable surplus of such crops as ground-nuts, palm oil and cocoa, but also to expand the consuming power of the peasant cultivator and thus to encourage manufacturing industries. At the same time, however, the plans aimed to extend the commercial infrastructure—roads, railways, docks—left by the former imperial powers.

The success of the plans, as measured by increased production, has not been great, owing in part to lax administration and in part to technological inadequacies. The greatest achievements have been made in the formerly British territories of Ghana and Nigeria. Both have had a series of development plans, each intended to be completed in Soviet fashion within a prescribed term of years, but these have been characterized more by *under*fulfilment than by their completion on time.

Nigerian plans included factories for processing locally produced materials, such as vegetable oils, cotton and timber, as well as for making consumer goods in wide demand. An iron and steel plant was envisaged, and a large hydro-electric development on the river Niger was completed in 1969. The industrial situation of Nigeria has been transformed since the late 1960s by the discovery and exploitation of oil and natural gas. In addition to supporting an oil-refining and petrochemicals industry, this new resource brings in 94 per cent of the country's annual income in foreign currencies. This has made possible the expansion of the cement industry, a pre-requisite of industrial development, and the building of docks and harbours. Nigeria must rank as one of the more successful instances of economic development among the Third World countries, but this owes much to the exploitation of internal resources such as are possessed by few developing countries.

Ghana's development plans date from the period of British rule, but they became more ambitious after independence in 1957. They included the construction of factories to make a wide range of consumer goods, but did not aim to expand agriculture so as to increase the cash income of the peasant cultivators who would constitute most of the consuming public. The result was a disastrous situation, with overproduction and underconsumption, leading to a drastic cutback in the plans.

Nevertheless, the Ghanaian plans did result in the creation of a small steel mill and also the completion of the Volta project, the largest feature of Ghana's industrial development: this involved building a dam across the Volta river at the point where it drops from the West African plateau to the coastal lowlands, and the creation of the largest artificial lake in Africa. Power from the dam is used to smelt aluminium as well as in other manufacturing industries.

The effect of these planned developments has been to raise Nigeria and Ghana above the economic level of most African states. But even the modest achievements of these two countries appear to be beyond the scope of most of their West African neighbours, which lack their natural resources. The northern tier of West African states, from Mali to Chad, are among the poorest countries in the world. They lie across the border of the Sahara desert and the savanna—the Sahel, as it is called. They have no significant mineral resources, and rainfall is low and highly unreliable. Agriculture is practicable only over small districts and in recent years a sequence of droughts has destroyed even the rough grazing that provided the only resource over large tracts of land. Such countries do not even merit the description of 'developing': they, and others like them in Latin America and Asia, as well as elsewhere in Africa, are totally undeveloped. Many areas which are thus lacking in resources for development are merely backward regions of otherwise developed and developing countries, and their scanty population can share the wealth of the more developed parts of their own country—as, for example, in Australia and Canada. Where, however, the whole country is made up of such marginal land, as in Niger and Chad, it is difficult to see how any form of development is possible.

(b) India

In 1947 the British withdrew from the vast Indian subcontinent, leaving it poverty-stricken and overpopulated. The population was rising rapidly, and dependence on the uncertain monsoon was overwhelming. Manufacturing had scarcely developed beyond the craft stage and up to three-quarters of the population was engaged in an unprogressive agriculture. In order to break the cycle of backwardness and poverty the Indian government introduced its first Five Year Plan in 1951, and this has been followed by a sequence of plans which is likely to continue indefinitely

Soviet industrialization provided a model for the Indian, but there are significant differences between the two. Indian development has relied substantially on private capital, and there has been no nationalization of either resources or capital assets. On the other hand it has, as in the USSR, emphasized the capital goods industries at the expense of consumer goods. On this point there was a prolonged controversy. Many believed that the manufacture of consumer goods such as textiles was better suited to India than heavy industry, and that education should be greatly developed. In fact the iron and steel and the chemical industries were very much expanded, and little attention was given in the earlier plans to the reform and modernization of agriculture.

India's economic progress was held back by drought and consequent famine, and by short wars with Pakistan and China. Nothing happened, however, to hinder the growth of the population. This increased from 361 million in 1951 to 439 million in 1961, and to 635 million in 1978, far outstripping the rate of growth in the agricultural and industrial sectors of the economy. This is also in marked contrast with the USSR and China, where the rate of population growth has remained below that of agricultural production. On a *per capita* basis, these countries are becoming richer; India is growing poorer.

Every successful industrialization has been preceded or accompanied by a reform of the system of land tenure and an increase in agricultural production; this is especially true of the British and Soviet examples. The Indian plans have included proposals for land reform, but these have never been fully implemented, vested interests generally proving too strong. This means that the rural sector has not been able either to generate a food surplus, or to provide a growing market for factory production.

The Indian case has focused attention on one of the most important arguments among development economists: whether to invest in large-scale industrial projects, as the Indian government has done, allowing the economic benefits to 'trickle down' through the increased demand for food and the higher wages of the workers to the humblest peasant at the base of the social and economic pyramid, or to start by reforming agriculture. In countries that have adopted the former method, it has taken a very long time for benefits to percolate downward. Furthermore, this mode of development increases demand for energy and scarce resources, does little to increase food production, and benefits only a narrow segment of the population.

The alternative method is to use available resources to improve agriculture and the structure of rural society. Land reform, consolidation of scattered parcels of land, the creation of farm units of adequate size, the construction of irrigation projects, the use of better seed and the adoption of a more scientific attitude to agriculture all contribute to an improved standard of rural life and a greater production of foodstuffs. At the same time, the government may encourage the development of small-scale manufacturing which can be carried on in the villages as a supplement to farming, as is happening in India and also in China. In time reforms of this kind will increase the rural demand for consumer goods and thus make manufacturing more profitable. In this case the prosperity is created at the base of the pyramid and communicates itself upwards. All the evidence suggests that it is this latter mode of development that provides in general the better prospect of improving the lot of Third World countries.

(c) China

China is a special case among the developing countries. It is of exceptional size — the most populous country in the world; it is richly endowed with resources for both agriculture and manufacturing, and it has a long history as a civilized, cultured country with a developed sense both of its own unity and of its exclusiveness. It is potentially a giant among the developed countries. Its present relative backwardness is due in part to foreign exploitation in the past and the destruction from endemic civil war, and in part to an innate Chinese reluctance to innovate or to accept the innovations of others.

The heart of China is a vast plain, built on the alluvium laid down over a period of many thousands of years, and intensively cultivated by methods that scarcely changed for four thousand years, until a decade or two ago. Surrounding the plain lies a belt of hilly country, well-watered and subtropical in the south but continental in climate toward the west, and increasingly dry to the north. Beyond this lie the high mountains, plateaux and desert that provided a natural protection for Chinese civilization, insulating it both from cultural contacts with the rest of the world and making invasion and conquest difficult and rare.

China has a plentiful supply of both energy and mineral resources. Recent estimates ascribe no less than a fifth of the world's coal resources to China. Known reserves of oil are proportionately less, but are nevertheless far greater than those of any other Asiatic country except those of the Middle East. There are large deposits of iron and of many non-ferrous ores, including some of those essential in modern steel-making. China is indeed far more richly endowed than many developed countries.

Development was slight before the Japanese invasion began in 1931, and was limited to coastal sites where European interests were active. After the expulsion of the Japanese in 1945, the Communists, led by Mao tse-Tung, took over the country, though not without a long and disastrous war. The Communists applied what they considered to be Marxist methods of development, though these were greatly modified by attitudes traditional among the Chinese. Faced with the continuing hostility of both the Soviet Union and, until about 1972, the United States, the Chinese attempted to develop their resources without aid from the rest of the world. They were obsessed with the idea that, given the proper motivation, economic miracles were practicable. The Soviet Union had found that this was not so. Nevertheless, the Chinese achievement since about 1950 has been immense. With utterly inadequate tools and equipment they

Fig. 15.5 The terraced hillsides of Shensi province in north-west China; the terracing counteracts both drought and flooding and has increased grain production in the area

constructed vast irrigation works, brought large areas of steep hillside under cultivation and built thousands of miles of roads and railways. Communist folklore celebrates the achievement of the Tachai brigade of peasants which, near Sian in Shensi, cut a huge hillside into terraces for cultivation (Fig. 15.5); each acre is said to have required twelve to fourteen hundred man/days of labour. A widely publicized attempt was made to boost iron production by encouraging peasants to build and operate small furnaces in their yards and gardens as a kind of part-time activity, but it proved a failure. Modern technology cannot be instantly adopted and applied by an unskilled, unlettered peasantry, however strong its political motivation.

Nevertheless, China did succeed in 'pulling herself up by her own bootstraps', if only to a limited extent, during the 1950s and 1960s. Production of energy and of iron, steel and basic consumer goods like textiles was increased. Food production grew at least as fast as population—perhaps faster, for China appears to have overcome the danger of recurrent famines. But development in this way caused immense strains within China. The people, docile, intelligent and immensely hard-working, accomplished an enormous amount during these years, but they failed to achieve a rapid and sustained economic growth. These events contributed to the intellectual ferment which came to be called the 'Cultural Revolution'. China emerged from it ready to compromise with her ideological adversaries and to accept technical aid and guidance from the developed countries. America's foolish involvement in the affairs of China's neighbour, Vietnam, delayed the reconciliation with the world's foremost industrial power. But since the early 1970s, China has gradually been opened up to influences from the developed world. Trade has increased, technical aid has been provided and sophisticated, high-technology hardware supplied. A rapid and sustained economic growth appears to have been achieved.

A condition of this growth has without question been the control of population increase. Statistics are somewhat uncertain, but the rate of growth was certainly very rapid during the first half of this century. Estimates put the population of China before the Second World War at from 400 to 500 million. A census in 1953 showed about 583 million, and current estimates suggest a total of 930 million, with perhaps 1 200 million by the year 2000 if the present rate of growth is sustained. It appears, however, that alone among developing nations, the Chinese have been able to reduce their birth rate drastically. The government refuses to allow early marriages—the permitted ages are twenty-eight for men and twenty-six for women—and regards large families as anti-social. The result is that increased production will not, in the future, be mopped up by a rapidly rising population.

15.3   Investment in the Developing World

Economic development within the Third World countries is more likely to be achieved with the technical and financial aid of the more advanced nations than by their own internal initiative. The Soviet model may be admired, but is likely to attract very few imitators. The developing world appears rather to assume that it is the duty of developed countries to assist them, while such countries, whether for political or humanitarian reasons, find it very hard to evade this responsibility. Aid to today's developing world is furnished at two levels, which may for convenience be termed the private and the public.

(a) Private Investment

Much of the fixed capital in development projects was installed by companies whose purpose it was to exploit resources and to make profits. Most of the developing world was at one time the colonial dependency of one European country or another. The imperial governments set out to ensure that political conditions were conducive to profitable investment, but as a general rule they did not themselves establish plantations, mines and factories. This was done by commercial companies set up for the purpose; even some railways and docks were built by private enterprise.

These companies were in business in order to make profits, and have consequently been accused of exploiting the dependent territory, using up its resources without adequate compensation and paying local labour less than a proper wage. There are well-advertised examples of this, the seamier side of imperialism, and the Marxists have erected an important theoretical model on the linkage between imperialism and capitalism. Yet capital investment by

Fig. 15.6 The Pacific island of Banaba has supplied vast quantities of phosphates to the rest of the world, at the cost of the destruction of its environmental quality and the displacement of the indigenous people

commercial companies in colonial territories seldom reaped any great rewards. The final balance sheet of imperialism is yet to be struck, but in the end the imperialists may well be found to have made an overall loss.

Yet in the context of backwardness and development, their achievement was significant. They prospected the dependent territory and opened mines, they laid out plantations and built factories to process or use the raw materials grown or extracted, and, above all, they created an essential infrastructure for development: roads, railways, docks, telecommunications, marketing organization. The imperial age has ended, and the assets and activities of many commercial companies have been taken over by the new governments; but private enterprise continues to play an important role in economic development. The exploitation of fuel and mineral resources is still largely in private hands, and in the case of oil drilling only private enterprise possesses the necessary expertise. There is, however, a tendency for the government of the developing country to accept a financial share in such undertakings.

Companies continue to invest in economic undertakings in the developing world, even though the risks may be higher today than under imperial rule. A company nowadays must make its decisions in the light of possible local hostility and even of the danger of nationalization, and the role of private investment in the developing world is probably declining relatively if not also in absolute terms.

(b) Public Investment

The role of assisting the economic progress of the Third World is today being assumed in the main by public bodies, both national and international. Only these can control resources of the size needed and deal on equal terms with the governments of developing countries.

(i) Government investment.

Investment by one government in the territory of another is a recent development. The earliest significant example began in 1947, with the provision of aid by the United States government to those countries willing to receive it. The purpose was to redevelop and re-equip the agriculture and industries of those lands which had been ravaged by the Second World War. This aid was in time phased out, but was succeeded by a number of other programmes designed to encourage growth in the less-developed countries. Similar, though smaller-scale, plans were adopted by other countries, especially the United Kingdom, France, West Germany and the Soviet Union.

There is a strong tendency for economic aid to be politically motivated. Aid from the Soviet Union has been available exclusively to its satellite countries and to those which it has wished to influence. The United Kingdom has directed its aid towards its partners in the Commonwealth, and France to members of the French Community. American aid has been strongly influenced by Cold War policy: Greece, Turkey, Afghanistan and Pakistan, countries which border the Soviet bloc, have received a volume of aid that contrasts sharply with the meagre expenditure in Latin America, where the need may have been very much greater. Aid given to the developed countries of western Europe outweighs all other,

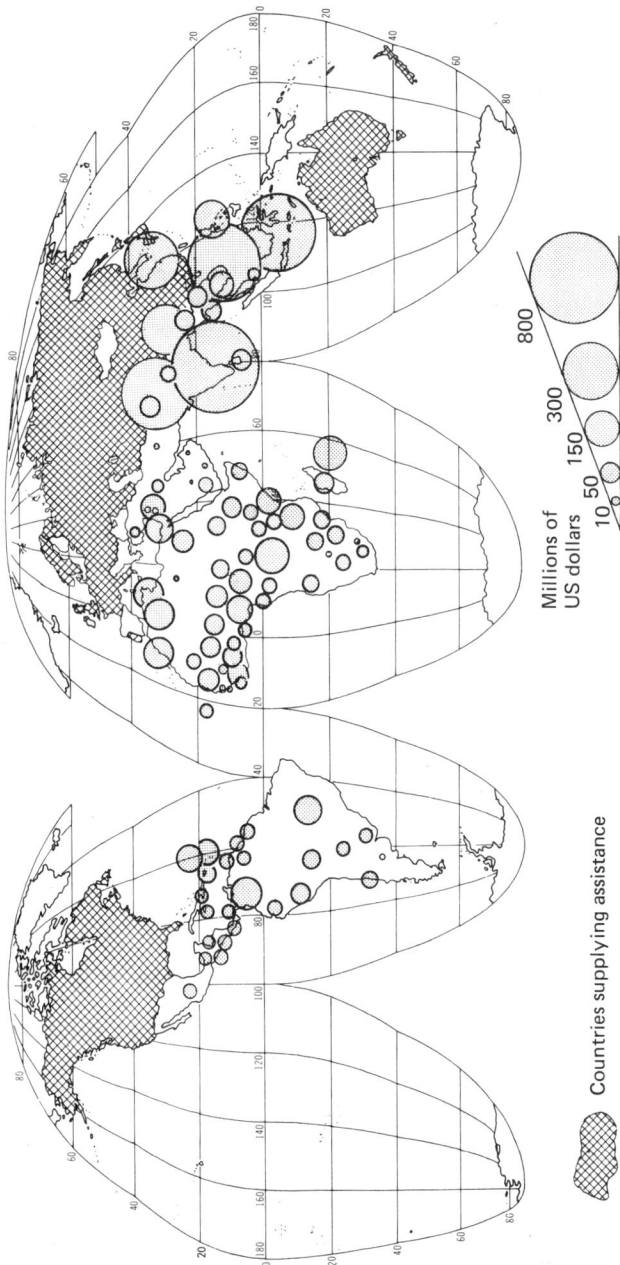

Millions of
US dollars

800

300

150

50

10

Countries supplying assistance

Fig. 15.7 World map of countries receiving assistance, and of countries supplying it, 1971–73

because it includes the vast amounts expended under the postwar programme mentioned above.

A map of total governmental foreign aid given in recent years to the developing world (Fig. 15.7) shows a very heavy concentration on south and south-eastern Asia and a considerable support for intertropical Africa, but comparatively little for Latin America. The legacies of the Cold War and of the wars in Korea and Indo-China are very much in evidence.

(*ii*) **World Bank.** The International Bank for Reconstruction and Development, known for short as the World Bank, is an agency of the United Nations. It was conceived at the Bretton Woods Conference in 1944 as a means of mopping up small amounts of investment capital and of channelling them towards major developmental projects. Its purpose is to increase production and raise living standards by means of capital investment. It draws its capital from its member countries but acts independently of them; its loans thus have no political conditions. Although no communist country except Romania has participated in the work of the World Bank, its actions have not been significantly influenced by the rivalry of the two great power blocs. The decision to make a loan is determined by the economic feasibility of the project in question and the availability of funds to cover it. The Bank, like any commercial bank, charges interest on the loans it makes and expects the invested capital to be repaid within a reasonable time. The projects which it supports are not restricted to the developing world, and, in fact, large loans have been made for undertakings in the developed countries. The Snowy Mountain irrigation and hydro-electric undertaking in Australia was financed in this way, and there has been a number of World Bank investments in western Europe.

The map of development loans made by the World Bank (Fig. 15.8) is in marked contrast with that of foreign aid given by governments. Although North America, China, the Soviet Union and the rest of the Communist bloc do not appear, either because they do not need such help or because they refuse to participate in capitalist enterprises, World Bank loans are more evenly distributed than is any other form of foreign aid. A correlation of Bank loans with the wealth of the recipients, however, confirms that the poorer countries have not been unduly favoured in the grant of loans for development. The practicability of the undertaking has been more significant than the applicant's poverty and need for a loan.

The activities of the World Bank and of the national governments which make development grants and loans are not mutually exclusive. They can unite to pursue an objective which all consider particularly worth while. The Indus valley development project was such an undertaking. In 1947 the Indian subcontinent was partitioned between India and Pakistan 'on the basis of ascertaining the contiguous majority areas of Muslims and non-Muslims'. As a result, the complex irrigation system of the Indus basin was divided in the least practical manner, with Indian rivers discharging across the new boundary into Pakistan. India cut off the supply of water to Pakistan, and twice hostilities broke out between the two countries. Economic development was inhibited, and the

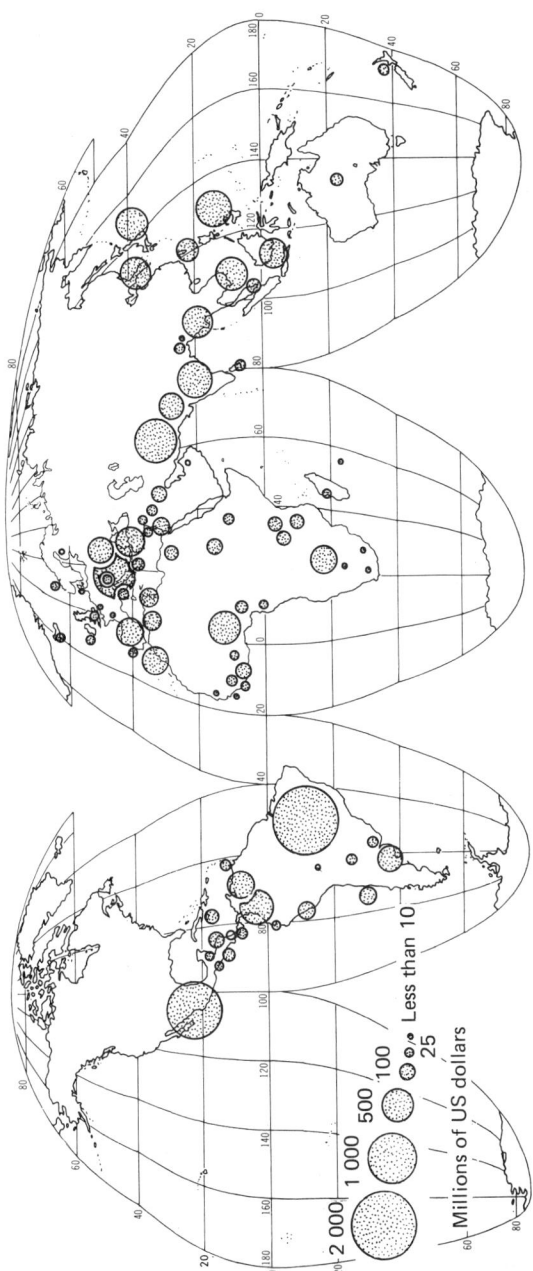

Fig. 15.8 Map of World Bank loans, 1975; note that loans are made to developed countries and that comparatively little is lent to the really poor nations

danger of full-scale war within the subcontinent increased. The Director of the World Bank himself suggested a solution: the construction of link canals, together with the necessary barrages, so that each country could be self-sufficing in the supply of water for irrigation. The agreement was negotiated by the World Bank and the governments of the two countries, and was underwritten in 1960 by the governments of the United Kingdom, the United States and other countries. At the time of writing, the works on the Indus rivers are nearing completion. In a sense this was an unnecessary investment, because the initial partition of the subcontinent could have been made in a way which took the irrigation works into consideration. When completed, however, it will greatly increase Pakistan's productive capacity.

15.4 A Model of Economic Development

Twenty years ago the economist W. W. Rostow proposed a four-stage model for the economic development of nations. In the first stage, he suggested, the necessary *preconditions of economic growth* begin to appear: an effective central government, the development of a scientific attitude to the material world and to innovation, the improvement of agriculture and the creation of 'social overhead capital'—means of transport, communication and exchange. This is followed by *take-off*—the period 'when the old blocks and resistances to steady growth are finally overcome'. Growth becomes normal and expected, and 'compound interest becomes built, as it were, into (Society's) habits and institutional structure'.

During the take-off period growth is commonly limited to certain leading sectors of the economy, such as textiles in Great Britain, or iron and steel in Germany. Take-off is followed by the *drive to maturity*, when growth spreads to other sectors and more sophisticated types of manufacture replace those that sparked the initial take-off. Machine tools, chemicals and electrical and electronic equipment supersede the simpler products of the steel industry, and plastics and synthetic fibres replace earlier textiles woven from natural materials. Lastly, there comes a *phase of high mass-consumption*, of cars and electronic equipment, of refrigerators and washing machines, of built-in obsolescence and frequent replacement.

Rostow set no time scale for this developmental process. He only suggested that Great Britain experienced 'take-off into sustained growth' in the closing decades of the eighteenth century, and reached maturity in the mid-nineteenth. France, the United States and Germany experienced these changes about fifty years later. Japan's take-off occurred toward the end of the nineteenth century, and her maturity between the two world wars. For Russia and Canada take-off followed in the early twentieth century. Australia, Turkey, Argentina and Mexico 'took off' about the time of the Second World War, and China and India in the 1950s. Some of these countries have now reached maturity and even the phase of high mass-consumption. Others, like Brazil and South Africa, have taken off and are approaching maturity. Most of the Communist countries can be considered to have reached maturity but not yet the stage of high mass-consumption.

Rostow's concept is, of course, a model—a generalized behavioural picture. In detail it is not fully accurate, and it is difficult to fit all developed and developing countries into the pattern. It nevertheless offers us a most useful way of making spatial comparisons of development. It stresses the nature of development as a continuing process, that the developed countries are themselves still developing, and that some underdeveloped countries are unlikely ever to catch up with the developed nations. We live in a very unequal world. The gulf between developed and undeveloped, rich and poor, *might* perhaps be narrowed; it is unlikely ever to be closed. The basic, unalterable reason is that resources and the capacity to use them are themselves spread unevenly about the surface of the earth.

Questions

1. Examine the thesis that some parts of the so-called developing world are incapable of development.
2. 'The greatest enemy of economic development is population growth.' Discuss.
3. Is an energy base a necessary pre-requisite of economic development?
4. Western economic development has taken the form of the creation of manufacturing industries. Must Third World development take the same course?
5. Terms of trade have in the past generally favoured the developed countries. Is this likely to change?
6. What are the obstacles to economic development in (a) Bangladesh, (b) Nigeria, (c) Vietnam, (d) Zaïre?
7. Examine the role of the World Bank in the economic development of Third World countries.
8. Does the Soviet or communist model offer a way to develop the Third World countries?

Assignments

The following assignments are appropriate to the BEC National Level Option Module in Economic Geography. They are designed to cover the general objectives of this module as specified by BEC, and integrate the tasks of data collection, presentation and analysis with written description, interpretation and explanation, using a variety of techniques.

Much of the basic information needed for each assignment may be obtained from the relevant unit or units of this book. The purpose of BEC assignments is, however, to encourage students to explore issues in greater depth, and the *Further Reading* list (page 362) provides a valuable guide to other sources of information.

Most of the assignments also require some research into published statistics, and the following publications should provide all that is necessary. They are available in most, if not all, reference libraries: you should always use the most recent edition available.

Abstract of Regional Statistics, Central Statistical Office. HMSO (London, annually).

Annual Abstract of Statistics, Central Statistical Office. HMSO (London, annually).

Demographic Yearbook. Statistical Office of the United Nations (New York, annually).

Digest of Energy Statistics, Central Statistical Office. HMSO (London, annually).

General Statistics. EEC (Luxembourg, monthly).

Fullard, H. (editor): *Geographical Digest*. George Philip (London, annually).

Regional Statistics Yearbook. EEC (Luxembourg, annually).

Statistical Yearbook. Statistical Office of the United Nations (New York, annually).

Transport Statistics of Great Britain, Central Statistical Office. HMSO (London, annually).

Yearbook of International Trade Statistics. Statistical Office of the United Nations (New York, annually).

Assignment One

Types of economic activity; regional contrasts: Units 1 and 13

(a) Using the primary, secondary and tertiary classification of economic activities, calculate the percentage employment in each sector for each region of the UK.

(*b*) Illustrate the data graphically on a map of the UK regions, using an appropriate technique.

(*c*) Comment on any significant differences between regions.

Assignment Two

Urban functions; urban distributions: Units 2 and 11

(*a*) Define and exemplify the concepts of range and threshold.

(*b*) With reference to the area in which you live, show how range and threshold have influenced the pattern of urban settlement.

(*c*) Identify those factors which are responsible for any pronounced irregularity in the distribution and structure of settlements.

(If you find it difficult to study a wide area, you may choose instead a large town, substituting local shopping centres for settlements. You should then survey shopping facilities in the various centres, so that you can identify central places of different orders.)

Assignment Three

Urban morphology: Unit 2

(*a*) Using a large-scale Ordnance Survey map (at least 1:25 000), prepare a base outline map of your local urban area. Plot the components of major land on this map, using chorochromatic techniques (colour shading). Your basic land use classification scheme might be: Residential, Services (retail and other), Industrial, Transport, Public buildings, Open space/recreation, Derelict/unused. Adopt a more detailed breakdown if it is appropriate.

(*b*) Compare the land use pattern that emerges with those proposed by the various models of urban land use discussed in Unit 2.

(*c*) Describe in detail the form and characteristics of the area you have identified as the Central Business District. Explain the concentration of service industries in the CBD, with special reference to agglomeration economies and accessibility.

(This assignment will also require field work. In addition, you will need to examine transport flows and networks to answer (*c*) (see Unit 12.2).)

Assignment Four

Population growth: Units 3 and 13

(*a*) Calculate crude birth rates and crude death rates for England and Wales for census years (ten-year intervals) from 1841 to 1971 inclusive. Plot these vital rates and the total population on one graph, showing their interrelationship.

(*b*) With reference to the graph, assess critically the validity of the demographic transition model as a means of explaining population growth.

(Information for 1841 onwards can be found in the first and second *Abstract of British Historical Statistics*, Cambridge University Press (London, 1962 and 1971), by Mitchell and Deane and Mitchell and Jones respectively.)

Assignment Five

UK population profile: Units 3 and 13
(a) Construct the age–sex pyramid for the population of the UK.
(b) Illustrate by means of a graph the post-war changes in the UK population.
(c) Map the present distribution of the UK population.
(d) Consider the value of this population profile to a large manufacturing firm.
(In (a), you should use five-year age-groups—0–4 years, 5–9 years and so on—
and express the population of each age–sex group as a percentage of the total
population of either sex. In (b) you should consider birth and death rates, natural
growth, and international and interregional migration. You can find data on
interregional migration in *Regional Statistics Number 11* (1975). In (c), you may
use regional population densities, but you should also identify and locate the
principal urban centres of population.)

Assignment Six

*Demographic contrasts associated with different levels of development: Units 3, 4,
14 and 15*
(a) Select two key population indicators (for example, crude birth rate and
    infant mortality rate) for the countries of western Europe and continental
    South America. Summarize the two sets of data for each region (by finding
    their means and standard deviations) and compare them.
(b) Combine the figures for the two regions and, using an appropriate statistical
    technique, discover whether there is a significant relationship between the
    two variables.
(c) List any other features which may be used to distinguish different levels of
    development.
(You will find it useful to refer to Units 14 and 15 when answering part (c).)

Assignment Seven

Spatial variations in welfare: Units 4 and 14
(a) On an outline map of the EEC, illustrate the *per capita* incomes of the
    member states, using choroplethic techniques (density shading).
(b) Consider the effectiveness of the map as a means of showing spatial
    variations in economic welfare.
(c) Outline the incentives available under EEC regional policy and identify
    areas eligible for assistance.
(d) State what criteria might validly be used to identify areas in need of
    assistance.
(This assignment could be applied to the UK or other individual countries, using
regional data and national government regional policy.)

Assignment Eight

Spatial variations in welfare: Units 4 and 15
(a) Select a representative sample of thirty countries of the world, and plot on a

graph, their *per capita* national income against *either per capita* energy consumption *or* the percentage of their employed population working in agriculture.

(*b*) Draw the 'best-fit' regression line through the scattergraph.

(*c*) Comment on the results of (*b*).

Assignment Nine

Agricultural land use: Units 5 and 13

Identify and assess the importance of the various physical and socio-economic factors influencing the pattern of agricultural land use in Great Britain.

(This assignment should be presented in essay form. Give examples to illustrate the operation of each factor, and include statistics and maps.)

Assignment Ten

Policies for agriculture: Units 6 and 14

(*a*) Identify the primary goals of the Common Agricultural Policy of the EEC.

(*b*) Consider the conflicts inherent in these goals.

(*c*) Outline the methods by which the CAP is implemented, and discuss their impact on agricultural land use in the EEC.

Assignment Eleven

Resources; reconciling supply and demand: Units 7 and 13

(*a*) Prepare a map of Great Britain showing (*i*) areas of high precipitation, and (*ii*) areas with a high density of population.

(*b*) Analyse the major problems involved in reconciling the spatial pattern of demand for water with the spatial pattern of supply.

(*c*) Consider the measures which have been taken to overcome these problems. Locate and name on the map the major supply projects.

(For (*a*) use the 1 000 mm isohyet to distinguish between areas of high and low precipitation; regard areas with a population of more than 100 per square kilometre as having a high density.)

Assignment Twelve

Changing patterns in energy production and consumption: Units 8 and 13

(*a*) Illustrate, using suitable graphic techniques, the changes in total primary energy consumption and the primary energy mix in the UK between 1952 and 1977.

(*b*) Discuss the main reasons for the changes that have occurred during this period, and their spatial consequences.

(*c*) In the light of the UK energy resource base and current trends in the world energy market, outline likely changes in UK energy production and consumption up to the year 2000.

(For (a) it may be necessary to refer to an older *Annual Abstract of Statistics*. For (b), consider not only the spatial impact on the energy supply industries but also its effect on other types of economic activity.)

Assignment Thirteen

Development of offshore energy resources: Unit 8 and 13
(a) Draw a map showing the distribution of UK offshore energy reserves and extraction and distribution facilities.
(b) List the problems involved in exploiting these offshore reserves for the UK market.
(c) Examine the spatial impact of the development of the offshore oil industry in Scotland.

Assignment Fourteen

UK transport sector: Units 12 and 13
(a) Illustrate by means of a graph the changes in the volume and share of different media in total passenger and goods transport in the UK during the decade 1967–1977.
(b) Analyse the pattern indicated in terms of the relative advantages and disadvantages, including costs, of each transport mode.
(c) Review the main developments in the UK transport system during the last twenty years.
(For the graph, use tonne–kilometres and passenger–kilometres given in the *Annual Abstract of Statistics*.)

Assignment Fifteen

Industrial location: Units 9, 10 and 13
(a) Select a major manufacturing industry and map its spatial distribution in the UK.
(b) Analyse the operation of those factors which have given rise to this distribution.
(c) Consider the likely impact of technological innovation on the location of the industry.
(Choose a major industry such as vehicle production, iron and steel manufacture or textiles. The answer to (c) will clearly depend on the industry selected, but the increasing rôle of scale economies and micro-electronics, and the speed of their adoption in other parts of the world, are likely to be important factors in the future.)

Assignment Sixteen

Network analysis: Unit 12
(a) Draw a simplified topological map of the UK motorway network; construct

the shortest-path matrix and determine the most accessible node in the network.

(b) Explain the value of this exercise to a manufacturer wishing to locate a new plant in order to supply the national market.

(c) Draw a simplified topological map of the French motorway network and compare its connectivity with that of the UK.

(d) Discuss the value of network analysis as a means of analysing and comparing different transport networks.

(Information is readily available from any road atlas. The networks may be simplified by treating complex motorway meeting-points as one node—for example, the London, Manchester and Paris regions may be regarded as single nodes. In addition, you may ignore outlying, isolated motorways which are not part of the main system.)

Further Reading

General

Alexander, J. W.: *Economic Geography*. Prentice-Hall (Englewood Cliffs, N.J., 1963).

Bradford, M. G. and Kent, W. A.: *Human Geography: Theories and their Application*. Oxford University Press (Oxford, 1977).

Chisholm, M.: *Geography and Economics*. G. Bell and Sons (London, 1970).

Fryer, D. W.: *World Economic Development*. McGraw-Hill (New York, 1965).

Haggett, P.: *Geography: A Modern Synthesis*. Harper Row (New York, 1975).

Hammond, R. and McCullagh, P.: *Quantitative Techniques in Geography: An Introduction*. Oxford University Press (Oxford, 1974).

Hodder, B. W. and Lee, R.: *Economic Geography*. Methuen (London, 1974).

Jones, E. and Eyles, J.: *An Introduction to Social Geography*. Oxford University Press (Oxford, 1977).

Science in Geography Series:
1. Fitzgerald, B. P.: *Developments in Geographical Method*.
2. Daugherty, R.: *Data Collection*.
3. Davis, P.: *Data Description and Presentation*.
4. McCullagh, P.: *Data Use and Interpretation*.
   Oxford University Press (Oxford, 1974).

Tidswell, W. V.: *Pattern and Process in Human Geography*. University Tutorial Press (London, 1976).

Toyne, P. and Newby, P. T.: *Techniques in Human Geography*. Macmillan (London, 1971).

Economic Atlases

Oxford Economic Atlas of the World. Oxford University Press (Oxford, 1972).

Ginsburg, N.: *Atlas of Economic Development*. University of Chicago Press (Chicago, 1961).

Population

Beaujeu-Garnier, J.: *A Geography of Population*. Longman (Harlow, 1966).

Brown, L. R.: *World Population Growth, Food Needs and Production Problems*. University of Wisconsin Press (1965).

Clarke, J. I.: *Population Geography*. Pergamon Press (Oxford, 1972).

Clarke, J. I.: *Population Geography and the Developing Countries*. Pergamon Press (Oxford, 1971).

Kosinski, L. A.: *The Population of Europe: A Geographical Perspective.* Longman (Harlow, 1970).

Lowry, J. H.: *World Population and Food Supply.* Arnold (London, 1976).

Trewartha, G. T.: *A Geography of Population.* Wiley (New York, 1969).

Wrigley, E. A.: *Population and History.* Weidenfeld & Nicolson (London, 1969).

Zelinsky, W.: *Prologue to Population Geography.* Prentice-Hall (Englewood Cliffs, N.J., 1970).

National Income and Welfare

Coates, B. E., Johnston, R. J. and Knox, P. L.: *Geography and Inequality.* Oxford University Press (Oxford, 1977).

Donaldson, P.: *Worlds Apart.* Pelican (London, 1973).

Freeman, T. W.: *Geography and Planning.* Hutchinson (London, 1971).

Hall, P.: *Urban and Regional Planning.* David and Charles (Newton Abbot, 1975).

Smith, D. M.: *Human Geography: A Welfare Approach.* Edward Arnold (London, 1977).

Agriculture and Rural Land Use

Bridges, E. M.: *World Soils.* Cambridge University Press (Cambridge 1971).

Bunting, B. T.: *The Geography of Soil.* Hutchinson (London, 1967).

Chisholm, M.: *Rural Settlement and Land Use.* Hutchinson (London, 1966).

Clout, H. D.: *Rural Geography: An Introductory Survey.* Pergamon (Oxford, 1972).

Coppock, J. T.: *An Agricultural Atlas of England and Wales.* Faber & Faber (London, 1964).

Cruickshank, J. G.: *Soil Geography.* David & Charles (Newton Abbot, 1972).

Grigg, D. B.: *The Agricultural Systems of the World: An Evolutionary Approach.* Cambridge University Press (Cambridge, 1974).

Morgan, W. B. and Munton, R. J. C.: *Agricultural Geography.* Methuen (London, 1971).

Trudgill, S. T.: *Soil and Vegetation Systems.* Oxford University Press (Oxford, 1977).

Fuel, Minerals and Mining

Chisholm, M. (Editor): *Resources for Britain's Future.* David & Charles (Newton Abbot, 1973).

Guyol, N. B.: *Energy in the Perspective of Geography.* Prentice-Hall (Englewood Cliffs, N.J., 1971).

Macgregor Hutcheson, A. and Hogg, A.: *Scotland and Oil.* Oliver & Boyd (Edinburgh, 1975).

Manners, G.: *The Geography of Energy*. Hutchinson (London, 1971).

Odell, P.: *Energy: Needs and Resources*. Macmillan (London, 1977).

Odell, P.: *Oil and World Power: A Geographical Perspective*. Pelican (London, 1977).

Patterson, W.: *Nuclear Power*. Penguin Books (Harmondsworth, 1976).

Simmons, I. and Simmons, C.: *Resource Systems* (Aspects of Geography Series). Macmillan (London, 1974).

Smith, K.: *Water in Britain*. Macmillan (London, 1972).

Warren, K.: *Mineral Resources*. David & Charles (Newton Abbot, 1973).

Manufacturing Industries

Alexandersson, G.: *Geography of Manufacturing*. Prentice-Hall (Englefield Cliffs, N.J., 1967).

Bale, J.: *The Location of Manufacturing Industry*. Oliver & Boyd (Edinburgh, 1976).

Bloomfield, G.: *The World Automotive Industry*. David & Charles (Newton Abbot, 1978).

Estall, R. C. and Buchanan, R. O.: *Industrial Activity and Economic Geography*. Hutchinson (London, 1980).

Hoover, E. M.: *The Location of Economic Activity*. McGraw-Hill (New York, 1963).

Pounds, N. J. G.: *The Geography of Iron and Steel*. Hutchinson (London, 1966).

Riley, R. C.: *Industrial Geography*. Chatto & Windus (London, 1973).

Smith, D. M.: *Industrial Location*. Wiley (Chichester, 1971).

Warren, K.: *The Geography of British Heavy Industry since 1800*. Oxford University Press (Oxford, 1976).

Transport and Trade

Alexandersson, G. and Nordström, G.: *World Shipping*. John Wiley & Sons (New York, 1963).

Bird, J.: *Seaports and Sea Terminals*. Hutchinson (London, 1971).

Briggs, K.: *Introducing Transport Networks*. Hodder & Stoughton (London, 1972).

Davies, R. L.: *Marketing Geography*. Methuen (London, 1976).

Fullerton, B.: *The Development of British Transport Networks*. Oxford University Press (Oxford, 1975).

Lobley, D.: *Success in Commerce*. John Murray (London, 1976).

O'Dell, A. C. and Richards, P. S.: *Railways and Geography*. Hutchinson (London, 1971).

Sealy, K. R.: *Airport Strategy and Planning*. Oxford University Press (Oxford, 1976).

Taaffe, E. J. and Gauthier, H. L.: *Geography of Transportation*. Prentice-Hall (Englewood Cliffs, N.J., 1973).

Thoman, R. S. and Conkling, E. C.: *Geographical Aspects of International Trade*. Prentice-Hall (Englewood Cliffs, N.J., 1968).

Urban Functions

Berry, B. J. L.: *Geography of Market Centers and Retail Distribution*. Prentice-Hall (Englewood Cliffs, N.J., 1967).

Carter, H.: *The Study of Urban Geography*. Arnold (London, 1977).

Dwyer, D. J.: *The City in the Third World*. Macmillan (London, 1974).

Everson, J. A. and Fitzgerald, B. P.: *Settlement Patterns*. Longman (London, 1969).

Everson, J. A. and Fitzgerald, B. P.: *Inside the City*. Longman (London, 1972).

Goddard, J. B.: *Office Location in Urban and Regional Development*. Oxford University Press (Oxford, 1975).

Hall, P.: *Urban and Regional Planning*. Penguin Books (Harmondsworth, 1975).

Hall, P.: *The World Cities*. Weidenfeld & Nicolson (London, 1978).

Johnson, J. H.: *Urban Geography: An Introductory Analysis*. Pergamon (Oxford, 1972).

Robson, B. T.: *Urban Social Areas*. Oxford University Press (Oxford, 1975).

Scott, P.: *Geography and Retailing*. Hutchinson (London, 1970).

Shepherd, J., Westaway, J. and Lee, T.: *A Social Atlas of London*. Clarendon Press (Oxford, 1974).

Sjoberg, G.: *The Pre-industrial City: Past and Present*. Free Press (US), Collier Macmillan (1965).

Smailes, A. E.: *The Geography of Towns*. Hutchinson (London, 1966).

The United Kingdom

Carter, H. *et al*: *An Advanced Geography of the British Isles*. Hulton (Amersham, 1974).

Graves, N. J. and White, J. T.: *Geography of the British Isles*. Heinemann (London, 1974).

House, J. W. (Editor): *The UK Space: Resources, Environment and the Future*. Weidenfeld & Nicolson (London, 1977).

Scargill, D. I. (Editor): *The Problem Regions of Europe Series*. Oxford University Press (Oxford).

Wreford Watson, J. and Sissons, J. B. (Editors): *The British Isles: A Systematic Geography*. Nelson (London, 1964).

The Developed World

Clout, H. D.: *The Geography of Post-War France*. Pergamon (Oxford, 1972).

Dewdney, J. C.: *A Geography of the Soviet Union*. Pergamon (Oxford, 1979).

Estall, R.: *A Modern Geography of the United States*. Penguin (London, 1976).

Harrison Church, R. J. *et al*: *An Advanced Geography of Northern and Western*

Europe. Hulton (Amersham, 1973).

House, J. W.: *France: An Applied Geography*. Methuen (London, 1978).

Kerr, A. J. C.: *The Common Market and How it Works*. Pergamon (Oxford, 1977).

Minshull, G. N.: *The New Europe: An Economic Geography of the EEC*. Hodder & Stoughton (London, 1978).

Pounds, N. J. G.: *North America*. John Murray (London, 1971).

Thompson, I. B.: *Modern France: A Social and Economic Geography*. Butterworths (London, 1970).

The Developing World

Donaldson, P. W.: *Worlds Apart*. Pelican (London, 1973).

Gilbert, A.: *Latin American Development: a Geographical Perspective*. Penguin (London, 1974).

Grigg, D.: *The Harsh Lands: a Study in Agricultural Development*. Macmillan (London, 1974).

Hodder, B. W.: *Economic Development in the Tropics*. Methuen (London, 1973).

Johnson, B. L. C.: *Pakistan*. Heinemann Educational Books (London, 1979).

Morriss, A.: *South America*. Hodder & Stoughton (London, 1979).

Mountjoy, A. B.: *Industrialization and Developing Countries*. Hutchinson (London, 1975).

Mountjoy, A. B.: *The Third World: Problems and Perspectives*. Macmillan (London, 1978).

Odell, P. and Preston, D. A.: *Economies and Societies in Latin America: a Geographical Interpretation*. Wiley (Chichester, 1978).

Tregear, T. R.: *China: a Geographical Survey*. Hodder & Stoughton (London, 1980).

Index